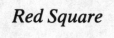

Red Square

Red Square

Edward Topol and Fridrikh Neznansky

QUARTET BOOKS
NEW YORK LONDON MELBOURNE

First published in the United States of America 1983
by Quartet Books Inc.
A member of the Namara Group

360 Park Avenue South
Suite 1300
New York, NY 10010

First published in Great Britain
by Quartet Books Limited, London, 1983

Translated from the Russian, *Krasnaya Ploshchad*

ISBN 0-7043-2378-8

Manufactured in the U.S.A.

CONTENTS

All the characters in this book, including Brezhnev, Suslov, Andropov, Tsvigun, their wives and children, as well as all the events described in it, are entirely fictitious. If, by chance, any of them should happen to coincide with Soviet reality, then so much the worse for the latter.

'There are some cases of murder when it is difficult to decide whether the killing was a justifiable necessity (e.g. self-defence), culpable negligence, or even a subtly executed, devilish plan'

Vladimir Lenin, *Complete Works* volume 41, p.52

'I only say, suppose this supposition'

Lord Byron, *Don Juan* part I, stanza LXXXV

LIST OF PRINCIPAL CHARACTERS

Igor Iosifovich SHAMRAYEV, Special Investigator at the Chief Public
    Prosecutor's Office
Anton, his son
Nina MAKARYCHEVA, circus acrobat, his mistress
Valentin (Valya) Nikolayevich PSHENICHNY, Investigator from the
    Prosecutor's Office
Taras Karpovich VENDELOVSKY, Senior Special Investigator from the
    Prosecutor's Office
Herman KARAKOZ, Head of Investigation at the Prosecutor's Office
Aleksandr Mikhailovich REKUNKOV, Chief Public Prosecutor

Nikolai Anisimovich SHCHOLOKOV, Minister of Internal Affairs (MVD)
Colonel Nadezhda (Nadya) Pavlovna MALENINA, Deputy Chief of the
    MVD Anti-Fraud Squad
General Aleksei KRASNOV, head of MVD Intelligence
Colonel G. OLEINIK, Deputy Head of MVD Intelligence
Captain Pyotr Stepanovich KHUTORSKOI, MVD Intelligence
Nikolai (Kolya) Afanasyevich BAKLANOV, Investigator from the Prose-
    cutor's Office, seconded to the MVD Anti-Fraud Squad

Yury Vladimirovich ANDROPOV, Chairman of the KGB
General Vladimir Petrovich PIROZHKOV, Deputy Chairman of the KGB
Lieutenant-General Boris V. KURBANOV, Head of the KGB Investi-
    gation Section
General Semyon Kuzmich TSVIGUN (deceased), First Deputy Chairman
    of the KGB, brother-in-law of Leonid Ilyich Brezhnev
Vera Petrovna TSVIGUN, his wife

Svetlana (Sveta) Nikolayevna AGAPOVA, gynaecologist, his mistress
Major SHAKHOVSKY, KGB agent in charge of surveillance in the Hotel
National

Colonel Marat Alekseyevich SVETLOV, Head of Third Section, Moscow
CID
Lieutenant-General Anatoly VOLKOV, National Chief of CID
Colonel V. Yakimyan, Chief of District CID
Colonel Vladimir GLAZUNOV, Chief of Moscow CID
Major V. OZHERELYEV
Captain P. KOLGANOV
Captain E. ARUTYUNOV } of Third Section, Moscow CID
Captain LASKIN

Galina (Galya) Leonidovna BREZHNEVA, daughter of Soviet Premier
Leonid Brezhnev
Boris (Borya) BURYATSKY, 'The Gypsy', entertainer, playboy, specu-
lator, lover of Galina Brezhneva
Givi Rivazovich MINGADZE, Georgian playboy, adventurer and specu-
lator
Anna (Anya) Arkadyevna FINSHTEIN, fiancée of Mingadze
Marusya SHEVCHENKO, soothsayer, sorceress, and dealer in stolen
goods
Kostya, the trombone player
Boris Yegorovich MOROZOV } housebreakers
Eleonora (Lena) SAVITSKAYA
Mikhail BELYAKOV
Volodya ('Gold Fang') AZARKIN } former criminals employed occasionally for special work by Colonel Svetlov of the Moscow CID
'Bossman'
Aleksei Igorevich VOROTNIKOV ('Korchagin'), escaped robber and
murderer
'Teacher' GRUZILOV, former criminal, now CID 'plant' in the Butyrka
prison
Tamara Viktorovna BAKSHI, circus-artiste and hooker

Leonid Ilyich BREZHNEV, Soviet Premier, Secretary General of the
CPSU Central Committee
Mikhail Andreyevich SUSLOV, Secretary of the CPSU Central Committee,
member of Politburo
Konstantin Ustinovich CHERNENKO, member of Politburo and close
associate of Leonid Brezhnev, Secretary of the CPSU Central Committee
Pavel Romanovich SINTSOV
Suren Alekseyevich PCHEMYAN } of Brezhnev's personal advisory staff
Eduard Yefimovich ZOLOTOV

Nikolai Ivanovich SAVINKIN, Head of Central Committee Administrative
    Section
Major-General Ivan Vasilyevich ZHAROV, Commander of Brezhnev's
    personal bodyguard
Dr Yevgeny Ivanovich CHAZOV, Brezhnev's personal physician
Professor Aleksandr (Sasha) SOROKIN   } of the Moscow Forensic
Alla SOROKINA, his wife   } Institute
Dr Boris (Borya) GRADUS   } of Medical Institute
Dr Aleksandr ('Sandy') BOGOYAVLENSKY   } Number One
Captain Andrei Pavlovich KOPYLOV, Captain of Militia, responsible for
patrolling élite residential area
Katya UZHOVICH, nine-year-old music student
Colonel Boris Ignatyevich TRUTKOV, Head of Special Intelligence, Soviet
    Forces General Staff of East Berlin
General I.D. BOGATYRYOV, Chief of the Main Directorate of
    Corrective Labour Institutions
Vadim BELKIN, author and journalist

NB Russians are often addressed formally by 'Comrade . . .' or else by their
name and patronymic (e.g. Igor Iosifovich in the case of Shamrayev). More
familiar address uses just the Christian name (e.g. Nikolai, Galina) or else
various affectionate or casual contractions of it (Kolya, Galya, etc.). The
common contractions used in this book are indicated in this list in brackets
after the Christian name.

Part 1

The Death of Tsvigun,
Brezhnev's Brother-in-Law

Sochi, 22 January, 6.15 a.m.

TOP SECRET
URGENT

By Special Military Telegraph

To Special Investigator Shamrayev Igor Iosifovich Hotel
Zhemchuzhnaya Room 605 Sochi Krasnodar Region
CHIEF PUBLIC PROSECUTOR USSR INSTRUCTS YOU INVESTIGATE
REASONS FOR DEATH FIRST DEPUTY CHAIRMAN KGB GENERAL SEMYON
TSVIGUN STOP FLY BACK URGENTLY STOP FINISH SCREWING GIRLS
LATER STOP INVESTIGATION SECTION HEAD USSR PUBLIC PROSECUTORS
OFFICE HERMAN KARAKOZ

MOSCOW 22 JANUARY 1982

Only half awake, I read this telegram three times. Only a bastard like
Herman Karakoz would have used special military telegraph to send a
message mentioning girls like that. It had taken half an hour to be trans-
mitted via Soviet Army General Staff to the head of the North Caucasus
Military Command, General Agapov, and had then reached me along with
his adjutant, Major Averyanov, and two officers with captain's epaulets on
their greatcoats.

They knew its contents, of course, these soldiers, even though the telegram was plastered with wax seals and marked 'Top Secret'. That was why
they were now in my room grinning at each other as they looked at Svetlov
snoring on the sofa and at the young circus-girl, Nina, curled up beneath the
sheets on my bed. In their eyes we must have been a sight: Marat Svetlov,
the head of Moscow CID's Third Section, myself, Special Investigator Igor
Shamrayev of the USSR Public Prosecutor's Office, and Nina, the eighteen-
year-old trapeze artiste (the 'little babe', as Svetlov had called her when he'd
rushed into my room at daybreak) looking for all the world like a little girl as

3

she lay beneath the bedclothes. And there on the table were some empty brandy bottles. I thought I'd better get the soldiers out of the room as quickly as possible to stop them smirking so brazenly.

I cleared my throat: 'All right, lads! You'd better sit in the hall, I'll be down right away.'

'Comrade Shamrayev,' said Major Averyanov, 'the commander gave orders for you to be taken urgently to Adler airport. A plane is waiting for you there. But the roads are terrible – the only way to get through is by military sno-cat. So you've got about fifteen minutes to get everything together. You'll have to give in the key to your room and . . .'

'I know very well what needs to be done,' I said, interrupting the major. That was all I needed, having him tell me how to get rid of a girl.

But it was quite true. Two days earlier Sochi had been hit by such low temperatures and heavy snowfall that the town had been paralysed. No public transport was operating, the schools had been closed and the lucky children were having a fine time having snowball fights on the roadways. But the snow at Sochi was actually no problem for the caterpillar tracks of an army sno-cat. The army is prepared for all contingencies.

'Go and wait for me downstairs,' I said, seeing them out of the room. I went into the bathroom, still clutching that damned telegram. Bits of the sealing-wax had dropped off it and somehow got into my slipper, pricking my foot. I shook off the slippers, went back into the room barefoot and tried to wake Svetlov, who was still snoring. I thrust the telegram into his hand. Let him read it while I was having a wash. But Svetlov didn't wake up. Instead he uttered an obscenity, rolled over to face the wall and carried on sleeping – hardly surprising since he'd got to bed only three hours ago, after spending the previous twenty-four arresting the leaders of the Sochi underworld. That was why he'd flown into Sochi the night before. So I had to open the venetian blinds and the window. That would wake them up quickly enough, both the 'little babe' and Svetlov. God! What an incredible sight outside! The palm trees were covered in snow, and so was the hotel beach with its famed golden sand imported from Anapa. The Black Sea waves lapped against the beach drawing snow from the ice crust at the water's edge.

The Hotel Zhemchuzhnaya had been built seven years earlier exclusively for foreigners, and was the last word in resort architecture. But then détente had collapsed, the number of foreign tourists fell drastically and this almost western degree of luxury became accessible to the Soviet citizen, thank God. Not to everyone, of course. In the summer the only people who could get rooms in this hotel were very high-up Party bosses or big black-market operators. I didn't belong to either group, so I modestly reserved myself a room in the winter. So it was that on 10 January I was already recovering here from the freezing temperatures of Moscow. By 13 January, the old Orthodox New Year, it was so warm that the oleanders were in flower, and under the green avenue of box trees the bold bosses of Krasnodar were entertaining their 'important' guests from the Transcaucasian underworld to

4

shish-kebabs and high-quality crayfish marked for export. There was obviously some dark deal going on, but even if I was an investigator from the Public Prosecutor's Office, why bother about it when I was on holiday? You can't get everybody, and for every one that is brought to trial, another turns up to take his place. To hell with them! I'd got my room at the Zhemchuzhnaya, a balcony with a view over the sea, and Nina from the nearby theatrical holiday home. But straight after the old New Year everything suddenly began to change. First of all there were rumours about Operation Cascade which was taking place in Moscow; that's to say there were mass arrests among the black-market bosses (and even here in Sochi the restaurants started to empty). Then the whole town was swept by blizzards and the beaches emptied. And yesterday, at four o'clock in the morning, Marat Svetlov crashed into my room, drank a glass of brandy straight off and said that he'd arrived with a special police squad to arrest the leaders of the Sochi mafia. At the same time, like a little bird, he told me of a vague rumour running through police circles that Brezhnev's brother-in-law, General Semyon Tsvigun, the First Deputy Chairman of the KGB, had committed suicide. Supposedly Mikhail Suslov, Secretary to the Communist Party Central Committee, had evidence linking Tsvigun with these black-market dealings and the latter had shot himself.

But I hadn't believed this rumour. Who ever heard of somebody in our government committing suicide? Let alone Tsvigun, a KGB chief. But now I was made to think otherwise by this telegram with its two red stripes, a sign of particular confidentiality.

Why had the Chief Prosecutor involved me in the affair, and not the other 'specials' he'd got at his disposal, like Baklanov, Ryzhov and Khmelnitsky? Why had the telegram been sent not by post or even through the Kremlin telephone network, but by army telegraph? Why all this hurry – the military escort, the army sno-cat and the special aircraft at Adler airport, almost as if I were a member of the Politburo? And why hadn't the newspapers printed Tsvigun's obituary yet? Damn – that Major Averyanov had had a copy of today's *Pravda* in his hands, and I'd seen him out of my room without asking him for it. . . But above all, God help us if Svetlov's rumour turned out to be true. What would I have to do then – cross-examine Suslov? Accuse him of driving Tsvigun to commit suicide? No, if he really had killed himself and it was done with the connivance of the Secretary of the Central Committee himself, then they would hardly be likely to involve a nonentity like me in such Byzantine goings-on. This must be about something else not connected with Suslov, thank God! But what? Perhaps he died screwing some girl or perhaps some girl was screwing him?. . .

Nina started to move about in the bed, tucked her legs up from the cold and said mournfully: 'Igor, cover me up, I'm cold.'

I cursed these official duties of mine and Karakoz – fancy having to abandon such a girl and such a hotel room because of some Tsvigun or other! But there was nothing for it, they had to be woken up!

At this point Marat stopped snoring and said from the divan: 'What are you doing? Have you flipped? Shut the window!'

He opened his eyes, saw the red-striped telegram near his hand, looked at it sleepily, then sat up with a jerk and gave a slow whistle: 'Now *that* I understand.'

That's what I like about Svetlov – he's really quick on the uptake. I needed eight minutes and God knows how many draughts of salt air to realize what a whirlpool I was being thrown into, yet he grasped everything in a second. And bear in mind that he'd been up till three in the morning dragging the directors of the Sochi Resort Trading Organization from their beds, along with the bosses of the Regional Consumer Goods Company and the actual head of the MVD's Anti-Fraud Squad in Sochi, Major Makarov. Then, fearing reprisals from the Sochi mafia, he decided not to go back to his own hotel, where relatives of the arrested men might have been waiting for him with knives, or thousand-rouble notes as bribes, but came to my hotel room instead, where he crashed out on the sofa. And now after three hours' sleep all he needed was a few seconds to understand everything and say: 'There you are, I told you I could smell something going on in Red Square!'

At that moment there was an insistent knock at the door. I opened it a little.

'Comrade Shamrayev,' said Major Averyanov, 'the plane is waiting.'

'I know,' I replied sharply. 'Bring me a copy of today's *Pravda*.'

You have to treat an adjutant like an adjutant. A couple of minutes later he knocked again, but didn't look into the room. Instead he handed the paper to Svetlov who had gone to the door. I didn't even put my head around the bathroom door: they could wait. I took a cold shower and had a careful shave, while Svetlov stood in the doorway and read me the report of Tsvigun's death.

'The Soviet government has suffered a heavy loss. We have to announce the death on 19 January 1982, after a grave and prolonged illness, of General Semyon Kuzmich Tsvigun, Member of the Central Committee, Deputy of the Supreme Soviet, Hero of Socialist Labour and First Deputy Chairman of the KGB. For more than forty years S.K. Tsvigun laboured to ensure the security of our Soviet motherland. He began work in 1937 as a teacher and then as headmaster at a secondary school in the Odessa region. In 1939 he was sent by the Party to work in State Security, and since then his whole life has been connected with the far from easy work of the Cheka. During the Second World War he saw active service on the south-west, southern, North Caucasus, Stalingrad, Don and western fronts. He played an active part in the partisan movement. After the war he occupied leading positions in the security organs of Moldavia, Tadzhikistan and Azerbaidzhan. In 1967 he became Deputy, and then First Deputy Chairman of the KGB. The name of Semyon Kuzmich Tsvigun, this loyal servant of Party and State, will live on in the hearts of Soviet security personnel and of all Soviet citizens. Signed: Andropov, Gorbachov, Ustinov, Chernenko, Aliyev, Bugayev,

Shcholokov and so on down the list of KGB generals,' said Svetlov in conclusion.

I felt uneasy. Neither Brezhnev nor Suslov had signed the obituary. Tsvigun's name wouldn't continue to live on in their hearts, was the implication. And that meant that there was no 'grave and prolonged illness' – after all, you don't punish somebody after his death just because he was ill. Apart from that, I couldn't remember that Tsvigun had ever been absent from the KGB on sick-leave. This was obviously a *Pravda* fabrication. Either he really *had* committed suicide, or what was more likely, he had had a heart-attack resulting from sexual over-exertion, aggravated by excessive consumption of alcohol. A similar thing had happened to the great Soviet producer Pyryev, for example, who had been the same age as Tsvigun. He'd been having an orgy with a group of girls in a sauna, that was the reason. And we don't like advertising the fact. What's the point of discrediting members of the government in the eyes of the people?

'Have you got the message?' asked Svetlov. 'Brezhnev doesn't put his name to his own brother-in-law's obituary! Tsvigun must have put Brezhnev in a real spot in that case. But there's one thing I don't understand. Why have they sent a plane to pick you up? Why the great rush? The plane will come in very handy, as far as I'm concerned. You'll be able to take me und my prisoners with you I'll ring up my boys straight away to get the suspects moved from the prison.'

'Hey, you two! What's happened?' The sleepy figure of Nina, trembling with cold, stood by the bathroom door, dressed in my pyjama jacket and slippers. The jacket came down to her knees and was a good substitute for a dressing-gown, though her arms stretched only halfway down the sleeves, which were hanging loosely. She was a kid really, not a lover.

'I'm frozen and need to use the loo.'

'There you are, sister,' Svetlov said decisively. 'Do you see this telegram? The motherland is summoning Igor to heroic deeds. I'm off with him by plane to Moscow in ten minutes. Kiss him goodbye, use the bathroom and get dressed. We'll drop you at your holiday home, and then we're off to serve Party and government. Understand?'

'Why?' she replied, with a hurt expression in her round blue eyes.

'Because that's how it is,' said Svetlov.

'But I want to go to Moscow, too!' she announced.

Svetlov looked at me, curious to see how I would extricate myself from this situation.

Quite frankly, I didn't know myself. It was one thing to have an affair in Sochi, but quite another to take this girl with me to Moscow. I might be a bachelor for most of the week, but on Saturdays and Sundays my fourteen-year-old son Anton came to stay with me, and Nina would be there. In any case, he was taller than her. Why! she might become *his* girlfriend!

'Nina,' I said, as gently as possible, 'look, you've got the whole of your holiday ahead of you. Just wait a couple of days, and it'll turn warm again.

You'll be able to lie in the sun, go bathing . . . And in Moscow what would you do? It'll be freezing cold with snow everywhere. And in any case, I'll be deluged with work.'

'You should be ashamed of yourself,' she said, suddenly grown up. 'Marat's arrested a whole gang of thieves and comes to our hotel room to hide from their friends. He may be a colonel in the militia, but he's still afraid. While you're willing to abandon me here all alone. You're going away, and yet I'm supposed to stay?'

Marat and I exchanged glances.

'Hm!' he said. 'From the mouths of babes . . .' His lively eyes switched from me to Nina and back, till he suddenly announced, as if he were in his CID office: 'All right, sister. You're right. You can come with us.' Then, turning to me, he said: 'You've got to pay for your pleasure, old lad, there's nothing else for it!'

That was another remarkable thing about Svetlov. Once he saw he was wrong, he would never insist. We'd often worked together, especially when we were a bit younger, when Svetlov was a police investigator in the Krasnaya Presnya district of Moscow and I was a simple member of the Public Prosecutor's Office in the same area. Sometimes Svetlov would come up with brilliant schemes for exposing criminals, or what seemed to him to be 'cast-iron' ways of catching them. But it only needed somebody to point out a flaw in them, and Svetlov would submissively bury the whole plan and come up with a new one. I had noticed long ago that only very talented and imaginative people react in this way, and Svetlov was one of them. Even his promotion to the headship of a CID department hadn't spoiled him, nor had the colonel's epaulets which he'd received two and a half years ago, when we'd worked on our last joint operation (we'd taken ten days to discover the whereabouts of a favourite young journalist of Brezhnev, Vadim Belkin, who had been kidnapped by a gang of drug-traffickers).* He had not acquired the witless self-assurance of a bureaucrat.

Five minutes later the caterpillar tracks of the sno-cat were already ploughing across the unprecedented Sochi snowdrifts, and we were speeding towards the prison to pick up Svetlov's 'lads' and their prisoners, as well as calling off at the holiday home to pick up Nina's belongings.

The same day, 6.35–9.05 a.m.
I won't describe our journey from Sochi to the airport. Instead I'll quote the accurate and laconic account which Svetlov gave in his official CID report.

'On the morning of 22 January, with the help of the officer commanding the Northern Caucasus military district, General Agapov, the prisoners were transported by armoured troop carrier from Sochi to Adler airport. With the mountain roads completely iced over, especially on the section between Matsesta, Khosta and Kudepsta, the prisoners and members of my

---

* The full story of this case is told in *Deadly Games* by Edward Topol and Fridrikh Neznansky.

section selflessly cleared the road of drifts, sometimes at considerable risk to their own lives. This allowed us to transfer the prisoners in the shortest possible time from the Sochi area, where they might have been illegally released from custody, to the transport plane at Adler airport, which was also made available thanks to the help of General Agapov. I would suggest that the MVD send a letter of thanks to the latter, and also that the co-operation afforded the members of my section by the prisoners should be taken into account while they are held in solitary confinement, pending investigation. . .'

Adler, 9.05 a.m.
The terminal at Adler airport was filled with passengers. The bad weather and heavy snowfall had prevented people from leaving the Black Sea coast for the last three days. They were sleeping on the floors and window-sills. Children were screaming. Harassed airport officials were being bombarded by the complaints of overwrought passengers. Boxes filled with black-market mandarin oranges and flowers, which local speculators were taking north for sale in Moscow, Leningrad and Murmansk at three roubles apiece – all this merchandise was perishing in the luggage department. In other words, thousands of roubles were literally rotting away at that very moment, but because of the bad weather, no bribe was large enough to get those goods delivered to their place of destination. And the despairing black marketeers were gloomily drinking brandy in the restaurant, which was the one place in the airport where for the price of a bottle of cognac you could at least spend a couple of hours sitting on a chair . . .

Meanwhile we – that is to say, Svetlov's team, the prisoners, Nina and myself, accompanied by a military escort – were quietly taken to a special lounge reserved for members of the Supreme Soviet on the first floor of the airport, where there were comfortable leather armchairs, carpets, flowers and a refrigerator with Narzan mineral-water.

Through the windows we could see the airfield which was completely covered with snow. Only a single runway had been cleared by army bull-dozers, and a Yak-40 was on it, warming up its engines. The prisoners realized very well that no local connections would help them now, and that they were about to be loaded on to this special plane and taken away to Moscow. And if their co-operation earlier on the mountain road had been brought about not so much by their desire to help the police, as to save their own lives (after all, the road was perched right over the sea, and at every bend we could easily have hurtled down on to the ice-hummocks of the Black Sea, unexpectedly frozen), these dozen or so heroes of the black market now became obsequious and servile. The first to come up to Svetlov was Ashot Simonyan, the director of the Sochi Resort Trading Organiz-ation. (While arresting him, Svetlov had needed a pair of scales to weigh the thirty-six kilos of gold ingots which had been secreted in various parts of Simonyan's *dacha*.)

9

'Comrade Colonel, old man!' he said. 'Will you allow me to bring some food for the journey? I'm absolutely starving, word of honour.'

Svetlov said yes.

Whereupon Simonyan picked up the receiver of an internal phone and said to the operator: 'Get me the restaurant manager, it's urgent! Rafik? This is Simonyan. You see the Yak-40 outside? That's my plane. I'm flying off to Moscow in a few minutes . . . Yes . . . I'm not travelling by myself, but with some very important people. Very important, do you understand? There are nineteen of us and one girl. A very important girl! Everything must be de luxe, quality stuff, do you understand?'

After this the rest of the prisoners rushed to the phone. They envied Simonyan his sharp wits and tore the receiver from his hands. The next person to ring was Major Makarov, the MVD officer in charge of the Sochi Anti-Fraud Squad. Makarov had grown fat on the many thousands of roubles he had received in daily bribes from all over the rich Kuban area. He had this to say: 'Rafik, this is Major Makarov speaking. Get in touch with the State citrus farm and get them to bring over five crates of mandarin oranges at the double. . .'

I looked hard at these men. I don't know what impelled them more – the desire to grease our palms or this last opportunity to enjoy their power. Only yesterday they'd been rulers of the region and country, earning easy money from their underworld dealings. They possessed cars, *dachas*, yachts and women, while losing no opportunity at Party conferences to read out speeches written by their subordinates calling on workers 'not to allow the squandering of State resources', 'to conserve the people's money' etc. And now in the course of a single night they had been put under investigation for corruption and embezzlement. Yet so used were they to exercising power that even when arrested they nearly came to blows over a telephone which would allow them to say once more with the authority of an important Party member: 'This is Major Makarov speaking . . .'

At that moment Major Averyanov appeared, accompanied by the airport manager.

'The weather reports are bad. There are blizzards covering the whole route, so I've called out the best crew,' he said. 'Are you going to take off or wait for the route to clear?'

I weighed up the alternatives in my mind. If there was no mention in the paper that a State Commission was being set up to supervise the funeral, this meant that Tsvigun was probably being buried quickly and with a minimum of fuss, perhaps that very day. Damn it all! Instead of watching these prisoners and philosophizing about them, I should have rung Moscow a long time before to find out when the funeral was being held. Idiot! You had to examine the corpse, after all!

'Where can I make a phone call to Moscow?' I asked the airport manager.

'You can do that from here.' And he took the phone away from the prisoners, clicked the receiver rest a few times and said to the operator:

'Valya, get Moscow. What number, Comrade Shamrayev?'

I gave him the number of the Public Prosecutor's Office, Karakoz's extension, grabbed the receiver and said coldly: 'Hello, Herman? This is Shamrayev. Thanks for your cheerful telegram. I'm ringing from Adler airport. When is the funeral?'

'Today, old man. At half-past one the coffin will be carried out of the Dzerzhinsky Club. What's the weather like in Adler?'

I felt like shouting 'You son of a bitch!', but I controlled myself and said icily: 'By the way, wasn't there anybody besides me to drag into the case?'

'It wasn't our decision, old man, word of honour!' Karakoz replied with a note of sincerity in his voice. 'You were nominated.'

'By whom?'

'I can't tell you over the phone. But do you remember the journalist business? You made quite a name for yourself then . . .'

Could it really have been Brezhnev? Did Brezhnev himself put me forward for this job? In that case, this was no suicide and Suslov had had nothing to do with it. They wouldn't let Special Investigator Shamrayev near such a big Party wheel as Suslov, and Brezhnev would be the last to do so. It was all a lot simpler. Tsvigun must have been guilty of immoral behaviour, that was all. Karakoz was pulling my leg with all this talk about me 'making quite a name for myself', of course, but all the same, everything was clear. Two and a half years earlier, ten days before Brezhnev was due to meet Carter in Vienna, a member of Brezhnev's press group, the young and talented journalist Vadim Belkin, was abducted in Moscow in broad daylight. The then Chief Prosecutor commissioned me to find the journalist. Together with Svetlov and some other assistants, I discovered that Belkin had been kidnapped by some drug-traffickers, whom he'd been intending to write an article about in his newspaper. These crooks had injected him with large doses of aminozine but we managed to 'un-fix' him, as they say. It caused quite a stir at the time. Brezhnev had obviously remembered my name and had now 'personally nominated' me to find out the reasons behind his brother-in-law's death. You're becoming an investigator at the court of King Brezhnev, Shamrayev, I said to myself. You'll be able to make a great career for yourself, in spite of your half-Jewish origins!

'We're leaving right away,' I said to the airport manager.

It was only 9.37 a.m. There would still be plenty of time for me to examine Tsvigun's corpse before the burial.

11.45 a.m.

The amount of food and drink which the restaurant manager at Adler airport loaded into our plane would have been enough for a crowded TU-144, let alone the nineteen of us. Two crates of brandy, a case of pink champagne, a case of Tvishi white wine, a load of grilled chickens, dishes of *satsivi* and other Caucasian delicacies, fried chicken hearts and kidneys,

11

salad, grapes and five boxes of sweets and Turkish Delight especially for the 'very important girl' Nina.

So we had a marvellous breakfast. Nina was swimming in chocolate, Svetlov's boys were exchanging jokes and doing crosswords, while the prisoners, knowing full well that this was their last break, made a determined attack on the wine and brandy.

Svetlov allowed them to eat and drink and then, half an hour later, with a glass of champagne in his hand, he made the following short speech: 'Citizen prisoners! Although I'm a Muscovite, I want to make a toast in the Caucasian manner. I am proud to have had the honour of arresting such talented folk as you. No, I mean that seriously. For example, citizen Ashot Gevorkovich Simonyan. Together with the Chairman of the Sochi Town Executive Committee and other persons arrested or not yet arrested, he opened a fake account at the State Bank into which he transferred the income from all the black-market factories and workshops in the area, and used this account as if it were his own. Your health, Comrade Simonyan! The thirty-six kilos of gold which you had piled up will be a great gift to the motherland! Or let us take citizen Nukzar Gogievich Baratashvili. For six years he has been supplying all the oriental restaurants in Moscow with fresh lamb from Georgia and Azerbaidzhan. Not by himself, of course; a whole mafia has been working with him, but on the other hand his income amounts to millions of roubles, more even than the Moscow Restaurant and Cafe Trust. Your health, Comrade Baratashvili! The six million roubles, one and a half million dollars and kilo of diamonds which we have confiscated from you are enough money to build a whole factory. Congratulations, old fellow!'

Svetlov cast his eye over the rest of the prisoners.

'My friends! As you know, Operation Cascade is going on at the moment, and I want to say to you, as one friend to another, that only one thing can make your fate easier: a frank confession and the realization that the valuables which you have amassed will help the motherland!'

'And that's not all!' said Baratashvili. 'Without my lamb there wouldn't have been any fresh meat in Moscow restaurants at all . . .'

I laughed inwardly at Svetlov's ruse. He'll now start persuading them to make a 'frank' confession. And although these confessions, made as they are under the influence of brandy, can't be admitted into the investigation as official evidence, all the same, when he's interrogating them and the prisoners start to deny their testimony, twisting and turning, keeping silent or simply lying, it's an easy matter to stick these confessions made in the heat of the moment under their noses. In other words, their backs are to the wall . . .

Then the captain of the plane entered the passenger section and said: 'Moscow airport is closed through snow. There's an opening at Zhukovsky. Shall we land there, or fly on to Moscow on the off-chance that it will open?'

I looked at my watch. It was 11.45 a.m. There was little more than an hour and a half before Tsvigun's body would be borne out of the Dzerzhinsky Club. You could get from Zhukovsky to Moscow by police car in about forty minutes.

'Let's land at Zhukovsky,' I said. 'Marat,' I went on, 'get in touch with the Zhukovsky CID by radio so that they can have a car to meet us at the landing steps.'

Moscow, 1.15 p.m.
The Dzerzhinsky Club, which belongs to the KGB, was surrounded by troops. Tomorrow's TASS report would run as follows: 'On 22 January, workers of the capital, employees of the State Security organizations and soldiers of the Moscow garrison gathered together to accompany Semyon Kuzmich Tsvigun, First Deputy Chairman of the KGB, on his last journey.' But in fact there were no workers at the funeral. Siren sounding, we rushed through the centre of Moscow, bringing all the traffic at the crossroads to a halt. But when we sped down Kuznetsky Most Street and screeched out opposite the Lubyanka, even our police car was compelled to stop. Soldiers of the Moscow garrison were blocking our path.

'Show your passes!'

My own identity card bore the words 'Chief Prosecutor's Office of the USSR' in gold letters against a red background, and was enough to get me into the Dzerzhinsky Club, but however much I tried to persuade the patrol officer to let Nina accompany me – 'She's my niece after all, I'll vouch for her' – the Armenian captain was quite implacable. 'It's not allowed.' So I had to give Nina the keys to my flat and ask the driver to take her back to my place. I got out of the car and walked down the empty pavement to the club. There was a slight frost, about minus seven. The snowfall was light but relentless. Outside the Dzerzhinsky Club, which was usually used as a meeting-place and conference centre for high-flyers in the security services, there were a dozen or so black government Chaikas and Zils, along with another dozen black KGB Volgas with radio aerials.

Then there was another line of soldiers, this time dressed in KGB uniforms.

'Show your pass.'

If it was simple enough to get past the ordinary soldiers by showing my identity pass, then it was a lot more difficult with the KGB. The Public Prosecutor's Office has a complex relationship with the organs of State security. Formally we have the right to intervene in any of their affairs, but in practice – just you try! The KGB colonel told me haughtily that without a special pass he wasn't allowed to let me through. So I had to insist. And meanwhile time was passing: there were only another six or seven minutes to go before the coffin would be carried out by the pall-bearers. At that moment the massive glass doors of the club opened and Andropov's deputy, General Vladimir Pirozhkov, came outside, looking gloomy in his dress uniform.

13

'What is it?' he asked the colonel.

I introduced myself and showed my papers. 'I've been instructed to investigate the circumstances surrounding the death of General Tsvigun. I need to examine the body.'

'What?' said Pirozhkov, his face showing a mixture of dissatisfaction and mistrust, as if he had been distracted from important affairs of State by a minor misunderstanding or somebody's ineptitude.

I repeated what I had said, trying all the while to retain my composure.

'What investigation?' he asked, brushing the snowflakes off his new uniform. 'We've already carried out an investigation ourselves. Don't you read the newspapers at the Public Prosecutor's Office? There was a government announcement today. General Tsvigun died of a grave illness . . .'

He'd already turned to go, but I grabbed him by the sleeve. 'One moment . . .'

'Take your hands off me,' said the colonel, rushing towards me and pulling my hand roughly away from the general's sleeve. He was all vigilance.

I laughed and looked him in the eye: 'Vladimir Petrovich! *I know what Tsvigun died of.*' I uttered this falsehood extremely slowly, emphasizing each syllable, to make him realize that I knew more than was in the government announcement. 'I have been instructed to deal with this affair. According to the due process of law, I am obliged to examine the corpse before burial. If you won't let me, I shall delay the funeral.'

He looked at me with curiosity. For the first time his grey eyes took on a lively, intelligent expression. 'And how would you do that, I'd like to know?'

'Do you want me to show you?'

We were now engaged in a silent battle. The colonel eyed the two of us obtusely, ready to knock me to the ground with his heavy fist at the slightest gesture from the general. Out of the corner of my eye I could see his tense figure inclining towards me and three more KGB soldiers standing next to him, turning their heads in our direction.

I was bluffing, of course. How could I have stopped the funeral if I didn't yet possess an official document from the Prosecutor's Office instituting proceedings? But then, he wasn't to know that I had only just flown in from Sochi . . .

'All right,' he said. 'Come with me.'

He dismissed the guard with a glance, and we walked through the massive glass doors of the club. The entrance hall was empty apart from fifteen or so KGB operatives who were standing around the edge and near the coat-stand, which was filled with generals' greatcoats.

'Who put you in charge of this business?' asked Pirozhkov as we were walking along.

'The Chief Prosecutor,' I replied, already playing cat and mouse with him since I knew perfectly well that he was really asking something completely different.

14

'I know,' he said with a wry face. 'But who gave instructions to the Chief Prosecutor?'

Naturally, he wanted to get his bearings by discovering what power was daring to encroach upon the authority of the KGB. No special investigator would risk offering such open resistance or adopt such a threatening attitude if he wasn't backed up by some imposing authority. What was it, did it need to be taken into account, and if it did, then to what extent? – these were the questions now exercising Pirozhkov.

The simplest thing would have been to tell him that I was acting on the personal instructions of Comrade Brezhnev. This would have had a greater effect than any official warrant, but . . . I hadn't yet been to the Prosecutor's Office, I hadn't spoken to my boss, and I didn't know whether this was a name that I could officially conjure with. Besides, I didn't particularly want to make things easy for Pirozhkov. Let him sweat a bit.

So I said: 'You'll understand, Comrade General, that such actions as these are not undertaken by the Prosecutor's Office on its own initiative. It is the responsibility of the General Committee.'

I turned left out of the vestibule and walked towards the concert hall, where the coffin was on view. It turned out that Pirozhkov was following me, rather than vice versa,

'Wait,' he said, and grabbed me by the arm, repeating my gesture of a few minutes earlier. 'What are you doing? Are you seriously intending to inspect the corpse *now*?'

'Of course.'

Soldiers with black arm-bands were standing guard at the doors of the hall. I walked past them. The coffin was lying in the centre by the concert platform on a table covered with red calico. The guard of honour consisted of the KGB Chairman himself, Yury Andropov, his Deputies, Tsinyov and Chebrikov, the Commander of the Frontier Guards, Matrosov, and the Deputy Chairman of the Supreme Soviet, Khalilov. Next to them was Savinkin, the head of Central Committee Administration and a dozen or so other no less influential Kremlin personalities. So this was why there was such massive security outside the building. But Brezhnev wasn't there. Nor was his wife, Viktoriya Petrovna, Tsvigun's sister-in-law. Instead of them, Brezhnev's close friend and right-hand man in the Kremlin, Konstantin Ustinovich Chernenko, was there, standing next to Tsvigun's widow, who was dressed in black, and his grown-up son and daughter. There had been much discussion in the Prosecutor's Office over the last few years about how this low-ranking provincial Party functionary from Dnepropetrovsk had suddenly reached the summit of Kremlin power . . .

'Just wait here for a moment,' said Pirozhkov.

He walked right through the hall to where Andropov was standing, and whispered something to the heavy, impassive features. Andropov shook his head. I realized that I wouldn't be allowed to examine the body. Then Pirozhkov made another deliberate movement. He didn't return straight away to where I was standing, but turned towards Savinkin, the head of Central Committee Administration. Some three or four years earlier, the KGB, MVD and other departments concerned with the administration of law and order had been under the control of the Council of Ministers, while we in the Public Prosecutor's Office were responsible directly and solely to the Politburo, i.e. to Brezhnev personally. But during a period of friction between Kosygin and Brezhnev, the latter, just to be on the safe side, had brought the KGB under his own control, and then, on 5 July 1978, had simply renamed it KGB USSR, thereby omitting all reference to the Council of Ministers in its official designation. And I realized why Pirozhkov was acting as he was. I would be refused permission not by Pirozhkov or Andropov (they weren't formally entitled to refuse) but by Brezhnev's lieutenant, Savinkin.

Ignoring Pirozhkov's order to stay where I was, I crossed the hall and went right up to the coffin. Out of the corner of his eye Pirozhkov had noticed my action. A shadow of annoyance passed over his features, and he started talking to Savinkin more quickly. The latter, meanwhile, didn't finish listening to him but began moving towards me. He greeted me and I listened, but I didn't once take my eyes off the body. If he had shot himself, then where had he done it? In the heart or in the head? At any rate there were no obvious external signs of the wound.

I looked at Tsvigun's fleshy open face with its double chin and thinning hair. He wore a general's uniform over a khaki shirt. His heavy, unwieldy body seemed to have spread out slightly in this somewhat narrow coffin . . .

'Comrade Shamrayev,' Savinkin was saying meanwhile, 'I realize that you are obliged to carry out your official duty, but it would be inexpedient to do so now. Moving the coffin now in front of so many people would give rise to slanderous rumours . . .'

'Especially as we have the medical certificate stating the cause of death signed by all the doctors involved,' added Pirozhkov somewhat irritably. 'I can't understand why the Central Committee has suddenly instituted a new investigation. I don't think that the Public Prosecutor's forensic experts are any better than ours.'

'What kind of death certificate do you have?' I asked, fully realizing that he'd got the better of me in what really counted: inspecting the corpse. 'Is it a fabricated one or is it genuine?'

He went red with indignation. Not even the Chief Prosecutor would have had the effrontery to say such a thing, let along a minion like me. But I couldn't resist the chance of being rude to a Deputy Chairman of the KGB, and Savinkin was a witness to it. I wanted to get my own back for being out-manoeuvred over the corpse.

'What do you mean?' he hissed.

I put on an innocent expression and said: 'I mean that you have a death certificate made for official dissemination in the press. But is there another document proving that. . .?'

To be honest, I didn't know myself what this other document might have contained, but I made it look as if I had stopped in mid-sentence for purely conspiratorial reasons. In any case, the word 'fabricated' probably applied to this second document, too, because for some reason Pirozhkov suddenly lost his temper.

'We don't deal in *fabricated* documents!' he said. 'The press announcement about General Tsvigun's illness was a decision of the Politburo. And as far as the death certificate signed by our forensic doctors is concerned, you can come and inspect it at any time.'

Ah! So he had already admitted that the statement about Tsvigun's illness was a bluff.

'There's no point in my visiting your office,' I said. 'Send all the documents to the Chief Prosecutor's Office. And do it today, please. I shall be waiting for them.'

Then I approached the coffin resolutely. I put on a sad expression, as it is customary to do on such occasions. Now that I was at close quarters, I could see that Tsvigun's head was resting on a special cushion which covered his right temple. So there *was* a wound! Expert pathologists had, of course, succeeded in masking it and had also stuck the cushion to the temple, just in case the body moved during the funeral and the bullet-hole became visible. But there *was* a wound, so it *was* suicide! Just imagine, a suicide in the Soviet government, and in Brezhnev's own family!

Shamrayev, you were a fool to delude yourself into thinking this was going to be an easy business! For the first time that day I realized with total clarity what I was getting myself involved in. What had yesterday seemed little more than a supposition based solely on Svetlov's rumours, what from a long way off, from Sochi and Adler, had seemed only a curious and entertaining adventure, albeit one which, I admit, was grist to the mill of my self-esteem (after all, Brezhnev knew my surname and had personally nominated me to investigate the affair), this now appeared to me in all its frightening simplicity. The worst thing that could happen, had happened. Brezhnev wanted me to find out what had driven his brother-in-law to commit suicide! And not only to find out. That wasn't enough, of course. If Brezhnev had initiated this investigation, it meant that he wanted documentary evidence of what happened, so that the Party could crush the villain (or villains?). But if Tsvigun had shot himself after talking to Suslov, that meant that the first, or one of the first people whom I should have to question was the Secretary of the Central Committee himself, Mikhail Andreyevich Suslov! Who gave him the documents incriminating Tsvigun? And generally – whose purpose did this suicide serve? Who was he getting in the way of? Andropov? Or did somebody want to take over his job? Pirozhkov, perhaps, or one of those other Deputy Chairmen, Tsinyov, or Chebrikov, or Matrosov . . .? And was I supposed to investigate all of them? There they were, standing before me now: Andropov, Tsinyov, Chebrikov and Matrosov, all dressed in generals' uniforms with smug expressions and cold, commanding eyes. Each of them had control over dozens of operations, secret or otherwise. They would make mincemeat of me, as soon as they discovered that I was delving into their affairs. They'd arrange a fatal car accident, a heart-attack or a chance attack by hooligans – they're past masters at that kind of thing. And no Communist Party Secretary General would be able to help me then. It would be too late . . .

I started to sweat. I think that for the first time in all my years as an investigator I suddenly felt really scared. Even the palms of my hands were wet.

'Comrades! The lying in state is over,' announced the chairman of the funeral commission. 'All those who are travelling to the cemetery are requested to get into their cars. The body of the deceased will be borne out in one minute . . .'

The widow started to sob and pressed her hand to her mouth. Her children and Chernenko patted her on the shoulder. I saw Andropov go up to her to say some formal words of consolation, but at that moment she stared at him with eyes so full of fear and hatred that he stopped awkwardly in his tracks. Her tears dried up and her sobbing died away. But all this lasted only a moment. It seemed to me that if Andropov had moved any closer to her, she would have spat in his face. And it wasn't just Andropov and I who noticed it. For a moment the whole hall was gripped by this scene, like an audience at the turning-point in a play.

Andropov turned away, and the release of tension was palpable. The drama moved on to its formal dénouement as the marshals, generals and other state dignitaries walked to the exit after Andropov's departure. Four hefty soldiers lifted the coffin, while the guard of honour, consisting of Pavlov, Savinkin, Dymshitz and Khalilov, walked next to it, each of them supporting it lightly by the palms of their hands, as if they were the ones bearing General Tsvigun on his last journey . . . After them came the children and the widow, who was sobbing frenziedly, while Chernenko and his two bodyguards disappeared through a side entrance on the stage. I realized that neither he nor Andropov would be travelling to the cemetery.

In fact, there was nothing for me to do at the cemetery either. They could play out the drama without my presence. The hearse with its military escort would deliver the corpse to the cemetery, which was doubtless already cordoned off by troops and KGB men. Then somebody would utter a regulation speech about the deceased's great service to the motherland, about how he had been a wonderful husband, a good father and a model Communist. Then the widow would start to weep again and the mourners would throw handfuls of earth and snow on to the coffin . . .

In the entrance hall I found a public telephone, inserted two kopecks and dialled my home number.

Nina lifted up the receiver immediately. 'Hello,' she said.

'It's me. How are things?'

'Where are you? I'm bored.'

'I'm still tied up at work. I'll not be home for another two hours at the earliest . . .'

'Oh dear,' she said in an aggrieved voice.

'Now be a good girl and watch TV.'

She didn't reply, and all I could hear was the dialling tone. Damn it, a show of female temper was all I needed today.

I hung up the receiver and without meaning to, heard part of the conversation going on in the next phone booth. A man with lively Jewish eyes, aged about fifty and dressed in a fur-lined jacket, a deerskin hat and blue jeans, was speaking. 'You wouldn't have some other screenplay up your sleeve, old man? The studio will pay you for this adaptation, of course. It's not your fault that the author has died. But they won't let me begin shooting it. Who needs Tsvigun now?'

I remember that a few years earlier there had been several films based on Tsvigun's books, *Front without Flank* and *The War behind the Front*. Most probably a third film had been planned, but the words I had just heard were entirely true! Who needed films based on pot-boilers written by the former Commander of SMERSH on the south-western, southern, northern Caucasian and other fronts?

I moved silently towards the exit. Outside I caught Pirozhkov staring at me. He was just getting into his car, a black Chaika, probably en route to the cemetery. So what? That was his duty. I wondered whether he had already arranged for the documents relating to Tsvigun's death to be sent to me at the Prosecutor's Office. I turned away and began walking down Kuznetsky Most Street. The funeral cortège was moving along behind me. It was snowing as relentlessly as ever. I really wanted a drink. I remembered that I hadn't eaten since the flight from Adler. But all the same, why did Tsvigun's widow look at Andropov in that way?

2.00 p.m.

The cafeteria at the Prosecutor's Office was busy in a way that happened only on Fridays. Just before the weekend there would be a delivery of groceries from the Third Special Supply Depot attached to the Council of Ministers. All kinds of things would appear – frozen Dutch chickens or meat, sausage, cheese, buckwheat, tinned fish and goose pâté. Since food had generally disappeared from Moscow stores and meat was only sold by coupon – one and a half kilos per person per week – a large number of government institutions had begun supplementing their employees' diet by selling such food through the internal cafeteria network. For some years now the State Planning Commission, ministries, committees, editorial offices and other government departments had been competing for the right to be attached to the highest quality supply depot: Number One, which provided food for the Kremlin, the Supreme Soviet and the Council of Ministers. In the days of the previous Chief Prosecutor, Roman Rudenko (who gained fame at the Nuremberg trials), our office was way behind in this competitive game. Marshal Rudenko himself used to have his food delivered at home direct from the special Kremlin supply centre, while everything else – from clothing to toilet paper – he would get from the special section at the GUM department store on Red Square, reserved for high government officials. For that reason he was far from sharing the daily burdens of us lesser mortals in his department, and he was of the opinion that all those who worked under him should carry on a modest way of life without any luxuries like chicken or fresh beef. They were all married, let their wives stand in queues like ordinary people . . .

But Rudenko had died the year before. The First Deputy Prosecutor, Aleksandr Mikhailovich Rekunkov, was appointed to succeed him. Now this was a person who had always had to play second fiddle, whether as Second Secretary to the Regional Party Committee, or as a Deputy Prosecutor, or finally as Deputy to Rudenko himself. Now that his hour had finally come, he showed his mettle. He removed the wall which had separated his own office from that of his predecessor, and made a luxurious suite for himself, complete with Finnish soft furnishings. He transferred Rudenko's secretaries over to internal administrative duties and chose a group of efficient young prosecutors who had graduated from the Higher Party College to be his own personal assistants. Moreover, he concerned himself with the state of our food procurement. If Rudenko's authority over his employees had derived from his links with Suslov, Brezhnev, Kosygin, Gromyko and other influential members of the Kremlin Old Guard, then Rekunkov was able to win over his subordinates in a completely different way. He managed to get our cafeteria attached to Special Government Supply Depot Number Three. Of course, Number Three wasn't the same as Number One. We weren't supplied with Pepsi-Cola from the factory at Krasnodar, with cigarettes imported from abroad, or with caviare, Finnish boiled pork, Austrian sausage meat or whatever. But all the same, the very fact that on Fridays it was possible to buy meat, chickens, vegetables and fruit in our cafeteria without having to queue for hours to get it, this alone meant that the employees of the Public Prosecutor's Office were even willing to work overtime for their boss.

And today turned out to be rather special. There was fresh fish on sale at the cafeteria, pike, perch and a new variety fished from the depths of the Antarctic Ocean. For this reason there was an almost festive atmosphere in the building. Ignoring the timetable whereby employees from different offices and departments are sold food in the cafeteria at different times, women from all five floors of the building had descended simultaneously. And that wasn't all. Even prosecutors, investigators and some of Rekunkov's own personal assistants were there, standing in the queue. Auntie Lena, the old woman behind the counter, had only one problem: there was no paper to wrap the fish in. There had long been a shortage of wrapping-paper in Moscow, and she was busy shouting to all her potential customers, even prosecutors and special investigators: 'Don't bring me any of your official documents! I won't wrap fish up in them! The Chief Prosecutor has forbidden me to wrap food up in your official papers!'

'But these are from the archive, as old as the hills,' some attempted to say.

'I'm not bothered whether they're from the archives or not! I've not time to read them and check! Kulebyakin wrapped some smoked sausage up in secret documents last time, and I was given a reprimand! Anybody that hasn't brought their own paper along needn't stand in the queue. I won't serve you! Couldn't you go outside and buy a newspaper, you lazy lot! Petya, what are you giving me your briefcase for? It'll stink of fish and so will your papers . . .'

'I'll wash it out, Yelena Ignatyevna. Give me three perch and one of the Antarctic variety,' the ingratiating request came from Public Prosecutor Pyotr Borisovich Remizov the fabled scourge of innumerable famous trials.

'You can only have *two* perch. Take a pike instead . . .'

I was sitting in the corner eating sausage and fried egg, waiting for my turn to come and wondering whether to take another perch for tonight's supper with Nina, or whether to take the whole selection on offer. You can make fantastic fish soup out of pike, after all. The only thing was that I didn't know how to cook it, but maybe Nina did.

To be quite honest, I should have called on Karakoz and the Chief Prosecutor long before this, to give them an account of my journey and what had happened since, and also to take official charge of the Tsvigun affair. But that would mean questioning Suslov, Andropov, and Tsinyov. It was frightening just to think about, let alone actually start. So that was why I was delaying, putting off the evil hour by munching away at my food, reminiscing about Rudenko and other nonsense like that. I didn't fancy any fish and all the fun I'd had with Nina seemed like a distant dream. Get dead drunk right away, that's what I'd have liked to have done, and make a great row in a restaurant, so that they'd have to give me the sack for unseemly conduct . . .

But at that moment Herman Karakoz ran into the cafeteria. Somebody had obviously managed to tip him off that I'd arrived.

'Well, just look,' he said indignantly. 'Here I am, waiting with the Chief Prosecutor for you to arrive, and here you are stuffing yourself with fried egg! Come on, get a move on!'

'I'm in the queue for fish, Herman.'

'You'll survive. Come on!'

'I'm not going anywhere,' I said, in a sudden fit of stubbornness. 'I've got an empty refrigerator at home, and I've only just arrived back.'

And that was how I really felt. They could go to hell with their endless rush to curry favour with the bosses!

Karakoz realized that there was no way I was leaving the restaurant without my fish. He turned to the woman serving behind the counter and said loudly: 'Lena, put some fish to one side for Comrade Shamrayev, as much as he's entitled to. And a couple of perch for me, too.'

'All right, Comrade Karakoz,' she replied. Auntie Lena bowed and

21

scraped to the head of the Investigation Department, more even than to the Chief Prosecutor himself – she knew that Karakoz was in command of the Anti-Fraud Squad and for cafeterias and restaurants there was no more terrifying institution.

Karakoz and I took the lift to the third floor, where the Chief Prosecutor's office was situated. On the way I gave him a laconic account of what had taken place at the Dzerzhinsky Club, about how Pirozhkov, Andropov and Savinkin had refused me permission to examine Tsvigun's body.

'Well, we'll have it exhumed in that case,' he said forcibly. 'What a lot of nonsense! And while you were eating your sausage and egg all the papers arrived from the KGB. I've already drawn up a draft version of the order instituting proceedings. As soon as the boss signs it you'll have all the powers you need. Do what you like.'

In general, Karakoz never saw any problems anywhere. Lively and cynical, he was about forty-five years of age, of medium height and somewhat on the fattish side with the dark shining eyes of an Armenian. He was invariably dressed in a smart general's uniform made of fine English wool, bought in a special foreign-currency shop, although the fashionable shirts and stylish French ties which he sported were out of keeping with it. He was a great one for pretty women and enjoyed long drinking sessions with his cronies at restaurants on the outskirts of the city. About eight years earlier he had married the niece of Ustinov, Minister of Defence, and had made a meteoric advance in his career, from being an investigator at the Moscow office to head of the Investigation Branch of the entire Public Prosecutor's Department of the Soviet Union, thereby outstripping all his contemporaries at the institute, including yours truly with his suspect, half-Jewish background . . .

We avoided the birchwood elegance of the reception-room where two of the Chief Prosecutor's assistants were on duty, and went straight into Rekunkov's office. The latter was sitting at a large empty desk. To the left, on a separate table, were four telephones, including two which were red. One was linked to the general government telephone network, and the other was a 'hot line', straight to the Politburo in the Kremlin. The big, wide windows looked out on to Soviet Square and the statue of Yury Dolgoruky, the founder of Moscow. Meanwhile, outside, the desultory snowfall continued, with the result that at three o'clock in the afternoon it seemed like evening and the Chief Prosecutor had had to switch on the lights in his office. Fifty-eight years old, Aleksandr Mikhailovich Rekunkov was tall and grey with something of a stoop caused by years of having to bow to his superiors. He was examining the documents contained in a thin folder marked 'KGB', which lay before him on the table.

I greeted him. He stood up from his chair and offered me his dry, leathery hand. 'Hello. Sit down,' he said tonelessly.

However, Herman quickly interrupted this awkward, official manner. 'What do you think of this, Aleksandr Mikhailovich?' he asked loudly.

'Leonid Brezhnev nominates him for an important task, and where is he? In the cafeteria waiting for perch! Who ever heard of such a thing?'

'Yes,' said the Chief Prosecutor in a deadpan voice. He removed his glasses. 'Tell me, Igor Iosifovich, do you know Comrade Brezhnev personally?'

'No, Aleksandr Mikhailovich, I have not had that honour.'

'But you did once carry out a task on his instructions, I think.'

'Yes, that was in 1978, just before he was due to travel to Vienna to meet Carter. Along with Svetlov from the Moscow CID I succeeded in locating a kidnapped member of the government press-group, Vadim Belkin, a journalist on *Komsomolskaya Pravda*. It was a routine affair, nothing out of the ordinary.'

'He's being modest,' exclaimed Karakoz. 'A routine affair, indeed! They turned all Moscow upside down, and half the Caucasus and Central Asia to boot. They uncovered a huge drug-trafficking network. It was even mentioned by the Voice of America!'

Rekunkov knitted his brow. He'd been working in the Russian State Prosecutor's office at the time and didn't know all the details of the affair. But even so rumours had reached him.

'Yes, I heard about it,' he said. 'There was some friction between you and the KGB at the time, wasn't there?'

I shrugged my shoulders. 'No more than on other occasions . . .'

'Friction' there had of course been. If it hadn't been for the KGB, four important witnesses who were going to testify about links between the underworld and several government ministers would still be with us today. KGB agents even got one of these witnesses in Switzerland, where they arranged for him to have a fatal car accident. Still, what's the point of opening up old wounds?

'Well, whatever happened, it's thanks to your prowess that Comrade Brezhnev has once again decided to honour the Public Prosecutor's Office by entrusting us with an affair of utmost importance to the State . . .'

That was certainly very subtly put. On the one hand, Brezhnev had decided to 'honour' us, but on the other, if it hadn't been for this upstart Shamrayev, God would have spared the Chief Prosecutor the necessity of conducting this investigation and of interfering in Lubyanka and even Kremlin affairs.

There was no avoiding the institution of proceedings. Tsvigun had been forced to commit suicide, any first-year law student could see that. But who was the Prosecutor to proceed against? Suslov, Secretary of the CPSU and its chief ideologist? Were we to pin five years' prison on him according to Article 107 of the Criminal Code? The Chief Prosecutor obviously regarded this case as poison. That was why he was leafing through the KGB's file so carefully.

'Of course, it's a complicated case,' said Karakoz, suddenly changing his tone of voice and drumming his fingers on the polished wood of the

Prosecutor's desk. He settled back in his armchair, as if dissociating himself from the whole business.

One of the red telephones began to ring – *not* the hot line to the Kremlin, however.

The Prosecutor picked up the receiver. 'Hello . . . Yes, we've received it . . . I don't know yet, Comrade Tsinyov . . . Through usual channels. The case is being handled by Special Investigator Shamrayev . . . Of course, it's top secret. We understand that perfectly well . . . Very good, I'll keep you informed, of course . . .'

So, Tsinyov was already on to the case, and he was Andropov's right-hand man. Just you wait, Suslov himself would be ringing up next!

Meanwhile, the Prosecutor had replaced the receiver very carefully and sighed heavily. 'Well, carry on, what more can I say?' he asked, and pushed the file across the table towards me. I thought he did this with some measure of relief, as if he, too, were washing his hands of it.

'But before you go, read this,' he said, opening a drawer and passing me a sheet of creamy-white paper with the following legend printed in red at the top: 'Secretary General of the CPSU Central Committee, Chairman of the Presidium of the Supreme Soviet and President of the Defence Council, Leonid Ilyich Brezhnev'.

Beneath this imposing heading, an uneven, jerky hand had written the following message: 'To Rekunkov. Instruct your investigator Comrade Shamrayev to find out the reasons for Tsvigun's death. Give him full authority – and let him get to the bottom of it. He must report by 3 February at the latest. L. Brezhnev.'

That's what it said. Short and sweet, and with Party directness. *Comrade* Shamrayev was to have full authority – while his immediate superior, the USSR Chief Prosecutor, was simply referred to by his surname, as though he was a nobody. There certainly wouldn't be any help or protection forthcoming from that direction!

I took the file and sighed. After reading something like that, it was obvious there'd be no escaping it by feigning illness and retiring to hospital: the doctors would have orders to get you out of your grave if need be. You couldn't resign, either. It would be written into your work book and you'd never get another job, even as a caretaker. I remembered some words from Griboyedov: 'Worse than any sorrow are a master's anger and a master's love.' Well, I hadn't escaped the love. What would the anger be like?

Printed on the front of the file were the words: 'KGB. Top Secret. Case No. 16/1065'. It wasn't tied up with the usual ribbons, but had a metal clip to secure it. They don't manufacture such files in the Soviet Union, so it was obviously imported from abroad. The KGB's procurement department seemed to work efficiently, unlike ours.

I opened the file. Lying on top of all the other papers was the draft order which the obliging Karakoz had prepared for me, enabling me to begin criminal proceedings:

Authorized by A. Rekunkov
Chief Prosecutor of the USSR

ORDER INSTITUTING A CRIMINAL INVESTIGATION

Moscow, 22 January 1982

Having examined evidence concerning the death of S.K. Tsvigun, Special Investigator of the USSR, I. Shamrayev, Senior Juridical Councillor has established that:

At 14.37 on 19 January 1982 at one of the safe apartments belonging to the Operations Branch of the KGB (16-A, Kachalov Street, apartment 9), the corpse of General Semyon Kuzmich Tsvigun, First Deputy Chairman of the KGB, was found by his personal bodyguard, Major A.P. Gavrilenko, bearing the marks of violent death.

In view of the exceptionally responsible position occupied by Comrade Tsvigun in the Party and the State apparatus, the Politburo has decreed that the real circumstances of his death shall not be made public. Newspapers will report that his death occurred as the result of prolonged illness and to this end the KGB has prepared an appropriate post-mortem report, to be found in the accompanying file.

According to documentary evidence provided by the KGB, a Special Commission of Enquiry headed by the head of the KGB Investigation Section, B.V. Kurbanov, visited the scene of General Tsvigun's death on 19 January. The Commission established that his decease was the result of a bullet-wound in the area of the right temple. The shot was fired from the deceased's personal weapon, a 9mm 'PM' revolver. The used cartridge-case was discovered and removed during the inspection of the premises.

The KGB Special Commission of Enquiry concludes that Citizen Tsvigun was not murdered, but died by his own hand. Their decree confirming the decision not to proceed with a criminal investigation is appended.

However, at 5.40 a.m. today, 22 January, the Chief Prosecutor's Office received personal instructions from the Secretary General of the CPSU, Comrade Leonid Brezhnev, to begin forthwith a more detailed investigation of the reasons for General Tsvigun's death.

As a result, the Chief Prosecutor's Office orders that a criminal investigation shall go forward on the grounds that Citizen Tsvigun may have been forced to commit suicide.

For these reasons and in accordance with articles 108 and 112 of the Soviet Criminal Code, the Chief Prosecutor's Office has ordered:

1) that the decision of the KGB Central Investigation Department not to proceed with a criminal investigation, as confirmed by KGB Chairman Comrade Yu.V. Andropov, is rescinded as being not in accordance with all the evidence.

2) that a criminal investigation of the causes of Citizen Tsvigun's death be instituted,
3) that the Public Prosecutor's office will take charge of the said investigation.

Signed
Special Investigator
I. Shamrayev

'Well, do you see how I've been working on your behalf?' said Karakoz, when I had finished reading through the order. 'Anything to say?'

'One or two things,' I replied. 'You've forgotten to add your own stamp of approval.'

I gave him a frank stare, and he caught my meaning.

Of course, he hadn't *forgotten* to stamp his approval. He'd purposely not done so. Why should he get involved in an affair like this, so closely connected with the KGB and Suslov? There was no way I could avoid it, that was quite obvious, though I should dearly have liked to use this document to wrap up my fresh fish at the cafeteria. All the same, if Karakoz saw fit to send me urgent official telegrams in the middle of the night with gratuitous advice about women, then I would get my own back. Let him sign the order, too.

'Incidentally,' I said, 'why did you contact me by military telegraph?'

Karakoz looked anxiously, first at Rekunkov, then at the telephones next to him and said: 'Because otherwise there would have been no way of getting you out of Sochi within a week. And who was to conduct the investigation if not you? Let's go. Will you be making some changes to the wording of the order now, or is it all right as it is?'

'I want to examine all the documents first,' I said, 'and then I'll decide.'

Heavens above! You have to keep your mouth firmly shut even in the Chief Prosecutor's personal office, in case it is being tapped by the KGB too. Just try working in a place like this!

'Come on,' said Karakoz loudly, 'or else all the fish will be sold out!'

Part 2

A Second Version of Events

Moscow, 22 January, 3.00 p.m.

'Either you're a fool or making a good pretence of being one,' said Karakoz, as we entered the corridor outside the secretary's office. 'What are you playing at? Don't you realize that the phones might have been tapped?'

I started to get angry. Of course I knew that the KGB might have been listening in. Even though the Chief Prosecutor's Office is responsible only to the Head of State and has the right to investigate the affairs of the KGB, the MVD and every other ministry including the Ministry of Defence, it's an open secret that for a week or two every year the KGB taps our telephones both here and at home, so as to gather information about each of us. And since Brezhnev had given us a job like this, the KGB were probably already plugged in to our offices as well as my phone at home. It was no accident that Tsinyov had rung at the very moment I was sitting in the Prosecutor's office. He was just giving us a reminder! But if that was how things stood, how was I supposed to investigate the case?

I stopped in the middle of the corridor and said spitefully to Karakoz: 'Listen, what's going on in Moscow? Only don't try to conceal anything from me!'

'Idiot! I wasn't intending to.' Karakoz put his arm around my shoulder and directed me down the corridor towards the lift, turning round to make sure that nobody was listening to us. 'Only what was the point of hanging about in a place that might be bugged? Now I can tell you what's been going on. Two weeks ago Operation Cascade started in Moscow. You've heard about it. On the surface it's nothing unusual – the fight against corruption, black-market dealings undermining the fabric of Socialism, and all that. But there is one strange feature. Neither Tsvigun nor Brezhnev knew that this operation was being planned. Note that it's being carried out by the MVD's Anti-Fraud Squad and their internal Intelligence service. When have you heard of anything like this going on without the knowledge of the Politburo or even of Tsvigun? The second point to bear in mind is that, as it turned out, they immediately arrested people from whom Tsvigun had been receiving bribes for years. And furthermore they passed all this information on, not to Brezhnev, but to Suslov! So, as you can see, this was no ordinary fight against crime. They knew whom they were out to get and why! They were preparing a case. But against whom? After all, Tsvigun isn't just Tsvigun, but a close relation of Brezhnev. Get it? That's obviously what Brezhnev is thinking too. That's all. You can read about the rest in the file . . .'

'Wait a minute! Does this mean that I've got to interrogate Suslov?'

'You won't be asking him any questions. He's in hospital with a heart-attack. He's been there since the nineteenth and nobody knows when he'll be on his feet again . . .'

'What? You mean he was taken ill on the nineteenth of January too?'

'Well, what do you think? Tsvigun shot himself after talking to Suslov. It's no joke. Brezhnev blew his top at Suslov, and now both of them have been struck down by illness – one of them's in hospital, the other one's at his *dacha*. But there'll be a session of the Politburo on the fourth of February to discuss the results of Operation Cascade. That's why your report has to be on Brezhnev's desk at least a day before the meeting. See you later,' he said, lighting a cigarette as we got out of the lift on the fourth floor.

I realized that I wouldn't squeeze any more out of Karakoz. We were on the floor which contained the offices of the Investigation Department, and there were too many eyes and ears around. This was why Karakoz was in a hurry to be off.

All the same, I stopped him. 'Look, just one more question. How did you get to know about the girl I had down in Sochi?'

Herman gave a start and his brown eyes flashed: 'Ah! So that's what's been eating you! Agent's information, old man!'

'All right, stop playing the fool! Where did it come from?'

'Eighteen years old, a trapeze artiste from the Vologda State Circus, five feet tall, blue eyes, fair hair,' said Karakoz slyly. 'You went to a number of restaurants together – the Akhun, the Riviera, the Kosmos, the Kavkazsky Aul. Need I say more?'

'That's enough. Who was doing the spying?'

'Nobody was. It was simply done for a joke, out of envy. It was your friend Kolya Baklanov.' Karakoz glanced towards the office of my friend and colleague, Special Investigator Nikolai Baklanov. 'He's attached to the Anti-Fraud Squad now. As soon as he finished with the caviare business, he was transferred to Operation Cascade.'

'Well, how does that involve me?'

'The point was that he had a whole squad of men working for him in Sochi. They're after people with big money. They bring them in, then take them apart. If you want to find out how much you spent on your circus-girl in all the Sochi bars, just go and ask Baklanov, he'll tell you. Just between ourselves, old lad, was she any good? Has she got any girlfriends?'

'Haven't you got enough of your own?'

'I can never get enough, you know yourself,' he said with a hint of pride.

'Never mind, you'll manage,' I replied. 'See you later.' I turned round and walked towards my office at the end of the corridor.

On the way I wanted to drop in on Baklanov to tell him what I thought of him and his gossip, but the door of his office was locked. He was probably down in the cafeteria queuing up for fish, or off on business somewhere. The other offices were also closed. Behind their doors, in the silent security of the special investigators' safes lay the documentation concerning scores of the most hair-raising administrative crimes, each one of which would have caused a sensation in the West. I wandered off to my own room still trying to distract my thoughts from the KGB case-file which I had in my hand. So Kolya Baklanov was involved in Operation Cascade. Why not? It was logical. He'd managed to uncover a huge black-market operation at the Ministry of Fisheries after all, and he'd done that by himself, arresting two hundred people in the process, including the Minister and his top officials. For eight years or more they'd been quietly sending quantities of black caviare abroad, concealed in tins marked 'Sprats', and they'd pocketed the proceeds. The lion's share of the profit had gone to their contacts in the West, however, so they'd also been guilty of undermining the economic foundations of Socialism and of a major crime against the State. They'd get the severest punishment for that. Meanwhile, the same Baklanov, who had exposed this gang and had probably saved tons of caviare for the State, worth hundreds of millions of gold roubles, was now queuing downstairs for fresh pike and perch . . .

The thought of this made me laugh and I stepped into my office. There was nothing for it, Comrade Shamrayev, you'd have to open the file and immerse yourself in the details. That's why you're paid your salary. And that's why you're sometimes able to get fresh fish through the government special supply network . . .

The top sheet had the red emblem of the KGB on it – the Soviet coat of arms above a sword and shield. After this was written the following:

TOP SECRET
CONCERNING THE DEATH OF SEMYON KUZMICH TSVIGUN
Begun: 19 January 1982   No. of documents: 9
Concluded: 21 January 1982   No. of sheets: 16

Document No. 1
TOP SECRET
To the Duty Officer, KGB, USSR. Telegram received by telephone. Special report.

At 14.37 hours on 19 January 1982 I, KGB Major A.P. Gavrilenko, personal bodyguard to General S.K. Tsvigun, First Deputy Chairman of the KGB, discovered the General's body at safe apartment No. 9, 16-A, Kachalov Street, Moscow. There is a bullet-hole in his right temple.

Until receiving further instructions, I shall stand guard over the place where General Tsvigun's body is lying.

Telegram received – 19.1.1982 at 14.37 hours.

Comrade Andropov informed personally – 19.1.1982 at 14.37 hours.

Duty officer, KGB Major-General O.S. Nikitchenko.

Moscow, 19.1.1982

Document No. 2

REPORT

(Examination of scene of crime. External examination of corpse)

Moscow, 19 January 1982

On the instructions of Comrade Andropov and in accordance with Article 178 of the Criminal Code, I, Lieutenant-General B.V. Kurbanov, Head of the KGB Central Investigation Section, proceeded to the place where the corpse of General S.K. Tsvigun had been discovered and conducted an examination in the presence of the following witnesses: S.I. Kuravlyov and V.V. Lemin and forensic experts Dr A.P. Zhivoduyev from the Moscow Health Department and Dr P.I. Semyonovsky from the KGB Central Forensic Institute.

The examination was started at 15.50 and ended at 18.03. It was conducted under electric light and at a temperature of 22° centigrade.

The following facts were established:

Apartment No. 9, 16-A, Kachalov Street was the scene of regular meetings between General Tsvigun and his 'sources', i.e. agents of the KGB. The three-room apartment is situated on the second floor of a twelve-storey block. The disposition of the rooms is as follows: a large entrance hall (18 sq. metres), a corridor, a living-room (12 × 8 metres) to the right, a kitchen (15 sq. metres) to the left, and a bedroom and study at the end of the corridor. The living-room contains a 'Zarya' piano, a stereo record-player, a television set and a large table in the middle of the room.

On either side of the table are two cherry-coloured, leather sofas and a coffee table and drinks cabinet each made of mahogany. Two windows give on to the courtyard, both of them covered by dark blue blinds. The floor is covered with a hand-woven, Persian carpet. Along the left-hand wall there is a bookcase containing works by popular Russian and foreign writers – Pushkin, Tolstoy, Dickens, Dreiser, as well as some recent western publications like *The KGB*, *The Great Terror*, *Gorky Park*, and *Life* and *Time* magazines . . .

The furniture in the bedroom, study and kitchen is of Czech manufacture, while the floors are covered with hand-woven Persian carpets. The study contains a writing-desk, sofa, safe, armchair and three chairs. The safe contains two packets of banknotes (115,840 roubles in one, 91,000 American dollars in the other, all in 100-dollar bills).

General Tsvigun's body is to be found in the living-room in a sitting position, in an armchair drawn up to the dining-table, his head facing the table and inclined slightly to the left, a 'PM' revolver in his right hand, his eyes half open and his face covered with blood. The corpse is still warm to the touch. At the level of the right temple there is a circular wound marking the place of entry of the bullet. The wound is surrounded by a narrow, dark brown circle about 0.25 mm. wide. The surface skin has been stripped away. The epidermis has dried somewhat. Close to the left temple is a wound (2 × 2.5 cm.) with torn uneven edges which mark the bullet's point of exit.

According to the forensic experts, the shot was fired at a distance of 4 or 5 cm. from the surface of the skin. This is indicated by the lack of damage caused to the skin by gases and unexploded gunpowder. The barrel of the revolver was probably held horizontally, to the surface of the skin, as the lesion is at right angles to it.

The 9 mm. 'PM' revolver No. 2445-S, found in the right hand of the deceased, was General Tsvigun's personal weapon. A used cartridge-case from this revolver was found on the floor next to the corpse.

In the middle of the table in front of the body a suicide note was found, written on General Tsvigun's own official notepaper. It contained the following message:

'Goodbye. I beg you not to blame anyone for my death, I am to blame for everything. Tsvigun.'

The gold Parker ball-point pen used to write the suicide note was also found on the table.

According to the forensic examination of General Tsvigun's corpse, death had occurred approximately ninety minutes before.

The apartment was dusted for fingerprints and other evidence.

The following objects were removed from the scene of the crime and are appended to this report: the 'PM' revolver, a magazine containing eight bullets, one used 9 mm. cartridge-case, the suicide note, the Parker ball-point pen.

Also appended to the report is a schematic plan of the apartment.

The body and its clothing have been dispatched to the mortuary at Medical Institute Number One on Bolshaya Pirogovskaya Street, pending further instructions from the leadership of the KGB. Head of the KGB Central Investigation Department, Lieutenant-General B. Kurbanov.

Forensic experts: A.P. Zhivoduyev
P.I. Semyonovsky
Witnesses: S.I. Kuravlyov
V.V. Lemin

Document No. 3
EXTRACT FROM THE REPORT OF THE AUTOPSY CARRIED OUT ON
THE BODY OF GENERAL S.K. TSVIGUN
On 21 January 1982, in the mortuary at Medical Institute Number One,

I, Major-General Dr Boris Stepanovich Tumanov, chief forensic expert attached to the KGB Frontier Regiment and corresponding member of the USSR Academy of Medical Sciences, together with forensic expert Dr A.P. Zhivoduyev, and in the presence of the Head of the KGB Central Investigation Section, Lieutenant-General B.V. Kurbanov, conducted a post-mortem examination of the body of General S.K. Tsvigun, First Deputy Chairman of the KGB.

As a result of this post-mortem examination I reach the following conclusions:

The death of S.K. Tsvigun at the age of 64 years occurred on 19 January 1982 between 2 and 3 o'clock in the afternoon as a result of a gunshot wound in the region of the right temple. The bullet was fired from a 9 mm. 'PM' revolver. Death occurred as the result of destruction of cerebral tissue vital to the functioning of the organism. Death was instantaneous.

Data provided by the microscopic and spectroscopic analysis of the bullet's points of entry and exit, of the lesions to the skin and particularly of the blackened and charred shreds of skin around the entry wound, indicate that the shot was fired almost at point-blank range, from a distance of 4–5 cm.

The direction of the shot, the absence on the body of any other injury other than the bullet-wound, the absence of any signs of struggle or self-defence, details given in the report of the KGB Special Commission of Enquiry and other forensic evidence – all this leads one to suppose that the injury to General Tsvigun's temple was inflicted by his own hand, i.e. that *his death occurred as the result of suicide.*

Signed: B.S. Tumanov
    A.P. Zhivoduyev
    B.V. Kurbanov
Official seal.

Document No. 4

To KGB Chief Duty Officer Major-General O.S. Nikitchenko
From the Personal Bodyguard to General S.K. Tsvigun, KGB Major A.P. Gavrilenko

REPORT

On 19 January 1982 myself and KGB Captain M.G. Borovsky, General Tsvigun's personal chauffeur, were accompanying the General in Chaika registration No. MOS 03-04 on his official duties.

At 11.53 General Tsvigun and I arrived at the headquarters of the CPSU Central Committee where I accompanied him as far as the office of Central Committee Secretary, M.A. Suslov. I waited for him in reception.

At 13.47 Comrade Tsvigun left Comrade Suslov's office and ordered his chauffeur to drive to Kachalov Street. When we arrived at 16-A, I accompanied the General into the building. Here he ordered me to wait for him in the entrance hall on the ground floor. Since government instruction No. 427 of 16 May 1969 envisages situations where it would not be desirable for a bodyguard to be present at meetings between the person under his protection and the latter's secret contacts, and bearing in mind the fact that apartment No. 9 in this building was a 'safe apartment' in which General Tsvigun could meet his informants and agents, I carried out the General's instructions, as on previous occasions, and waited down below in the entrance hall.

While I was waiting there, nobody either entered the building or left it.

About 20 minutes later the chauffeur, Captain M.G. Borovsky, entered from the street and asked me whether I knew how long the General would be delayed and where he would be travelling next. 'If he'll allow me,' said Captain Borovsky, 'I'll get the petrol tank filled down at the garage at Tishinsky market, it'll only take me a couple of minutes.' Not wishing to disturb General Tsvigun, we waited for another ten minutes or so, after which Captain Borovsky used the phone in his car to get through to the KGB telephone operator, asking to have his call transferred to apartment No. 9. The telephonist replied that there was no answer from the phone in the apartment. Disturbed by this, but assuming that Comrade Tsvigun was resting, I took the lift to the apartment and cautiously knocked at the door, according to our prearranged signal. Without waiting for a reply, I rang the bell but could get no answer. Acting in accordance with instruction No. 427, point 11 about 'emergency situations', I forced open the door and saw General Tsvigun dead in the living-room, the body in a sitting position at the table, with a gun in the right hand and a bullet wound in the right temple. I immediately informed you, the Chief Duty Officer, by telephone.

I found no unauthorized persons in the apartment, the front door had been locked, and I have no reason to suspect anybody of the murder of General Tsvigun. As far as I am concerned, I personally committed no crime, since I was acting according to instruction No. 427 and the orders of Comrade Tsvigun.

Following your instructions given over the telephone, I immediately left the apartment without touching the body of the deceased or any other object, and stood guard outside until the investigation team arrived, headed by General B.V. Kurbanov.
KGB Major A.P. Gavrilenko
Report accepted by KGB Major-General O.S. Nikitchenko
19.1.1982, 16.45 hours

Document No. 5
To KGB Chief Duty Officer Major-General O.S. Nikitchenko
From KGB Captain M.G. Borovsky, Personal chauffeur to KGB General S.K. Tsvigun

REPORT

On 19 January 1982 myself and KGB Major Gavrilenko, Comrade

Tsvigun's personal bodyguard, accompanied the General on his official business.

At approximately 13.55 hours, following the instructions of General Tsvigun, we arrived in Chaika registration No. MOS 03-04 at No. 16-A, Kachalov Street. The General entered the building accompanied by Major Gavrilenko.

After waiting for twenty minutes, I assumed that Comrade Tsvigun was being delayed and that I might, with his permission, drive to the garage at the Tishinsky Market to fill up with petrol. I mentioned this to Major Gavrilenko, who, as often in the past, was standing guard in the entrance hall of No. 16-A. Major Gavrilenko advised me to wait for a few more minutes. If Comrade Tsvigun hadn't appeared by then I was to try to contact him by radio-phone, which I attempted to do at 14.25 hours. However, the telephone in General Tsvigun's 'safe apartment' wasn't answering, and I immediately informed Major Gavrilenko about this. He went up to the apartment No. 9 and discovered the dead body of General Tsvigun there. I found out about this later, as I did not go up to the apartment myself, but stayed on guard by the entrance below, as Major Gavrilenko had instructed, allowing nobody to enter the building until the arrival of the KGB investigation team headed by KGB General B.V. Kurbanov.

I observed nothing suspicious while I was at No. 16-A, Kachalov Street, nor did I disobey any of General Tsvigun's orders.
KGB Captain M.G. Borovsky
Report accepted by KGB Major-General O.S. Nikitchenko
19.1.1982, 16.55 hours

Document No. 6: sheet of personalized notepaper torn from the writing-pad of General Tsvigun:
First Deputy Chairman KGB
Deputy of the Supreme Soviet
General S.K. Tsvigun
Text written in a firm, legible hand:
> Goodbye. I beg you not to blame anyone for my death, I am to blame for everything. Tsvigun

He certainly had guts. I spent some time examining this document. The message was short, clear and to the point, as befits a military man. The signature was expansive, but legible; the handwriting, rounded and even. After all, he had been a schoolteacher in his youth, and a person's handwriting doesn't change much as he gets older. I wrote the following in my own notebook: 'Why didn't the bodyguard accompany him to the second floor?' – and read on.

Document No. 7

EXTRACT FROM THE MINUTES
OF A MEETING OF THE COLLEGIUM OF THE KGB, USSR

On 20 January 1982, at 16.00 hours in Moscow (No. 2 Dzerzhinsky Square) a special meeting of the Collegium of the KGB was held.

In view of the urgency of the meeting those members of the Collegium who are chairmen of the KGB in the other constituent republics of the USSR were not summoned to Moscow.

Those present: KGB Chairman, Comrade Yu.V. Andropov, Deputy Chairmen, Comrades G.K. Tsinyov, V.P. Pirozhkov, V.M. Chebrikov, L.I. Pankratov, Yu.A. Matrosov and other executive members of the KGB.

Present from the Central Committee of the CPSU: Chief of Administrative Section N.I. Savinkin

Total present: 14

Chairman: Yu.V. Andropov

Secretary to the Collegium: Head of Chancery Comrade Yu.N. Baranov.

Subject of the meeting: Comrade Yu.V. Andropov's report on the exceptional situation arising as a result of the demise of Comrade S.K. Tsvigun.

Comrade Andropov reported that on 19 January 1982 Comrade Tsvigun had shot himself in the head at one of the KGB's 'safe apartments'. The reason for his suicide was the discovery of the links which he had over many years with the illegal activities of State embezzlers and other economic crimes, information about which had come to light during the operation code-named Cascade, which had been carried out by the Anti-Fraud Squad of the MVD. In view of his impending removal from office and his being called to account by both Party and judicial organs, the said Comrade Tsvigun had taken his own life.

Comrade Andropov put forward a series of measures designed to preserve equilibrium in the central and provincial organization of the KGB, to reveal General Tsvigun's violations of his administrative duty and also to place the KGB machine in a position actively to avoid in future the negative and corrupt consequences of actions such as those which took place during Comrade Tsvigun's incumbency as First Deputy Chairman.

The meeting was also addressed by: Comrades Savinkin, Tsinyov, Chebrikov, Pirozhkov, Matrosov, Cherkasov.

Items decreed:

1. That the speeches made should not be reproduced in the minutes.
2. That particular attention should be paid to Comrade Andropov's announcement that General Tsvigun's suicide occurred as a result of cowardice.
3. That the Collegium should act on Comrade Savinkin's observation that the government considered it undesirable for its own organs and

those of the KGB to be compromised at home and abroad by the revelation of General Tsvigun's suicide.

In this connection it has been decided:

a) to keep the fact of General Tsvigun's suicide strictly secret,
b) to prepare a death certificate attributing his death to a grave illness,
c) on the basis of this medical certificate to instruct TASS to issue an announcement about the death of Comrade Tsvigun, First Deputy Chairman of the KGB,
d) to apply cosmetic treatment to Comrade Tsvigun's face with a view to concealing the traces of his bullet-wound,
e) to allow his body to lie in state at the Dzerzhinsky Club for two hours on 22 January 1982, so that his close relations and colleagues could take leave of him, but that no unauthorized persons or foreign correspondents should be allowed into the hall,
f) to bury the body of Comrade Tsvigun at the Vagankovskoye cemetery with second-class military honours.

4. That the official functions of the First Deputy Chairman of the KGB should, for the time being, be divided amongst Comrades Tsinyov, Chebrikov and Pirozhkov.

5. That the decision should be taken not to institute a criminal investigation into the death of Comrade Tsvigun in view of the self-evident nature of the case.

Signed:

Chairman of the Collegium of the KGB: General Yu.V. Andropov
Secretary to the Collegium: Major-General Yu.N. Baranov

There was no point in going on to read the fabricated death certificate (about hypertonic crisis, cardiac insufficiency, and so on) or the formal refusal to institute a criminal investigation. All right, so let's sum up. Now, how did my Jewish grandmother used to put it?: 'What's left over from the goose?'

A) Tsvigun shot himself after visiting Suslov, but was that the only reason? B) Where were the documents which helped Suslov to incriminate him? C) Why didn't the bodyguard go with him to the second floor? D) Where were Tsvigun's pistol and ball-point pen, along with the spent cartridge and the keys to the flat? On second thoughts, the fact that they didn't send any of those along with the file, had nothing to do with Tsvigun. That was simply Pirozhkov or Kurbanov's little revenge. They wanted me to drag along to the KGB to get them for myself. So we could forget about point D). So that left three unanswered questions – and God knows, that was quite enough to be getting on with!

I thumbed through the file once again from the beginning. Karakoz's draft order, made out in the name of Shamrayev, lay before me, pristine and as yet not signed either by myself or by the Chief Prosecutor. Well, what shall we do, Comrade Shamrayev? Shall we sign it? Shall we tackle the case?

I lit a cigarette and suddenly became aware of myself making this instinctive gesture. Now that was interesting! Before putting my name to this potentially lethal document, I had lit a cigarette. And what had Tsvigun done before killing himself? After all, he was a smoker – and a drinker too. I'd seen that myself many times. The last time I'd seen him was three months earlier at a meeting of Party activists in the Hall of Columns in the House of Unions – or rather, at the cafeteria there. He'd been seated at a table with Brezhnev's son and somebody else, drinking brandy and smoking. I can remember it very well. Is it really likely that before firing a shot into his head he wouldn't have lit a cigarette and poured himself at least one glass of brandy? Yet the report of the KGB investigation made no mention of any cigarette-end or brandy.

I looked at the clock. It was about 5.00 p.m. In a few minutes Kurbanov and the whole KGB Investigation Department would be off home with all the punctuality of professional soldiers. I found their number in the special government telephone directory marked 'Secret. For Official Use Only', and dialled.

'Lidiya Pavlovna, good afternoon! This is Shamrayev from the Public Prosecutor's Office. May I speak to Comrade Kurbanov?'

'Just a moment,' said Kurbanov's secretary, and a few seconds later her boss's voice came through the receiver

'Hello, Kurbanov speaking.'

'Good afternoon, this is Shamrayev. What chance is there of my receiving the other objects in the Tsvigun case today – I mean his gun, the spent cartridge-case and the keys to the flat on Kachalov Street?'

'Why the urgency?' he laughed.

I said nothing. That was my business.

'All right, if you need them, drop in at our office. The packet will be waiting for you downstairs with the duty officer. Only bear in mind that the revolver has already been cleaned. There's no smell of gunpowder any longer. How were we to know that there was going to be a second investigation?'

'And what about his diaries? And I'd also like to cross-examine the people that worked with him, including his bodyguard and chauffeur.'

'You've got their testimonies in the file. In our opinion, that's enough. You must understand that General Tsvigun and those around him weren't only involved in the internal affairs of the country. The specific nature of their work . . .'

'My questions won't concern the specific nature of their work.'

'I don't know about that. Only Comrade Andropov can authorize the cross-examination of KGB agents,' he said with finality.

'I'm sorry, Comrade Kurbanov, but the Chief Prosecutor's Office, as you know, doesn't require the permission of anybody,' I replied angrily. 'All I need is their addresses. And also the addresses of the witnesses who were present when the body was first examined.'

'I don't think that they will answer your questions without permission from Comrade Andropov,' said Kurbanov, laughing once again. 'And the witnesses are also our employees. You must understand you can't involve people in an affair like this at will.'

During this conversation, without even seeing Kurbanov, I could feel all the arrogance which a KGB general displays towards a tiresome little nobody at a public prosecutor's office somewhere or other. Pirozhkov had adopted exactly the same tone of voice three hours earlier.

'Tell me then, are *you* allowed to answer questions without Comrade Andropov's permission?'

'Which ones precisely?'

'Did Comrade Tsvigun smoke?'

'What? What?' he asked in astonishment.

'I'm asking whether Comrade Tsvigun smoked.'

'Yes, what of it?'

'Thank you very much. Can you give me the address of the widow?'

'For what reason?' he asked suspiciously.

'My dear Comrade Kurbanov,' I said in a conciliatory tone, 'you surely understand that I cannot conduct this investigation without even talking to his widow. Or do I need Andropov's permission to meet her, too?'

'All right,' he muttered. 'I'll put a note of her address into the packet along with all the other stuff . . .'

5.40 p.m.

Tsvigun's 'safe apartment' on Kachalov Street was exactly as it had been described in Kurbanov's report. There were the Persian carpets, the imported furniture and the soft leather sofas. The Yale lock of the door forced by Tsvigun's bodyguard had been repaired, and the door had now been officially sealed, but you could still see signs of the repair. All the rooms were decorated with vinyl wallpaper, imported from Finland and embossed with a pleasant design – wallpaper that would have been the dream of many a Moscow housewife. There were dark blue blinds at the windows, and in the middle of the living-room ceiling was a Cascade chandelier with a special three-way switch, the last word in Soviet electronics.

But I didn't pay much attention to the chandelier. The first thing I noticed about the apartment was its exemplary cleanness. This apartment, which had witnessed a suicide and had seen investigators, witnesses and forensic experts coming and going, was absolutely spotless. That is to say, Kurbanov had been so convinced that no further investigation would be carried out after his own, that he had ordered the apartment to be cleaned right through. I'd have to question the woman who did the cleaning, of course, although she was also bound to be an employee of the KGB.

I looked around for the ashtrays. They were empty, of course. But there they were, made of crystal, porcelain and metal, and to be found in every room. The one in the living-room was on the dining-table near where traces of blood had been removed. Now, if Tsvigun had given up smoking so much as a day before he died, there wouldn't have been any ashtrays around. People who give it up put all their ashtrays away and don't allow their visitors to smoke either. I know this from experience. So this meant that, although Tsvigun was a smoker, he didn't take a drag at a cigarette before he died, or else the cigarette-end would have been one of the exhibits in the case, along with everything else.

Next I examined the drinks cabinet.

It was of Czech design, made of darkish wood with a light inside it. It contained an array of bottles – French and Armenian brandy, imported and Soviet vodka, Rigan balsam in an earthenware bottle, Scotch whisky, Georgian wine, champagne – in a word, something to suit everyone's taste. Some of the bottles of brandy and vodka had been opened. Of course, this didn't necessarily mean that the occupant of the apartment kept all these bottles for his own personal use, though it certainly didn't argue against the fact that he liked to tipple. Nevertheless, he didn't have anything to drink just before he died. If he had, the post-mortem report would have referred to traces of alcohol being found in his blood. So he didn't pour himself a drink and he didn't light up a cigarette. All right. He arrived from Suslov's office (why did he come here, instead of going home or back to his own office?), sat down at the table, opened his writing-pad, wrote the suicide note, put the gun to his temple and pressed the trigger. He didn't waste any time, I'll say that for him!

I sat in the same chair. I placed the suicide note and ball-point pen in front of me and reached into the side pocket of my jacket, as if to get the gun. Wait a minute! Where was his overcoat or greatcoat? After all it was January. Or did he enter the apartment wearing his coat, forget to take it off, sit down at the table and shoot himself on the spot? None of the KGB reports mentioned what he was wearing – greatcoat, dress uniform, civvies, or what.

OK. Instead of Tsvigun's revolver, which I didn't have on me at that moment, I got a packet of Bulgarian cigarettes from my coat pocket, struck a match and walked over to the small ventilation window to have a smoke. At that moment I thought that Tsvigun might well have done the same thing just before his death. Gazing down at the relentless snow and at the brick wall of a garage outside in the courtyard, he might well have said his farewells to this marvellous, sinful world, where he had spent his sixty-four, admittedly far from dismal, years. Then he'd lit up his last cigarette and . . . In his place I would have thrown the cigarette-end out of the ventilation window at the top of the window-frame. What then? Would I have walked back to the table? Would I have sat down in the chair again, reread the note and got out my revolver? Or would I have shot myself there and then, while standing at the window? I knelt down, hoping to find some ash on the carpet by the window. No such luck! Could he have flicked it out of the ventilation window, I wondered? But when I stood on tiptoe and stretched out my arm to do this very thing, I noticed something which made me forget all about cigarettes, brandy and all those other subtleties of deductive and inductive procedure.

41

The upper edge of the open window-fame had been grazed in two places. The splinters were covered with powdered snow but the grazing was obviously of fairly recent origin, a day or two, say.

I moved a chair to the window and brought a desk lamp in from the study, so as to examine this interesting discovery more closely. I'd forgotten to bring my black bag with me, with its magnifying-glass and other instruments. What a goddammed fool! But who would have thought that I'd need it? I'd only been interested in ashtrays and bottles, after all . . . Besides, even without a magnifying-glass, I had a good view of a narrow, semi-circular furrow, about 3 mm. in diameter, torn through the fibre of the wood. I reached for the sealed, cellophane packet which contained the yellowish steel bullet which had put a sudden end to General Tsvigun's existence three days earlier. I removed the bullet and could see that, although its tip had become slightly flattened on impact with the skull, its cylindrical 9 mm. body had remained undamaged. I held it by its bottom edge and pushed it down the narrow furrow in the wood. It was a perfect fit. Of course, it would be necessary to carry out some ballistic tests, but it appeared perfectly obvious that the bullet had been fired through the room in the direction of the window, and had caught the edge of the frame as it passed.

Once through the window it must have hit the first or second floor of the apartment block opposite, which was identical with this one, and then dropped down into the snow below, which was three feet deep at least. It had been snowing continuously for days and the janitors had given up snow-clearance as a bad job, preferring to wait for the blizzards to end.

I jumped off my chair and rushed out of the apartment. I rang the doorbell of a neighbouring apartment at random. There was no reply. I could hear loud music in the next one along, so I tried there and a plumpish girl dressed in a wedding-veil appeared at the door.

'Excuse me,' I said, 'you wouldn't happen to have a pair of binoculars?'

'What?' said the bride in amazement.

It turned out that she didn't have one, but four doors down I did manage to get a pair of Zeiss field-glasses and even a child's telescope from the grandson of a former Navy Minister. I went out into the street. By the entrance was the Volga, the car which had been allocated to me for the evening by one of the Chief Prosecutor's assistants. Inside it, listening to the 'Beacon' on the radio, was my young, blue-eyed driver, Sasha Lunin. I ordered him to drive into the courtyard and to focus his headlights on the wall of the apartment block opposite, between the first and second floors.

That wasn't easy. Sasha scratched his head, but managed to do it by placing a couple of stones behind the back wheels and jacking up the front of the car. The powerful headlights were enough to light up the right spot, even at that distance.

Standing right by the wall, I focused the binoculars on the place in question and found what I was looking for – a blackish indentation in the white wall of the building.

I did a geometrical calculation in my head and ordered Sasha to lower the car and light up the area of snow vertically below the indentation at the foot of the building. To his astonishment, I then started to root around in the snow with my bare hands, precisely where he was focusing the light.

It didn't take long for my hands to become frozen stiff and I was cursing myself for my inordinate haste. Of course, it could all have been done much more professionally the following day and I could have called out a company of soldiers to sift the snow bit by bit. But there are times in any job when it's not manly to give up. Sasha looked at me ironically, while the yellow lights from neighbouring windows taunted me, along with domestic sounds of laughter, loud music and the flickering of television screens. In the pleasant warmth of these new, super-quality apartment blocks, built on quiet Kachalov Street especially for the governmental and scientific élite, people were drinking wine or tea, listening to music, celebrating weddings or simply watching the next episode of the TV detective serial 'Seventeen Moments in Spring' with Tikhonov in the main part. And there was I, like a janitor, rummaging around in the snow beneath their windows. But the angrier I became (and who was I angry with? Myself?), the more stubbornly I shoved my hands into the snow, as if it were a test of character. Only when I could hear my heart beating from the cold, would I drag out my hands, attempt to warm them by breathing on them, and then force myself to carry on searching. On top the snow was soft and new, but as I went further down, I encountered snowfall from yesterday and the day before, which had already half turned to ice. And I needed to go down to the level of three days earlier. I knew that I was being stupid, and that sooner or later I was bound to cut my hands on a piece of wood or metal or broken glass, and that would be that. My shoes were already soaking from the snow that had managed to get into them, as were the legs of my trousers and the sleeves of my coat and shirt which I'd stupidly forgotten to roll up. But just as I was about to give up the whole thing as a bad job, I suddenly felt something smooth, cold and metallic between the first and second fingers of my left hand. I could scarcely believe my luck. It was the bullet! I dragged it out, just as I had found it, between my two fingers. As I did so, I nearly dropped it! The digits of my right hand were so frozen that they simply wouldn't do what I wanted them to – grasp the bullet by its flattened nose. So, without even looking at the bullet, I stuffed it and my left hand into my coat pocket and almost ran indoors. It wasn't so much that I was in a hurry to examine the bullet, as that I was frozen to the marrow.

'That's enough!' I said to the driver. 'Turn off the headlights.'

A young couple were standing under the concrete awning by the entrance, dressed in imported, fleece-lined coats and deerskin hats. They looked at me in amazement, as if I were a tramp or crook who had rushed in from the courtyard. But I had no time for them. With great difficulty I managed to fit the key into the lock of the outer door and went into the entrance hall. Without even waiting for the lift, I rushed upstairs to the second floor and entered No. 9. Leaving wet marks all over the carpet, I headed straight for the drinks cabinet, grabbed hold of the first bottle I could (it happened to be Finnish vodka), undid its metal stopper with my teeth (my frozen fingers still wouldn't do what I wanted) and swallowed a great mouthful of liquor straight from the bottle. I did the same thing again, and again. Then with my mouth wide open I gasped for air, feeling the pure spirit rescue my frozen, frozen soul.

Now that I'd warmed myself up, I grabbed the telephone and dialled Svetlov's home number. After it had rung three times, I heard the voice of Olya, his wife.

'Hello!'

'Good evening,' I said. 'This is Igor. How are things?'

'Good evening,' she replied, in a strained, suspicious voice.

'Where's your other half? May I talk to him?'

'Humph!' she said sarcastically. 'He's already been at your place an hour, according to him. In future you ought to agree beforehand what you're going to say!' Whereupon she slammed down the receiver, so that all I could hear was the dialling tone.

So, I'd done Svetlov a bad turn. Still, it wasn't for the first time. I dialled the number of my own apartment, not really expecting anybody to answer. Nina would surely have gone by now, leaving me a note to the effect that I could 'go to hell', or something along those lines. After all, I'd sent her home before Tsvigun's funeral and then had disappeared completely.

But somebody answered straight away, and I could hear Nina's happy voice obviously struggling to make itself heard over the loud jazz music in the background: 'Hello.' And, then, talking to somebody else who was in the room, 'Tamara, turn the volume down a bit. Hello. I'm listening.'

'Who's Tamara then?' I asked.

'Is that you, Igor?' The music at the other end of the apartment got a little quieter. 'Where are you? We've got visitors.'

'What visitors?'

'Who do you think? Marat Svetlov.'

'And who's this Tamara?'

'She's a friend of mine from the Circus school. Marat asked me to invite her along so he'd have somebody to talk to. Come home quickly, or else all the food will have gone . . .'

'Let me talk to Marat.'

There was a short musical interlude, and then Marat came to the phone. 'Hello, old lad! Where are you?'

'Kachalov Street where Tsvigun died. Look, grab the girls and get over here as fast as you can!'

'What for?' he said with surprise.

I couldn't tell him over the phone. Both the telephone here and at my place were bound to be bugged, so I started to make it up as I went along. 'All right, I'll tell you. There's whisky here, and brandy. It'll go nicely with

44

the food the girls have prepared.' Then I put an end to his objections. 'No discussions.'

These words were an old signal of ours dating back to the time when we had worked together in the Krasnaya Presnya district of Moscow. He knew now that I wasn't really talking about carrying on the party in another place.

I went on talking in a relaxed manner. 'So take the food, put it in the black case on the window-sill behind my desk, and come over here, all right?'

The window-sill behind my desk was where I kept the tools of my trade.

'OK. And shall I bring the girls?' asked Marat suspiciously.

'Of course, what kind of party would it be without girls, idiot! 16-A, Kachalov Street, apartment 9. Ring the doorbell below. See you soon – and don't forget to bring the food!'

Let those who were taping and listening in to our conversation think that Special Investigator Shamrayev was abusing his official position to entertain his friends with French brandy and other spirits, taken from the drinks cabinet of the late General Tsvigun and therefore the property of the government. Tomorrow they'd make a note of this in my personal file which sits in the KGB archive along with files on all the other employees of the Public Prosecutor's Office, from the Chief Prosecutor himself down to Auntie Lena. But I didn't give a damn. What I needed more than anything were two witnesses and Svetlov with his born bloodhound's instinct. Because this was a very strange suicide. Not only did the victim not light up a cigarette before he died. For some reason he also fired a shot through the ventilation window.

9.00 p.m.

Of all the legal processes in which a lawyer is involved, the most interesting, to my mind, is the preliminary investigation. The barrister, judge and the public prosecutor always have their clients or the authority to think of. They urge on the lawyer, as if he were the driver of a carriage, they dictate the route he should follow and his final destination. In fact, these pressures can be so great that Soviet jurisprudence is often little better than legalized lawlessness.

But Article 127 of the Russian Republic's Criminal Code states that 'during the preliminary investigation *all* decisions regarding the direction and conduct of the investigation are the *independent* responsibility of the investigator, except when the law stipulates the Public Prosecutor's intervention'. Thus, any investigator is his own master. He has to deal with the concrete facts and actions of individual people. He comes face to face with life in all its poverty and splendour, with all its passions, accidents and bloodshed. No novel is so full of human passions as even the simplest, most routine of crimes. Jealousy, the desire to make money, the will to power – you come across everything. Often a single fact will involve the investigator in collecting details of the lives, characters and actions of everybody even remotely connected with the crime – including those who have cast-iron alibis, whether they have anything to gain from the crime or not. It's not unlike what the novelist does, except that you, as investigator, don't have the right to juggle with facts or invent them. You must seek only the truth. You're not dealing with some invented Othello or Raskolnikov, but the fate of any number of real, flesh and blood Ivanovs, Petrovs, Rabinoviches and Brezhnevs. Your own destiny is involved in it, too, which isn't the least of considerations.

In itself, the 9 mm. calibre bullet which I had found in the courtyard was of no importance. It was just a piece of metal, after all. Even the fact that it was shot through the ventilator wasn't of importance in itself. But the fact that I found it outside in the presence, not of two witnesses, but of a simple chauffeur, was already a deviation from the law on my part. Any court of law could reject the evidence. Of course, with the prevailing atmosphere of judicial arbitrariness, it was possible to neglect these formal niceties by writing the report of the discovery of the bullet later. But I don't seem to remember professionals like Comrades Shakespeare or Dostoyevsky disregarding the formal laws of grammar and punctuation in their works, full stops, commas and all the rest. In the same way, the formal correctness of a judicial investigation is the sign of an investigator's professionalism.

This was why I was waiting in the kitchen of the late General Tsvigun's safe apartment, drinking tea out of a glass, which I'd already checked for fingerprints, and waiting for the witnesses to arrive – Nina, a Tamara whom I didn't know, as well as Svetlov, who would be arriving with my black case. Something other than suicide had taken place in this apartment, and I wouldn't leave until Svetlov and I had examined every inch and every fibre of those luxurious Persian carpets and every little mark on that imported Finnish furniture. But now it would be done fully in accordance with the law – in the presence of witnesses and with the aid of simple but entirely adequate investigative tools. Svetlov was even better at this than I was. In his CID work he had to examine the scenes of crimes almost daily. He could see and sniff out anything.

My thoughts were interrupted by a ring at the door. It was Svetlov, Nina and Tamara announcing their arrival very loudly. They'd brought everything with them, including my black case, a tape-recorder, bags of food and even a bottle of champagne.

Nina had scarcely crossed the threshold and seen the spacious entry hall with antlers on the wall and a collection of African masks, before she said: 'Well, what a place! Is there anything for us to wipe our feet on?'

There were little globules of melting snow on her black, high-heeled boots.

'It doesn't matter, just walk in as you are,' I said magnanimously. But this didn't stop Nina looking round domestically for a doormat or at least a brush to wipe off the snow. Then she sat down firmly in a chair and started to take off her boots.

'Who ever heard of such a thing!' she said 'I won't leave dirty marks all over the parquet flooring. Let me introduce you. This is my friend Tamara, a bareback rider.' Then she stopped to listen. 'But who owns the apartment? Where are they?'

Svetlov and I exchanged glances. He obviously hadn't told them what it was all about. He'd probably said to them: 'We're going somewhere. You'll find out where later.' And he'd been right to do so. But now we'd either have to lie our way out of it, or tell them everything.

I decided on the latter. 'Look, girls,' I said. 'A crime took place in this apartment a few days ago. So you just go and sit quietly in the kitchen for a bit, but mind you don't touch anything, especially the crockery. Marat and I will work in here for now.'

Tamara was a tall, black-eyed girl with a thin, delicate waist, but she had shapely legs and firm strong shoulders. She said nothing at first, but soon grasped the situation. She gave her coat to Svetlov and then offered him her right leg for him to remove the boot. She already seemed to have control over the head of the third section of the Moscow CID, and no wonder! She lifted her leg so high that you could see right up her skirt.

Meanwhile, Nina had turned her lively blue eyes in my direction. 'A crime, you say!' she exclaimed. 'Is it the one that Marat was telling you about in Sochi?'

So she hadn't been the empty-headed child I'd taken her for!

'That's enough!' I said testily. 'No questions. Into the kitchen with you. And let me have something to eat. I could eat a horse.'

A few minutes later, Marat and I began our inspection of the apartment. I brought him up to date, showed him the damaged window-frame and the bullet. I didn't need to tell him anything else. He understood right away. His brown eyes flashed with excitement, his movements became at once deliberate and automatic.

'OK,' he said, donning the rubber gloves which he'd brought along in my black case. 'Girls, you sit in the entrance hall! You can breathe, but you mustn't move – and above all, don't touch anything. When we've finished checking the kitchen, you can move in there.'

'Could we switch on some music?' asked Nina timidly.

'All right, you can do that,' he replied.

'And can we watch you working?' asked Tamara.

He couldn't say no, but he did add severely: 'You can watch, but only from a distance. And don't ask any questions!'

After this he seemed to forget about her. Or rather, he probably remembered in his mind that they were there and played up to his audience slightly, but only the tiniest bit. In other respects, he was a model of serious concentration, attentive to the slightest sign and saying nothing. We probably resembled a couple of surgeons, putting on our rubber gloves and about to begin a complicated operation. Svetlov was in charge, however, and I readily agreed to be his assistant.

'Tweezers! . . . Magnifying-glass! . . . Give me some light from the side!

'. . . Powder! . . . Magnesium oxide! . . .'

Every tumbler and wine glass was taken by Svetlov, turned upside down and examined under the electric light. Every suspicious mark on the furniture was dusted with special powder to reveal any fingerprints. And all this he did with a speed acquired from long years of habit.

'Nothing . . . Nothing . . . Nothing . . .'

We dealt with the kitchen fairly quickly, in about a quarter of an hour. There were no traces of anything on either the crockery or the furniture. Cups, glasses, refrigerator, chairs – all clean. Svetlov gave me a meaningful look: there was nothing even to discuss. Obviously, somebody other than a cleaning-woman had been at work in the kitchen.

We moved the girls into the kitchen and allowed them not only to listen to the tape-recorder, but to get some supper ready. Then we moved into the main part of the flat. As we walked from the entrance hall to the living-room, Svetlov made the first discovery – though Nina later claimed the credit for it herself.

'Hey, old lad,' he said. 'Look over here, at the floor.'

I looked, but couldn't see anything. Just the traces of our wet footprints on the clean parquet flooring.

'Petya!' he said, mocking slightly, just as he used to when we were students living in Room 401 on the third floor of the Moscow University Law Faculty hostel on Losino-ostrovskaya Street. There were four of us sharing the same room then, and, instead of using our real names, we all used to call each other 'Petya'.

'Your girlfriend's got the look of a born police investigator. I'll take her into CID and make her a lieutenant. Look, there are carpets everywhere in this flat, apart from the entrance hall, where there isn't so much as a mat to wipe your feet on!'

This was quite true. There were carpets in the living-room, bedroom and study, and a runner in the corridor. But nothing in the hall. It didn't make sense. Svetlov got on all fours and, armed with a magnifying-glass, began to examine all the skirting-boards. A moment later he stood up and triumphantly showed me a thread of thick green carpet which he'd picked out of a gap between the skirting-board and floor.

'There you are! Of course, there was a rug here,' he said. 'There had to be somewhere to wipe your feet. Get married to Nina. She'll make a good housewife!'

In the living-room and bedroom we found nothing except what we already knew about from the KGB report. The traces of blood on and below the table had been more or less obliterated. All the same, we took some traces, more for form's sake than anything else.

Our second and last discovery came an hour later, when the girls were already tired of waiting for us and had begun to get bored. In Tsvigun's study, behind a radiator, hidden by his desk, we found a pile of yellowing sheets of paper, with columns of figures and other pencil-marks written all over them – the kind of notes scribbled down by card-players when they are playing 'preference'. I know nothing about the game at all, but Svetlov was an old hand at arresting card-sharks, and he said immediately: 'They were playing for high stakes. And these sets of initials will come in handy.'

The most interesting thing about the sheets of paper were not the notes about how much each individual was bidding, or had lost and won, but the initials of the players. I'd have to rack my brains over those.

When we'd finished checking over the flat, our last act was to photograph the window-frame and saw off the section of wood which had been grazed by the bullet. Only after we'd done this, did we sit down with the girls to drink tea and champagne. It was about midnight, and our two companions were almost nodding off from boredom and tiredness. Tamara wanted to slip home, but Svetlov had a simple way of dealing with that. He put his official identification papers on the table in front of her, a red booklet with the words 'Criminal Investigation Department, MVD, USSR' printed in gold on the front. Inside it read: 'Colonel of Militia Marat Alekseyevich Svetlov, Head of the Third Section'.

'Witness Tamara!' he said. 'We are detaining you, not as admirers of your beautiful legs, but in connection with an urgent matter of State. Sit quietly and stop moaning. In half an hour we'll want you to sign a report of our examination of the apartment, and then we'll drive you home. Understand?'

In my opinion, this had a greater effect on her than any amount of cajoling or flirtation.

'And where will you be going yourselves?' she asked.

'First we'll drop these items off at the Forensic Institute for tests, and then Marat will come back to my place. We've still got a few things to discuss,' I said.

Marat looked at me in surprise. He'd been intending to go home.

Then I added: 'I'll deal with your wife. I really need your help right now.'

'Perhaps I could come over to your place too,' said Tamara. Whereupon I realized that there was no way Svetlov would leave me now, not tonight at any rate.

The same night
'Whoever removed the traces of blood and took away the rug in the entrance hall, also killed your Tsvigun,' remarked Svetlov.

'And fired through the window?' I asked sarcastically.

'I don't know. If it wasn't suicide, then it must have been murder. There's no other alternative . . .'

'Very profound,' I replied.

'Wait a minute. Let's make a hypothesis. A) The conversation with Suslov and the accusations about black-market dealings are the best cover for staging and motivating the suicide, right? B) Tsvigun arrived here from Suslov's office. He's bumped off and they make it look like suicide. And C)

49

Suslov goes into hospital to make it appear that he has nothing to do with the whole affair.'

'But why shoot through the window?' I persisted. 'And how could they have known that he wouldn't go home to his wife, or back to his office, but that he would come here and walk into a trap?'

'I don't know . . . But if it was suicide, why the second bullet?' Svetlov persisted in his turn.

Our conversation was taking place at 2.30 a.m. in my one-roomed flat near the 'Airport' metro station. Marat and I were sitting in the toilet. The reader must forgive this mundane detail, but the exhausted girls had fallen fast asleep – Nina on a mattress which I had laid down on the floor in the kitchen, and Tamara in my bed, which Nina and I had relinquished. Svetlov's wife, needless to say, didn't believe me when I tried to persuade her over the phone of the urgency and importance of our business. I made several attempts, but after my third phone call she simply left her receiver off the hook.

'Don't bother,' said Svetlov. 'She won't change her tune, however many times you phone.'

By two o'clock the girls had dropped off to sleep, and Marat and I locked ourselves in the bathroom. We smoked one cigarette after another and quietly discussed the possible versions of Tsvigun's death.

'But suppose it was simply a burglar who knocked him off? Or a western intelligence agent,' I suggested.

'Do you really think so?' said Svetlov. 'How could they have chosen the precise day when Tsvigun had a quarrel with Suslov?'

'Well, I don't know,' I said with a sigh. 'We'll have to examine all the possibilities. It's a pity that the Forensic Institute isn't working tomorrow. We won't find out until Monday whether it was Tsvigun who fired through the window or somebody else . . .'

Out of my pocket I produced some of the standard forms, which I'd filled in an hour or so earlier when Svetlov and Tamara had been busy with less prosaic matters. One of them was a plan of investigation. It included everything: exhumation of the body, graphological analysis of the suicide note, forensic and ballistic tests on the two bullets, interrogation of all Tsvigun's relatives and associates, cross-examination even of Suslov, Andropov and Kurbanov. I'd also divided it up into a series of sections with titles like: 'possible motives for murder,' 'the circle of people with something to gain from the death of Tsvigun', 'ways of entering the flat', 'weapons used', 'examination of the deceased's clothing', and so on.

Svetlov whistled. 'Have you drawn it up already? When did you have time?'

'While you were screwing Tamara,' I replied.

'Let's have a look . . .'

He read through the plan, nodding here, shaking his head there. I couldn't help laughing as I watched him. He didn't yet know why I had been in such a hurry to draw it up. He was like a professor checking the work of one of his first-year students. Yet this wasn't the first case we had tackled together, and we'd known each other for more than twenty years. The point was that both of us thought he was professionally better than the other, though we would never have admitted it. It was my view that CID detectives didn't have the breadth of vision which would enable them to see the wider social ramifications of a case, that is to say, they had no criminological flair. He, on the other hand, was convinced that we 'specials' lacked the ability to sift through a mass of concrete facts and details, and extract the clues which lead straight to the criminal – in other words, that we had no investigative flair. You might have thought that he was giving me an examination in the latter, to judge from the occasional remarks he made as he read through my plan ('What's the point?' 'Nonsense.' 'No need for that.') It sounded as if I'd scarcely passed.

'Not to worry, old lad. Your little plan will do,' he said condescendingly. 'But I'm sorry, there's no way you're going to keep the timetable you've set yourself.'

'Well, I won't manage it alone, of course,' I replied. 'But it might be possible if you were to help.'

'Me?' he said in amazement.

'On Monday I'll ask your boss whether he can transfer you to my unit. Along with your entire team.'

'Oh no! I want nothing to do with it,' he said, and stood up decisively. 'In the first place, they won't let you have me. I'm on loan to Malenina and the Anti-Fraud Squad. And besides, I haven't the slightest desire to get mixed up in this affair. I don't mind helping you with a bit of advice, especially if Nina has more friends like this. But as for getting mixed up in the affair officially, you'll have to look elsewhere. I've got a family, and I want to carry on living. Get involved with Andropov and Suslov? Not on your life! You must be joking!'

A shuffling noise behind the door made us look round. Svetlov unlocked it. There was Tamara, half dressed and wearing my dressing-gown.

'What on earth's going on?' she said, pressing her legs together with impatience. 'I thought the toilet was engaged and here you are – smoking!'

Part 3

Saturday – a 'Non-Working' Day

Saturday, 23 January, 10 a.m.
And still it snowed. White flakes like pawprints blurred the outlines of houses and trees. The streets were deserted, apart from groups of alcoholics hanging around outside wine and vodka shops, waiting for them to open. But it was more lively in the metro: cheerful young people in woollen and flannel ski-suits were making their way noisily to the Belorussky and Savelovsky stations in order to get out of town to the snowy forests around Moscow. They couldn't care less about Tsvigun, Suslov, and Brezhnev. They had their own lives, skiing, laughing, tumbling in snowdrifts, kissing wind-chilled lips, unaware that during these days perhaps the fate of their government was being decided, and therefore their own fate.

I myself did not know it on that Saturday morning; I just quietly slipped out of my apartment while Nina, Svetlov, and Tamara were still asleep, and set off for the Prosecutor's office so that I could sit in the quietness of my room and continue to plan the investigation with a clear head.

Saturday silence reigned in the Prosecutor's office too. Locked office doors, empty, clean-swept corridors with their velvet runners. Only on the fourth floor, in Baklanov's office, was a typewriter tapping. Since we were friends I opened the door without knocking. And I got the impression that Nikolai Baklanov, my friend and colleague, was startled and gave a slight jump, but then quickly got over his fright and said: 'Oh, it's you? Hello. Did you get the new case? Oh, I've heard all about it! So how's it going?' and with a seemingly casual movement of the hands he covered some typed sheets with a folder.

'I'm getting into it,' I said. 'What about you?'

When I first came to the USSR Public Prosecutor's Office eight years ago, Baklanov, tall, thin, well past forty, was already a leading figure there, an experienced special investigator. He had been happy to teach me the ropes, especially over a glass of beer in the local pub on Stoleshnikov Lane. But for the last couple of years we were more or less level both in experience and in the importance of the cases we were handling. And although I still con-

55

sidered Baklanov to be more experienced and better qualified than myself, for some reason we had begun going to the pub less and less often, and we confided in each other less and less often over our cases.

That is probably why he said: 'Me? Oh, just routine stuff,' and he stuck a cigarette into his customary amber cigarette-holder.

'Some routine!' I laughed. 'Karakoz said you were the one who stirred it up over Cascade . . .'

I exaggerated about 'stirring it up', I was just trying to get a rise out of him, but he leant back in his chair and said drily: 'Me? I didn't stir anything up. I was seconded to Anti-Fraud, and that's all. And if Karakoz is going to start these rumours . . .'

The telephone cut him short, and he picked up the receiver. 'Hello, Baklanov speaking . . . Good morning, Nadezhda Pavlovna . . . Hmm . . .' He glanced at me. 'Can I ring you back in about five minutes? Are you at home or . . . No, I have everything ready, but . . . Yes, you guessed right. I'll ring you back in five minutes.' He hung up and stared silently at me, obviously waiting for me to get out of his office.

'Was that Nadezhda Malenina?' I asked.

'Yes,' he replied reluctantly, 'what of it?'

'I need to see her. Is she at home or at the Anti-Fraud Squad office?'

'She's at work. What do you need her for?'

'Oh, nothing much . . .' I laughed. 'Routine stuff . . .' I began to go out, my hand already reaching for the door.

But Baklanov suddenly stood up. 'Igor, I want to say something to you. It would be better to do it in the pub of course, but there is no time. Listen. This case that has been foisted on you. It's not for you. Wait, don't get insulted. You'll simply break yourself for nothing over it, and that's just what you don't need to do, believe me.'

'Why?'

'Old man, I can't reveal everything to you,' he said. 'It's just that I want the best for you, you know that. And I ask you as a friend, take sick-leave and get out of this case. Even for a week. Go to a holiday home. I'll fix you up in any one you like. Take a girl with you, three girls if you like! And in ten days everything will have changed, believe me . . .'

'What will have changed?'

'Stop probing me, chum. Just believe me, you don't need to get into this business.'

'Kolya, you and I are very close,' I said with complete calm. 'The next Politburo meeting is in ten days' time. Is that what you have in mind when you say something will have changed?'

'You really keep at it, don't you?' he said, shaking his head in annoyance. 'This constant suspiciousness! Sit down, we'll talk about it. I don't really have the time, but . . .'

I did not sit down, but continued to stand by the door. Baklanov came round the desk and closed the door behind me.

'Igor,' he said quietly. 'I am not anti-Semitic, you know that. Yes or no?'

'No, you're not,' I said sincerely, for it was true.

'Now listen. *Where, when,* and *what* is going to change,' he uttered with emphasis, 'I shall not tell you. But remember: don't sink your teeth too deeply into this case, and after all no one is forcing you to sink them all the way in, but just conduct it . . . well . . . it's not for me to tell you how, understand?'

I was silent.

He did not wait for a reply and continued: 'I'll be brief. Look to the future. Anything can change, and we need people like you.'

'Kolya, is it a ministerial post you have your eye on?'

'Idiot!' he said in a pained voice. 'I'm just telling you as a friend . . .'

'As a friend – what? Are you trying to get me to hush up . . . murder?'

For a long time he looked me straight in the eye. Almost a minute. And it was so quiet that it seemed as if he and I were the only two people in the whole of snowy Moscow.

Then he turned, walked round behind the desk, sat down in the chair, and said wearily, almost indifferently: 'Sorry, old chap. Consider we never had this conversation.'

I shrugged my shoulders and grasped the door handle.

'But bear in mind,' I heard behind my back, 'if our paths cross . . .'

'Then what?' I turned round in the open doorway.

He looked me in the eye and smiled, showing nicotine-stained teeth: 'Then we'll see . . . Sorry, I have to work.'

I closed his office door tightly. To all intents and purposes Nikolai Baklanov had silently confirmed that Tsvigun had been murdered and had challenged me at the same time to a professional duel. In that case I could not do without Svetlov.

I went down to the third floor and said to the man on duty: 'I need a car. For the whole day.'

And while he was ringing through to the garage for a car I sat down at my typewriter and on a sheet headed USSR Public Prosecutor's Office tapped out first a normal covering letter – to the head of the main Post Office in Moscow, Comrade I.I. Mescheryakov, and after that my first order relating to the case of General Tsvigun's death.

ORDER

(concerning the seizure of postal and telegraphic correspondence)

Moscow, 23 January 1982

In connection with the institution of legal proceedings in the matter of the death of General S.K. Tsvigun and in pursuance of Article 174 of the Criminal Code of the Russian Soviet Federal Socialist Republic, Senior Juridical Councillor I. Shamrayev, Special Investigator at the USSR Public Prosecutor's Office, hereby orders:

1. That all correspondence (without exception) addressed to Semyon

Kuzmich Tsvigun and arriving by post and telegraph, irrespective of address, including work address: KGB of the USSR, 2, Dzerzhinsky Square, Moscow; and also home address: Apt. 9, 16-A Kachalov Street, Moscow; and also *dacha* address: 2, Garden Road, Malakhovka Platform, Moscow Region, shall be intercepted.

2. That all postal despatches arriving for Citizen S.K. Tsvigun, including letters, telegrams, parcels, printed matter, postcards, money transfers, etc., shall be forwarded immediately by courier to the USSR Prosecutor's Office: 15-A, Pushkin Street, Moscow, c/o Special Investigator I. Shamrayev (personally).

3. That it be explained to all personnel working in sorting, examination, and delivery departments of the Post Office that in the event of postal or telegraphic correspondence addressed to S.K. Tsvigun being delivered to other persons, those guilty will be held criminally responsible under Article 75 of the Criminal Code of the RSFSR – for divulging state secrets and for violating the present Order of the USSR Public Prosecutor's Office.

I. Shamrayev, Juridical Councillor
Special Investigator at the USSR Public Prosecutor's Office

Having dashed off this document and stamped it with the round seal, I put it on the desk in front of the Duty Prosecutor and requested him to send it, please, to the main Post Office by courier.

'Fine,' he said, 'the car is down below. MOS 16–54. The driver is Aleksandr Ruchov; you know him.'

10.35 a.m.

It is a long time since I have seen such a panic as was going on that Saturday morning in the Main Directorate for Combating the Embezzlement of Socialist Property (the Anti-Fraud Squad). The building occupies an old green detached house on Sadovo-Sukharevskaya Street, whose ballrooms and drawing-rooms have long since been partitioned into investigators' offices, and on all five floors the work was noisy and intense – inspectors, senior inspectors, special inspectors of the MVD's Fraud Squad together with militia inspectors, were in their offices questioning those involved in underground business who had been arrested in Operation Cascade: shady dealers from Moscow, the Caucasus, and Central Asia, dismissed directors of large trading organizations, wine factories, meat and dairy combines, and shops. The corridors were crowded with people. Fat, sun-tanned Georgians, pale, freckle-faced people from the Baltic states, and Muscovite kings of the unofficial economy in their fleece coats, stood or sat, wearily waiting their turn to be interrogated. The militiamen from the special regiment who formed the escort were smoking and joking by the open windows and on the stairs.

I went up to the second floor to see Colonel Malenina, Deputy Chief of

58

the Main Directorate, but a smartly dressed inspector, Sasha Sychov, a pupil of mine who had done his investigative practical under me about five years ago, popped out of her office and said: 'Oh, hello! Are you coming to see Nadezhda Pavlovna?'

'Yes.'

'She's not here.'

I nodded in the direction of the half open office door: 'Who's in there?'

'I'm interrogating another lemon man, head of the Sochi Resort Trading Organization. By the way, he said it was you who fetched him up from Adler. Thanks, he's a useful fellow.'

'But what's going on around here? What's all the panic?'

'Terrible! Don't even talk about it!' Sasha smiled. 'Operation Cascade – heard about it?'

'A little,' I smiled.

'And do you know where they got the name from? A suburban light-bulb factory was putting out these modern chandeliers with a three-way switch; they're called Cascade – the housewife's dream. My wife nagged at me to get one, but how? The whole line went underground, with a hundred per cent mark-up. As for auditing, no way, you couldn't get near the factory because the director was Tsvigun's nephew. But about ten days ago Malenina gave the go-ahead, and that's when things took off! We grabbed the nephew, and hundreds of others – we are unravelling corruption and mafia, as you used to teach us . . .'

I smiled again. Here it was, the irony of fate. General Tsvigun's life was cut short beneath a Cascade chandelier produced with his protection by his own nephew. Wondrous are the thoughts of the Lord, are they not?

'But why the panic? Why have interrogations on a Saturday? That's against the rules, isn't it?' I asked the talkative Sasha.

'Oh, who has time for formalities right now? We're cleaning out such pig-sties that we're making up to a hundred arrests a day! The whole MVD is on alert!'

'And the Forensic Institute too?'

'You bet! They're up to the eyes – working two shifts and no days off.'

'And where's Malenina?'

'She's in the new building, on Ogaryov Street, by the Central Telegraph. Do you want me to put you through to her? We have a direct line.'

'No thanks, I'd better drop in on her myself.'

'Suit yourself, so long!' and Sasha Sychov ran down the corridor into another office, where I could hear his young petulant voice: 'Tanya, you've been promising to give the tape-recorder back for an hour. It's impossible to work like this – one tape-recorder to three investigators! And this is the electronic age!'

I went downstairs to my car. There at the entrance to the Main Directorate stood yet another police van, and a new party of prisoners was being brought in for questioning by the escort. Among them were my acquaintances from

Sochi – the 'meat king', Nukzar Baratashvili and Major Makarov, head of the Sochi Anti-Fraud Squad. As they got out of the van they took a deep breath of fresh frosty air and looked up and down the street. On the other side of the Garden Ring Road there was a queue outside the Forum cinema. The Forum was showing a popular melodrama, *Moscow Doesn't Believe in Tears*.

'Hurry up! Don't gape!' the escort policeman yelled at the prisoners and Major Makarov, his shoulders drooping, trailed obediently into the Main Directorate.

I got into the black 'MOS' Volga and said to the driver: 'Ogaryov Street.'

Then I fished the radio-telephone out of its nest and gave the operator my home number. But nobody answered – either they were all still asleep, or they had gone for a walk. I was sorry I had not rung earlier – I really should have warned Svetlov that I was coming to Malenina on His Svetlovian Highness's behalf not on Monday, but right now. These alerts in the Main Directorate and the Forensic Institute merely strengthened my resolve.

The Garden Ring Road sped beneath the car's wheels; we made a left turn on Petrovka and in half a minute passed the famous No. 38, the Main Directorate of the MVD, where the legendary Moscow Criminal Investigation Department is housed. Here too, at the gate of the CID control-room, there was an unusual amount of life for a Saturday: about eight brand new West German Mercedes police cars painted in the livery of our militia, Volgas with souped-up engines, militia inspectors with dogs, and plain-clothes agents.

'Has something happened in Moscow then?' the driver asked me. I shrugged my shoulders. Moscow looked just the same – a quiet, peaceful snow was falling.

11.10 a.m.
Everyone knows the Moscow Central Telegraph on Gorky Street. Right behind the Central Telegraph on the quiet, short Ogaryov Street is a long, seven-storeyed, sandy-coloured building – also famous – the USSR Interior Ministry. Lorries are forbidden to pass through here, and every car that drives down this street is closely watched by the militiamen patrolling outside the building and five or six plain-clothes agents who dutifully walk up and down both sides of the street. No private car has a right to stop – the duty traffic-controller will immediately run up and ask sharply: 'What's going on? Move along! Hurry up!' Why should this be? Why such strictness? Even the KGB building at the Lubyanka does not have such blatant and intense protection.

To be honest, I never used to attach much significance to this. So Shcholokov, the Interior Minister, wants to show his power – well let him. The Ministry filled the empty plot between the Central Telegraph and themselves by putting up another narrow, modern-looking nine-storey building looking exactly like the Ministry of Communications. It catches few people's attention, and does not even carry a sign, so one would think it is a new wing of the Central Telegraph – and good luck to them. Which ministries are not expanding these days? Every clerk wants to sit in his own office, and there are more and more of them, especially in the Interior Ministry. But I realized that on that morning it had nothing to do with Shcholokov's ambitions. Our black Volga with its MOS number-plate braked beside the militiaman who was patrolling the pavement. I handed him my ID as Investigator of the USSR Prosecutor's Office. He compared the photograph on the ID with my face, and then waved his hand: 'Carry on.'

The snow at the entrance to the new building was covered with car tracks. Another MOS Volga drew up behind us, and at the entrance stood two militia Mercedes, a Zhiguli, two vans marked 'Repairs', and a meat and dairy lorry. In each vehicle there was a driver in plain clothes and also plain-clothes militiamen – just as in times of a really hot operation. Cascade, I thought; they've really pulled out all the stops.

I walked past the cars, nodded to an agent I knew, and once again showed my ID to the captain of militia on duty.

'Who do you want?' he asked.

'Malenina,' I answered.

'Did you order a pass?'

'Me?' I asked in amazement. 'I am a Special Investigator!'

'One moment.' He picked up the intercom and reported to someone: 'Somebody from the USSR Prosecutor's Office for Colonel Malenina . . .' Then he listened to the answer and asked me: 'Are you from Comrade Baklanov?'

'Yes,' I lied without blinking, so as not to waste any more time. From Baklanov, so be it – what's the difference?

'First floor please,' he said and gave back my ID. 'You can take your coat off in the cloakroom.'

I walked along to the cloakroom, hung my well-worn overcoat on a peg, and now, in my uniform of Senior Juridical Councillor, looked just like the various ranks of militia scurrying about the vestibule. Yes, they hadn't done badly for themselves in the new building, I thought, looking at the tall arched windows that reached up to the first floor, the marble finish on the walls, the soft carpeting in the corridors, and the noiseless lift with its steel plate: 'Made in Germany'. Not like our dilapidated Prosecutor's Office. But the next minute I was no longer able to continue my admittedly envious curiosity.

In the bright empty corridor of the first floor I clearly heard the imperious and throaty feminine voice of Nadezhda Pavlovna Malenina: 'What the fuck has happened to the sound?! Gurevich, I'll have your balls! Turn the sound on immediately!'

So, I laughed, Nadya Malenina was in her element. Swearing by no means suits all women, and I personally don't think it suits anyone, but this thirty-eight-year-old blonde with the beautiful figure, ex-Master of Sport in

61

artistic gymnastics, wife of a professor in the Military Academy of the General Staff, Colonel of the Militia, Nadezhda Malenina, told me more than once that her reply to such Soviet etiquette was to 'lay it on thick'. She enjoyed swearing, and enjoyed showing off her blue colonel's tunic (and it certainly did go with her blue eyes, white skin, and slightly reddish hair). But more than anything she enjoyed openly and loudly laying into the whole system, the corruption in the ministries, the collective farm set-up – everything that we talked about only at home with our very closest friends, and even then only after the third bottle of vodka. As the wife of a general and Deputy Head of the Anti-Fraud Squad, she could afford to do that.

'Do you hear me, Gurevich? Fuck your mother!' her imperious voice resounded right down the corridor.

'Nadezhda Pavlovna, I . . . Comrade Colonel, I thought . . . There is even . . . after all it is Leonid Ilyich's daughter . . .' came the voice of some Gurevich, slightly distorted by the ether and evidently embarrassed.

Oho! Brezhnev's daughter? *This* was getting interesting. I approached the half open door and saw that it was not an office at all, but a hall, exactly like the one in the Moscow CID, only with much newer equipment – television surveillance screens, tape-recording points, video-recorders, long-distance bugging terminals . . . Malenina was standing with her back to me, her whole body straining towards the central terminal. Next to her stood three generals and two colonels, while at the terminal a captain in the engineering and technical service sat on a rotating stool with some other technical personnel at small screens on either side of him.

'None of your business whose daughter it is, Gurevich!' Malenina said furiously into the microphone. 'Sound!'

'Yes, Comrade Colonel,' replied the voice of the poor Gurevich, and immediately, heavy breathing could be heard, languid female groans, the rhythmical sounds of naked bodies, then a woman's voice: 'More! . . . That feels good! . . . More!!!'

'But why can't you help Givi?' asked a soft, well-spoken baritone.

'Forget it! I've already told you why! Don't get side-tracked! More! . . .'

'When did she tell him?' exclaimed Malenina in the hall. 'So, Gurevich! You missed that bit! I won't forgive you for that! We're going to drive those dirty Jews out of the security services, Comrade Minister, we're going to drive them out!'

The generals turned slightly sideways towards Malenina, and I recognized one of them as General Nikolai Shcholokov, Interior Minister of the USSR, while the other I recognized as Major-General Aleksei Krasnov, the new head of Intelligence at the MVD following the death, in Afghanistan, of Paputin.

'No!' the female voice said suddenly and immediately changed to a sob: 'I can't! I can't . . . I'm old! I'm too old! My God, why can't I come?'

'Stop shouting,' said the baritone. 'It's embarrassing, there are guests.'

'Oh, to hell with your guests! They can go and get knotted!' screamed the woman's voice. 'My life is finished, finished! I'm already a grandmother! An old woman! . . .'

'Stop, stop,' the man's voice admonished. 'You're just not on form today, come again tomorrow. Bring Givi's diamonds with you, since you can't do anything for him.'

'All you think about is the diamonds!' the woman's voice exploded. 'There! There! There are your baubles!'

Over the ether could be heard the sound of objects falling on the floor.

'Bitch!' commented Malenina. 'She's chucking diamonds about!'

'Wait! Wait!' the baritone began softly again. 'What are all these earrings and bracelets for? Here, let me wash you. There. Silly, I'm not asking for myself. I realize that while Tsvigun was around nothing could be done for Givi, no amount of diamonds could help, but now . . .'

'She won't give them back to me!' the female voice wept.

'Who?'

'Irka Bugrimova!' sobbed the female voice. 'She promised me she would get her sugar daddy to free your Givi, but he refused; he was afraid of Tsvigun.'

'But Tsvigun is dead . . .'

'Well, I don't know what to do . . . Let him wait a little!'

'He's already waited three years . . . All right, I know what to do,' said the man decisively. 'I shall collect the diamonds from her myself and give them back to Churbanov, and everything will be all right . . .'

'Yury won't take them,' said the woman's voice. 'He's playing the saint right now.'

'We'll see about that! No one's ever refused diamonds like that. All right, let's go, or the guests will be sulking. Come on, I'll sing you your favourite song. "I was on my way home . . . I was thinking of you! My anxious heart was sometimes confused, sometimes eager . . ."'

The baritone's song was lost, but only for a moment, then it could be heard clearly again in another room against a background of male and female voices: 'Well, why are we all sitting around, not drinking? Where's the guitar? A glass each – there we go! Now we're living! "The apple trees and pear trees were in blossom, the mist was floating over the river! Out onto the bank came Katyusha!",' he sang in a jolly dancing rhythm.

'To hell with it!' said Malenina angrily. 'I've already got reels of his songs! It's time to get that singer. If we take him she'll squeal straight away, she'll sell her own father . . .'

I moved about twenty paces away from the door, towards the window, just in case. I would have done better never to have stood next to her, to have stayed home with Nina. I should not have left Sochi, but stayed there as a doorman, a guard, a lifeguard on a children's beach. Karakoz was right – this was what Cascade was really about! Not racketeers, like the ones they were arresting right now by the dozen, not the anti-corruption campaign for the purity of the Soviet economy – that they really laid on thick! Cascade was

Tsvigun, Galya Brezhneva, and one wondered who would be next? And they were taking in the racketeers and all sorts of big underground men just to get material to compromise the Brezhnevs. 'We'll drive those dirty Jews out of the security services!' Malenina had said, and I thought: you bitch! Wasn't it you who tried to press me to take an official trip with you to Alma-Ata, and openly offered me a fabulous journey in a compartment for two in the Moscow–Peking train? Wasn't it you who got interested in the difference between circumcised Jews and uncircumcised Orthodox? And at Novosibirsk didn't you sleep with half the population of Akademgorodok while you were supposedly checking on the huge sums earmarked for some atomic physics research?

My recollections were interrupted by the agitated voice of Malenina: 'I can't believe she doesn't know about these tapes! I'm not going to let that whore out of my sight!' her voice suddenly stopped about six feet away from me. I turned away from the window and saw her face, distraught and pale. 'Igor?'

Shcholokov, Minister of Internal Affairs, and Aleksei Krasnov, head of MVD Intelligence, were walking along beside her. The three of them didn't even say 'Hello' to me. Malenina looked straight at the door of the hall, mentally calculating the distance from me to that door and trying to work out if I could have heard anything, while Krasnov – a small, lame fifty-year-old with a stick – scowled: 'How did you get in here?'

I shrugged my shoulders: 'Actually I came to see Nadezhda Pavlovna.'

'And how long have you been here?'

'About half a minute . . .'

Apparently I said it sufficiently naturally – the suspicious shadows left their faces. Shcholokov and Krasnov moved off down the corridor, and Malenina immediately took me by the elbow with exaggerated warmth: 'Igor! Let's go to my office. Haven't seen you for ages! How's your son? How are things?'

'You've got your own office here too?'

'Of course! We're on the way up! It's time to clean out these pig-sties. I heard you were on holiday somewhere in the south. Some people have all the luck!'

It seemed as though she was talking this rubbish just in case any more sounds should reach my ears from the surveillance-room. And so, holding me by the arm and seemingly accidentally brushing against my shoulder with her firm breast, she guided me to the far end of the corridor and unlocked an unmarked office. Yes, it was a luxurious suite, almost ministerial! A reception-room panelled in Karelian birch, soft furniture and a desk for the secretary, and beyond the reception-room was the actual office – with huge windows looking out onto Ogaryov Street, a Cascade chandelier above the desk, two leather sofas, a cocktail cabinet in the corner, and Persian rugs on the floor. Malenina sat me down on the sofa near the bar and poured some French Napoleon into crystal glasses.

'For old times' sake! You're the only fellow I've never had it off with, though I must say there were times when I really wouldn't have minded! D'you think I've aged? Cheers!'

She downed a full glass in one and watched me sipping and savouring mine. 'Not one of us!' she commented with a smile and poured herself some more. Then she unbuttoned her tunic and sat down next to me on the sofa, very close. 'What's the matter, aren't you a real man? Can't drink? With a woman like this sitting next to you!'

The woman certainly was a bit of all right – not a wrinkle on the neck beneath the tunic, and under the officer's shirt and tie were full breasts without a bra.

She intercepted my glance and laughed with pleasure: 'And the legs? Take a look at that!'

Quite unceremoniously she pulled up her officer's skirt, already much shorter than regulation, and stretched out her leg in its leather boot. 'Well? Will it do? Let's have another! Only you drink it all down in one! I'll be honest with you – I'm a bit drunk. We've just been doing an old bird, listening – you know, there's this American gadget, it can hear you screwing your girl in the bathroom a kilometre away. You can hear everything! And can you imagine – this old cunt was at it forty minutes and couldn't come. Couldn't get a climax. And the man, he was terrific, kept banging away. It quite took my breath away. I got really worked up – terrible! So now's your chance!' She placed my hand on her breast and gave me an impudent, challenging look.

'Listen,' I said. 'I came to you on business . . .'

'Oh, fuck off!' She seemed genuinely annoyed. 'Isn't a woman business? Come on! You don't expect me to fuck Krasnov!' With a single movement she removed her tie and unbuttoned her shirt collar revealing luxurious white breasts with erect cherry-coloured nipples.

'Well?' she said proudly, 'any good? And the waist? Look . . . Let's have another drink.'

'Listen, somebody might come in . . .'

'I'll give them come in. I'll tear their balls off. Although they're all impotent here, nothing to tear off. But what about you?'

And she boldly undid my flies . . .

About half an hour later Malenina lay exhausted on the sofa, her eyes closed, limply holding an American Malboro which she slowly brought to her lips, pulling on it deeply, without opening her eyes. Her colonel's uniform lay on the floor – tunic, tie, shirt, skirt, boots, and underwear.

I got dressed, finished my glass of brandy, and lit a cigarette too. I had no regrets. There was even a certain vengeful pleasure in crushing, bending, breaking open the body of that anti-Semite. Besides, this vengeful feeling had obviously given me extra energy, and that prolonged her pleasure.

'What a performer . . .' she said, not opening her eyes. 'A real man.' And she sighed: 'What are we to do with you lot?'

'What do you mean – "you lot"?'

'Well, I don't mean you. You're like us. You're not even circumcised. Give me a glass. So what's your business?'

She got up from the sofa. I thought she would get dressed straight away, but she had no such intention. Stepping over her colonel's uniform with strong bare legs, she walked to the tall window and stood there beneath a portrait of Dzerzhinsky against a background of snow falling outside the window. She was truly beautiful. If I were an artist I would have made a picture of that – naked, with a beautiful figure, her reddish braid falling loose down her back, Malenina stands framed by the cold metal of the window, beneath the portrait of Dzerzhinsky, while on the floor, on the Persian rug, is her uniform of Colonel of the Militia. Nearby is the edge of a desk with push buttons and a red government telephone, and through the window is snowy Moscow. I would call the picture simply – 'MVD Intelligence Section' . . .

But I was not an artist, I was an ordinary investigator and moreover one who had just sinned – I went up to her and said: 'Nadya, let me have Svetlov.'

She shook her head. 'I know you came for that. Listen, Baklanov already told you – chuck this case. And now I'm asking you as a woman: take your circus-girl and get lost with her for ten days or so. What about it?' She looked pleadingly at me, so that I almost gave in to those green eyes.

She continued: 'Why do you have to poke around asking why Tsvigun shot himself? So, he shot himself; fuck him! Anyway he was such a swine! He took millions in bribes, you can believe me as head of the Main Directorate.'

'Surely you're not head already?'

'Well, I will be,' she said lazily. 'And maybe even higher. That's not the point. But that whole family! Neither fish nor fowl, they've fucked up Afghanistan, and very nearly fucked up Poland. It's a good thing Jaruzelski turned up, he's one of us, he trained under my husband. Otherwise . . . No, we need a strong power, an iron fist!' She actually clenched her strong militia fist, and I realized that I would not give up the Tsvigun case or go anywhere with Nina. It was already clear to me that the true purpose of Cascade was to compromise and topple the Brezhnev family, but with all the charms we already enjoy in our country, all we need is that fist over our heads. People choose the lesser of two evils, and I chose.

I said: 'So you won't give me Svetlov?'

'Listen,' she said. 'I realize you can't just chuck this case. You're afraid. Let's do it like this: we'll give you not the Third Section of the Moscow CID, not Svetlov, but the First Section, Voznesensky. He has a bigger staff. And if you like, I'll throw some of my Anti-Fraud men in as well, say twenty of them. Then you can have lots of activity going on, but just for appearance. Well? And then afterwards, everything Baklanov promised you you'll get, I promise. Well?' and she pressed her body against me and flung her bare arms over my shoulders. 'And now, let's do it again, Igor. Can you manage?'

But beneath the egg-shell white velvety skin of her bare arms the tensed muscles had not yet relaxed.

I laughed and removed her arms from my shoulders. 'Sorry, Nadya,' I said, falling in with her tone. 'Then I wouldn't have enough left for tonight, for my circus-girl.'

12.00 midday

When I came out into the street several vehicles, including a Repairs van, had already gone and the sprightly driver of an 'ambulance' nearby was sitting in the front seat of my Volga chatting with my driver. On seeing me, he got out of the car and withdrew.

Sasha, the young driver of my Volga, started up the engine. 'Where to?'

'Just keep driving for a while.'

Almost immediately, just by the Central Telegraph, the Repairs van began to tail us. I realized that the driver of the 'ambulance' had stuffed a radio-microphone somewhere under the seat and that right now in the surveillance-room, on the first floor of MVD Intelligence, Nadya Malenina and General Krasnov could hear every word I said.

I pulled the radio-telephone out of its nest and gave the operator my home number.

Nina's voice answered almost immediately: 'Hello? Is that you? Come home, I've got the soup nearly ready! And we've got company again – your son. Come on home quickly.'

'I'm not sure yet . . .'

'No discussions! We're waiting for you! We're not eating without you! D'you understand?'

There was something new, slightly odd, about her voice, and then there was that phrase, Svetlov's and my password – 'No discussions!'

'Where were you an hour ago? I rang.'

'I went to the shop to get some onions for the soup. Come on home!'

'All right, I'm coming,' I replied, and said to the driver: 'To my place,' and in order to head off any unnecessary talk in front of a concealed microphone I nodded at the heap of fresh newspapers on the seat next to him: 'Well, what are they saying in the papers?'

'Same as usual,' Sasha laughed. He was a great lover of football and politics. 'Unemployment is increasing in West Germany, racial tensions are growing in England, and in the UN they wanted to condemn Israel for grabbing the Golan Heights, but the Americans blocked the resolution. In Washington Reagan is putting on some TV show about Poland, but in Poland itself everything is very peaceful.'

After about ten minutes we drove up to my house, and I took the lift up to the tenth floor. Jazz music was blaring away in the apartment, you could even hear it from the lift.

'Keep the noise down!' I said with a frown as I entered.

I surveyed my lair in amazement – it had been completely tidied up, floors

67

washed, not a speck of dust on the table. My fourteen-year-old-son Anton was swabbing the bathroom with some sort of powder! And from the kitchen came an unusual smell – real soup!

'Fantastic!' I shouted above the shattering noise of the jazz. 'But turn the music down, for Pete's sake! Nina!'

Nina popped out of the kitchen wearing a flowery apron, put her finger to her lips, and led me over to the table where there was a sheet of white paper with a few words written on it in the regular, almost schoolboyish hand-writing of my son: 'Dad, a man from Moscow Gas just came. He checked the kitchen stove and changed some fuses in the hall in the meter. But I don't think he was from Mosgas at all, and those fuses are just microphones. What do you think? Anton and Nina.'

I laughed. Even the children were getting involved in my work. Anton came out of the bathroom with a cloth in his hand and looked at me anxiously.

I took out a pen and wrote on the same sheet: 'And what made you decide that?'

Nina grabbed the pen and wrote: 'Because Mosgas doesn't work on Saturdays.'

'That's the first thing,' added Anton. 'Second – what has Mosgas got to do with an electric meter. Well?'

So my son was acquiring the deductive method of investigation. The last thing I would want was for him to become an investigator. A doctor, engineer, musician, even a footballer – but just steer clear of politics.

I took the pen from him and wrote: 'All right. But why the loud music?'

'So their ears will pop listening to us!' wrote Nina.

I went up to the tape-recorder and turned down the hellish din. Then I opened the door onto the balcony and looked down. On the other side of the street stood the van marked 'Repairs'. Were they really such idiots that even children could find out what they were doing? Or . . . or were they deliber-ately trying to frighten me?

'OK, kids!' I said reassuringly to my son and Nina and, holding it in the air, burned the sheet of paper. 'The weather is perfect. Let's go skiing. A quick lunch and get ready!'

The plan was made; it merely remained to carry it out: to lose the shadow during the skiing and contact Brezhnev's favourite journalist Belkin. I had met him at the end of last year in the bar of the House of Journalists. 'I don't seem to have read anything by you in the papers for a long time,' I had said to him at the time over the beer and lobsters.

'We're writing books!' he had laughed without enthusiasm, almost sar-castically.

'Oh! Congratulations! When's it coming out?'

'One's already out,' he said gloomily. 'We even got the Lenin Prize.'

'All right, that's enough fibbing!'

'I'm not fibbing. I'm bibbing!' he quipped and looked at me bitterly.

'What book? Why didn't I hear about it?' I asked, trying to recall who got the Lenin Prize for Literature that year. Then I remembered: 'Wait. It was Brezhnev who got the Lenin Prize, for *Rebirth*.'

'Exactly,' said Belkin. 'That's our pseudonym, our collective one! We sit in Pravda Village at a government *dacha*, eight writers, and we write . . . And the pseudonym comes out once a week, and reads . . .'

Now all I had to do was find this Belkin, but first get to the Forensic Institute to find out whose bullet it was that hit the ventilation window.

2.20 p.m.

We travelled out to the ski-centre at Serebryanny Bor along the Khoroshevskoye Highway, still escorted by the same Repairs van. There was a noisy throng of young people at the ski-centre and, as always, an immense queue to hire skis. People stood around waiting for them to be handed in by skiers returning from the woods. This was precisely what I had counted on when I fixed this outing. I let our driver go and pushed my way through to the front of the queue where I was greeted by the tough wench in charge of the ski-store: 'Hey, you! Where d'you think you're going? Ain't no skis here. Ain't any!' But once I thrust my red Prosecutor's Office identity card under her nose, she immediately changed her tone: 'Word of honour, Comrade Prosecutor, there are no skis! Honestly and truly! Look, they're only just coming in from the woods.'

And sure enough, a group of men and women on skis were just emerging from among the trees.

The crowd started shouting at the kiosk window: 'There's a queue here, you know! There's a queue waiting here!'

'So what?' she snarled at them. 'Comrade Prosecutor booked his skis by phone this morning! What's all the shouting for? Quiet while you wait! You'll get the next lot.'

She had told an obvious lie about the phone booking – there was no telephone in her cabin – but the crowd quietened down as usual when faced by someone in authority. I knew the passengers in the Repairs van would be rushing to grab the next sets of skis, since they couldn't have been provided with any in advance; and at some point the next group of skiers would be coming out of those woods. It was not very pleasant taking the skis from under the noses of the sullen crowd, and my son looked at me reproachfully. But ten minutes later, in the woods, he had forgotten the incident. All around us was that fairy-tale beauty to be found only in Russia. As the snow continued to fall, the woodland with its broad-boughed pines, looked as if it really were made of silver, and along the smooth intertwining tracks bounded the energetic figures of young men and women on skis.

I took Nina and Anton further and further into the wood, changing direction sharply, switching from one ski-track to another, until I was convinced there was no one on our trail. Then Anton, who was boasting about his fine prowess in front of Nina, forged on ahead and I was left skiing

69

along next to her. Wearing a sky-blue knitted ski-cap, and with her neat little figure and blue eyes she was devilishly attractive. If it had not been for the dim figure of Anton looming in front, I would have embraced her there and then and rolled her in the snow. They could all go to hell – the Tsviguns, the Suslovs, and the Brezhnevs. In that forest I had forgotten about them anyway.

'What did you tell Anton about us?' I asked Nina as we went.

'I said I was the daughter of your friend from Vologda, and now he's started taking an interest in me,' she smiled. 'I couldn't tell him I was your mistress, though!'

So now we'd got a love-triangle in the family. As if I didn't have enough worries!

'Just you come here!' I said to her sternly.

She stopped and I embraced her. But at that moment the woodland was filled with the roar of engines. We turned round. Along the forest road a formation of tanks was moving in the direction of Moscow, their caterpillar tracks crushing the fresh, silvery snow. There was something ominous about that roaring column of iron machines with their gun-barrels trained on Moscow.

Groups of skiers stopped in bewilderment. Anton came skiing up to us and looked at me in alarm. But what could I say to him? They might in fact be the tanks of the KGB's Dzerzhinsky Division, but they might equally well be the regular troops of Marshal Ustinov engaged in a perfectly routine change of location. There had certainly been a 'relocation' operation in the days following Stalin's death and during the conspiracy against Khrushchev . .

The tanks moved on, drowning us in powdered snow and in the sound of roaring engines.

'Right now, lads,' I said to Nina and my son. 'We're going to have a quick bit of cross-country to the nearest taxi-stand, and from there we'll flit back into town. You can go the cinema or wherever you like, only not back to my place. I'm going off on some business. We'll meet at about six, say, on Red Square by the Mausoleum. OK?'

'And what about the skis?' asked Anton. 'We've got to return them.'

'Drop the skis off at the Prosecutor's Office. Just hand them to the man on duty. Forward march!'

3.35 p.m.

After seeing everyone on emergency duty at the Anti-Fraud section of the Ministry of Internal Affairs, and after that roaring column of tanks, I was not surprised when I got to 1905 Square to find all hands were on deck too at the Forensic Institute. In the old residential house painted a desolate barracks-grey colour, there was a fury of activity on all five storeys – especially in the forensic research laboratory of Professor Aleksandr Sorokin. This leading laboratory employs experts on graphology, biology and ballistics, and there are more than thirty specialists working there, including Sorokin's wife,

70

Alla. She and I had been in the same year at our institute, and it was through her that I intended to 'squeeze' her husband, so as to get as soon as possible his report on the materials handed in last night.

But I did not have to squeeze at all. The forty-year-old brunette with green eyes, a former Law Faculty beauty whom Sasha Sorokin had captured from seven other admirers, greeted me with 'Aha! There you are! Come with me.'

She led me into the depths of the laboratory to her husband's empty office. She closed the door and immediately turned to me: 'Let's be hearing!'

'What is there to tell?' I said with surprise.

'Don't try and make out you're an idiot!' she said severely. 'You're not getting the results until you spill the beans. I want a report on when they're going to topple Brezhnev and what exactly is going on in Moscow.'

'Have you already done both analyses?'

'You bet! When you get materials like that to work on! On the death of your actual Tsvigun! We've dropped everything else since early morning, even an urgent case from Baklanov.'

'And what was it that he gave you to look at?'

'Come on, cut out your Jewish habit – answering one question with another! I'm asking the questions, not you. Is it true Brezhnev is finished?'

'Alla, I only flew back yesterday from holiday in Sochi. And I landed in the midst of this affair, like a chicken ripe for plucking. My word of honour, I know nothing. You lot here know more than I do, I swear it! What makes you think that Brezhnev is finished?'

'Get on with you!' she said. 'What makes me think that? Because our Institute keeps getting assignments from all over the place – from the Anti-Fraud Squad, Criminal Investigation, the Ministry of Internal Affairs, the Prosecutor's Office, and even from the KGB. Somebody probably sees each matter as an isolated affair, but here we have an overall view of the whole scene, and we've put two and two together. What would you make of it, when Baklanov and Malenina ask you to look at mountains of notebooks from all sorts of shady dealers, and each of them contains the home phone number of Tsvigun, and of Galya, Yury and Yakov Brezhnev? And when Tsvigun's notebook has the phone numbers of these dealers. That must mean something, wouldn't you say? They've got Brezhnev cornered like a hunted animal!'

'What, you've had Tsvigun's notebook?'

'We most certainly have!'

'I've got to see it.'

'You'll be lucky! Baklanov has already taken it back. He never once left the laboratory while we were working on it. We had to reconstruct a dozen or so passages that had been crossed or rubbed out. He even took all the copies away with him. But we do have something that will interest you. Read this.'

She pulled out from her husband's desk the typed, but still unsigned, draft

71

of a report by the medical and biological analysts on the bullets I had handed in the previous evening. Then she went out of the office.

I picked up the sheet, and leaving out the standard preliminaries, I read the following:

Extract from the Combined Report by Forensic Medical and Biological Consultants

The barrel of General Tsvigun's revolver presented for examination was evidently cleaned after use; nevertheless, from other traces left in the internal bore of the barrel and on the firing-pin, and from other indirect evidence, it proved possible to establish that both bullets submitted for examination had passed through the barrel of this revolver and were fired by the weapon not later than 20 January and not earlier than 18 January of this year.

Microscopic medical examination of bullet number one showed that it had not impacted against the human body, but it bears the signs of passage through some slight wooden obstacle, such as the fragment of window-frame submitted for investigation.

Analogous examination of bullet number two shows that it carries microscopic fragments of human skin, bone and blood. From the deformation characteristics of this bullet, it can be concluded that it passed through human bone. Since the bullet in question was presented in connection with the infliction of a fatal bullet-wound to the head, the specialist investigators observe that no traces of brain-tissue could be discovered on the bullet.

Moscow, 23 January 1982

Signature of investigating specialists: A. Sorokin

B. Golovlyova

I read the last line once again and went with the report to Sorokin's laboratory. Sorokin was a tall man of fifty with a shaggy red mane framing his round and freckled face. Together with his wife and three laboratory assistants he was working on a piece of graphological analysis.

I went straight up to him. 'Listen. What exactly is this?'

'Where?' he said with an innocent look.

I showed him the paper and he shrugged his shoulders.

'It's an examination report, so what?' Laughter sparkled in his eyes. I realized that he was bent on exasperating me, and was trying it on. In fact he was well known for this idiotic habit of mocking investigators and for inserting all sorts of personal digs into otherwise official documents.

'I can see it's a report. I'm not blind.' I said with restraint. 'But what does this mean – "no traces of brain-tissue could be discovered"? This bullet went right through Tsvigun's head!'

He said nothing. In addition to those working next to him, the lab assistants from the whole laboratory had now left their work and were looking curiously in our direction.

'Well,' I said, persisting, 'have you nothing to say?'

'You understand . . .' he said, drawing out the story with calculated effect, 'on this bullet there are no traces of brain-tissue. Now, if you are going to insist that it passed through the head of Tsvigun, then that means that the head of the First Deputy Chairman of the KGB, member of the Central Committee and Deputy to the Supreme Soviet, contained no brains. But I wouldn't let that surprise you, old chap, it's not a unique phenomenon. I know some legal investigators who don't have very much up there either.'

He got what he wanted – the whole laboratory rocked with laughter. He went on: 'But if I were you, I would cease this slander of members of our government, and I'd have a look at Tsvigun's body to see if there aren't any traces of other wounds.'

'You mean to say it was not this bullet which killed him?'

'I mean to say nothing. We don't draw conclusions; even less do we make assumptions. We say only what we can see. On the bullet there are no traces of brain-tissue. And on the final note that Tsvigun wrote before his death there are no signs either of the sweat secretions typical of him; and six of the letters in the note raise some doubts.'

'A forgery?'

'I repeat: we do not draw conclusions. It's simply that I recently held in my hands the notebook belonging to Tsvigun, and I observed that Comrade Tsvigun had sweaty hands whenever he wrote. These sweat secretions are present even on the charts he made when he played preference. It's quite natural. Fat people like Tsvigun perspire on any pretext, and especially when they are under stress. But on this note written before he died there are absolutely no traces – neither fingerprints, nor papillary marks, nor sweat secretions. And there are six characters which are written not quite in his hand – almost but not quite . . . Any more questions?'

I went back to his office in silence. On the desk lay exactly the same sort of telephone directory as I had, stamped 'Secret. For Official Use Only'. In it I found the home telephone number of B.S. Tumanov, chief forensic medical expert in the Soviet Frontier Forces, who had carried out the post-mortem on Tsvigun, and I rang him.

The conversation was a short one: 'Boris Stepanovich? Good evening. Sorry to disturb you. This is Shamrayev speaking, from the Prosecutor's Office. I am conducting the case concerned with Tsvigun's death. Please, excuse me for ringing you on Saturday. I have just one question to ask: since you performed the post-mortem . . . apart from the head-wound, were there any other signs of injury on Tsvigun's body?'

'My dear chap, you offend me,' replied a gracious and gentlemanly baritone. 'Everything I found on the body went into my report. I can assure you of that.'

'Did you open up the skull?'

'But naturally! We traced the path of the bullet through the brain. I did

73

everything perfectly properly, old chap.'

'But you see, on the bullet which went through the head of the victim, the investigators have found no trace of any brain-tissue.'

A prolonged gust of booming laughter was all I heard in reply. Then, when he had finished laughing, he said: 'That's a real killer! That, old chap, is a real killer! I'll have to tell that one to the students at the Academy. What was it you said? "On the bullet that went through the head of the victim, the investigators found no trace of brain-tissue"?! Well, there are your experts for you! I shall put that in the textbook I'm writing. Thanks for helping an old man out! And exactly what sort of experts were these, may I ask?'

'Boris Stepanovich, where did you carry out the post-mortem?'

'In the anatomy department of Medical Institute Number One. Why?'

'Thank you, Boris Stepanovich, forgive me for disturbing you!'

Actually, I need not have asked that last question – post-mortems on government figures are always carried out at Institute Number One.

I made a second call – to Pravda Village, the government residential estate. The telephonist on the switchboard answered immediately: 'Pravda Village speaking.'

I explained I was ringing from the USSR Prosecutor's Office and asked them to find me the journalist Belkin who was working with some literary team at one of the *dachas*.

A few seconds later I heard Vadim's voice: 'Igor Iosifovich, welcome back!'

'How did you know I'd been away?'

'Well, I can't tell you on the phone,' he answered hinting at the inevitable phone-tapping. 'What can I do for you?'

'I need to meet your "pseudonym",' I said, lapsing into Aesopian language.

'Who? . . . Who?' he said, taken aback.

'Three months ago over a beer at the House of Journalists you were telling me you now write under a pseudonym.'

'I get the message. I can't promise anything. But tell me where you're calling from, and I'll ring you back.'

I gave him the number of Sorokin's office. Then I sat there in the stillness, pondering the situation. Outside the window in the thickening dusk, snow was falling. So Svetlov was right: it was not suicide – most probably, it had been rigged to look that way. It was a piece of double duplicity in fact: first of all to make it look like suicide; and then, for the public benefit, to claim that Tsvigun had died a natural death. Of course it is well known even to students of the Law Faculty that a rigged suicide is set up most often by people close to the actual victim, in which case there could be several rings of suspects. First of all there was Andropov and his deputies, for whom Tsvigun was an obvious burden – being Brezhnev's personal supervisor of the KGB, as it were. But it would be extremely stupid to suspect Andropov of such clumsy work: the case also involved Suslov, Kurbanov, and Tumanov, and various other experts, investigators and bodyguards. If Andropov had been so very anxious to get rid of Tsvigun, he could have removed him quietly – the KGB is well practised in such things: poison that leaves no trace, a paralysing gas . . . and the doctors would have no doubt about confirming natural death as a result of acute hypertonia or a stroke. The second ring of suspects were all those underground dealers who used to hand Tsvigun bribes. They were a shady set of people, often capable of anything, but why should they choose to kill Tsvigun if he was in cahoots with them? And how could they have reckoned on Tsvigun coming to his apartment at two o'clock in the afternoon? The third circle of suspects was his own family – wife, children, and possible mistresses. But in that case why had the KGB made so many crude mistakes? They had missed the damaged window-frame, immediately cleaned up the suicide weapon, failed to make a forensic examination of the bullet or a graphological analysis of the suicide note. If indeed there was a conspiracy against Brezhnev and his family, then some scandal to discredit the whole clan would have suited them ideally. No, it was all beyond comprehension, a matter of mere conjecture. Except for one thing: it was clear that I could not deal with this case single handed, especially in a situation where I was being tailed and not being allowed to interrogate witnesses. These reflections were interrupted by the telephone ringing.

I lifted the receiver and heard: 'Igor Iosifovich? Good evening. This is the CPSU Central Committee. In a few minutes' time a car will come to collect you.'

4.17 p.m.
It was a government Chaika – a long, black, armoured limousine. On the front seat next to the driver sat a man of about thirty – a silent type, who throughout the whole trip was to say only a few words, and then only when the car first drew up to the Forensic Institute.

'How do you do?' he said, 'are you Shamrayev? Could I see your documents?'

I showed him my identity papers, and when he was convinced that I actually was Shamrayev, he said: 'Please get in. Leonid Brezhnev is sick, but his personal doctor Yevgeny Ivanovich Chazov would like to meet you.'

And there we were, sweeping along through Moscow in the evening, along the reserved priority lanes of the Garden Ring Road first of all, and then Kutuzovsky Prospect. We drove at a hundred kilometres an hour, and all the traffic-control points gave us the green light, and the controllers at the crossroads stood to attention and saluted. To be honest, it was my first ride in a government limousine. Not only could you stretch your legs inside to their full length but there was also a television set and a bar with glasses that gave a musical clink. And in front, next to the driver, sat the escort who radioed all the nearby traffic-control points to give us green. I guessed where we were going – either to Brezhnev's house on Kutuzovsky Prospect, or else to his *dacha* along the Rublyovskoye Highway. But the car shot past the house known to every Muscovite, where Brezhnev, Andropov, Kirilenko, and Shcholokov all have their two-storey city apartments. And before reaching the turn onto Rublyovskoye Highway, we suddenly bore away to the left and I realized at last where we were going – to the Kremlin Hospital at Stalin's former *dacha* in Kuntsevo. Sure enough, as it crossed the picturesque snow-bound bridge over the frozen river Setun, the car reduced speed and slid along the winding woodland road with its surface ironed smooth by snow-ploughs. To the left was a birch wood, to the right – a grove of tall dense spruce trees that held out shaggy paws laden heavily with snow – a genuine thick forest. In the depths of that wood, I thought, even a perfectly honest man might be tempted to commit a crime – was that why Stalin had chosen this retreat for himself? The road curved away to the right and we came to a nine-foot-high fence with metal gates – the Cardiac Hospital of the Fourth (Kremlin) Medical Directorate of the USSR Ministry of Health.

There was a short exchange over the radio between my escort and someone outside. Then the gates opened and we were in the hospital grounds, on a road that had been cleared down to the asphalt and strewn with sand which had then frozen hard. Away to the right was Stalin's former *dacha*, a low, two-storey hunting-lodge. It was here in the days gone by that Stalin had filled his 'companions-in-arms' with food and drink – Voroshilov, Kaganovich, Mikoyan, Beriya, Khrushchev, and Suslov. But now the little house looked abandoned and uninhabited, and beyond the courtyard gleamed the lights of the new twelve-storey wing of the Kremlin Hospital. Along the snowy paths around it, each accompanied by a personal nurse, there walked the men of the Kremlin, sick with various geriatric afflictions, and the highly-placed officials of other important government departments.

The car rolled directly up to the vestibule, and still accompanied by my silent guardian, I went up in the lift to the first-floor office of the Head Doctor of the Kremlin Hospital, Candidate Member of the Central Committee, Academician Yevgeny Ivanovich Chazov. Whatever people may say about Brezhnev, one thing which they cannot deny is his success in promoting his own people to positions of importance: he made his son First Deputy Minister of Foreign Trade; his son-in-law, Galina's husband, Yury Churbanov, was made First Deputy Minister of Internal Affairs; his brother-in-law, Tsvigun, became First Deputy Chairman of the KGB; his personal pilot, Bugayev, was appointed to Minister of Civil Aviation; and his doctor, Yevgeny Chazov, was appointed head of the so-called 'Kremlyovka' and became a Candidate Member of the Central Committee, although even the Minister of Health himself was not in the Central Committee! And Chazov's office corresponded with his position – it was spacious and had comfortable imported furnishings. Chazov himself was a wiry fifty-three-year-old of medium height, with hazel eyes, a refined and intelligent face, and was prematurely balding.

He stepped from behind his desk, came to meet me, shook my hand and addressed me immediately on familiar terms: 'Have a seat. What'll we start with? A glass of French brandy maybe? As a doctor, I can recommend it . . .'

He poured out a glass for me and for himself. The two of us were now sitting alone.

He went on: 'Well, then. The situation is a simple one. Leonid Brezhnev is staying at his *dacha*. He's ill, but not fatally so, just stunned slightly by the business with Tsvigun. But he'll be on his feet again in a couple of days. Suslov, though, is in a critical state. He is lying here in Stalin's cottage. He has got his personal doctor with him, my namesake Yevgeny Ivanovich Schmidt – he is the best neuro-pathologist in the country. It was at my insistence that you were dragged back from holiday, as soon as I learned the history of Suslov's illness. It is a very interesting case-history, especially for an investigator. But first of all tell me what you've got on Tsvigun. No need to be shy. Tell me everything just as it is. In two hours I'll be paying my evening visit to Leonid Ilyich.'

'I have nothing to be shy about,' I said, and I briefly told him the story of the second bullet and the results of the experts' examination.

'Just as I thought!' said Chazov. 'The night before last, as soon as Leonid Ilyich had come to himself a bit, I was the first to tell him that I didn't believe in the suicide of Tsvigun. Tsvigun was a healthy fellow. At sixty-five he could down a bottle of brandy and give a twenty-year-old girl all she wanted. And for him then to go and put a bullet through his own temple? I'll never believe that. Of course, I can't prove that he was killed by Suslov, Andropov or Shcholokov – that was what we summoned you for, to investigate. But one thing is a hundred per cent certain – that it was Tsvigun who put paid to Suslov – and I'm telling you this as a doctor.'

I looked at Chazov in astonishment, and he burst out laughing.

'Aha! You don't follow me? I ought to tell you that doctors too are investigators. Have a look.' He returned to his desk and pulled from a drawer a thick folio with several markers in it. 'This is the medical history of Comrade Mikhail Andreyevich Suslov. We open it up: childhood illnesses – measles and mumps – let's leave them out. And let's pick up from about his forties, when Suslov first went into the Kremlin Hospital. So, the year 1937. Mikhail Suslov, Senior Inspector of the Central Control Commission of the Party, a very close colleague of Yezhov, came to the hospital with a diagnosis of "sugar diabetes, and a seizure of the vascular system and the vessels supplying the brain". Now, recall what the Central Control Commission was engaged in and what was going on in 1937, and the reason for the illness will be clear to you. On Stalin's orders they had been busy destroying thousands of the most talented old bolsheviks; the whole of the Leninist old guard were shot. But by 1937 Stalin had already shot Yezhov himself and half of the staff of the CCC. As a result of this, Comrade Suslov had his first attack: there was a sharp increase in the amount of sugar in the blood and a seizure of the vessels supplying the brain. But it was that which saved his life – for Stalin didn't shoot him and didn't send him off to Siberia. We don't know the details and we won't try and guess at them . . .'

Chazov leafed through the file to his next marker. 'When did Suslov go into hospital the next time? When do you think? It turns out it was in 1953, in March. Suslov, Stalin's comrade-in-arms, and now a member of the Presidium of the CPSU Central Committee, suffered another sharp rise in his blood sugar content: the vascular system was affected and another brain-seizure followed. Why? Because, as you remember, Stalin died in March; Beriya was killed; and almost the whole of the Central Committee went to hell. And, putting it simply, Suslov had another attack because he feared for his life. Well, of course, such things leave their mark: an increase in blood sugar and seizures of the brain change a man's character. He cannot drink, eat, or have women, and the result is that his whole psyche changes. He becomes aggressive and starts taking vengeance on others for his own ailments. Suslov outlived Stalin and stayed on in the government, and by concealing his impotence and sickness, he created for himself a legend that he was some sort of Party ascetic, a Marxist holyman. But in private his illness took its toll. At home he beat up his wife and son, and drove both of them to alcohol, while at work he wore down his subordinates with his Marxism and betrayed his own allies. Look at the year 1957, in June. The same diagnosis: sharp rise in blood sugar and a brain-seizure. Look through the newspapers for that period and you'll see what was happening: at the June plenary meeting of the Central Committee Suslov made the main speech against his colleagues Malenkov and Molotov and helped Khrushchev to seize power. The conspiracy was successful, Khrushchev came to power, and two days afterwards Suslov landed in hospital – because the blood sugar increase comes with any powerful emotional stimulus, whether negative or positive. And it was at this point, as a doctor, that I made my diagnosis: Suslov was not to blame for the fact that he was a conspirator – rather it was the result of his sickness, a form of compensation for personal discontent. In theory he ought to be kept, if not in a psychiatric hospital, then at least in isolation. But – he's on the Central Committee, and he's involved in nothing less than the international Communist movement. And there is a vast stamping-ground there for an aggressive maniac like him: Cuban terrorists, Palestinian terrorists, the Italian "Red Brigade", and the American "Panthers" . . . He ends up hating the whole world just because he can't tuck into a piece of roast! Well? What do you make of it? Interesting? But that's not all. We turn on and come to October 1964 – an epileptic attack immediately following Khrushchev's overthrow. And who was it who was first to speak out against Khrushchev? Who was it who was intoxicated by his own power and was simply a new tsar in disguise? Of course, it was the holy Marxist, the high-principled Leninist, Mikhail Suslov. It was he who spoke at a plenary meeting on the "twenty-four mistakes of Khrushchev". And from that meeting he went straight into hospital, and no shots of insulin could control his rocketing blood sugar count. Well, you see now what I'm leading up to?'

'I'm beginning to guess.'

'Splendid. And as a doctor, I can tell you that he has never been able to tolerate his own close friends. It has been a mania of his to help some man to climb up and seize power, and then subsequently to topple the same man. But as you know, in this country you can't do anything without the KGB. And in the KGB it was Tsvigun who stood in his way. Hence Operation Cascade which he instigated in secret from Brezhnev, and hence the death of Tsvigun. That's what I think. If only because each of his attacks has been tied up with some conspiracy in the Kremlin. And here now we have all the same signs again – in the afternoon of the nineteenth the death of Tsvigun, a strange sort of suicide, and already that evening Suslov was feeling sick. Treatment did not help, and on the twenty-first there was a sharp disruption in the circulation of the blood to the base of the brain, loss of consciousness, and the kidneys and liver ceased to function.'

And ignoring two further markers, Chazov closed the folio. 'So I assume that this was one of his routine anti-government conspiracies, but this time the old man overestimated his strength. The death of Tsvigun caused him his usual seizure which this time he will not recover from. But at the moment it's not that which interests us.'

Chazov came and sat down next to me at a table with magazines on it. 'Whether he dies in an hour or a week from now, to hell with him – not a single dog will shed a tear.'

'Apart from myself,' I said.

'Why?' he asked, amazed.

'Because I need to interrogate him. How the material against Tsvigun turned up in his hands, where this material is now, what did he talk about to Tsvigun? I can't move without answers to those questions.'

'But, you know, he would not have told you anything anyway. On the nineteenth he promised Leonid Brezhnev on the phone that he would send him all the material about Tsvigun's connections with unofficial traders. But then he went to hospital and sent nothing at all. But it's no longer just a matter of Tsvigun or of Suslov. It's important to know who was involved in the conspiracy. And even more important to have proof of the conspiracy. Because on the outside it all looks perfectly clean, in best Party manner: the militia pick up various common crooks, the crooks confess that they gave bribes to Tsvigun, and Tsvigun commits suicide. You couldn't fault it if you didn't know that Suslov was a man who couldn't live without conspiracies, and that Tsvigun was the one man who stood in his way.'

'But in the militia, though, there's Churbanov, Brezhnev's son-in-law. Operation Cascade could not have started without him.'

'I think that Churbanov has simply got fed up with Galya's whoring around. But he can't get rid of her while her Dad's in power. So therefore he's away on a month's leave. He's holidaying on the Belovezhskaya Pushcha reserve. You see, it's all a big game. On the surface it looks like a series of coincidences, but in actual fact . . .'

The intercom gave a gentle but commanding buzz, and Chazov shot out a hand and pressed a button: 'Chazov here.'

A man's voice came over the speaker: 'Yevgeny Ivanovich, his condition's worsening, trouble with breathing!'

'I'm coming!' said Chazov and nodded to me: 'Come with me!'

Chazov picked up Suslov's case-history and quickly left the room. I followed. Without putting on a coat and wearing just a doctor's smock over his suit, Chazov descended the stairs at a run, then went out quickly along the path cleared of snow, making for the two-storey lodge that had once been Stalin's *dacha* at the edge of the park. From the half-darkness at the door of the lodge two male figures emerged and barred our way, but with a nod in my direction, Chazov told them, 'He's with me.'

We went inside. I don't know how the lodge had looked earlier, in Stalin's day, but now it was as cheerless as a barracks, and there was a strong hospital smell. And since there was a guard in the very first room by the entrance, it almost looked like a prison hospital. Further on there was a desolate hallway with a low ceiling and traces on the floor of where a billiard table had once stood. Then there was a room for the medical staff where there was some bulky – obviously important – medical equipment. And finally, in the next room, on a high surgical couch, covered by a sheet and with an oxygen mask over his face, lay the long, emaciated body of Mikhail Andreyevich Suslov. A nurse sat on duty at the head of the bed and kept an eye on the oxygen and various monitoring instruments; to the left, bending over the patient, stood a tall grey-haired seventy-year-old with eyes of Aryan blue and a sharply hooked nose – Suslov's personal doctor, Academician Yevgeny Ivanovich Schmidt. With him was another staff-nurse of the Kremlin Hospital, Leonid Viktorovich Kumachov.

Chazov flung the folio with Suslov's case-history onto a table and started talking with the doctors in rapid bursts, and in professional medical jargon. My ear picked up only individual phrases such as 'disturbance of the functions . . . fails to pick up . . . arrhythmia . . . heart-stimulator . . . infarction of the brain . . .' I made no attempt to work out exactly what they were saying, and simply looked at what lay there covered by a sheet on the raised hospital bed. I wasn't a doctor, though of course with twenty years' experience as an investigator I had paid literally hundreds of visits to the morgue and seen hundreds of corpses. But even without any medical diagnosis, I could tell that Suslov had reached the end. He had the skin of a corpse, and the smell of death hung over him. Now no authority over the international Communist movement, no conspiracies or quotations from Marx could help this old, emaciated, almost lifeless figure with his thin, pointed nose and yellowish skin stretched over his face. I picked up the folio with Suslov's medical record and went over to the window. The two markers which Chazov had ignored when talking to me aroused my curiosity. I opened the dossier at the first of them. I didn't even have to think hard about the medical terminology because a note had been made on the first page in thick red pencil: '27 May 1976 – Necrosis, sharp rise in blood sugar, seizure of heart-muscle, infarction.' Strange, I thought, in 1976 there were no upheavals.

I leafed through the sheets of the folio till I came to the next marker. The same thick red pencil noted: '17 July 1978 – sharp rise in blood sugar, brain-seizure, digestive functions disturbed.'

I closed the file and replaced it. Why had Chazov not mentioned these dates to me? Or did they fail to fit his theory? But if he had put these markers in, that must mean that he had shown the history of Suslov's case to someone, maybe to Brezhnev himself. Chazov was standing behind me together with Schmidt and Kumachov as they bent over the now almost lifeless patient. The doctors were trying artificial breathing, and the old man's body was racked by gurglings and wheezings. Meanwhile as I stood by the window looking at the quiet park surrounding Stalin's *dacha* and the snowflakes circling round the outside lights, I mentally repeated those dates: '27 May 1976, and 17 July 1978'. Something had happened then. Something must have happened. Chazov did not give the impression of being an adventurer who might have shuffled the facts around; indeed it seemed rather that they wanted to conceal something from me. What could have happened on 17 July?

With one more glance at the busy doctors, I went out of the ward into the room where a young doctor with a red beard was on duty beside the medical equipment. To his left on a table together with today's issue of the newspaper *Vechernyaya Moskvu* stood a telephone. I lifted the receiver.

'If you're phoning out, you need to dial 9 first,' the doctor said as he watched his instruments and an oscillograph which traced out on a long strip of paper the last echoes of Suslov's life.

I dialled 9, and then 02 – the switchboard of the Moscow militia.

'Militia,' said a woman's voice.

'I want the Third Section of Criminal Investigation,' I said.

'Putting you through,' she answered and immediately a deep male voice sounded in the ear-piece: 'Third Section – duty officer Lieutenant Kravtsov here!'

'This is Shamrayev from the Prosecutor's Office. Is Svetlov there?'

'No, Comrade Shamrayev, he is at home.'

'Who is there from the head of staff?'

'Major Akopyan.'

I did not know this new chief of the Third Section sub-department very well, but said nevertheless: 'All right, put me through to him . . . Comrade Akopyan? This is Shamrayev. I am a friend of Svetlov's.'

'I think I know you, Comrade Shamrayev,' said a man's voice with a gentle southern accent.

'Fine. Then just for friendship's sake would you order from the archive a round-up of events in Moscow for 25 to 27 May 1976, and from 15 to 17 July 1978. And I'll ring you back in about ten minutes' time.'

81

'Igor Iosifovich, you know, there'll be up to a hundred events mentioned for each day! I can't read all of them out on the phone!'

'I don't need them all. Just cast your eye over them and look for anything unusual and striking. We can sort out the rest later.'

I rang off and immediately dialled another number – the newsdesk of *Vechernyaya Moskva*. The journalists from this paper were forever plaguing the Prosecutor's Office to get material for their features, so why shouldn't I call on them?

A breezy young voice answered immediately: '*Vechernyaya Moskva*. Drannikov speaking!'

I introduced myself and heard in reply: 'For the Prosecutor's Office we'll do everything we can. I'll just run and get the file for May '76 and July '78 and read it straight from the column . . . Are you there? The 25 May – opening of Pioneers' summer season. Don't want that? Right. On the twenty-sixth a she-bear at the zoo gave birth to twins. No good? New tram-route opened – no good either? It's funny, you know, at your Prosecutor's Office you never give us anything spicy, yet now you're asking me for something interesting! Well, I can tell you what it was that they forbade us to print then. Here I see that instead of my report on the fire in the Hotel Rossiya on 26 May, the paper carried an article with pictures on birds in the forests around Moscow. Does that interest you?'

'That is certainly more interesting,' I laughed.

'Splendid! So on we go! . . . 15 July 1978. A raid of our newspaper – people caught speculating on the sale of lilac were arrested at the Yaroslavsky station. Do you need that? On 16 July in Moscow, a Week of Turkmen Literature and Art; on 17 July the sudden death of Politburo member Fyodor Kulakov, aged sixty . . .'

'Excellent!' I cried, losing all restraint.

'What's excellent?' Drannikov asked suspiciously. 'The death of Kulakov?'

'No, of course not. But read me the whole report. Is there any medical explanation?'

'Certainly: "On 17 July 1978, the sudden death occurred in the sixty-first year of his life, of Fyodor Davydovich Kulakov, member of the Politburo, member of the CPSU Central Committee, deputy of the Supreme Soviet of the USSR, and Hero of Socialist Labour. His death removes from our ranks a prominent figure in the CPSU . . ."'

'Let's leave that out,' I said. 'Any medical details?'

'Certainly: "During the night of 16 May 1978, he developed an acute cardiac-vascular insufficiency, which caused a heart-stoppage."'

'Any doctors' signatures?'

'No surnames. It's just signed by a "Medical Commission of the USSR Ministry of Health".'

'Thank you.'

From talking to Akopyan again shortly afterwards, I knew that in the period from 25 May to 27 May 1976, there were two murders in Moscow sparked off by jealousy, a fire in the Hotel Rossiya, the robbery of a perfume store, three rapes and 214 cases of malicious hooliganism.

And in the period 15 July to 17 July 1978, there were 317 cases of malicious hooliganism, five rapes, and not a single murder out of jealousy; on the other hand, four fishermen got drunk and drowned in the Moskva River, and Politburo member, Supreme Soviet Deputy and Hero of Socialist Labour, Fyodor Davydovich Kulakov died suddenly in the sixty-first year of his life . . .

When I was finishing copying this list into my notepad, Chazov appeared from Suslov's room. We went out into the park now lamplit in the evening.

Chazov said: 'Of course, he may hold out another couple of days. These old men have an amazing hold on life. I had one research student, a talented young chap, who was burnt up by cancer at the age of twenty-eight. And yet that shit continues to live . . . And the main thing is: nobody needs him. Not even his own son has been to visit him. He's probably drinking somewhere . . .'

He lit a cigarette and after a pause said: 'Hmm, yes . . . a funny thing – life! Especially when in the last days of your life there's only one person at all interested in you – and he turns out to be an investigator!'

'What sort of terms was he on with Kulakov?' I asked

Chazov looked at me keenly: 'With Fyodor Kulakov? Now why have you suddenly thought of him? He died three years ago.'

'In the early hours of the seventeenth of July,' I said, 'And that same day Suslov suffered a seizure.'

'So-o-o!' Chazov drew out the word. 'It looks as if Brezhnev did right to think of you when things got difficult. He has a good nose for men of intelligence. Come over to my place. We must have another drink.'

Back in his office he poured out another glass of brandy and said: 'You know, you don't need to go into these stories inside the Kremlin. All that's required of you is that you find out whether this was suicide or murder, and if it was murder, who killed him. That's all! And never mind what happened in the past. It bears no relation to the present. When a surgeon is summoned to perform an emergency operation, he doesn't bother asking about what sort of stool the patient produced three years before. He cuts at what he can see in front of him. As you can see, I keep dragging Suslov back from the edge of the grave, although I think that that's the only real place for him. But it's my professional duty to treat patients, and it's yours to uncover crimes. That was what they called you in for. We trust neither the KGB nor the militia now, but you are an almost neutral character. And remember: if you do what you've been entrusted to do, you will not be forgotten. Leonid Brezhnev knows how to promote people that are needed.'

'Yevgeny Ivanovich,' I said with a laugh, 'this morning an attempt was made both to bribe and intimidate me. But I can't work in that sort of atmosphere. I am being followed and my phone is being tapped. If an official inquiry has been ordered into the Tsvigun affair, I must have some freedom of action. It was this that I wanted to tell Leonid Ilyich.'

Chazov stood up and went to the window. Outside the window was the forest, and beyond the forest – Moscow. He said: 'I too would like to engage in pure science, in sterile hospital conditions. Or do you think it's such a great pleasure to be Brezhnev's nursemaid, sitting there catching his every sneeze? But the one thing is impossible without the other. And if you want to know – we need them as much as they need us. Today at various ends of Moscow two old men are lying in their beds. One of them is already pegging out. The other can hardly move his jaw. And behind them stand two phalanxes of men lined up, like you and me. I am not authorized to speak to you on behalf of our whole company, but I'll tell you one thing: if anyone has no place on the other side, then it's you. As soon as Brezhnev leaves his post, the Politburo will become one hundred per cent anti-Semitic. I'm telling you this as chief doctor of the Kremlin Hospital who has been over every member of the Politburo right down to their spleen.' He glanced at his watch. 'OK. It's time for me to go and see Brezhnev. What shall I tell him?'

I opened my notepad and wrote on a clean sheet: 'Dear Leonid Ilyich! I thank you for the trust you have put in me. Unfortunately, I cannot investigate this case single-handed in such a short period. At the very minimum, I need those helpers I had when investigating the case of journalist Belkin: the chief of the Third Section of Moscow Criminal Investigation – Svetlov, and the investigator from Moscow City Prosecutor's Office – Pshenichny. Without them I cannot guarantee to fulfil the task you have entrusted me with. Respectfully yours, I. Shamrayev.'

Chazov took the note and I got up.

As I was about to leave, I nodded towards the folio with Suslov's medical record which was once again lying on his desk: 'Did Tsvigun ever see that case-history?' I asked.

'No,' said Chazov. 'I only began studying it myself the day before yesterday. Before that Suslov never allowed anyone near him apart from his own doctor Schmidt.'

6.00 p.m.

No forms of transport other than government vehicles are ever allowed on to Red Square. With its tyres softly rustling over the fresh snow, our Chaika passed the traffic-control point and moved on to the cobble-stones of the Square. I could see Anton and Nina a long way off, as we made our way across the half empty Square with its occasional groups of foreign tourists. Their sporting dress stood out sharply against the background of ladies' luxurious fur coats and the fleece jackets of foreign tourists. Nina and Anton were gazing along with the tourists at the changing of the guard outside the Lenin Mausoleum. As the Kremlin chimes struck six, the soldiers of the Kremlin garrison marched with clockwork precision from the Spassky Gates to the Mausoleum to relieve the sentries who had done their turn. The tourist cameras flashed. In the evening silence, the guards coming off duty left their posts and stamped away, and in their place at the doors of the Mausoleum the new ones froze into position. Few of the tourists or other idlers hanging around on Red Square could suspect that what the soldiers hated above all else was to serve in the Kremlin garrison, despite the choice food and the supposed honour of guarding the remains of the great leader. For in the Kremlin garrison there is special drill – three hours a day of parade-drill, and four hours of political training, so apart from having to stand like that without stirring or blinking in front of gaping onlookers and the cameras of half the world – they have an added torment. But the ceremonial is kept up without fail from hour to hour, through years and decades, in times of war and peace, under Stalin, Khrushchev and Brezhnev, both when there is calm inside the Kremlin, and also when revolutions go on behind the scenes. The façade of the Kremlin must be kept perfectly clean, the ruby-red stars must gleam unwinking, and the sentries at the Mausoleum must stand eternally at their posts as a symbol of the country's and the government's faithfulness to the legacy of Lenin. The world must see that whatever may happen elsewhere, within our country complete calm and order reign. And for that reason, there was now this festive splendour – at least on this side of the Kremlin wall. Quiet, almost Christmastide snow circled in the beams of the floodlights illuminating the Mausoleum . . But once the spectacle of changing the guard had finished, the tourists' and spectators' attention switched to our government Chaika rolling up to the Mausoleum. I realized it was somewhat immodest to come here in this Kremlin limousine to collect Nina and Anton. But damn it, you only live once! Let them see that I had achieved something in life!

I lowered the window and called out to them: 'Nina! Anton!'

They glanced towards the Chaika in surprise and disbelief.

I called again: 'Anton!'

They both dashed towards me.

'Is that you?' said Nina in amazement.

'What are you doing here?' Anton asked. 'Have they arrested you?'

'Get in!' I ordered them.

'Phew!' Anton whistled, slapped Nina on the shoulder, and they both jumped into the limousine. It drove off smoothly as the foreign tourists watched.

Our Kremlin escort turned round from the front seat and asked: 'Shall we perhaps take your young folk for a ride around Moscow?'

'Can't we go through the Kremlin?' Anton immediately asked.

The escort hesitated and said: 'Perhaps not. It's late now. Another time. But we could have a run round Moscow for half an hour.'

'Thank you,' I said, 'but I think they are rather tired today. We'll take Anton home to Krasnaya Presnya, and then I need to go to Medical Institute Number One, to the Anatomy Department.'

'What? Aren't I sleeping at your place tonight?' asked Anton.

I had been waiting for that question. On Saturdays Anton usually spent the night at my place. But there was no call for that tonight, now Nina had moved in.

'I've told you, I have still some things to see to. You can spend the night at your mother's this time.'

Anton turned away and looked out of the window, and he did not say another word that evening. When we stopped outside the house on Krasnaya Presnya Street, he got out of the car without saying anything, and his thin, erect figure never turned as it disappeared into the entrance. And I then noticed for the first time that his jacket was far from new, and his rabbit-fur *shapka* was worn. The son of an investigator engaged on specially important cases looking like a tramp, I thought. But his father had not yet earned the money for a new overcoat and a deerskin cap – or, to be more exact, he had already spent that money on high living while on holiday in Sochi. I had to earn some more quickly. I must solve this case, and then there would be more earnings. They might even put me up to four hundred a month, and that would be enough for a coat for my son, and for all my Ninas.

'Zubovskaya Square,' I said. 'The Medical Institute.'

And little Nina, her eyes all bright, squeezed up to me on the back seat.

6.40 p.m.

We released our car and its crew at the entrance to the Anatomy Department of the Medical Institute.

'Just bear in mind,' I told her, 'that the Anatomy Department is not one of your circuses. It's quite simply a morgue. And corpses stink. If you're not used to it, it might nauseate you.'

'I want to be with you everywhere. And I shall not be nauseated,' she insisted as we went together down the stairs, past the 'freezer' where the corpses were kept, and down to the Anatomy Department.

In various parts of the large room below there were several men working at dissecting-tables.

Boris Gradus – one of our best, if not *the* best, expert on morbid anatomy – was a strong man, broad in the shoulders, with a large head, bald as a billiard ball, and with a luxuriant growth of bluish-black beard. With his bloody apron and a scalpel in his left hand, he looked the genuine Jewish butcher.

He turned to us from the table where a body lay half covered by a sheet. 'Oho, look who's come!' he said. 'Greetings! Are you bringing some tourists?'

'Almost,' I said.

'I thought at first it was just the next accident victim coming in. As soon as there's ice or snow in Moscow, we simply can't cope here. People just don't know how to drive. There are crashes every ten minutes.'

'Let me introduce you,' I said. 'This is Nina, my niece.'

'I understand,' said Gradus meaningfully. 'Forgive me, miss, I've got gloves on.' After sizing Nina up with the disrobing glance of a professional, he said reproachfully, 'Couldn't you find anywhere else to take a girl like that? Did you have to take her to the morgue, instead of a restaurant or the theatre?'

'I'm here on business,' I said.

'I bet you are! Nobody would come to the morgue for anything else! Excepting the bodies, of course, but they get *brought* here. They don't come of their own accord.'

Nina had turned pale, and she looked away from the slit in the sheet covering the corpse that lay there on the table. I tried not to look myself – the intestines of the victim had been torn out in a car crash and had not yet been sewn back. The lungs were stained dark and emitted a thick nicotine slime – the dead man had obviously been a heavy smoker. But there was little else to look at in the room: at the far end more corpses were being worked on by two other medics and a young girl assistant whom I didn't know – probably she was a student from the Institute, or a postgraduate whom Gradus had managed to charm. She and her colleagues, whom I also hardly knew, were working on the body of a dead woman who had had part of her skull hacked away. They had washed the blood from the hair and were now sewing the head together.

'Another street accident?' I asked Gradus, nodding towards them.

'No, an axe,' he said. 'A small family quarrel following the fourth bottle of vodka. Well, Nina, how do you like it here?'

'Very interesting . . .' said Nina, putting on a bold face.

'Oho! You're doing well! You don't feel like enrolling at the Institute, do you? I can fix you a place if I pull a few strings.'

'OK, let her be,' I said. 'Listen. I am conducting the inquiry into Tsvigun's death. Tell me, who was it that made up the body for the funeral? Was it you?'

'No, they don't trust me to darn up anyone of that rank. I'm not a Party member. And thank God for that. I've enough to do as it is with this lot. What is it you want?'

'I want to talk with whoever prepared the body.'

'The post-mortem was done by our kosher brigade of Party members – Tumanov, Zhivoduyev and Semyonovsky.'

'Precisely. But you must realize there's no point in talking to them. They'll never say anything other than what they have written together with Tumanov in the official autopsy report.'

'Well,' said Gradus, dropping his voice, 'the man standing over there is Sandy. He was the one who made up Tsvigun's corpse. But I would advise you not to try talking to him without a bottle of Armenian brandy. Run and get some, but mind it's decent stuff. Meanwhile I'll take your niece on a tour of the Anatomy Department. Nina, what about a nip of spirits? You're not going to turn your nose up now, are you? It's absolutely pure alcohol.' And he took out a round flask of surgical spirit from a small cupboard containing his instruments, saying, 'Don't be afraid. It'll give you courage.'

'But mind you don't get her drunk!' I said as I left the room.

When I got back fifteen minutes later, I found Gradus and Nina standing there using two glass phials as drinking-glasses.

'Back already?' said Gradus. 'Getting scared for your niece's safety? That means he loves you, Nina, and takes good care of you. Come on, man, let's pour you some too. And here are some olives. Dip in!'

I looked dubiously at several olives that lay there on a white enamel dish. One could expect anything of Gradus.

I nodded towards the open stomach of the corpse: 'Borya, tell me honestly: they're not out of there, are they?'

Gradus made an offended grimace: 'Shame on you! What are you talking about? They're from a fresh New Year's consignment – delicious Algerian olives!'

At that moment Sandy came past us on his way back from the 'freezer'.

'Sandy,' said Gradus, stopping him, 'I know that you normally spurn our surgical spirit, but we've just got some brandy here. How about it?'

'I could certainly manage a brandy,' said Sandy approvingly. He was about sixty and had a face that looked as strong and brown as a walnut.

'Let me introduce you,' said Gradus, 'my old friend Shamrayev, special investigator, and Nina, his niece.'

'Bogoyavlensky,' Sandy announced his name and looked eagerly at the brandy gurgling into the phials as Gradus poured it out. 'What's it like outside? Blowing a blizzard?'

'It is indeed,' I said, clinking glasses with him. 'Your health! Much work these days?'

'A lot. Sometimes crashes, sometimes brawls, and sometimes people snuff it just like that. My normal quota is ten good Christians a day. I tart them up, of course, so they're not ashamed to appear before the Lord. After all, you really can't turn up in the next world all sinful and indecent with your brains mangled.' He drank up and held his phial out for a refill.

'Do you really find it interesting cutting up ten corpses a day?' asked Nina.

Sandy looked down and studied her, then answered solemnly: 'But, my child, this is profitable work. We cut up nine bodies and put them in the "freezer", and the tenth we keep for ourselves.'

'But why?' Nina was dumbfounded.

'Well, you know the difficulties getting meat these days, and bones too. The shops are empty. So that's how we manage. The bones help to make jellied meat, and the flesh goes into . . .'

Gradus roared with laughter, and I too couldn't withhold a smile. Only Sandy looked serious.

'All right, that's enough leg-pulling,' said Nina, still not too sure of herself.

Of course, so far as the flesh and the bones were concerned, Sandy was indeed pulling her leg, but he wasn't joking about the profitability of the work. The mortician's job is an extremely well-paid occupation. Who of a dead man's friends would begrudge the money to have his body set in order, so it looked well in the coffin, and seemed almost 'lifelike'? And for the sake of this lifelike appearance, the relatives of the deceased would hand fat bribes to Sandy and similar men of his trade.

'And did you do Tsvigun's cosmetics too?' I asked.

Bogoyavlensky hauled from his pocket a packet of Belomor cigarettes, silently lit one, inhaled, cast a glance in my direction, then turned to Gradus: 'What was that about the brandy? Is it all for me, or do I only get it by the glass?'

'It's all for you,' Gradus assured him hastily and handed him the bottle. 'He brought it specially for you.'

'Aha,' said Sandy and silently gathered up the bottle. He tucked it in the pocket of his smock and just as silently moved off to the far end of the room. Gradus motioned me to follow. I caught up with him, and as we walked he said morosely: 'You don't behave properly. That was wrong of you, even if you are one of the "specials" . . .'

'What do you mean?' I asked.

'Why did you mention Tsvigun in front of the girl? That's government business, it comes under official secrets. What do you want to know?'

'Apart from the bullet-wound in the head, were there any other injuries on the body? Any abrasions, cuts or fractures?'

'I didn't inspect the body. I only put the head in order and changed his clothes. Because the jacket he had on was covered in blood and was split down the back . . .'

'The jacket had split down the back? Do you remember that for certain? Where is the jacket?'

'His wife collected it. She brought in a tunic for him and I handed the jacket back to her . . . But just you remember, I've told you nothing.' Sandy went over to his dissecting-table where the next corpse was waiting, and resumed his work.

I rejoined Gradus, who was busy buttering up a now thoroughly intoxicated Nina.

"OK, that's it for today,' I said. 'Off we go back home!'

I glanced at my watch. It was only 7.27 p.m., but the events of that Saturday had so exhausted me, I felt as if I hadn't slept for three days. When my last five roubles went on a taxi home, I regretted having let the government Chaika go an hour before . . . Opposite the house entrance there stood the same Repairs van that had followed us that morning. I had honestly thought they merely meant to give us a scare and then leave us alone, but I now no longer had the energy to get annoyed or even swear at the dolts. Nina, though, thought differently. She wriggled free of my hand that supported her elbow, and quickly ran across the street. Skipping up to the window of the van where two MVD men were sitting, she stuck her tongue out at them and gave them the two fingers, then came running back to me, laughing.

11.48 p.m.

We were woken in the middle of the night by an insistent ringing at the door. I glanced automatically at the glowing dial of my watch. It was twelve minutes to midnight. The bell continued jangling. In the dark my bare feet groped and completely failed to find my slippers – Nina had them on last when she ran to the bathroom, and goodness knows where she had left them. With her, there was no chance to get bored. First she went cocking snooks at the MVD, and then, five minutes after we arrived at the apartment and I had flopped straight into the bath feeling like a corpse, she came plunging in, and brought me back to life by massaging me. She began by pummelling my back and shoulders with her little fists, and I merely moaned slightly with pleasure. But following this, games of another sort began, and only the roar of the shower concealed our noise from the listening microphones.

Then Nina settled down next to me in bed, covered herself with two blankets against eavesdroppers, and breathed into my ear: 'Are you still alive?' And her hand slipped down to the spot where there was now no sign of life.

'Go to sleep, you little hooligan!' I said. 'Anyway, tomorrow I'm packing you off home.'

'Why?'

'Because it's forbidden to spend more than three days in Moscow without registering. You have to be registered with the police. And what do I register you as? My niece? They could come bursting in here at any minute and charge me with immoral behaviour. And then they'd throw you out of the Komsomol.'

'Fat lot I care about Komsomol!' she laughed. 'I'm never going to leave you!'

'What? Never?'

'Aha. I'm going to be your mistress in perpetuity. Don't you enjoy being with me?'

I recalled how only a few days ago in Sochi, I had woken up in a hotel room at night and been surprised to hear her steady, almost childlike breathing next to me. I had got up and parted the curtain, and the moonlight illuminated her little figure on the white bed. I had sat on the edge of the bed and had wondered at this gift which fate had sent me so unexpectedly on the shore of the Black Sea. To think that this jolly little girl, full of life and youthful audacity, had come to me, a divorcee of forty-five, no playboy or philanderer, indeed no expert at all in such amorous affairs. And of course I did enjoy being with little Nina – both in Sochi and in Moscow . . .

'But probably you're bored with me, though,' I said. 'I'm almost thirty years older than you.'

'Silly!' she whispered into my ear. 'With you life's very interesting!'

'Just because I turned up in a Chaika today?'

'No . . . I mean, that was interesting as well, but . . . You're simply very intelligent.'

'What gives you that idea?'

'You have intelligent eyes. Intelligent and sad. And I like that.'

I embraced her and pressed her to me. Once upon a time my wife had left me, having decided that I would achieve nothing in this life and that she was simply wasting her time with me. She had always said I had the sad eyes of a Jew who wouldn't make it, and that I'd never get beyond being an investigator at some district prosecutor's office. But recently I had begun to notice that at forty these same eyes made quite a different impression on women. I embraced Nina and she began kissing my chest and shoulders . . . Nevertheless, in half an hour we finally dozed off. But at 11.48 came that loud ringing at the door. I had no doubt that these were emissaries arriving from Krasnov, Malenina and Baklanov. They had evidently taken a long time deciding when to give me a serious fright – either today or tomorrow – and they had finally decided that tonight would be best, before the girl departed. Hastily I flung a blanket and pillow on the settee to give at least the appearance that Nina and I were sleeping separately, and then made my way to the door where the bell was still jangling with militia-like insistence.

'Who's there?'

'The fucking Gestapo!' came Svetlov's voice. 'And you're asleep! Open up!'

I opened the door. On the landing stood a sullen Marat Svetlov, Valentin Pshenichny, and the solid figure of an elderly major-general with shoulders like barn-doors and a strangely familiar face.

Behind my back, Nina dashed into the bathroom to get dressed, and the major-general said: 'Sorry to wake you, Comrade Shamrayev. Leonid Brezhnev has given orders to place these comrades at your complete disposal. The national head of all criminal investigation and the Moscow Prosecutor have been informed that these comrades are working with you. May we come in?'

'Yes, yes . . . please do . . .' I said, somewhat confused.

They came in. Svetlov surveyed the pillow and blanket on the settee with a crafty smirk. Valentin Pshenichny was a tall, gaunt, thirty-five-year-old. He had blond hair, grave blue eyes, and an elongated face like the poet Aleksandr Blok. He had lost his earlier, hunched appearance of the hard-driven rank-and-file investigator, but otherwise seemed totally unchanged in the two and a half years since last I saw him.

Pshenichny hung back modestly in the entrance, while the general asked: 'Are you having any other difficulties in your work, Comrade Shamrayev? Please don't hesitate to say.'

'Difficulties? Yes, I think there are a few. Can I have a word with you for a moment?'

I threw a fleece jacket over my pyjamas, threaded the slippers onto my bare feet at last, then opened the door onto the balcony and motioned him to follow me. Despite the slippers, my bare feet were frozen by the snow, but I gritted my teeth. Down below on the street I saw two black Volgas standing outside the house entrance, and on the opposite side of the road the Repairs van was still parked.

The general followed me on to the balcony and I pulled the door to behind us and asked: 'May I know who you are?'

'Of course. I'm sorry for not introducing myself. Major-General Zharov, Commander of Comrade Brezhnev's personal guard.'

Only then did I remember where I had seen him – of course, I had seen his face a hundred times on television whenever official government functions were being covered. He always walked slightly behind Brezhnev, but close to him, and then behind him came the rest of the Politburo. He was also the one who supported Brezhnev's arm and helped him down aircraft gangways.

'General Zharov, do you see that Repairs van? Well, it is really a radio-monitoring van from MVD Intelligence. My quarters are chock-full of microphones. They are trying to scare me into abandoning the case.'

'I understand,' he said. 'But let's go inside, or you'll catch a chill.'

Inside Nina had already been introduced to Pshenichny and was adroitly straightening the bedding on the couch. Without a word the general left the apartment, and a minute later we watched with curiosity from the window as he emerged from the block and went up to the two black Volgas. Immediately five hefty sportsmanlike figures sprang out of them and crossed the road, heading for the Repairs van. The driver sheepishly started up and tried to extricate the van from a snowdrift. The general unhurriedly pulled a pistol from his pocket and fired a muffled shot that punctured the van's back tyre. The five men closed in on the van, the general tore open the side door and pointed his gun at the three frightened radio sleuths. They got out. A minute later all three of them were up in my apartment. Cowering and working hastily, they changed all the fuses in the electricity meter in the entrance, they took two microphones from under the gas-ring in the kitchen, removed a further one adhering by a suction cup to the bedside table and finally unscrewed one from the telephone receiver.

'Is that the lot?' Zharov asked.

'Yes, sir, Comrade Major-General.'

'Ragimov,' the general ordered one of his men, 'Go down with them and take all their tapes. And then they'd better get the hell out of my sight, while they're still alive. This will not occur again, Comrade Shamrayev. You can carry on working in peace. Anything more we can help with?'

'Have you got the address of Tsvigun's bodyguard?'

'I'd be glad to oblige, but that's something I don't have. He had his own bodyguards from the KGB.'

Nina appeared from the kitchen wearing a neat apron and bringing tea on a tray.

'Would you like some tea, General?' she asked.

'Thank you,' said the general, 'but I'll not get in your way.' He looked at Svetlov, Pshenichny and myself. 'I think you've probably a lot of work ahead of you today. Comrade Shamrayev, can I talk with you a moment?'

He looked round the apartment for a place to go with me alone, then stepped through into the kitchen. 'Hmm, well your apartment's not much to write home about,' he said when we were in the kitchen. 'But, when you've finished this case, you'll get another one, and a better one. But I've called you out here for something else. Leonid Brezhnev asked me to urge you to do everything you possibly can in this case. There are no limits on expense or on your freedom of action. Take this now.' He took a small sealed packet from the inside pocket of his tunic and laid it on the kitchen table. 'And write down my phone number: 253-17-17. You can ring at any hour of the day or night and they'll put you through to me. I want you to understand perfectly clearly that Comrade Brezhnev's fate is now in your hands . . . and your own fate as well.'

'Can you tell me any details at all? Can you tell me what you know, General?'

'What details do I have? At the moment nobody really knows anything about what was on Suslov's mind when he started Operation Cascade, or who is in his team, and what they intend doing. At any rate, we have transferred the Kantemir Division to Moscow. That I do know. But there won't be any fighting on the streets. That can happen only at some Politburo meeting. Only now Suslov's out of action, nobody knows who is going to start things up, and what trumps they might hold. Before, everything rested on Tsvigun. He suspected that Suslov was planning some government coup. And Brezhnev therefore allowed him to put Suslov under surveillance. That was a month ago. A month later Suslov invited Tsvigun for a talk, after which Tsvigun committed suicide. That's all that we know.'

'Tell me, where is Yury now, Brezhnev's son?'

'He has just flown in from Luxembourg. He was there as head of a trade delegation. Why?'

'He would do best for the time being to stay at home with his father. At any rate he should stay somewhere where there's no possibility of his phone conversations and personal contacts being monitored. And the same goes for Galina, Brezhnev's daughter.'

'Oh-oh-oh!' Zharov gave a real old man's sigh. 'There's no holding that girl! OK. We'll have a think about that one . . . Anyway, here's wishing you success.' He proffered his hand. 'And ring me at any time.'

I shook his hand.

Suddenly he asked: 'Do you have any brandy?'

'Yes, I do . . .'

'Pour me a glass. My heart just gave a twinge.'

'Do we need to call an ambulance?'

'No, no,' he laughed. 'The doctors would say I was completely healthy. It'll pass off.'

I handed him a glass of brandy.

He drank it down in one and paused a few seconds. 'That's it,' he said, grey in the face and obviously steeling himself against some internal pain.

93

'Wish you luck,' he said, and went out with shoulders hunched.

I watched him leave. So even the guardians of our government get old and have heart complaints! I undid the sealed packet. It contained a wad of new hundred-rouble notes tied round with banker's tape and marked '10,000 roubles'. There was also a letter on headed paper with a red signature-stamp. It read as follows:

The Chairman of the Presidium of the USSR Supreme Soviet
Secretary General of the Central Committee of the CPSU
Leonid Ilyich Brezhnev
This is to certify that Senior Juridical Councillor Comrade Igor Iosifovich Shamrayev, Investigator from the Office of the Chief Public Prosecutor of the USSR and concerned with matters of national importance, is carrying out a government assignment. All national, military, administrative and Soviet institutions are instructed to assist him in his work and to carry out his every requirement.
Leonid Brezhnev

The Kremlin,
Moscow,
23 January 1982

I placed this letter and the money in my jacket pocket and went through into the living-room to hold my council of war with Svetlov and Pshenichny.

Part 4

Contenders for Killer

Sunday, 24 January, 6.17 a.m.
Moscow was still sleeping when Senior Investigator of the City Prosecutor's Office Valentin Pshenichny arrived by the first morning train at Arbatskaya metro station. The empty escalator brought him up to the still dark and snow-swept Arbat. From there it was another ten minutes on foot to Kachalov Street, where former Deputy Chairman of the KGB Tsvigun had his secret apartment. Pshenichny crammed his porkpie fur hat even lower on his head, pulled up the collar of his tawny overcoat, and set off. The main quality for which I had included Pshenichny in my investigation team, was his thoroughness.

So that night, when the three of us worked out our plan of action, I detailed him to question all the residents of 16-A, Kachalov Street – perhaps one of them might have seen or heard something suspicious on the day of Tsvigun's 'suicide'. I realized full well that at the minimum Pshenichny would interrogate not only all the residents of the house but those at 15 as well. But I had not imagined he would immediately slip out of my apartment at six in the morning and start work straight away – not on a Sunday! Later, in his report, Pshenichny put with typical laconic modesty: 'Wishing to familiarize myself with the scene, I arrived at Kachalov Street at 06.17 hours.'

Named after the celebrated Russian actor, Kachalov Street is a quiet thoroughfare even at noon on a working day, and at such an early hour it was dark, empty and snowbound. The blizzard had also streaked the several new twelve-storey housing blocks that were built specially for high-ranking figures in the Council of Ministers. In front of the breadshop on the ground floor of No. 14 trays of fresh rolls and loaves were being unloaded from a van. All Moscow knows that fresh bread made from pure wheat flour can only be bought in four places: on Kutuzovsky Prospect near Brezhnev's house, at the Yeliseyev Shop on Gorky Street, by the Arts Cinema on the New Arbat, and here, next door to the so-called government houses. The

97

smell of freshly-baked bread reached Pshenichny some distance away. He made for the shop, showed the woman in charge his investigator's identity card, and apart from having a general chatter he also received a low-calory loaf and a cup of coffee. The woman at the shop turned out to be a sprightly, cheery soul and knew the names of almost all the regular customers from the houses around. Soon Pshenichny was noting down all those who usually came to buy bread in the afternoon: Kseniya, the housekeeper of Kosygin's daughter; Masha, housekeeper of the actor Papanov; Ivan Polikarpovich from the Council of Ministers; Roza Abramovna, the professor's wife from 16-A; nine-year-old Katya Uzhovich, a pupil at the Junior Music School on Merzlyakovka, who each day after classes called in to buy a nice French pastry; and so on – sixty people, including twenty-seven housekeepers, six Academicians, eight diplomats and three actors. Pshenichny was intent on questioning them all, since each of them might have walked past 16-A on the afternoon of 19 January and have seen something interesting. At this point, into the shop came the local inspector of militia, Captain Andrei Kopylov. He was a thickset man; his greatcoat was powdered with snow and he wore felt boots. He felt the loaves in the tray in managerial fashion, selected for himself the crispiest and also took several French loaves – his daily tribute, free of charge – and he was about to leave when Pshenichny stopped and questioned him too. According to Kopylov, 16-A was a quiet and orderly house, with no noisy drunken parties and no cases of hooliganism, since all the people living there were solid folk from the government. It was true, they did go to bed late, there were many lights still burning after midnight, and often black Volgas, Zils and Chaikas rolled up during the night. Sometimes the people in them were merry, slightly tipsy, but that was, as they say, nothing out of the ordinary. The people had money, so they could afford to go to restaurants, or throw wedding celebrations. In apartment No. 11 on the second floor, for instance, there had been the din of music and feasting for ten days from morning till night. But for all that, during all the six years that Kopylov had worked here, there had been only one incident, and that had involved traffic on the road: three or four years ago somebody's drunken guest, a Georgian from Tiflis, had smashed the bumper of his Volga through the door of the new Zhiguli belonging to the wife of Academician Tsipursky. But everything passed off without a scene – the Georgian had immediately paid the cost of repairs, and the traffic-controllers who wanted to confiscate his licence for drunken driving were bought off with a hundred-rouble fine. Nevertheless, the assiduous Kopylov had entered the incident in the local 'journal of events' which was kept at the Krasnopresnensky district station No. 45. After that, the Georgian had disappeared, and Captain Kopylov had never seen him again. Other Georgians had sometimes turned up, but not that one.

And although in itself this affair was three years old and bore no relation to the case in hand, Pshenichny took the trouble to go with Kopylov to station No. 45, and consult their duty records for 1978 and copied into his pad: 'July 12 1978. Duty went smoothly. 21.20 hours: dark-blue Volga GRU 56-12 smashed the door of Zhiguli MKE 87-21. Traffic-controllers fined driver for driving in drunken state, did not confiscate licence. No other incidents. District inspector, A.P. Kopylov.'

Following this, Captain Kopylov handed Pshenichny the 'House Book' for 16-A, which contained a complete list of residents in every apartment. Studying the register, Pshenichny discovered that in the space for 'Apartment No. 9' no names were given; there were simply the words 'Special Apartment'. Pshenichny recruited Kopylov as his assistant, and now armed with the names of the forty-eight residents and the sixty regular afternoon bread-buyers who might have passed by on 19 January he could get down to the main task of interrogating all of them in order to reconstruct every minute of the day's events of Tuesday 19 January in the many-mansioned house at 16-A.

8.55 a.m.
The official Volga summoned from the Prosecutor's Office stood outside my entrance, and the driver as usual was Sasha Ruchov.

'We're coming down!' Nina called to him from the balcony. But before getting into the lift, I put my own seal on the door of my apartment – now let them try and fix microphones there!

But Svetlov laughed sarcastically: 'If Krasnov sees fit, they'll take your seal off and put it back again, and you won't notice.'

'But what about this?' Nina suddenly pulled out one of her own flaxen hairs, deftly wound one end round some snag under the door and the other round the uneven edge of the doorstep, and knotted it.

Svetlov gave a whistle of admiration, and said to Nina: 'Here, what's your name? Richard Sorge?'

'I saw them do that once in the cinema,' she said.

Then we went without further ado to Petrovka No. 38. Here Svetlov took Nina with him to his office at the Moscow CID, while I went on to Kotelnicheskaya Embankment to see Tsvigun's widow.

9.20 a.m.
Vera Petrovna, widow of Tsvigun, lived, by government standards, in a fairly modest four-roomed apartment. Considering that both her son and daughter were already grown-up and lived away from their parents, the four rooms and a spacious kitchen were perfectly ample for two elderly folk. That was what Vera Petrovna told me, and then immediately corrected herself: 'It *was* ample, but now I am alone, I don't need anything at all.'

She showed me round the quarters. There was old furniture dating from the forties, carpets and armchairs were worn through, there was an old Underwood typewriter, and all over there were signs of a spartan, even impoverished existence – quite the opposite of the 'special apartment' on Kachalov Street. In the drawing-room Vera Petrovna showed me her family

99

photographs – here was her father in Chernigov, and here she was herself with her sister Vika aged twelve; this was Vika's wedding at Dnepropetrovsk, when she married a young, dark and bushy-browed Party worker called Leonid Brezhnev; and here were Semyon and Vera Tsvigun in the Crimea in '39 – both of them former teachers who had joined the Cheka; and there were the Tsvigun and Brezhnev families relaxing. Yes, all those years they had been friends, and now the Brezhnevs did not even come to Semyon's funeral!

In typical Moscow fashion, this conversation took place not in the drawing-room but in the kitchen. Although it was warm in the apartment, Vera Petrovna wrapped herself about with a scarf. She fed me tea and doughnuts, and in a miserly trickle poured out her offended soul. She was mainly insulted by her sister and brother-in-law – Brezhnev had not signed the official obituary notice and had not gone to the funeral; not even her sister had come. She had also taken offence against their circle of acquaintances – at one time they had all tried to push their friendship but now even her own children would ring her up only out of a sense of duty; they would ask their mother how she was and then immediately hang up. The only decent person had turned out to be Geidar Aliyev from Baku, First Secretary of the Central Committee of the Azerbaidzhan Communist Party. Twenty years ago, when Tsvigun was head of the KGB in Azerbaidzhan, Aliyev was his pupil, assistant, and close friend. From that moment his star had been in the ascendant. Not without Tsvigun's assistance, he had become virtual manager of the whole republic and even a candidate member of the Politburo – in fact, he had overtaken his one-time mentor. But he had not forgotten their old friendship or become too headstrong, and in the evening of 19 January, the day of Semyon's death, he had rung her up from Baku and announced that he was flying immediately to Moscow in order to be with her at the funeral. But evidently someone else had also listened in to the conversation, for an hour later Aliyev had rung again and said that the Politburo had refused to let him leave Azerbaidzhan, since a government delegation from Angola was expected in Baku on the twenty-first.

'Well, who could have listened in – you realize well enough yourself!' Vera Tsvigun laughed. 'Who is it that decides where to send these tar-brushed Communists? It's Suslov and Andropov! Only they have such authority! Scoundrels they are, nothing more than scoundrels!'

Vera Petrovna rocked on her chair. 'And they must have filled Brezhnev's ears with such things about Semyon that even Vika didn't come to the funeral, and Aliyev even was stopped from attending! The scum! Suslov at least had the conscience not to turn up at the funeral and pretended to be ill, but Andropov put in an appearance!'

'Vera Petrovna, aren't you afraid that they might be able to eavesdrop on you even now?' I asked, somewhat shocked at such open abuse of Andropov and Suslov.

'Oh, I wish they would! I wish they would listen in! What can they do to me? Put me in prison? Me, Brezhnev's sister-in-law? They can't! And it's a fact that they're all scoundrels – so let them hear it! Semyon stopped them from bringing Brezhnev down, since he had the whole of the KGB in his hands. So they went and spread slander about him and Brezhnev believed it, the idiot! That's how it always is! Semyon served him like a faithful hound for thirty years, and Brezhnev wouldn't even visit his grave. And what cemetery did they give him? Not even the Novodevichy! The Vagankovskoye! Well, never mind, they'll still bring him down fairly soon now, it serves the bungler right. If they could stop Aliyev coming, they must already be running rings round him. That's just it! Aliyev would quickly have worked out who it was that pushed Semyon into the grave.'

But apart from the malice and the cruelty, perhaps unexpected in such an old woman, these lamentations did contain several details that were important to me. First of all, she had confirmed what she had heard from her husband about Suslov and Andropov scheming against Brezhnev. And secondly, it looked as if Geidar Aliyev really was a close friend of Tsvigun and had wanted to come on 19 January, when he would certainly have rushed immediately to the safe apartment where the suicide took place. But that was evidently undesirable and would have got in someone's way, so Aliyev's visit was stopped. Who by? Tsvigun's widow thought it was Andropov and Suslov . . .

'But, Vera Petrovna, did your husband have any concrete proof of there being a conspiracy against Brezhnev?'

She laughed. 'There we are! So that's why Brezhnev has sent you to come and see me! Sucks to him! I don't know anything. It's because of him that I've lost my husband – and you might say lost him twice over. Yes, I mean that! What sort of manner has Brezhnev adopted in recent years? Khrushchev used to take his wife all over the world, to America and Europe, but Brezhnev doesn't let Vika go beyond the *dacha*. Even at receptions he appears alone. And Semyon also stopped inviting guests home. It's about ten years now since I even went to the theatre with him.'

One needed the patience peculiar to investigators in order to fish out from this deluge what was actually useful for the inquiry.

'But have you kept any papers of your husband's? Even jottings or notebooks?' I asked.

She shook her head. 'No. They took everything away that same day. Six men appeared on the evening of the nineteenth. They turned the whole apartment upside down, they leafed through every book in the cupboard, and they took away all the papers with them and even the tape cassettes. I asked them: "What do you need the cassettes for? They are only songs by Vysotsky and Okudzhava – old favourites of mine – and there's nothing on them to do with any KGB secrets." But they said: "No, we have to listen through everything. You never know . . ." Idiots! Do you think if Tsvigun had had anything, he would have kept it at home?'

'And where might he have kept it?'

101

'I don't know . . .' she said. 'But they went through the whole *dacha* as well.'

'Who carried out the search? Did you ask to see their papers?'

'Why should I bother looking? I know them anyway. Kurbanov was from the KGB, General Krasnov from the militia – they were in charge. Yes, there was also a tall elderly man with them, in civilian clothes and with tobacco-stained teeth. He also behaved like someone in command and pounced immediately on the tapes.'

Could it have been Baklanov? The thought flashed through my head, and I asked: 'Do you remember his surname?'

'He didn't tell me his surname, but they called him Nikolai Afanasyevich. So I said to him: "Nikolai Afanasyevich, leave me at least just one cassette, my favourite, with Okudzhava's song about the last trolleybus." But he wouldn't, the bastard.'

So, I thought, Baklanov's path and mine have crossed! Not even a day had passed since his warning to me, and now it had come out already: on 19 January, a few hours after the 'suicide', Baklanov was involved in searching Tsvigun's apartment. And that meant that immediately after looking over the apartment on Kachalov Street, Kurbanov had rushed over here, together with Krasnov. And Malenina too had said something about tapes yesterday, when she came out from the secret surveillance-room. I remembered her words: 'I can't believe she doesn't know about these tapes! I'm not going to let that whore out of my sight!' That meant they were all hunting after some tape-recordings – Malenina, and Baklanov, and Krasnov, and even Kurbanov – they were all one company. Maybe Tsvigun was wary of committing to paper any information about Suslov's scheming against Brezhnev, and he therefore spoke it all onto tape. Or perhaps he had recordings of conversations between Suslov and Andropov and other conspirators? After all, Brezhnev did permit Tsvigun to put Suslov under surveillance . . . Oh, if only one could interrogate Tsvigun's agents! Only who could tell me who they were? Certainly not Andropov, at any rate!

'Vera Petrovna, tell me please, how did you spend the day of the eighteenth of January? Or even earlier, a couple of days before . . . Was your husband at all depressed or irritable?'

'My dear boy, if only you knew how rarely I saw him recently! He was away from home for days at a time – he was at work all the while. Well, – why should I hide it from you? – he had two apartments, here and one on Kachalov Street. Over there he used to play cards, or he even had women there. After all, he wasn't really old yet – only sixty-four. It was me that was old at sixty-two, but he wasn't old even at sixty-four. But as far as I was concerned, if he wasn't at home, then he was at work. Especially since we've had such goings-on every day – first Afghanistan, then Poland, then the dissidents, then Sakharov – there was no peace. So he was nervous. His one saving was that he had plenty of flesh on him. He didn't want to slim. I forget how often he used to say that a thin man simply couldn't stand up to his sort of work. Dzerzhinsky, now, he was thin and in a few years he had burnt himself up, but Semyon after all spent almost his whole life in the KGB, since 1939.'

'So if you didn't see your husband on the eighteenth and nineteenth when did you see him for the last time?'

'No, I did in fact see him on the eighteenth and nineteenth. But prior to that he was away for three or four days. But the night of the eighteenth he spent at home. He was morose and tired, but in general his usual self. And on the nineteenth in the morning I made him some breakfast, and he ate it with gusto and went off to work.'

'Did he say anything to you before he left? I mean did he say anything special, unusual?'

'No. Nothing.'

'And what did you do after your husband had gone to work that day?'

'I went to the cinema,' she said.

I looked at her in astonishment, and there was a sad resignation in her voice as she explained: 'I tell you, the last few years I have been completely alone – the children live away, Semyon was away for days at a time at his work, and if he came home, it was only towards nightfall. So what was an old woman to do? I got to like going to the cinema, in the mornings. I would feed him his breakfast – he had lunch at the KGB anyway; they have a separate room there for the bosses. So I don't bother making lunch for myself at all, and I go to the cinema to the ten o'clock show – either here, there's a cinema near us, or I go into town, to the Rossiya. And whenever there's a picture of Semyon's on, I go to that.'

'What picture?'

'Haven't you seen them? – *Front without Flank* and *The War behind the Front*? Semyon wrote them, only under a pseudonym "Semyon Dneprov". Tikhonov himself plays him in that, and the actress Natasha Sukhova plays me.'

'And what did you see on the nineteenth?'

'*Mechanic Gavrilov's Woman*, a comedy . . . Had I known that it was just at that time . . .'

'So your husband left the house quite calmly, as usual, and a few hours later he committed suicide. Doesn't that strike you as strange? After all, it must be really terrible bringing oneself to do a thing like that. Especially at his age.'

She gave a laugh: 'My dear boy, they have terrible things happening every day. Look how self-possessed Vitya Paputin was, yet he put a bullet through his forehead when he failed to take Amin alive in Afghanistan. That was the first time that such a thing happened – that the MVD and not the KGB conducted operations abroad. What is more, Semyon warned Brezhnev that they would fail – and fail they did.'

I was left blinking, and could not comprehend – which Amin? What did she mean: 'take alive'?

103

Vera Petrovna laughed again: 'You see, you know nothing of all this, but in their work things of that sort happen almost every day. When the anti-Soviet demonstrations began in Afghanistan, my husband immediately suggested bringing Amin to Moscow and getting him to sign a request for our troops to move in and provide some friendly assistance for his government. Then everything would have been quiet and peaceful, just like in the United Nations charter. But Suslov said that he would deal with these Muslim fanatics through the Afghan Communist Party. But he failed. The fanatics attacked our embassy, killed thirty-six of the staff, and stuck their heads on poles and carried them in a torchlight procession through the town. Of course, there was a meeting of the Central Committee, and the military all shouted that they should go and occupy this Afghanistan place immediately. But Semyon was against it. He told them it was too late already. They should have acted earlier, but now there would just be a second Vietnam. Well, Suslov started sneering that if the KGB was not sure of its strength, we would entrust the matter to the MVD – let them show what they were capable of, since they also had an intelligence section. And Paputin was happy to oblige, and he landed in the soup. They planned an armed raid on Kabul, on the presidential palace, to take Amin alive and then make him sign a request for Soviet troops to be sent in. When we had suggested doing the same on the quiet – oh, no! But now the MVD would move in, and Paputin himself was to lead the raid. Well, they landed at night on the president's palace and dealt with the guards, but they'd not reckoned that Amin himself might shoot and refuse to surrender alive. One of our troops shot him with a sub-machine-gun, and the whole operation went haywire. And what a scandal there was – invading a foreign country and killing the head of state! And of course, after that Suslov would have made Paputin really eat shit. He'd have sent him to the uranium mines for the rest of his life. Because he is a Fascist, this Suslov, a despot, one of Yezhov's offspring. How many Communists did he and Yezhov kill – do you know? And who do you think invented international terrorism? The Arabs? Not likely! They'd never have been capable of that! It was Suslov! It was he who set up whole training-camps for them near Simferopol. So that Vitya Paputin knew what awaited him when he got home, and so in the plane he put a bullet through his head. And you say what a terrible thing! Terrible things like that can happen there every day! Shevchenko defected in America and gave away a whole agency network, and who was to blame for that? Tsvigun! Then Israel beats the Arabs, and again who was to blame? Tsvigun – for not supplying the Arabs with intelligence reports!'

Probably, if I had not interrupted her, Vera Petrovna would have told me a dozen such stories. But I could not afford to sit around over tea and doughnuts, so I cut her short: 'So you consider that your husband might have had grounds for committing suicide?'

She stopped short, looked hard at me, and something changed in her face – from an aggrieved and garrulous old woman she turned into one who was malicious and even hostile: 'Listen, young man! If you work for the Prosecutor's Office as an investigator, then you too have grounds for committing suicide. Do you understand?' she said, pursing her lips.

'Well, that is perhaps a somewhat philosophical approach.' I tried to smooth over this unexpected turn in the conversation. No, this old woman was not as simple as I had at first assumed – or as she had at first wished to appear. For all her complaints about life and loneliness, for all these touching little excursions to the cinema to see her husband's films, there was something much harder, something of the Cheka agent in her.

Then I had a sudden idea: 'Vera Petrovna,' I asked, 'what rank did you leave the KGB with?'

She looked me straight in the eye and suddenly burst out laughing: 'You young bastard! No, I *like* you! Oh, if Semyon was alive, I'd have persuaded him to take you on instead of Kurbanov, and you could have gone even higher. Want some vodka?'

'Vera Petrovna, perhaps we'll stop playing at being garrulous old women, shall we? What tapes were they looking for here? You do know!'

'No, I do not know,' she said drily.

'Or don't you want to say?'

She shrugged and laughed straight in my face: 'Listen, young man. I am not going to help your inquiry one iota. And not because Semyon Kuzmich Tsvigun died for me as a husband a long, long time ago – at the time when I found out he was deceiving me – for we stayed friends all the same. But because now neither he nor I require all this investigation of yours. Only Brezhnev needs it. Brezhnev doesn't believe that Semyon committed suicide, and he wants you to prove that Tsvigun was killed by Suslov and all that company – Andropov, Gorbachov, Kirilenko, and Grishin. Isn't that right? Then at one sweep he could throw them all out of the Politburo and stay on himself. And that is something which I do not want. I do not want that scum to stay in power again at the price of a man's life whose funeral he wouldn't even attend. Do you understand? That's it then, you can go. And you can tell him that.'

'Very well,' I sighed, getting up. 'One last request. I have to take back from you your husband's jacket which was given to you yesterday at the morgue in Medical Institute Number One.'

'I've burned it,' she said, without shifting from the spot.

'I don't believe you. You could not have known that I would be coming for it.'

'Nevertheless, I have burned it. If you don't believe me, you can search the place.'

'Tell me, when you got this jacket back, whereabouts did it have a tear on it?'

'It was absolutely undamaged.'

'That is not true. It was torn or had burst along the seam down the back.'

'Then I didn't notice it.'

'You noticed all right. An old member of the Cheka like you could not fail to notice and to realize that that split was the sign of a struggle. That was why you burned it. Before his death your husband had a fight with someone and perhaps even shot at them. It's strange, isn't it? First having a fight with someone and then putting a bullet through your own head. Well? . . .'

She did not answer.

I played my final card: 'And if it turns out that he *was* murdered, will you still refuse to assist the inquiry?'

She said nothing, but only pursed her dry old lips more firmly.

'Well then,' I sighed, after a pause, 'I'll be off. I should tell you, though, that you too are squaring accounts with the living at the expense of the dead. Good day!'

10.12 a.m.

Vera Petrovna Tsvigun's idea that she would not help the inquiry in any way, was in vain. Of course, when I left her, I was furious – and how! To think the wife of the victim could destroy evidence and refuse to give testimony! None the less, she had been useful to some extent. First of all, I was inwardly even more convinced that the suicide story was humbug. Whatever she might have told me about Paputin, she herself did not believe in her husband's suicide. Most likely, Suslov had simply found out that Tsvigun suspected him of scheming against Brezhnev. And it was because of this that he had the idea of neutralizing Tsvigun by blackmailing him with evidence gathered in Operation Cascade. So Suslov had invited Tsvigun to go and see him. How the conversation had ended I did not know. I knew only that Tsvigun went straight from Suslov's to Kachalov Street, and here in apartment No. 9 he was probably attacked. Tsvigun fought back. His jacket was split in the fray, and he fired two shots. But for the time being this was only hypothesis. Who attacked Tsvigun? Who was it he had fired at? Where were the tapes that Krasnov, Malenina and Baklanov were looking for?

I tried to collect my thoughts. If it was not suicide, then how could a bullet from Tsvigun's gun have gone through his head? Did someone wrest the gun from him and then shoot him? But in that case, why were there no traces of brain-tissue on the bullet? It was a cleft stick situation.

Sasha Ruchov, the driver of my official Volga, coughed impatiently and I awoke from my thoughts. Apparently, when I emerged from Tsvigun's widow I had simply got into the car and sat there without a word.

'Where to now, Comrade Shamrayev?' Sasha asked.

'To the cemetery,' I said sullenly.

He decided I meant this as a joke and said: 'Isn't it a bit early for that?'

But I looked at my watch. It was twelve minutes past ten.

'No, just right. Gradus will be there to meet me at half-past ten.'

'Ah, so you're being serious? Which cemetery?'

'The Vagankovskoye. We're going to exhume a body.'

As we arrived, a modest funeral procession was approaching the Vagankovskoye Cemetery – a hearse and a group of poorly-dressed people. I held Sasha back and told him not to overtake them – I cannot bear overtaking funeral processions. It is a bad omen. We patiently crawled along through the churned-up snow behind the procession. Together we passed through the cemetery gates, and then we turned off down a side track to the director's one-storey house.

A disgruntled Boris Gradus, who had been woken from his bed by a phone call at 9 a.m., was waiting for me in the director's overheated ante-room. Indeed, how could he have been pleased? Only yesterday he had asked me not to involve him in this case, and this morning I was ringing him and not asking, but demanding, ordering, him to act as specialist consultant at the exhumation of Tsvigun's body.

Apart from him, there were about ten other people sitting on the wobbly chairs in the waiting-room – all queueing to see the director. Damn it if we didn't even have queues for graves! In a country that stretched across two continents from the Baltic to the Pacific Ocean, they had managed to create a shortage of burial ground! Just try and get a place in a decent cemetery without bribery or a government directive!

I walked straight through the waiting-room towards the door of the director's office with its name-plate 'Doplatov'. The secretary rushed to intercept me with a shout of, 'Comrade, where do you think you're going?' But I reached the door of the office first and opened it.

Inside the office some act of extortion was evidently in progress. The director of the cemetery was young and rosy-cheeked, and looked very like some physical-culture leader from Komsomol. He slouched in his chair and was telling an old woman who stood before him, neatly dressed in a worn squirrel fur: 'Well if you're from Petersburg, then take your sister up to Leningrad to bury her.'

'But her husband is buried here. They lived fifty years together,' the old lady pleaded.

The director turned to me, obviously irritated: 'Wait in the waiting-room. I'm busy.'

But without a word, I went up to his table and laid before him my Prosecutor's Office ID and the paper from Brezhnev. On seeing the personal headed notepaper of the Secretary General of the Central Committee, the grave-monger sprang to his feet and obsequiously offered me a chair. 'Do sit down please!' Once again I was amazed how these sporting giants could turn within a second into servile pigmies.

'Comrade Doplatov,' I said, 'I give you two minutes to deal with all these people. And it is desirable that you should deal with their requests in a positive way. Your sister, dear lady,' – I turned to the old woman – 'will have a place beside her husband. Only I must ask you to stay on here for half an hour, because I need witnesses. What is your name?'

Certainly, I was slightly abusing the authority granted me, although to my mind this was a right rather than a wrong use of it. And I really did need witnesses.

'Nadezhda Pavlovna Kiprenskaya,' the old lady announced.

'Very good. Comrade Doplatov, send four workmen to Tsvigun's grave. We are going to exhume him. The special consultant is already here and waiting in the ante-room.'

'But . . . is this? . . .' He faltered and glanced again at my identity card. 'Comrade Shamrayev, what does this mean? We're to do an exhumation without the Moscow City Council's permission?'

'Correct!' I said firmly. 'The MCC is not working today, and I have no time to wait till tomorrow.'

'I understand, of course. But, er . . . could you give me a written directive at least? Just a few words, as a matter of form, in your name . . .'

I laughed and took pity on him: 'OK, give me some paper. While I write, you send your men to dig out the grave.'

Tsvigun had lain in the frozen earth slightly less than forty-eight hours, and when we took him to the chapel he was still nice and unspoiled, as though fresh from the refrigerator. His fat, slightly puffy face still wore a haughty expression. Boris Gradus tore away the pillow-case sticking to his temple and revealed the round wound from the pistol shot. Next, Gradus raised Tsvigun's head and with one movement of the scalpel slit open the three stitches of rough thread with which the skin of the dead man's head was attached to his neck. Then with his powerful fingers he prised up the scalp and pulled it forward over Tsvigun's face, revealing the bare cranium, sawn open by the recent autopsy and smashed by the pistol shot. The old women witnesses gasped in horror and rushed out of the chapel where we had brought Tsvigun's coffin for the examination.

I motioned to Gradus: 'Open it up!'

Readers with weak nerves may absent themselves from the next scene, just as I allowed my elderly witnesses to leave the chapel. But Gradus and I stayed. From somewhere in an inner pocket of his coat Gradus produced his inseparable companion – a smooth aluminium army flask containing surgical spirit. He drank a swig and also let me have a nip straight from the bottle. Then he placed under the head of the corpse a flat surgical dish and neatly removed the already sawn-through scalp from the rest of the head, like the lid of a saucepan. The marble-grey brain with its red veins and bullet-hole flopped out into the dish.

'As you see, the brains are in place,' said Gradus, making deep incisions in both hemispheres of the brain. 'And splendid brains they are – no sign of disease, not a single haemorrhage in his whole life. Now, let's try the bullet for size.'

I handed him the bullet, and he placed it against the bullet-hole in the temple bone – he did not push it in, but just placed it against the aperture, carefully holding the bullet by its base. Even so, it was clear that the bullet would have made a perfect fit, as though it belonged there.

'Well,' said Gradus, 'I can say one thing: it is the same calibre. That means that either your tame genius Sorokin is wrong when he maintains there are no traces of brain-tissue on the bullet, or else this is simply not the right bullet. The calibre is the same, but not the bullet. Did they compare the blood-groups?'

'I don't know,' I said uncertainly. 'I think not.'

'Idiots!' said Gradus calmly. 'Shall we look further?'

I placed the bullet back in its cellophane packet, mentally cursing both Sorokin and myself for not checking the blood-group on the bullet with that of Tsvigun himself. Meanwhile Gradus was already undressing the corpse, and beneath the general's tunic he revealed a long cut running down the body from chin to groin and fastened with stitches at only three points – tacked together as it were.

'What else are you interested in seeing?' asked Gradus, slitting the stitches with his scalpel. 'The internal organs? Any diseases?'

'No. I am interested in just two things. Are there any other injuries on the body? And why did his jacket split at the moment he committed suicide?'

'Right, let's begin with an external examination.' Gradus sized up the body with the keen eye of a tailor about to cut out material. 'There are no other injuries, but the jacket . . . the jacket split for a very simple reason. Look!' He picked up a heavy lifeless arm and showed me some dark blue bruising on the wrist. 'Do you see? They held him by the hands, and as you can see, held him very firmly. He tried to break loose. And that's how the jacket split.'

'But why didn't Tumanov see these marks?'

'Well, first of all, the man is a prick,' said Gradus dismissively. 'And secondly, five days ago these bruises would not have been so noticeable. Or it may be that Tumanov simply chose not to notice them . . . But apart from that there's nothing on the body . . .'

11.45 a.m.

Once again I was back at the Forensic Institute, and once again Sorokin was displeased. He was short of sleep and angry at having to work on a Sunday. 'I have never in my life carried out a repeat examination, and I'm not prepared to do so now.'

'But you didn't compare the blood-group of the corpse with that on the bullet!'

'Nor do I consider it necessary! There are only four different blood-groups, and one of those hardly ever occurs. So that, even if this bullet is not from Tsvigun's head but from your backside, there is a thirty per cent chance that the blood-groups will coincide anyway. So what, then, is the sense of doing such an analysis? It is clear in any case that Tsvigun was not killed by this bullet since I've not found any brain-tissue on it.'

'You haven't found any – but that doesn't mean that's an end of it! That is not proof! Tumanov, for instance, simply laughed when I told him about it.

And if these blood-groups *don't* coincide, then it will be clear immediately that he was not killed by this bullet, and I shall also know the blood-group of the person Tsvigun shot at. Because the bullet *is* out of Tsvigun's pistol. In a nutshell, I urgently need a comparative analysis of the blood.'

Sorokin rummaged silently among his papers. I looked beseechingly at his wife Alla. She lowered her eyelids reassuringly, as if to say: 'OK, we'll do it', and with a nod motioned me towards the corridor.

'I'm asking you in earnest! Please get it done for tomorrow!' I said to Sorokin.

'But I'm up to my eyebrows! Snowed under!' he suddenly burst out. 'Can't you see? We've not left the laboratory for two weeks! I've never in all my days had so much shit land on my head! Look!' He took some papers and files from the table and began hurling them in the air. 'All this lot – robbery, scheming, rapes, all manner of crimes! And where? Right up to Central Committee level! This is not a country, it's a suppurating sore full of shit! And now you come bringing your Tsvigun! I couldn't care a damn about him! He was another fine brute! There's no knowing how many folk he did for in his time!'

I went out into the corridor. Alla Sorokina was standing there in tears.

'What's the matter with him?' I asked her.

'We're tired,' she replied. 'And not so much from work, as from the wear on our nerves. We realize what we are doing and why. Only we're not convinced it's for the best. The whole country is wallowing in thievery and corruption. Yet on the other hand, if the Baklanovs and Maleninas come to power tomorrow, that will still be no better. Today they've already sent militiamen out on to the streets with dogs.'

'What? What?' I asked in surprise.

'Haven't you seen? Oh, of course, you travel round in your personal car! But you have a look – the streets and the metro are full of militiamen and official dog-handlers – militiamen and KGB men dressed up.'

And I remembered: during the night General Zharov had told me that on Brezhnev's orders the Kantemir Division had been moved into Moscow. And that meant that Shcholokov had put his militia on active alert, and Andropov similarly with the KGB Dzerzhinsky Division. But on Red Square, by the Mausoleum, all was still peace, quiet and solemnity.

'I need the results of that blood analysis, Alla,' I said.

'We'll do it. I'll tell the biologists. It'll be ready tomorrow. And, here, take this as well . . .' She pulled out a piece of paper.

'What is it?'

'I've managed to reconstruct from memory some of the team's report on Tsvigun. It may be of use to you. Bye!'

She disappeared into the laboratory, and I opened out the note she had handed me. There were only a few lines: 'Igor! First: judging by Tsvigun's notebook and preference papers that your friend Baklanov handed in for examination, in recent months Tsvigun has been playing cards with Aleksei

Shibayev, Chairman of the Central Trade Union Council, Boris Ishkov, Minister of Fisheries, and also a certain Kolevatov from the State Circus. In addition to them, the following names also appear on the preference papers, which I have not been able to identify: "Boris", "Sandro", "Sveta". Secondly: while deciphering the passages that had been erased in Tsvigun's notebook I noticed the following notes: "M.M. Suslov drunk" (presumably Suslov's son, Misha), the surname Kulakov, with his home telephone number heavily crossed out, and opposite the surname of a certain Givi Mingadze there were several question marks. I don't know whether you need all this, or not, Alla.'

12.10 p.m.
As we passed Krasnopresnenskaya metro station, I remembered Alla Sorokina's words. She was right: outside the station stood a double guard of militiamen with dogs. Later on I saw similar guards with alsatians at two other stations, Arbatskaya and Pushkinskaya, and at all the crossroads in the centre.

In the Prosecutor's Office there was the usual sabbath calm, and not even Baklanov was in his office. I went up to the second floor to the Chief Prosecutor's reception-room, took the keys to the archive from Zalensky who was on duty, and rang Svetlov at the Moscow CID. But Marat was not there. Major Pogorelov, the duty officer in his section, told me: 'They are all down at Ogaryov Street, Comrade Shamrayev, at the MVD Central Files Section. They are trying to match up the evidence with data in the records. Shall I put you through?'

'Yes please.'

I first heard him rap the cradle of the telephone, then give the switchboard operator the internal extension number of the MVD Central File Section.

Then I heard Nina's voice on the line: 'Hello!'

I laughed and said: 'I would like to speak to Nina Makarycheva, the investigator's assistant, please.'

'Is that you, Igor? Listen, it's really interesting here! We are comparing the Tsvigun case with other crimes. If you're free, come over here!'

'And may I speak to your deputy, Colonel Svetlov?'

'You may. Marat!' she called at the other end of the line.

I immediately heard Svetlov's voice: 'Greetings! I was about to try and find you.' He sounded serious and worried.

'Has something cropped up?' I asked.

'Not yet, but . . . Where are you?'

'In my office. Listen. We've got to find out who Kolevatov, Aminashvili and Givi Mingadze are.'

'I can tell you about the first two straight away,' said Svetlov. 'Kolevatov is director of the State Circus, and Aminashvili is Minister of Finance in Georgia. Both have already been arrested in Operation Cascade. I don't know Givi Mingadze, but I can look him up straight away in the records.'

111

'The name Givi also cropped up on the preference papers we found behind the central heating in Tsvigun's apartment.'

'I'll ask the computer straight away. Who else do you need to know about?'

'That's all for the time being,' I said, although I was, of course also interested in Shibayev, and the names Alla Sorokina had failed to unravel: 'Sveta', 'Boris' and 'Sandro'. But my sense of logic told me that if Baklanov had arrested the Minister of Fisheries for various machinations involving caviare, and if the arrests of others who figured in Tsvigun's notebook – such as Kolevatov and Aminashvili – had also taken place, then it was fruitless to inquire about the rest – they had either been arrested already, or were about to be! In any case, if Baklanov and Co. had a lead over me in this area then there was no point in mentioning names over the telephone. Already furious with myself for having named even those three, I went and searched in our own archive for the records of cases dealt with by the Prosecutor's Office in 1976 and 1978.

Having studied all the record folios and the register of cases under surveillance, I discovered that the Prosecutor's Office had not concerned itself with the death of Kulakov, and in July 1978 in general there were no cases on record of a restricted or secret nature involving higher Party echelons and connected with Suslov, Kulakov or Tsvigun. On the other hand, in May 1976 our special investigator Taras Vendelovsky had been involved in an inquiry into the causes of the fire in the Hotel Rossiya – case No. SL-45-76 for 1976. Anticipating Vendelovsky's typical engaging description of the fire which, if I remember correctly, destroyed almost half the west wing of the hotel, I went over to the shelves by the window and began searching among the cases for 1976 for a bundle of folios with the number SL-45. But the item was missing from the shelf. Immediately after the 120 folios comprising case No. SL-44 came the thin folio of 46. Surely Baklanov had not forestalled me here too, I thought. To hell with it! But that was silly of me – I could go and find Vendelovsky and get the story out of him . . .

However, while I was mulling over what to do – set out for Vendelovsky's home (he lived right out in the sticks, somewhere in Tyoply Stan), or hop over to Kachalov Street to see how things were with Pshenichny – on Svetlov's front some much more dramatic and urgent events began coming to a head.

SECRET

To Comrade I.I. Shamrayev,
Investigation Team Leader,
from Colonel M.A. Svetlov,
Head of Third Section, Moscow Criminal Investigation Department

REPORT

From the record of all criminals registered on the territory of the USSR, the MVD Computing Centre has made a computer selection of all persons who may have been in Moscow on 19 January of this year. This information was made available to the group under my control at 10.15 hours.

By 11.20 hours a preliminary list of criminals was made, consisting of 46 persons who could potentially be involved in the murder of Tsvigun. Then, for various reasons (such as their being under round-the-clock militia surveillance at sobering stations, at venereal disease clinics, or where other alibis were available) forty names were removed from this list. The remaining persons who may on 19 January have been in Moscow at 16-A Kachalov Street, were as follows:

1. Ignaty Stepanovich Kostyuchenko, born 1942, burglar, recidivist, four sentences, released from camp 12 January this year, having served his full sentence. Up to the present has not yet appeared at his official home address: 18, Chapayev Street, Poltava. Noted for special ability to open door-locks without leaving slightest trace, liable to use arms.

2. Arkady Israilevich Bach, born 1921, nicknamed 'The Dancer', 'Black', and 'Three of Spades'. No permanent address, whereabouts unknown. Plays preference, persistent defaulter on gambling debts. In 1942-4 served on the south-west front as German language interpreter with SMERSH detachment led by Captain S.K. Tsvigun of State Security.

3. Margarita Aleksandrovna Goptar, born 1948, recidivist, prostitute, two sentences, alias 'Rita', 'Bitch' and 'Crazy'. Released on 3 January of this year from Psychiatric Hospital Number Six in the town of Saratov. Present whereabouts unknown. In 1963, during General S.K. Tsvigun's chairmanship of the KGB of the Azerbaidzhan SSR, worked as waitress in Baku marine terminal and was KGB informer. Possibly closer personal relation with the deceased, since her illegitimate son born in 1964 carries name Semyon; father's surname not indicated in birth certificate.

4. Aleksei Igorevich Vorotnikov, alias 'Korchagin', born 1933, recidivist, murderer, three sentences, the last in 1979 for premeditated murder with intent to steal. Sentenced to be executed; this then commuted to 15 years' strict regime internment. During night of 31 December 1981, escaped from prison hospital in strict regime colony No. 26/29-SR, Potma, Mordovian Autonomous SSR. During night of 7 January of this year, committed brutal murder of militiaman on duty, Senior Lieutenant A.M. Ignatyev; using his uniform and weapon ('PM' revolver) on 12 January this year robbed the Agat jeweller's shop on Moscow's New Arbat. Search for Vorotnikov is being conducted by First Section of Moscow CID. The case is under the control of Lieutenant-General A. Volkov, head of Main Directorate of Criminal Investigation of the USSR Ministry of Internal Affairs.

5. Gerakl Isaakovich Faibisovich, born 1907, father of Mikhail Geraklovich Faibisovich, sentenced for Zionist propaganda who died in camp on 7 January of this year. No sentences. Recipient of special

pension, former colonel in Soviet Army. Having received notice of son's death on 14 January of this year, disappeared from home in Odessa. According to evidence of neighbours and his wife, Faibisovich is armed with a captured German 'Walter' type pistol and has set out for Moscow intent on revenge on KGB for the death of his son.

6. Unknown housebreaker (or group of such), responsible for over 120 thefts from apartments in Moscow over last two years, mainly in homes of high-ranking government employees, artists and leaders of trade and management.

Thus, the idea that Tsvigun's murder might have been committed by a person or persons with a criminal past, or for personal motives, has acquired factual support. Especially if one considers that those parties interested in the death of General Tsvigun could have used these persons for bringing about his death. Therefore I have issued a series of directives and requests for information on all six suspects, with the object of getting more detailed information from their places of residence, penal detention, or confinement for psychiatric treatment.

The telephone ringing distracted Svetlov from his extensive report. He automatically glanced at his watch. It was seventeen minutes past twelve.

Major Ozherelyev lifted the receiver and began rapidly taking down the text of a telegram. Over his shoulder he announced to Svetlov: 'Telegram from Poltava on the first suspect, Kostyuchenko . . . He has a cast-iron alibi: since 14 January he has been on a continuous drinking bout with his brother, because his wife would not let him into the house. While he was doing time, she got married again . . .'

Immediately a second telephone rang and the switchboard operator announced: 'The head of strict regime colony in Potma calling Colonel Svetlov.'

And from the MVD Computing Centre a Captain Laskin reported: 'We have not been able to clarify about Givi Mingadze. Our computer's blown, and it's out of action. The technicians say they'll have it repaired in an hour to an hour and a half.'

12.17 p.m.

Meanwhile there was a further telephone call to the Prosecutor's Office. The duty officer heard an agitated woman's voice, told her to wait one moment, and handed me the receiver.

I heard the following: 'This is Professor Osipova of Moscow University speaking. Your investigator has locked us all in the house and will not let us out.'

'What investigator? Which house?'

'Investigator Pshenichny, in 16-A on Kachalov Street. He is interrogating every one of us here as though we were criminals! And it's quite impossible for me to wait up to three hours in a queue in order to be questioned!'

114

'Very well, I'll come along there right away and sort things out.'

Ten minutes later I drove up to 16-A Kachalov Street, and immediately realized that Valya Pshenichny was not wasting any time there. The vestibule of the main entrance had been turned into a check-point. Here the local inspector Captain Kopylov had been drafted in and was using his militiaman's authority to detain everyone entering or leaving the house.

'Just one moment!' he said, holding before him a large sheet of drawing paper, ruled into squares representing each apartment. 'Which apartment have you just left? Thirty-two? Has the investigator already been to see you? No? Then please stay behind. The investigator wishes to speak with you.'

Thus, not a single resident of the house escaped being interviewed that day by Pshenichny. With characteristic thoroughness, he was spending a minimum of half an hour on each person, and quite naturally the rest of them did not want to wait for hours until their turn came. In the vestibule there was already a large queue of people irritated by the enforced wait – Academicians, artists, leading officials, and even more impatient wives and children. Someone had already rung the City Council to complain and made great play of all his offices, ranks and distinctions, and it seemed that I arrived just in time to quell the row that was brewing.

'Excuse me, Comrade, which apartment are you going to?' Captain Kopylov stopped me too, his pencil poised over the residence plan.

My answer was a loud announcement that filled the whole vestibule: 'Comrades! I must ask you to maintain your Party discipline and conscientiousness! We are working on a special assignment from the government. It is suspected that a crime has taken place in your house involving intrigues by foreign intelligence agencies. It's therefore necessary to interrogate each resident in order to help establish which outsiders visit this house, and who might have broken in here on the nineteenth of January . . .'

Regarding the activities of foreign intelligence, I simply invented that bit on the spur of the moment, since I know the psychology of the Soviet public. Such phrases as 'the intrigues of foreign intelligence agencies' have an almost magical effect on our people: the residents of 16-A quietened down immediately. Someone even brought some chairs out of his apartment to avoid having to stand while waiting. And the respectable elderly gentleman who had been ringing the City Council, now showed his civic initiative by coming up to me and whispering: 'If you're interested in what goes on in our house, I advise you to ask the old woman on the seventh floor in the house opposite – the third window from the corner on the left. She sits for days on end at that window and gapes across at our house. I have had to put blinds on my windows – her apartment is right opposite mine.'

I nodded to him, made a note in my pad and asked Captain Kopylov: 'Where is Comrade Pshenichny?'

'Up on the fourth floor at No. 24. He seems to have got held up there, it's forty minutes now.'

I went up by lift to the fourth floor and rang at the door of No. 24.

115

Valya Pshenichny came out to greet me, his blue eyes beaming joyfully: 'Igor! Listen to the lady who lives here! On the eighteenth of January this apartment was burgled. In broad daylight they removed from here three fur coats – one fox-fur and two mink, several gold rings and a diamond necklace. But the theft has not been registered at the district militia office, I've just rung them.'

'But did you inform the militia?' I asked the owner of the apartment, Roza Abramovna Tsipurskaya, wife of the Academician.

'Of course she did!' Pshenichny answered for her. 'That's the point! As I've discovered, over the last two months there have been at least eight thefts from the homes here, and the district militia have not registered one of them. They refuse to accept notifications from the victims in order not to lumber themselves with a backlog of unsolved cases! How about that, if you please?'

'Valya, in the house opposite, on the seventh floor, there's apparently an old lady constantly sitting in the window. She might well have seen something interesting.'

'If only she *could* see!' Pshenichny laughed. 'Do you think I don't know such basics? All sorts of managerial types in Moscow have been given luxury flats and they've settled grandads and grandmas in from the villages. Out in the country they sit on those mounds outside their peasant huts, but here in town there aren't any, so instead they sit for days by the window. I always make use of their observations. I've known all about these old women for a long time, and I've sought them out and been round all of them. Only the one you are talking about is blind; she simply sits there and basks in the sun. You can't get much sense out of her. But as for the burglars who go poking around in these houses, I'd dearly like to meet the person who tips them off! Not a single thief can get into a house like this without someone on the inside to point him to the target, and that means that the person who tips them off has to know the lie of the land.'

A knock at the door interrupted Pshenichny. Madame Tsipurskaya opened it, and there on the doorstep stood my driver Sasha.

'Comrade Shamrayev,' he said, 'Colonel Svetlov is calling you, and wants you to get in touch with him urgently.'

I went through the drawing-room with its rare crystal and Saxon porcelain, and on a carved eighteenth-century table I discovered a quaint old-fashioned telephone. I dialled the number of the MVD Central File Section on Ogaryov Street.

Colonel Svetlov's
report (continued)

At 12.17 hours I received the following telegram message from the head of strict regime colony No. 26/29-SR in Potma, Major G.B. Selivanov:

CHIEF OF SECTION 3 MOSCOW CID COLONEL SVETLOV STOP URGENT STOP

SECRET STOP RE YOUR INQUIRY CONCERNING PRISONER ALEKSEI
IGOREVICH VOROTNIKOV ALIAS KORCHAGIN WHO FLED 1 JANUARY THIS
YEAR I HAVE TO INFORM YOU TODAY 24 JANUARY AT 0930 HOURS CAMP
INFORMER KASHCHENKO REPORTED THAT HIS NEIGHBOUR RECIDIVIST
MUSREPOV ALIAS BALDY ON READING OBITUARY OF GENERAL TSVIGUN
IN NEWSPAPER PRAVDA OF 22 JANUARY SAID QUOTE WELL DONE
KORCHAGIN HAS FIXED THE BASTARD UNQUOTE WHEN SUMMONED FOR
INTERROGATION PRISONER MUSREPOV TESTIFIED THAT VOROTNIKOV
HAD ON SEVERAL OCCASIONS CITED GENERAL TSVIGUN AS RESPONSIBLE
FOR HIS TURN TO CRIME STOP VOROTNIKOV ALLEGED TSVIGUN
PERSONALLY SHOT HIS FATHER IN 1943 AFTER ACCUSING HIM OF
DESERTION STOP ACCORDING TO VOROTNIKOV-KORCHAGIN LOSS OF
FATHER AND LIFE IN ORPHANAGE PUSHED HIM TOWARDS LIFE OF CRIME
STOP QUOTE THE CIRCLE MUST BE CLOSED STOP BULLET SHALL ANSWER
BULLET UNQUOTE STOP I CONSIDER THIS REPORT EXTREMELY
IMPORTANT AND THEREFORE INFORM YOU WITHOUT DELAY STOP HEAD
OF COLONY 26/29-SR MAJOR G SELIVANOV 24 JANUARY 1982 1217 HOURS

In view of the exceptional nature of this report I promptly requested
Lieutenant-General A. Volkov, national chief of the CID, to provide the
search dossier on Vorotnikov-'Korchagin'. Following Vorotnikov's
recent bloody crimes, the CID issued teletype photographs of him to all
area centres of militia, railway stations, banks, and other public buildings. In addition, all local and district militia stations received instructions
to distribute photographs of Vorotnikov without delay to the shops and
other trading centres in their area.

Yesterday, on 23 January, the saleswoman in a grocery shop at
Vostryakovo in the Moscow Region recognized these photographs as
those of a man who had three times in the period January 6 to 22
purchased Georgian brandy, bread and processed cheese from her, and
he had also allegedly expressed annoyance at the absence of other
provisions. According to this saleswoman, her customer was not a local
resident, although each time he drove up to the shop in a white Volga
belonging to a well-known local fortune-teller and sorceress, the gypsy
Marusya Shevchenko.

A team from CID Section One headed by Section Chief Voznesensky
immediately went out to Vostryakovo and established by observing
Shevchenko's residence, that her white Volga, registration MKI 52-12
was not parked at the house. Marusya Shevchenko and her husband had
not left home and had not reported their car as missing. When questioned,
local residents confirmed that the same white Volga periodically
appeared at the Shevchenkos' house, driven by a man answering the
description given of A. Vorotnikov-'Korchagin'.

All traffic-control points were then immediately given instructions to
find the Volga in question. At the same time an ambush was set up at the

house in Vostryakovo, and members of CID Section One collected additional information about the activities and lifestyle of Marusya Shevchenko and her husband Viktor. According to this, Marusya Shevchenko enjoys great popularity in certain circles in Moscow, thanks to a recent fashion for parapsychology and healing by those claiming extrasensory powers. Among her clients are the wives of well-known academics, writers, architects, and of leading employees of several ministries and other institutions, including the Ministry of Foreign Affairs, the KGB and MVD. Yesterday during her afternoon consulting hours, no fewer than seventeen persons attended, including the wife of Malkov, the Moscow Council Deputy and City Prosecutor. Clients of Shevchenko questioned after visiting her, testified that in addition to healing and forecasting the future, she often tried to sell them diamonds and other jewellery, valuable fur items and imported radio equipment, which allegedly came her way by chance. It is therefore presumed that Shevchenko may also be involved in the purchase and sale of stolen property.

In view of the suspicion that Shevchenko has contacts with the world of crime, and in particular with the highly dangerous criminal Vorotnikov-'Korchagin', her telephone calls are now being tapped. At 11.30 hours a telephone call was intercepted in which a certain Aleksei asked her whether everything was ready and announced that he would call on her in a couple of hours. The call was made from a coin-box near Sokol metro station. Since that moment, several CID teams have been tracking the Volga car MKI 52-12 which is proceeding along the Kiev Highway in the region of Vostryakovo, where an ambush is being set up to apprehend the criminal.

The operation is being run from the Vostryakovo operational head-quarters by Deputy Chief of MVD Intelligence, Colonel G. Oleinik, Chief of the District CID Colonel V. Yakimyan and Chief CID Section One, R. Voznesensky; and from the Moscow Region Militia Head-quarters by Lieutenant-General A. Volkov, National Chief of CID, and the Duty Officer for Moscow Region Militia, Colonel V. Glazunov. I have also decided to participate with my own team in the capture of the criminal.

1.05 p.m.
Why did I permit Svetlov to take part in the operation to seize Vorotnikov? And why, when I left Pshenichny, did I rush over to the Headquarters of the Moscow Regional Militia? Because at five minutes past one my conversation with Svetlov was both briefer and clearer to us both than the whole of this long report which I received much later.

Svetlov said: 'Igor, I am phoning from a car on the road. No discussion. Take a pen and get this down. At 11.30 hours Vorotnikov, alias "Korchagin", was spotted in Moscow. At 11.45 hours Colonel Oleinik of

118

MVD Intelligence joined in. And at 12.17 hours I had a telegram from the camp where "Korchagin" fled from. It says that in 1943 "Korchagin's" father was shot for desertion by Tsvigun, and he has now escaped from camp in order to have his revenge.'

'I think I get it. Where is Oleinik now?'

'In Vostryakovo, in charge of the ambush. I am rushing over there with my team to help him. You get over to Belinsky Street to the Moscow Militia HQ – Volkov and Glazunov are there. That's all. I'll be in touch.'

I was just in time to shout 'Where is Nina?'

'I've sent Nina to Pshenichny. Bye!' was the answer.

I glanced at my watch. It was five past one. At any moment Colonel Oleinik might seize 'Korchagin', and once they got him to MVD Intelligence Section he would readily admit it was he who killed Tsvigun. They wouldn't even need to torture him. With other crimes on his record, he would simply be promised luxury conditions in camp, remission of sentence, and a Moscow residence permit when he came out. And it would then take me a fortnight to prove that he had lied, and even then it was uncertain whether I would succeed.

The control-room of the Moscow Militia Headquarters looked more like that of a television studio. At the main control desk sat the duty officer, an old stager, Colonel Vladimir Glazunov. Next to him in an armchair was the National Chief of the CID, youthful-looking and energetic Lieutenant-General Anatoly Volkov; in the past he had been proved one of the greatest masters of crime-detection. To the left and right of them, operating the controls, recorders, television screens and other equipment, were various assistants and technicians. There was a relief map on the wall showing Moscow Region pinpricked with various coloured lights and with labels for the various districts: Mytishchi, Pushkino, Odintsovo, etc.

But despite all this awe-inspiring equipment, the atmosphere in the duty area was far from business-like, and the sound of carefree prattle came over the radio intercom: 'I think perhaps I'll be a fortune-teller too! What about it? People pour in to see her. She never takes less than fifty per client. In one day she rakes in the whole of my monthly salary!' The voice was that of District CID Chief, Colonel Yakimyan, with his Caucasian accent coming loud and clear over the speaker.

'Can she cure lumbago?' Volkov asked into the microphone.

'And who's suffering from lumbago? Is it you, General?' asked Yakimyan.

'That's right,' Volkov confirmed.

'The best remedy, dear boy, is hot sand or hot salt! You heat the salt up in a frying-pan, put it in a small bag . . .'

He was interrupted by a clipped male voice: 'Sixteen kilometre check-point on Kiev Highway reporting. They're now on the eighteenth kilometre stretch – a white Volga has just passed through, registration MKI-52-12, carrying two passengers, heading for Vostryakovo.'

'Roger!' Glazunov leaned towards the desk and lightly pressed down a

119

key, and immediately on a large wall-screen appeared the projection of a detailed map of that sector of the Kiev Highway. I made a mental estimate of the distance – from the eighteen kilometre point to Vostryakovo by car was twelve to fifteen minutes. That meant that our man was about to land in a trap at any moment. But here in the control-room there was no tension whatsoever. On the contrary, Volkov was bent over the microphone and talking again to Yakimyan who was sitting somewhere in Vostryakovo at the headquarters of the ambushing force: 'So what do you do with this salt? Warm it in the frying-pan, and then what?'

'Then put it in a bag, wrap it in a towel and lay it across the small of your back. But it shouldn't just be warm, it should be baking hot,' Yakimyan answered.

I looked slightly amazed at Volkov. He was never known to be so carefree as this – he was definitely one of the best and most talented CID officers in the country.

At that moment another, stern and unfamiliar voice sounded over the intercom: 'No more irrelevant conversation please. Colonel Glazunov, is the traffic-control chopper ready to go?'

'Ready and waiting, Comrade Oleinik,' said Glazunov, who exchanged glances with Volkov and added: 'But we believe there's no sense in sending it up. With this heavy cloud and snowfall we'll see nothing from the air, and the noise might very well scare our man off.'

'We'd better play this one by ear. Tell the pilot and the snipers to be ready to scramble!'

Glazunov and Volkov caught one another's eyes again and exchanged a meaningful glance. Volkov shrugged ineffectually, and I realized what had happened: Oleinik had taken the running of the whole operation upon himself and left Volkov, Glazunov and Yakimyan as mere onlookers. Indeed this was precisely the style of MVD Intelligence: they had probably declared Vorotnikov to be not a common criminal, but guilty of a crime against the State, and on this basis they had virtually excluded from the operation even the National Chief of the CID.

There was another radio signal: 'Pursuit team reporting. He's passing the twenty-three kilometre post, approaching the turn-off for Vostryakovo!'

I stole another glance at my watch – by my reckoning Svetlov should already have been in Vostryakovo ten minutes ago. That meant it was time for me to enter the game. If these gentlemen from the MVD Intelligence Section wanted to palm Vorotnikov off on to me as the killer of Tsvigun, then we would be the ones to take him and not them! In such an event it would be interesting to discover how they would find out that it was he who had supposedly killed Tsvigun!

From the doorway of the control-room I stepped forward to the desk, briefly greeted Glazunov and Volkov, then bent forward to the microphone: 'Comrade Oleinik! This is Shamrayev speaking, investigator from the Prosecutor's Office.'

'Receiving you. What is it?' replied Oleinik guardedly.

'Please hand over the radio to Colonel Svetlov. And at the same time hand over to him the direction of this operation.'

Volkov and Glazunov looked at me astounded.

Oleinik's infuriated voice came over the intercom: 'Wha-a-at?! And on whose authority?'

'Don't argue, Colonel, there's no time for that. What is *your* authority for directing operations?'

'We have information that this criminal was connected with the death of General Tsvigun.'

'Precisely! And the case of the General's death is being handled by me on direct instructions from Comrade Brezhnev, and he has granted me extra-ordinary powers. "Korchagin" is therefore *my* man. That is, of course, if today's telegram from the camp in Potma was not a hoax designed to pin the murder of Tsvigun on "Korchagin"!' I added with a smile. 'So, please, hand over charge of operations to Svetlov.'

'You think you can take over the responsibility for capturing this criminal?' Oleinik tried intimidation tactics. 'Anything at all could happen. He's armed . . .'

'In the presence of General Volkov and Colonel Glazunov, I accept that responsibility,' I said calmly. 'And you also realize of course that our conversation is being taped here.'

'I understand,' said Oleinik. 'Very well then, I hand over the mike to Svetlov, and to you – the responsibility.' His voice was full of mockery, but I did not rise to this at all. Without saying anything, Volkov and Glazunov shook my hand as a sign of their support against Oleinik.

I spoke into the microphone: 'Marat, did you hear all that?'

'Yes,' answered Svetlov.

Then the voice of the pursuit party came on the air again: 'Attention! He's turning off the Kiev Highway onto the Vostryakovo road! I repeat . . .'

'Roger! Roger! We read you,' Svetlov interrupted.

I looked at Volkov and Glazunov and nodding towards the microphone, said: 'Please come in and lead the troops.'

I was not flattering them, or boot-licking. First of all, I realized clearly that in operational work I was a mere amateur compared with them. And secondly, it was simple human gratitude: if Volkov had delayed half an hour in passing the information on Vorotnikov to Svetlov, neither Svetlov nor myself would have managed to intervene in this operation, and Vorotnikov would have become the unchallenged murderer of Tsvigun. But in all of this beautifully played campaign, MVD Intelligence had failed to take account of just one factor: when the fruits of their labours are wrenched away from under their noses, people take great offence.

Volkov bent towards the microphone and said: 'Marat, report the position.'

'The men are not distributed here in the best possible way, Comrade

121

General.'

'Move them to where you want them.'

'Too late. I can already see the Volga. And there's some taxi making its way here too, to the fortune-teller's . . .'

Colonel Svetlov's
report (continued)

Unfortunately it was not possible to relocate the men in the ambush party. At 14.01 hours two cars entered the yard of Marusya Shevchenko's *dacha* – the Volga registered MKI 52-12 and a taxi, registration number MTU 73-79, with some other clients or patients of Shevchenko. The presence of passengers in this taxi made it impossible to seize the armed criminal. In order not to put their lives at risk, I decided to await a more favourable opportunity and assumed that Vorotnikov-'Korchagin' would enter the house, where a further ambush awaited him by our men disguised as Shevchenko's clients. However, Vorotnikov's behaviour thwarted this plan. He remained in the car, and the middle-aged man accompanying him went into the house and immediately emerged again, carrying a heavy kit-bag. Realizing there was no time to waste, I gave the order to seize the criminal. The men, who had been placed too far from the house, tried to rush Vorotnikov's car. But he managed to grab the bag through the open window of the car and push his accomplice over into the snow. Since we were unable to use firearms for fear of harming the passengers in the taxi parked next to him, he drove out of the yard at top speed. Taking advantage of the confusion, the falling snow and the already failing light, the criminal succeeded in breaking away from my men who were giving chase. At high speed he set off down the Ochakovo Highway in the direction of Vnukovo Airport . . .

The atmosphere in the control-area became nervous and tense. Volkov, Glazunov and I understood perfectly well what cards Oleinik and Krasnov held in the event of the criminal escaping or if the blood of innocent people was spilt. Svetlov too realized this. Gritting his teeth and hardly responding to our requests for information, he gunned his militia Volga after the criminal's white-painted vehicle. Two other pursuing cars fell back on the narrow Ochakovo Highway which was covered in snow preventing them from reaching high speed. But Svetlov clung to the tail of the fleeing car with the tenacity of a fox-terrier, and Glazunov, Volkov and I did everything possible to halt the flow of traffic along the Ochakovo Highway and force 'Korchagin' into a trap. As ill-luck had it, evening closed in early that winter Sunday and the road was filled with traffic travelling in the opposite direction. Muscovites were returning from their *dachas* in the surrounding countryside and none of them realized that a dangerous criminal with several murders to his credit was coming towards them in a white Volga, armed with the best Soviet Makarov type gun.

122

'Calling all traffic-control points on Ochakovo Highway and all side roads leading to it!' Glazunov sent out the message every minute. 'Halt all traffic immediately! Stop all cars and clear the roadway on the sector between the sixteenth kilometre and Vnukovo! A dangerous armed criminal is being pursued down that section! I repeat . . .'

Meanwhile private car-owners mercilessly slanged the traffic-controllers who were stopping them and under their breath they cursed the government even more – for these sudden rapid clearances of the roadways usually take place in this country for the benefit of government motorcades.

But the empty road of course also put the criminal on the alert. He realized that somewhere ahead of him a road-block would be set up, and by some sixth sense he guessed exactly where it would be. On two occasions he turned off onto the verge literally a hundred yards short of the militiamen who were waiting to ambush him, and relentlessly drove his car round the barrier and across the snow-covered fields of the Kommunarka State farm at Vnukovo. Svetlov's car repeated exactly the same manoeuvre. The supercharged engine of the militia Volga roared with the strain, and burly Captain Kolganov and Captains Laskin and Arutyunov banged their heads full-force against the roof of the car. It was growing dark. To the turn-off for Vnukovo Airport there were now eight kilometres, then seven, then six . . .

General Volkov frowned and leaned towards the microphone: 'Marat, can you hear me?'

'Yes,' Svetlov grated.

'He's approaching Vnukovo Airport. That's not good – there are people there.'

'I know. Set up two blocks – one at the airport, lorries, and another on the road.'

'Remember, though, he could turn off the road and cut straight across to the terminal building.'

'I can't help that! He's got a supercharged engine too. Tomorrow I'll tear the balls off those mechanics who changed his engine! What's happening about the barriers?'

'Six kilometres ahead Inspector Stepashkin has put two dump-trucks across the road. So get ready! He can't get round them – there are trees there.'

'What sort of dump-trucks?' Svetlov suddenly asked. 'Have they got tractor-units?'

'What difference does it make?' asked Volkov, surprised.

'I'm asking you: with separate tractors or not?' Svetlov bawled at his superior.

Of course, only twenty years of work together and the tenseness of the situation gave Svetlov the right to address Volkov in that manner.

Meanwhile Glazunov was already asking Stepashkin at the traffic-control post: 'Lieutenant Stepashkin, do your dump-trucks have separate tractor-units?'

'Yes, they're the MAZ tractor and trailer type,' Stepashkin reported.

'Give me a direct link with him!' Svetlov demanded.

'You've got it already. Keep your hair on!' said Volkov.

'Stepashkin, old son!' yelled Svetlov. 'Uncouple the trailers and put them across the road together with the tractor-units. Put the tractors on the outside curbs. And when I give the signal switch on the headlamps. Got it? Can you do it in time?'

'Got it. We'll try . . .' we heard the agitated response of the young traffic-controller.

Now we too grasped Svetlov's idea. When the criminal approached the road-block, the powerful headlamp beams of the MAZ tractors would blaze at him from the darkness on either side of the roadway. Between them would be a dark and seemingly empty space, and he would race blinded into the trailers that blocked his passage . . .

'Igor,' came Svetlov's voice over the intercom. 'I'm sorry, it looks as it we're not going to take him alive . . .'

It was a matter of seconds – would Stepashkin succeed or not in carrying out Svetlov's instruction? We sat there in the tense silence. Only the roar of Svetlov's car engine told us that the chase was still on. Mentally I had already bidden farewell to this imaginary murderer of Tsvigun. As it turned out, neither I nor Oleinik was going to get him . . .

'Done it!' we heard Stepashkin call on the intercom. 'We're ready! I can hear him already. He's close! Give the word!'

'Switch on!' grated Svetlov after a few seconds' wait, and we heard him telling his car crew: 'Doors open and get ready!'

And out there on the barrier, on the last curve of the Ochakovo Highway towards Vnukovo Airport, Lieutenant Stepashkin ran towards the drivers of the dump-trucks he had borrowed, and yelled 'Switch on!' The drivers could themselves either see or sense the Volga hurtling towards them through the falling snow and darkness. They switched on the headlamps and immediately sprang from their cabins to take cover in the roadside ditch.

By what miracle Vorotnikov managed to glimpse the barrier at the last instant and slam on the brakes, I do not know. His car skidded on the snow-covered surface, slid straight into the snare and smashed side-on into one of the MAZ trailers, and 'Korchagin' jumped alive and unharmed from the car and sprinted off into the nearby wood.

Colonel Svetlov's
report (continued)

Since a new opportunity had presented itself of taking the man alive, although there was still the danger of his breaking through to Vnukovo Airport, where people might be injured in any exchange of fire, I was forced to act according to the situation. Spreading out in a chain, Captains Kolganov, Laskin and Arutyunov, together with Lieutenant Stepashkin of traffic-control and myself, began pursuing the criminal through the wood.

Firing every time he heard our footsteps, the fugitive was crossing the wood in the direction of the Vnukovo air terminal building. Still leaving open the final opportunity of taking him alive, I did not give the order to open fire until we had practically reached the edge of the wood, and we used our weapons only when Vorotnikov had a real chance of slipping from the wood to the car-park next to the air terminal. I fired a warning shot into the air and shouted, 'Drop your gun and surrender! You're surrounded!' We rushed our quarry from various sides. In response we heard only obscenities and swearing. Suddenly I saw in the darkness the silhouette of Vorotnikov advancing towards me from behind a tree with pistol raised. A shot sounded and the same instant I realized I had been wounded in the right arm. Taking my pistol in my left hand I fired at the criminal. At the same moment Laskin and Kolganov who were running to right and left of me, also fired at him.

The following items were removed on examining the body of A. Vorotnikov-'Korchagin': one Makarov type gun – 'PM' No. 6912-A, three cartridge-clips of ninth calibre, 240,000 roubles, 16 items of jewellery of total value 824,000 roubles, also one passport issued in the name of Boris Yegorovich Morozov, address: 17 Lesnaya Street, Apt. 9, Moscow. The year of birth had been scratched out in the passport and corrected to '1941'; the photograph had been removed and replaced by one of A. Vorotnikov.

I take on myself full responsibility for the killing of this criminal who was so vital to the inquiry, and request you to review the question of my having exceeded the limits of necessary self-defence.
Chief of Moscow CID, Section Three,
Colonel M.A. Svetlov

This was the report which Marat Svetlov was eventually to hand to me. But at the time of the exchange of fire, the wounding of Svetlov and killing of Vorotnikov, there were more worrying things than Svetlov's confession of having 'exceeded the limits of necessary self-defence'. Despite the fact that he made light of it, and said on the intercom that the bullet had only grazed his arm, and that he would 'live to see his golden wedding', I gave orders for him to be taken to the Vnukovo staff sick-bay. Then I switched over and re-established contact with Valentin Pshenichny. Twenty minutes earlier the team of men headed by Major Ozherelyev had burst into Marusya Shevchenko's house and at the same time as the 'Korchagin' chase another series of events began to unfold, perhaps less spectacular, but probably more important for the course of our inquiry.

According to Major Ozherelyev, the Shevchenkos' house contained a treasure-trove of stolen property. The attic and cellar were bursting at the seams with crystal, furs, fleece jackets, fur coats and imported radio equipment. I immediately rang Pshenichny and asked him to establish from the wife of Academician Tsipursky any identifying marks on the fur coats and jewellery she had had stolen. He was also to find out whether she had ever been treated by the sorceress of Vostryakovo. Confirmation of the latter and a list of identification marks followed immediately. After this, there came a report from Vostryakovo announcing the discovery of the fox-fur coat produced in 1979 by the Kuntsevo Fur Factory and belonging to Roza Abramovna Tsipurskaya. I thereupon detailed Ozherelyev to find out from Marusya Shevchenko how she came into possession of this coat.

But our sorceress was an old stager, experienced at the game. She evidently relied on her highly-placed patients coming to her defence, and therefore did not crack immediately. According to her, the things with which her house was crammed had been brought to her for safe-keeping by several gypsy friends. 'You know yourself, chief,' she said to Ozherelyev, 'that gypsies are not given residence permits for Moscow. So the poor things are stuck without a roof over their heads. But they have to keep their decent possessions somewhere, so they bring them to me. It's no skin off my nose, so the things lie here. But I haven't the faintest idea where they get them from.'

'But someone like yourself, so skilled in divination, might be expected to divine that these things have been stolen!' Ozherelyev sniggered. 'OK, that's enough of your clever stuff. I'm going to summon all your clients out here whose homes have been burgled and whose things are lying here in your cellar. For instance, we might call Roza Abramovna Tsipurskaya.'

Thus they managed to establish that Shevchenko had a group of young men working for her, to whom she gave the addresses of her wealthy clients, and the rest was left up to their skills at theft. Shevchenko even named the leader of this gang – the same Boris Morozov whose passport had turned up in the pocket of Vorotnikov-'Korchagin'. And the members of the gang were a certain Lena, or Eleonora, and Kostya the 'Trombone Player' – whether the latter was a real musician, or just had that nickname, Marusya Shevchenko did not know. According to her evidence, all three of them had been at her *dacha* in Vostryakovo the day before yesterday, and here they had made the acquaintance of 'Korchagin'. 'Korchagin' had 'bought up' Morozov's passport with the object of using it to fly today from Moscow down to Yalta. Concerning the killing of General Tsvigun by 'Korchagin', she claimed categorically that she knew nothing of it. The man who had come out by car with Vorotnikov turned out to be a drunk whom he had chanced upon and hired two days ago as his chauffeur.

But while the CID men were making an inventory of the stolen property found on Vorotnikov, the doctors at Vnukovo Airport sick-bay were giving Svetlov an anti-tetanus injection and bandaging his wound, and while the traffic-controllers were reopening the Ochakovo Highway for normal traffic, Nina, Pshenichny and myself were far away – searching for a band of housebreakers who had burgled the apartment of Academician Tsipursky at 16-A, Kachalov Street. Both Pshenichny and I were very anxious to talk to the man who had tipped them off . . .

Meanwhile it was an ordinary January Sunday evening. And although Moscow was blanketed in snow and no amount of snow-clearing vehicles could devour from the pavements and streets all that had tipped out of the sky, Muscovites were not sitting at home. There were queues at the cinemas for Pyotr Todorovsky's new comedy *Mechanic Gavrilov's Woman,* the theatres were overflowing, pretty girls were walking along Gorky Street in imported fleece coats and high boots, and on the New Arbat a crowd of boys and girls who had scarcely come of age was eddying round the entrance to the Blizzard, a popular young people's cafe.

From upstairs on the first floor the sounds of a jazz band in the main room of the cafe reached the street, agitating the crowd even more, and the boys and girls surged in waves against the closed doors with the sign 'Full' hanging on them.

Pshenichny and I exchanged glances – how were we supposed to get through this dense, congealed crowd to the cafe doors? We could of course call a militiaman on point duty, and he would clear a path for us with his whistle, but that was just the sort of commotion we did not want to cause. Right now, inside the cafe were all three people the Vostryakovo fortune teller had named: Boris Morozov, Kostya the trombone player, and Lena-Eleonora. There were three of us, too, and we had to take them quietly, without any chases, shooting, or other nonsense. But to do that we had to get through into the cafe without undue commotion, or at least to the doors so that we could show the doorman our IDs.

It was Nina who saved us. Actually, 'saved' is not the right word, since one might say without exaggeration that Nina conducted this whole operation of arresting the gang of housebreakers, while Pshenichny and I merely acted as her assistants. Even back in the control-room, as soon as Svetlov had radioed that the passport of a Boris Morozov had been found in Vorotnikov's pocket, I found out through the directory that he shared an apartment with his mother Agnessa Sergeyevna and asked Nina to ring that apartment. We needed to know whether this Morozov was home, and if not, where he was. Nina with her Vologda accent was perfect for this and handled the job brilliantly. From this same apartment of Academician Tsipursky she rang Agnessa Sergeyevna, while at the control-room we heard the whole conversation – our phone-tapping technology is excellent.

'Hello! Agnessa Sergeyevna?' Nina said into the telephone so naturally that Agnessa Sergeyevna could have been her own aunt. 'Good evening, it's Nina. Is Borya at home?'

Of course, the twenty-year-old Borya had more than one friend called Nina, but Agnessa Sergeyevna wasn't about to betray her son.

Obviously flattered that even one Nina knew her name, she said: 'He took off long ago!'

'With Kostya?' asked Nina, 'or with Lenka – Eleonora?'

'All three of them are at the Blizzard right now. Kostya's working today!' said Agnessa Sergeyevna.

'Oh yes, that's right!' exclaimed Nina. 'How stupid, I forgot! I've been waiting for them here at the Lyre. *Ciao,* Agnessa Sergeyevna!' and she hung up.

'Superb!' General Volkov exclaimed, and said to me: 'Listen, she would make an excellent recruit. Why not send her to militia school? As soon as she graduates I'll take her into the CID, I promise . . .'

Now, in front of the entrance to the Blizzard, inspired by the general's praise, Nina herself took the initiative. 'Follow me!' she ordered Pshenichny and me, and like a corkscrew drilled her way through the crowd of people of her own age who were attacking the doors of the cafe. And, working with her little elbows and shoulders, she began to clear a path for us too, shouting somewhere ahead of her as she went: 'Zhenka, here I am! I'm here, I'm coming! Let me through, girls!'

'No pushing, it's closed!' Someone was trying to stop her.

'Belt up! My bloke's there waiting for me!' said Nina, waving her away, and once again shouted ahead of her to her imaginary 'bloke': 'Zhenka!'

So we reached the cafe entrance, where I showed the doorman my ID; he immediately changed from a lout and a bouncer into a grovelling lackey, and I asked him: 'Is Kostya working tonight?'

'Of course! He's playing the trombone.'

'And do you know Morozov?'

'Borya you mean? He's here, Comrade Prosecutor . . .'

'And is Lena with him?' asked Nina.

'Yeah.'

'Come on, you can show us,' Nina ordered him.

Even the wooden staircase up to the first floor was crammed with pimply long-haired youths with cigarettes in their mouths. Their voices were drowned by the deafening jazz. Pushing adolescents aside, the doorman made a path for us into the main room. The scene was unimaginable. Young people – girls and boys of sixteen to eighteen, sat crowded round closely-packed tables in a dense curtain of cigarette-smoke that hung over the dark room. On the tables in front of them they had Zhigulyovskoye beer, ice-cream, or the cheapest sour Aligoté wine. They were all smoking furiously and talking, while on the stage the jazz band roared: five strangely-clad musicians – a cross between Russian ploughboys and American cowboys – were grinding out of their instruments an almost unrecognizably jazzed-up version of the patriotic Komsomol tune 'Grenada, Grenada, my Grenada . . .' Thus the interests of all interested parties were safeguarded: in its daily report to the city culture directorate the band's repertoire looked ideologically sound, while the content of the song was lost on the listeners, since these jazz lads made even 'Grenada' sound completely western. That was enough for this place.

Meanwhile the doorman was pointing out to us across the room: 'Over there on the right, playing the trombone – that's Kostya. And in front of him right next to the stage, see that girl dancing in the green blouse? That's Eleonora. And that person drinking wine at the table near us – that's Borya Morozov.'

I could see that even my Nina was involuntarily jerking her hips in time to the music – she was in her element.

'We'll have to wait till they stop playing,' I said to Pshenichny.

'Why?' asked Nina. 'You go downstairs, and I'll bring them to you one at a time.'

'How?' I said in surprise.

'That's my business!' said Nina. She walked straight across the room to Morozov's table, and a minute later was dancing with him on a single spot next to the stage.

Yes, Nina from Vologda had really turned out an excellent member of the team – after dancing a couple of minutes with Boris, she easily drew him downstairs to the ground floor, as if to go to the darkened bar, and on the way handed him straight over to us – Pshenichny and me. And she herself went back to fetch Lena-Eleonora . . . Thus in half an hour or so all three of them ended up in the Third Section of the Moscow CID without any chases or shooting

FROM THE REPORT OF THE INTERROGATION
OF ELEONORA SAVITSKAYA

SAVITSKAYA: I began watching 16-A before the New Year. We knew a lot of rich people lived there from the fortune-teller Marusya Shevchenko in Vostryakovo. She gave us inside information and told us a couple of rich Jews lived there, some Academician and his wife. Actually we had already got the addresses of all sorts of rich people about a year ago. That was when Borya Morozov worked in the special service department of the grocer's on Smolensk Square. This department supplies all sorts of top people, stars, directors, other celebrities. For example, Maya Plisetskaya, Arkady Raikin, Muslim Magomayev, and lots of other top people. They have special permission to phone in and order whole crates of food – chops, caviare, cognac, sausage, etc. And all this while ordinary folk only get meat on coupons, and chilled meat at that, and they have to queue for three hours . . .

PSHENICHNY: Stick to the point, please, suspect. Let's get back to 16-A.

SAVITSKAYA: I am sticking to the point. I am just saying that Borya Morozov used to work in the order department of this shop and had the addresses of all these rich people. Whenever he had an order from them which was to be delivered, they themselves would tell him when they were home and when they were out. It was a cinch because I already knew roughly when the people wouldn't be at home. And I just had to check it out for a day or two so we wouldn't go and blow it as we did once when we

129

were doing one apartment and bumped right into some old bird coming out of the toilet.

PSHENICHNY: Still, let's get back to 16-A, Kachalov Street. You'll have time enough to talk about your other burglaries. This interrogation is confined to events occurring in 16-A. And bear in mind, if you come clean it will make things easier for you at the trial.

SAVITSKAYA: I am coming clean. I'm telling you that when Morozov quit his job at this shop it was easy enough for him: he just got the addresses for the new burglaries from this fortune-teller. But it got ten times harder for me, because this fortune-teller only gave the address and that was that, and I had to snoop around and find out when the people were out.

PSHENICHNY: Even so, shall we get back to 16-A?

SAVITSKAYA: We are. Anyway, so that's how it was. We got the address of this Jewish Academician just a month ago, just before New Year. And Boris ordered me to start watching the house. I was to draw up an exact timetable of when these Academicians leave the house and come back again. The first time I went there to watch, a Chaika drove up to the house right before my eyes and a KGB general got out with two others, either colonels or majors. And half an hour later another Chaika arrived with Podgorny in it. Anyway I told Borya we ought to keep away from this house, there were too many bigwigs living there, and there was bound to be a guard. But he says no. Bigwigs live there all right, but there's no guard. That's what the fortune-teller told him. She had managed to get out of Academician Tsipursky's wife that there wasn't even a lift attendant, and that you either get in the main entrance by key, or you have to know the telephone number of the person you are going to see, and on this sort of dial by the door you dial the last four figures. And then, if there's anyone at home they press some button and the door unlocks itself. In other words, just like in foreign films. And we're definitely going to take this pad, he says, and not just the one – the whole house is loaded. Well fine, what Borya says goes for me, he saved my brother's eyesight two years ago. I have a kid brother. He's seventeen now. Well, two years ago he had a motorbike crash and lost an eye. Absolute hell, it was! So Morozov put him straight on a plane and sent him to the Filatov Hospital in Odessa. He slipped someone five thousand, and they operated on my brother straight away. There's a three-year waiting-list for operations down there! Anyway, I began to wonder what to do about 16-A. It was winter, December, you couldn't stand about outside watching very long. So what did I do? I took a look at the house opposite and saw that it's not so special, no Chaikas drove up, not even black Volgas. So I went into this house with my notebook, calling in at all the apartments as if I was from Social Security, and there I found what I needed – on the fourth floor, right opposite the entrance to 16-A was a bachelor living alone. And not very old, only about forty or so. Some sort of engineer, a fitter. Well, after that everything went swimmingly – the next day I just happened to meet him by the metro, let him pick me up, and that night was already sleeping with him. Of course I made sure he went absolutely crazy over the sex, he'd never had such sex. You know, when a woman puts her mind to it she can make it so that no man will let her go. Anyway, next morning he begged me to move in with him. Well, I pretended I wasn't too keen on the idea, but in the end agreed. Anyway, from that day on I watched 16-A for days on end from that apartment, I even bought myself a pair of binoculars. And what a lot of interesting things I saw! When you look at the outside, it seems like a quiet, respectable building with respectable people living in it, top people, scientists, generals. But if you were to watch from morning to late evening, as I did! My fitter was out at work till late at night, installing some pipe-making machinery, and I sat for hours by the window watching that house through the binoculars. It's especially interesting in the evening and night. Anyway, what did I discover? Well, that this wife of Academician Tsipursky doesn't work anywhere and her lover comes to her twice a week in the morning – Wednesdays and Fridays. And on the other days she hangs round the shops, and once a week – Thursdays – has her hair and nails done at the Sorceress. A couple of times I followed her to this Sorceress. Borya has his own girls working at the Sorceress, people he supplied for a whole year from the grocer's on Smolensk Square. So they confirmed that this Tsipurskaya was there every Thursday from ten to twelve, regular as clockwork. Anyway, I soon had that apartment sorted out, two weeks it took. But while I was watching it I also noticed a few other things. For instance, would you be interested to know that Podgorny's daughter has a two-storey apartment? And Kosygin's daughter too. I've never seen that before, except in the cinema, where you can go from one room up a spiral staircase right up to the next floor. She's not just got all sorts of bedrooms, but even a swimming-pool. Honest! I'm not lying! They've got a bathroom as big as your office, except much nicer of course. Just like the pools at the Aragvi restaurant or the Berlin. And in this pool, or rather in the area where this pool is, this Kosygin's daughter keeps diamonds and all sorts of personal jewellery in a little white table. You should see them! I've never seen anyone with such things, honest. And we'd really combed the city for stones like that. In Moscow alone we cleaned out 317 apartments in two years.

QUESTION FROM INVESTIGATOR SHAMRAYEV: How many? How many?

SAVITSKAYA: 317. I have the record. You can check it from my notebooks.

PSHENICHNY: How do you explain the fact that far fewer burglaries are registered in the militia?

SAVITSKAYA: Quite simple! In the first place, not everyone reports losing valuables. For example, if we clean out the apartment of a furniture factory director or the secretary of a Party regional committee, they're hardly going to report the loss of diamonds, gold, pearls, or money – say

131

200,000 roubles – from their apartment, are they? They would ask them, 'And how did you get all that money, when your salary is at the most 200 or 300 roubles a month?' Well, nobody wants to look like a swindler and a thief, so they keep quiet and don't report to the militia. For instance, once we burgled the apartment of the chief of the Timiryazevsky district militia and took away all sorts of gold and valuables, I don't remember how much now. Well, is he going to report to someone that he, a mere major in the militia, has so many valuables? He'd do better to grab himself a new million in thefts and bribes than to expose himself. The only people who report our thefts are those who legally earn a lot – various scientists, Academicians, generals, and actors. But the militia doesn't always take statements from them because we don't leave any clues behind and nobody knows when the theft was committed. People don't check the safes where they keep their gold hidden every day.

PSHENICHNY: Understood. What else have you to say about the residents of 16-A? As many details as possible, please.

SAVITSKAYA: Sure! Well, first about this KGB general, if you're interested. His name is Tsvigun, he died recently, I saw his picture in the paper. Do you want me to tell you about that?

PSHENICHNY: Yes, tell us.

SAVITSKAYA: Well, in the first place, he died – nothing surprising about that. With that sort of living even a young man would kick the bucket, let alone an old boy like him. I read in the paper that he was nearly 65, yet he played cards every night till three in the morning, drinking whole glasses of brandy and fooling around with girls. At first I couldn't understand where his wife and children were. Then I twigged – this wasn't his home apartment, but just for whoring and cards. He only occasionally slept there, and always with the light on, that's right. He never put the light out, always went to bed with it on. I think he was afraid of the dark. Because as soon as he came into his apartment he would switch on the lights in every room. And I could see everything through my binoculars, as long as he didn't pull the blinds of course. But on the whole he didn't often spend the night in that building, but used to go off somewhere at three or four in the morning. I think he went home. And at 7.30 in the morning the cleaning-woman would go into the apartment, clean everything up, put food in the fridge, and leave, and there was nobody in the apartment for the whole day. So it would have been easy to burgle. But we decided not to touch this apartment, or the apartments of Kosygin's and Podgorny's daughters. Because there would have been such a row that the whole militia would have been after us, or the KGB. Is that any use to you?

PSHENICHNY: Can you describe the people you saw in General Tsvigun's apartment?

SAVITSKAYA: Yes, but not all of them. The ones that played cards with him I can. And one middle-aged woman I can describe. But I can't describe all the whores and tarts she brought him, because they were all alike and you can see them yourself any night in the Hotel National and the Metropole.

PSHENICHNY: Please describe those people you saw in Tsvigun's apartment.

SAVITSKAYA: All right, here goes! One – a Georgian. Fat with a moustache. And bald. Looked about fifty, maybe more. Drank nothing but wine. Many times I noticed that while they were all playing cards and knocking back the brandy or whisky, he had only wine. And he smoked a cigar. Two – a tall handsome bloke with dark hair, looked just like a gypsy. Always came in his own Volga wearing an overcoat with a diamond cross on his chest. I swear it! He had rings on all his fingers, all with real stones, and then on his chest this diamond cross, Komsomol's honour! I was even surprised that he would visit a general like that with a cross on his chest. I thought perhaps he was a priest or something. But not a bit of it! Priests don't go around in velvet jackets and jeans. And this one dressed like a real American actor, with a foreign coat. And the last time I saw him I noticed he wasn't in the Volga any more, he drove up in a gold Mercedes . . .

PSHENICHNY: When was that?

SAVITSKAYA: Well, we were working in the house on 14 January, Thursday. That means the last time I saw this actor was on Wednesday, the evening of the 13 January. Yes, that's right. Right on the old New Year's Eve he came to see the general in his brand new Mercedes. I even remember, it stunned me rather – gold-coloured and such a cool customer. If we hadn't had to do those apartments the next day I would have made a pass at him myself right then, honest! I've often dreamt of riding in a Mercedes! But of course the man had quite enough women without me. And he didn't just screw hard-currency prostitutes in this general's apartment, he also got off with a star in the same building – Izolda Snezhko. I saw her in a film recently; she's old already, older than him. She lives alone there with a dog, a Great Dane. So this actor obviously couldn't be bothered to go home at three in the morning, so he nips up to the eleventh floor, to this actress. And he sleeps at her place till about one in the afternoon. A couple of times his wife came for him. At least, I don't know if she was his wife, maybe not. She was about ten years older than him, if not more. But she threw such a scene! I saw through the window. This general tried to calm her down and she just chucked a bottle at him, only she missed. I was amazed – such a jealous old bird that she wasn't even afraid of a KGB general! And the second time she couldn't find her star, because at that moment he was on the eleventh floor, so she starts howling! An old bird like her howling about a fellow, and this Tsvigun was comforting her and stroking her head just like his own daughter. And then I looked closely through the binoculars, and you know who she looks like? Brezhnev, honest! Maybe it's his daughter?

133

QUESTION FROM INVESTIGATOR SHAMRAYEV: Tell me, Eleonora, have you ever seen this star, as you call him, singing or playing a guitar?

SAVITSKAYA: Sure! He always has a guitar in his car! He never went there without it. So you know him, do you? Is he really a star? What's his name?

INVESTIGATOR SHAMRAYEV: You mentioned some woman who you said brought girls to this apartment. Can you give us a 'verbal portrait' of her?

SAVITSKAYA: She's about 35 to 40. Reddish hair, possibly dyed, I don't know. Thin and very tall. She would come in her own car, a blue Lada. Sometimes with a briefcase, as if she was coming from work, sometimes without it. She would make tea or coffee in the kitchen and wait for everyone to arrive. Yes, I forgot to tell you that she and this star sometimes arrived before the general. They had their own keys to the apartment and the main entrance. And then they would either sit down to play cards or this red-head would go off somewhere in her car and half an hour later bring a whole carload of foreign-currency whores. But then they usually closed all the blinds, so that I only occasionally saw between the cracks that these girls were walking about stark naked. But that's natural, what else are they for? They're not going to start playing chess!

PSHENICHNY: You testified that your group burgled the apartment of Academician Tsipursky on Thursday the 14 January. But the victim, Citizen Tsipurskaya, reported to the militia that the theft was on the 18th . . .

SAVITSKAYA: Well that's quite early to catch on! Some people still haven't! She probably went to put on her fur coat. I told Morozov we shouldn't take any fur coats, only the valuables hidden in the sideboard. But he wouldn't listen, so we blew it! Right? Was that it?

PSHENICHNY: You just testified that your group robbed other apartments in that building. Which ones?

SAVITSKAYA: Altogether we were in four apartments, to be honest. I really wanted to get into that general's apartment, and Kosygin's daughter's. But we didn't take anything there, Komsomol's honour! To begin with, as I told you, we had decided not to touch the general or Kosygin's daughter, the hell with them. But I just wanted to have a look inside.

PSHENICHNY: So you just walked around those apartments without taking anything?

SAVITSKAYA: I swear it! Not a thing! We didn't even drink anything. Morozov doesn't allow drinking on the job. We just sat in the chairs, had a smoke, and flicked the ash into a matchbox . . .

QUESTION FROM INVESTIGATOR SHAMRAYEV: And did you see if there was a rug in the hallway of Tsvigun's apartment?

SAVITSKAYA: Yes, there was. The whole apartment was carpeted.

PSHENICHNY: And do you clearly remember that there was a rug in the hallway? Can you describe it?

SAVITSKAYA: Well what's there to describe? Just a rug, a Persian one, yellow with a green fringe. Is it missing or something? We didn't take it, honest!

PSHENICHNY: And which other apartments did you go into that day?

SAVITSKAYA: That actress on the eleventh floor, Izolda Snezhko, we were in her apartment too. Because I had seen her on the 7th getting into a car marked 'Film Studios' with the dog and two suitcases, and after that she was away all week. So we decided she must be off shooting a film, and we quite calmly walked into the actress's apartment and took a man's gold ring with a black agate off the bathroom shelf.

PSHENICHNY: Nothing else?

SAVITSKAYA: There wasn't anything else to take. Either that actress doesn't have anything or she took it all with her. I mean gold, of course.

PSHENICHNY: She took everything, but left the ring behind?

SAVITSKAYA: Well it wasn't her ring. It belonged to the star who used to visit the general. I've spotted that ring on his hand many times through my binoculars. He spent a couple of nights in the actress's apartment after she had left. And he must have forgotten that ring. Now I've got it hidden at home. That's the first time I've ever kept anything I've stolen, Morozov used to strictly forbid it . . .

QUESTION FROM PUBLIC ASSISTANT INVESTIGATOR MAKARYCHEVA: What's the matter, have you fallen for this star or something?

SAVITSKAYA: Well, yes! You should see him! You'd go crazy too!

QUESTION FROM INVESTIGATOR SHAMRAYEV: What other apartment did you visit that day?

SAVITSKAYA: We also went to No. 40 on the ninth floor. There's a type living there, either a diplomat or some sort of head from the Ministry of Foreign Trade. Anyway, his whole apartment is full of African masks and foreign things. Even the tiles in the lavatory are foreign, and there's a pink wash-basin marked 'Made in Sweden'. We took something like 30,000 American and Canadian dollars or more, and then various bits of gold and jewellery as usual . . . And that was it. We didn't go anywhere else, I swear. And what's more, I'd like to state that we have never taken a kopeck from the State or from ordinary folk, and even all these crooked top people we didn't clean out completely. They have enough left to live on, I can assure you! More than their salary entitles them to!

QUESTION FROM INVESTIGATOR SHAMRAYEV: So you're trying to say that your business was expropriating from the expropriators?

SAVITSKAYA: That's it! Absolutely! That's what Borya Morozov says! He says Lenin said: 'Take from the thieves what they stole from the people.' That's why I am calmly telling you everything. We're not afraid of justice. We're going to tell them such things in court about all these top people – how much they've got stashed away in every apartment, and how they live when there's not only no meat in the shops, but even queues for vitamins in the chemists . . .

The office door burst open and the interrogation of the latest disciple of Lenin was interrupted by the appearance of Marat Svetlov. Pale, with his right hand bandaged, he came over to his desk where we were questioning Savitskaya, shot a penetrating glance at the young 'expropriatress' with the magnificent bosom, and placed in front of me his typed report on the chase for Vorotnikov, alias Korchagin, and on the need to do a routine investigation into the 'legal justification for the use of a firearm by Colonel Svetlov leading to the death of the criminal'.

I read the report unhurriedly while Svetlov, gloomy and nervous, paced the office. He clearly wanted to talk, but the presence of Savitskaya prevented him.

I turned to Pshenichny: 'That's all for today, Valentin. Send the prisoners to the Butyrka.'

Pshenichny led Savitskaya away.

Svetlov asked Nina to run down to the buffet for a glass of strong tea and, when we were alone, sat down at his desk abruptly and said: 'Look, we've been had like kids! Do you know who Krasnov and Baklanov arrested while we were chasing after Vorotnikov and those house-burglars? You'll never guess!'

'Galya Brezhneva's lover,' I said.

'How did you know?'

'I worked it out only five minutes ago unfortunately, when Savitskaya testified that he used to play cards with Tsvigun almost every day. How did you find out they had got him?'

'In the typing pool. I was dictating my report, and the typists nearby were all in a flutter about some Buryatsky, a singer in the Bolshoi and Brezhneva's lover; he was trying to steal some diamonds from the apartment of the circus-star Irina Bugrimova today, and Krasnov caught him red-handed.'

'Now I expect they'll try to hang Tsvigun's murder on him,' I said.

'He expects!' exploded Svetlov, jumping up and pacing up and down the room. 'So where were you? The philosopher! He expects! Of course they will! They can kill two birds with one stone! They can write off the murder and completely compromise Brezhnev: if his daughter's lover murdered his brother-in-law, can you imagine the scandal? Listen, perhaps you could go down to the Butyrka Prison and have a talk with this Buryatsky?'

'I don't think Baklanov will let me in to see him,' I said, picking up the telephone and dialling the duty officer at the Butyrka. 'Hello! This is Shamrayev from the Prosecutor's Office. Who am I talking to? Captain Zoshchenko? Good evening, Timofei Karpovich. Was a Boris Buryatsky brought in today? You have him? He features in my case too, so make a note to have him sent to me in the morning for questioning. What? Of course. Thank you, I thought so. No, I realize it's nothing to do with you. Timofei Karpovich. Goodbye.'

I hung up and said to Svetlov: 'Buryatsky has a very high temperature, so no interrogations are allowed.'

'Rubbish!' said Svetlov. 'The swine!'

I laughed: 'Of course it's rubbish, but they won't let us in to him until they've worked him over. Sit down, stop fussing. I want to tell you something else.'

Pshenichny came back into the office and I now addressed them both: 'Tomorrow Baklanov and Krasnov may arrest another hundred people who have given Tsvigun bribes, played cards with him, drunk brandy or served with him at the front. And they'll try to hang Tsvigun's murder on every one of them. But why should we go running around after them proving that this one didn't do it and that one didn't do it? That's just what Krasnov wants – to draw us into this mess and waste another week. We've already lost three days!'

'So what do you suggest?' asked Svetlov glumly.

'I suggest we go straight to the pub and celebrate your being still alive. That's the main thing for me today. If "Korchagin" had aimed a few centimetres to the left I would consider myself to be your murderer.'

'Stop trying to fool me!' said Svetlov, waving me away. 'Of course it would be nice to hop down to the pub, but I haven't any money . . .'

Silently I pulled Brezhnev's packet of money out of my pocket – almost ten thousand roubles. Svetlov, Pshenichny, and Nina, who had just arrived with the tea, stared at me wide-eyed.

'Where did you get all that money?' asked Svetlov.

'I received a bribe from a client yesterday,' I said. 'What do you think, is it enough for the pub?'

'Incidentally,' said Pshenichny suddenly. 'They can pin Tsvigun's murder on any odd bod, as you say, but only if they know that the blood-group on the bullet coincides with Tsvigun's.'

Svetlov and I gazed at Valentin in amazement.

He explained unhurriedly: 'While you were chasing after "Korchagin", I summoned to Tsvigun's apartment the ballistics expert from the Forensic lab at Chistye Prudy. As you know, Article 133, footnote, permits that . . .'

'Get to the point!' said Svetlov impatiently, even banging his injured hand on the desk and wincing in pain.

'To get to the point, the expert measured the distance from the ventilation window to the wall of the building that Tsvigun's bullet hit,' Pshenichny continued calmly, 'then with his books of tables he worked out the ricochet angles, the resistance of the wood, and the coefficients and calculated that Tsvigun hit the ventilation window with his first bullet, shooting right across the room from the hallway. With that conclusion one can assume the following situation. Tsvigun entered his apartment and found some outsider or a group of people who then attacked him. He managed to fire two shots at them standing in the hallway. The first bullet hit the ventilator, the other hit one of his assailants. That person is either wounded or dead, I don't know which. I only know that Tsvigun's bullet passed right through his body, and that's why there are no traces of brain-matter on it, but there are traces of

137

skin and bone. After Tsvigun had fired two shots he was grabbed by the arms and held tightly. Hence the bruises on his arms and the split down the back of his jacket. Tsvigun wrenched himself free. Then, right there in the hallway, he was killed by a shot through the temple. They took away the spent cases and substituted the bullet, then they dragged him on the rug from the hallway into the sitting-room and sat him at the desk, rigging it to look like suicide. The bloodstained rug in the entrance hall they rolled up and took away. We cannot rule out the possibility that the person Tsvigun killed or wounded was carried out of the house in that rug. Therefore we have to look in the hospitals and mortuaries for a person with a bullet-wound going right through his body and with whatever blood-group the experts discover on the bullet . . .'

'And what about Tsvigun's bodyguard? And his chauffeur? And the neighbours?' Svetlov asked scornfully. 'What happened to them? Were they hypnotized so that they couldn't hear any shots or see a corpse being carried out in a carpet?'

'I don't construct hypotheses if I don't have a particular fact to hand,' replied Pshenichny calmly. 'Therefore I cannot say anything yet about the bodyguard and the chauffeur, except that at the time there was a wedding-party going on in the building, music filled the whole house, and the neighbours had got used to the popping of champagne corks. But that is not the point . . .'

'I'll construct a different scenario for you, if you like,' said Svetlov. 'Tsvigun entered the apartment and found *one* person there. This person attacked Tsvigun, grabbed the gun from him in the course of the struggle, his first shot went through the window, through the ventilator, and the second landed in Tsvigun's head. Then he dragged him into the sitting-room on the carpet, rigged the suicide, and so on. And all the details of the case – the split jacket, the bruises on the wrists. And do you want a third scenario? Tsvigun entered the apartment and *himself* attacked somebody, but missed and hit the ventilation window. The other person jumps him, twists his arms round, and when the hand with the gun is next to Tsvigun's head, forces Tsvigun to press the trigger. Then he drags him into the sitting-room on the carpet and so on . . . . That makes it not even premeditated murder, but self-defence, and you can hang that on anyone – on me, on you, on Nina! And certainly on "Korchagin" or Buryatsky . . .'

'You could, but only if the blood-group on the bullet coincides with Tsvigun's. You could also laugh off Sorokin's test showing the absence of traces of brain-matter, as Tumanov did, and insist that that bullet did go through Tsvigun's head. Only then could you pin the murder on me, you, or Nina,' concluded Pshenichny.

Svetlov turned towards me: 'When do we get the blood-test?'

'Tomorrow,' I said. 'Tomorrow morning.'

'Listen,' said Nina. 'Why are both of you so bent on cutting a dash? You're going round in circles, scared to call a spade a spade. I'll tell you what happened. Tsvigun arrived home to a KGB ambush. They killed him, then mocked up the suicide and ordered the bodyguard and the chauffeur to write that they didn't see or hear anything. That's all. Got it?'

Svetlov laughed and stroked her head: 'Clever little girl! How did you guess? Of course that's what happened, but you've got to prove it! And the important thing is to understand why they made such a meal of it. After all, the KGB can dispose of anyone quietly, even Andropov, and as for mocking up a suicide, you couldn't fault them on anything. But this is neither one thing nor the other – we'll never get to the bottom of it without a stiff drink. So let's go to the pub!'

After midnight
Nina and I got home from the Slavyansky Bazar restaurant after midnight. My lead seal still adorned the door of my apartment. But Nina's flaxen hair, which she had used that morning to attach the bottom of the door to the threshold, was broken. We looked at each other: once again our apartment was stuffed with hidden microphones. They couldn't care less about Brezhnev's personal guard and their commander, General Zharov. But we didn't have the energy to protest or complain. We tumbled into bed and fell into a dreamless sleep. The sound technician on duty somewhere nearby had nothing to record except our breathing.

Part 5

The 'New Course' Government

Monday 25 January, 7.30 a.m.
Doctors claim that one hemisphere of our brain is asleep all the time; in other words, it is switched off. I'm afraid that on that morning both my hemispheres were switched off. And not just mine – Nina's too. Three days of chasing non-stop after the shadow of Tsvigun's murderer had worn us out, and last night's booze-up at the Slavyansky Bazar had finally knocked us off our feet – so we didn't even hear the alarm clock. It began straining away at 7.30 and then went hoarse, only to be joined at 7.45 by the telephone. After about the fifth or sixth ring I shook myself awake with difficulty, reached for the phone, and picked up the receiver: 'Hello . . .'

'Good morning,' said an unfamiliar female voice. 'Sorry to have woken you up. Can I speak to Nina?'

'She's asleep. Who is it?'

'A friend of hers.'

'Tamara? Ring back in about half an hour.'

'I don't know if I'll be able to. I'm just off to work. Tell her I booked her in at my hairdresser for six o'clock, as she asked. So I'll meet her at Mayakovskaya metro station, on the right-hand platform opposite the last car. But she mustn't be late!' and she rang off.

I swore, pulled myself out of bed and went to the bathroom, trying to recall the agenda for the day. But neither hemisphere would switch on, my head ached, and I realized there was only one way to get myself into shape for work. I took an opened bottle of vodka out of the refrigerator, poured a third of a glass, and drank it with revulsion. And they call me a Jew! Who ever saw a Jew drinking vodka in the morning? Nevertheless I felt slightly better, though that was only half the treatment. I glanced out of the window. It was still snowing and snowing in the morning gloom. I turned on the hot shower in the bathroom, heated my feet up in it, then just as I was, naked except for my underpants, jumped into the snow on the balcony. I began to rub myself with snow – chest, shoulders, neck, stomach, arms. From the balcony I went back under the hot shower.

143

Hm, yes . . . The working week, and technically the first official day of the investigation into the death of Tsvigun, were beginning with a headache and the possibility that at any moment Krasnov and Baklanov would toss me a new gift – Galya Brezhneva's lover Boris Buryatsky, who would have 'confessed' to the murder of Tsvigun. I would have done the same in their position, and I would have tied the whole thing up in a bow: Buryatsky had the keys to Tsvigun's apartment – Savitskaya testified that he often got there before Tsvigun, that was quite normal. And so, as Pshenichny says, let's imagine the situation: Buryatsky arrived at Tsvigun's apartment at, say, midday. At two Tsvigun arrived from being with Suslov. Tsvigun was bad-tempered and irritated and vented his anger on Buryatsky. They swore at each other. Buryatsky will say Tsvigun even wanted to kill him. I don't know why, but let's say because Buryatsky is unfaithful to Galya Brezhneva, Tsvigun's favourite niece. Proceeding further: Buryatsky testifies that Tsvigun pulled a gun on him and fired at him, but missed and hit the ventilation window. Then he grabbed Tsvigun by the arms and a struggle began in which Tsvigun's jacket split. In the struggle Buryatsky managed to catch hold of Tsvigun's hand with the gun, but as he was twisting it (hence the bruises on Tsvigun's wrists) the gun was near Tsvigun's head and at that moment went off. That way it was not even premeditated murder, in fact not murder at all, but merely an incident in a moment of self-defence – Article 13 of the Criminal Code, no punishment. Any criminal will be willing to carry such a 'crime' if you promise either to reduce the punishment for his real crime, say, burgling the actress Bugrimova, or even to close the case altogether. Yes, the CID's version is perfectly plausible: Tsvigun died from an accidental shot during a quarrel or a fight with Buryatsky, but Buryatsky (or whoever else they shove into the role) got frightened that they wouldn't believe him and would accuse him of murder, so he staged a suicide and forged a suicide note, then rolled up the carpet, went up to the eleventh floor with it, to the apartment of his friend, the actress Snezhko. He sat it out there until night, when of course he chucked the rug into the Moskva River, and no one would be any the wiser. So, Investigator Shamrayev, take your killer – we picked him up for burgling the actress Bugrimova, and he has confessed to killing Tsvigun in self-defence. The bullet came from Tsvigun's gun and passed through Tsvigun's head – what more do you need, Comrade Prosecutor?

And suddenly a simple idea came into my head. Simple as a tear. If Tsvigun was killed by KGB or MVD agents, then they know the blood-group of the man Tsvigun shot. And if they are going to hang this murder on Buryatsky *before* Sorokin does his blood-test, it means they know the blood-groups *coincide*. Actually that was just what Pshenichny was trying to get through to us yesterday evening. Well, well, well! My brain was working feverishly. We must use this! There are two ways, two ways! First – get in to Buryatsky and find out if they are trying to get a confession out of him or not, and the second – Good heavens, it's even simpler . . .

144

Astounded at my discovery, I stood still under the shower and only now heard Nina knocking and banging on the bathroom door with her fists.

I opened the door in fright: 'What happened?'

'It's what happened to *you*?' she launched into me. 'You've been in here fifteen minutes already, and not a sound! I'm screaming and knocking. I was just going to ring for an ambulance!'

'Sorry, I was thinking . . .' I came out of the bathroom.

'You were thinking! The thinker!' Deeply offended, she slammed the bathroom door behind her.

'Tamara rang you, you're going to her hairdresser this evening!' I shouted to her through the door.

'Why?' came from the bathroom.

'How do I know? You were the one who asked her!' I answered, flicking through the telephone book.

'What did I ask her?' Nina thrust her head round the bathroom door.

'To make an appointment for you at her hairdresser's. You're meeting at 5.30 at Mayakovskaya metro station, right-hand platform, last car.' I copied Sorokin's home address out of the telephone book: 162, 5th Peschanaya Street, Apt. 14.'

Nina shrugged her shoulders and disappeared into the bathroom again, and I hurriedly got dressed and wrote her a note: 'Gone to the shops. Back in 15 minutes. Igor.'

With my shopping-bag in my hand I ran out of the house and rushed down to the nearest grocer's two blocks away. I looked over my shoulder as I went and saw I wasn't being followed. They had obviously put a secret microphone in the telephone receiver, and nothing more. Even so, when I got into the grocer's I went straight to the window to double-check that I had no tail. I had thought up a clever ploy, and I didn't need it to come unstuck through some silly mistake. But there was no one – the dark, snowy street was almost deserted; the intelligentsia in our region are what is called 'creative' – so artistic that they get up late. But you can't even get a taxi round here at this early hour – drivers know there's nothing for them to do in our area before nine or ten in the morning. I became nervous – I needed a car urgently – in ten or fifteen minutes the Sorokins might leave for work, and there was not a single vehicle on the streets except a snow-plough rumbling along and a milk-cart from which the men threw down at the entrance to the grocer's, not milk, but a few crates of yoghurt and then drove off.

'Take some yoghurt, there won't be any milk today!' said a saleswoman I knew, so I quickly went to the cash register and got chits for two bottles and a can of fish, some curd cheese portions, and some Roquefort – there was nothing else worth buying for breakfast; the windows were bare as usual. Packing my purchases into my shopping-bag, I darted out of the shop and then realized I had no choice. I had already wasted almost a minute and a half over that wretched yoghurt. Running across the street, I jumped up onto the running-board of the snow-plough.

'Hey! Where are you going?' the driver yelled at me.

I knew how to soften up his sort, and I showed him a green twenty-five rouble note that I had taken out in the shop: 'Can you give me a lift to 5th Peschanaya? Only fast – there and back in fifteen minutes. Can you make it?'

'Hop in!'

The engine roared and, with its snow scoop raised, the vehicle lurched away. About eight minutes later I was already running up to the second floor of 162, 5th Peschanaya, to the Sorokins' apartment. And I made it – Alla was just leaving for work and locking her apartment door.

'Hello!' she said in astonishment. 'What's happened?'

'Where's your Sorokin?'

'Behind the house outside in the snow with his Moskvich. But what's happened?'

'Nothing, I have to have a word with him . . .' and I ran down the stairs.

Outside, completely snowed in, stood four private cars – two small Zaporozhetses, Sorokin's Moskvich, and a Zhiguli. The owners, including Sorokin, were cursing away, digging them out of the snowdrifts, but it was immediately evident that so much snow had fallen in the night that they were going to be digging all day.

Wading almost up to the waist in snow, I reached Sorokin and said: 'Hello! I can pull you out of here with a snow-plough right now, but on one condition.'

'I know your condition,' he said meekly. 'You need a comparative blood-test. OK, pull me out.'

'No, it's a different condition. No matter what the result of the test, you will ring me at the Prosecutor's Office in an hour's time and say that the blood-groups on the bullet and for Tsvigun do *not* coincide.'

He shook his head: 'I can't give false reports. I've signed an undertaking.'

'But you're not going to give false reports! A telephone conversation is not a written document. People say all sorts of things over the telephone! The proper report of the analysis you'll give me later . . .'

'You want to check if they're tapping your office phone or not?'

'Exactly!' I lied.

'And if they are, then what?'

'Then precisely half an hour after that call Baklanov, Krasnov, or Oleinik will come to see you. Because that'll ruin their whole game. Either that, or I'm an idiot . . .'

'Well, one thing doesn't exclude the other,' he observed, and said: 'Listen, Igor, I can't do what you are asking.'

I looked him in the eye.

'Sorry,' he added. 'I don't play with fire like that, and I advise you not to.'

'But don't you understand, I can nab them this way!' I shouted at him. 'I'll know whether or not they're palming me off with a sham murderer. And all it costs you is one telephone call! If they come running to you, it means they've known for a long time that Tsvigun and the person he shot have the same blood-group! I'll nab them on that! Come on, Sasha, I beg you . . .'

'Igor, I've already given you my answer,' he said curtly, removing my hands from his coat collar, and resumed digging his Moskvich out with a shovel.

'Boys, what's happening down there?' Alla Sorokina shouted to us.

'Idiot!' I said to Sorokin; I turned back, trying to retrace my steps, but floundered up to my waist in snow. A brilliant idea had failed because of that coward.

'Igor!' Alla called me, but I walked past her without speaking.

Back on the street I climbed up into the cab of the snow-plough, angrily opened a bottle of yoghurt, took a mouthful, and said to the driver: 'Back to Airport Street.'

But after two blocks I ordered him to turn back. We turned into the courtyard of the Sorokins' house, and within a minute had pulled their Moskvich out of its snowy captivity. Then, without a word to the Sorokins, I drove off home.

9.15 a.m.

The Third Section of the Moscow CID was almost deserted – some of the inspectors had gone down to Kachalov Street to help Pshenichny question people, some had dispersed to the various hospitals and mortuaries in search of a person with a bullet-wound right through his body. But Captain Laskin, who was on duty, told Nina and me that Svetlov was here at the CID, in the 'Whores' Section'. This section is officially called the Second Section for the Exposure of Sexual Offences, but nobody gives it that long name. They simply say, 'Whores' Section'. It deals with the uncovering of rape, child molesting, prostitution, homosexuality, lesbianism and other sexual perversions in the Moscow area. However, its mandate includes more than just the struggle against these relics of capitalism. Of the forty thousand Moscow prostitutes, cocksuckers, nymphos, queers, and lesbians on this Section's books, two or three thousand co-operate actively with the CID as its agents in the various social strata of the city. Admittedly, just before the Moscow Olympics the CID's best cadres were taken over by the KGB – thousands of foreigners had to be serviced, and you couldn't entrust that sort of work to amateurs or girls that had not been vetted by the KGB. That is why Svetlov was now digging around in the drawers of the Records Department with his healthy left hand and pulling out cards marked, 'Now under the KGB'. At the same time he was examining each photograph with interest, studying the biographical data and the date of birth. As Eleonora Savitskaya testified the day before, Sveta, the forty-year-old red-head, brought young hard-currency prostitutes to Tsvigun's apartment, and now Svetlov was making a separate pile of girls not older than twenty-one or -two.

My appearance interrupted this entertaining pastime.

147

'In the first place, this Sveta doesn't work for the KGB,' Svetlov told me. 'Otherwise the lads from our Whores' Section would have known her – they are in close contact with the KGB. Colonel Litvyakov and Major Shakhovsky are the ones who deal with hard-currency whores over there.'

'Wait,' I interrupted him. 'Forget the girls; Ozherelyev or Laskin can take care of them. I need you to go to the Butyrka prison.'

'Why?'

I explained briefly how I had failed with Sorokin and told him my idea about Buryatsky: 'We've got to find out if they've started hustling him to take responsibility for the murder yet, or not . . .'

'But if they're not letting you in to see him, they certainly won't let me!' he said.

'Marat, in order to find out what's going on with a prisoner in the Butyrka, it isn't at all essential to talk to the man himself or his investigator,' I said.

He looked me in the eye and smiled: 'Do you always have such interesting notions when you've got a hangover?'

And we went up to his section on the second floor. There I left Nina in the care of Captain Laskin and asked him to load her with work. I reminded him about Givi Mingadze, and finally drove off to work at the Prosecutor's Office.

9.45 a.m.

Getting out of the lift on the fourth floor, the Investigation Section of the Prosecutor's Office, I heard the deep, indignant voice of a well-dressed woman with startlingly black eyebrows: 'Do you know who you have arrested?' she was shouting at Herman Karakoz. 'I'll put the whole lot of you in jail! He didn't rob anyone, he came to fetch his diamonds from her!'

I realized who this woman was, and Karakoz immediately confirmed my guess: 'Galina Leonidovna, what are you talking about?! We haven't arrested anybody!' he assured her in a velvety voice, almost dancing round her, his whole greasy figure exuding total innocence and righteousness.

'What do you mean, nobody? I know perfectly well! I rang the MVD!' countered Galina Brezhneva, looking, with her bushy eyebrows, incredibly like her father. 'Yesterday a friend of our family was arrested, Boris Buryatsky, a singer at the Bolshoi Theatre! And your investigator Polkanov is handling the case!'

'Baklanov?' asked Karakoz.

'That's the one! I rushed over here by nine o'clock and found total chaos! No one here, not the Public Prosecutor, not even this Balkanov!'

'Baklanov . . .' Karakoz corrected her.

'Oh, go to hell!' Galina Leonidovna suddenly said to him. 'Who are you to teach me? Balkanov, Polkanov! What's the difference? The main thing is that it's already ten o'clock and he's still not at work! Get rid of these parasites! I shall tell my father today!'

At that moment Nikolai Baklanov stepped out of the lift. From his

148

hunched shoulders, red eyelids, and blue shadows under his eyes it was obvious he had been conducting interrogations for at least two days and nights. He had a heavy briefcase stuffed with files in his hand, and a cigarette-end smouldered in his mouth.

Karakoz strode over towards him with relief. 'Kolya! Here . . .'

But Baklanov, without even saying hello to Karakoz, walked past to the door of his office, opened it, and at the same time said curtly to Galya Brezhneva: 'Galina Leonidovna, come with me.'

'What?' she was stunned by such a tone.

He pointed to the open door of his office and repeated: 'I said, come in.'

'And who are you?' she asked in amazement.

'I am Senior Special Investigator Nikolai Afanasyevich Baklanov.'

'Ah, so you're this Polkanov!' Galya put her hands on her hips like a cook in a provincial cafeteria. 'You don't come to work till ten o'clock! And look at you! What a sight! A Soviet investigator, and he turns up to work with a hangover! Let's smell your breath!'

You had to hand it to Kolya Baklanov – in front of the entire Investigation Section, who were hanging out of their offices gaping, he calmly heard Brezhneva out and said in the same quiet, even voice: 'Galina Leonidovna, I do not think it is in your interests to make this scene here. I want to show you certain documents concerning your friend Buryatsky. They concern you too. Come in,' and without waiting for her he went into his office.

Brezhneva had no option but to follow him in, obediently. But she contrived not to lose face in front of everyone. 'Scum!' she said to us all, pointing after Baklanov. 'Goes ahead of a woman!'

I laughed and went into the office of Investigator Taras Vendelovsky.

The same time
Svetlov's car stopped at the corner of Lesnaya and Novoslobodskaya Streets, by an art shop. One of his sergeants was driving, since Svetlov's right hand was still bandaged up and he couldn't drive the car, but instead sat rather grumpily next to the driver. After waiting while the pedestrians crossed the pavement, the driver slowly drove under the arch of a multi-storey building and came out into an area in front of a high, ancient brick wall that looked like the Kremlin wall – the same turrets and battlements, the same high quality of construction with bricks that had formerly been red, but were now a greyish brown. But it was not of course the Kremlin wall, but the curtain wall surrounding the Butyrka, the biggest and most famous prison in Moscow, built back in the days of Peter the Great.

Svetlov left the car outside the wall and climbed up the stone steps to the inner courtyard of the fortress. On normal days this little courtyard is empty apart from a few visitors clustering at the door of the parcel-reception-room, and investigators hurrying to question their prisoners. But now it was busy days in the Butyrka – the courtyard and the low-ceilinged parcel-reception-room were filled with crowds of well-dressed people. Fur coats, fleece coats, deerskin caps, real astrakhan, musk-rat, mink . . . The wives, children, and friends of fifteen hundred underground dealers arrested in Operation Cascade had converged from the entire Soviet Union to bring parcels and to try and visit their prisoners. It was hard to tell whether they were just using the chance to show off their clothes, or whether their wardrobes simply did not contain anything more modest. Svetlov walked in amazement through the expensive furs and the smells of French cosmetics that mingled with the aroma of roast chicken, Finnish brisket, Dutch cheese, Arabian fruits, almond pastries, and other delicacies that the Butyrka had probably never sniffed before . . .

In the reception room of the 'Grandad', the deputy governor in charge of daily routine, Svetlov greeted the four women from outside who worked in the office and the records department. He flirted with each of them in turn, and in a few minutes had a file in his hand with the dossiers of Buryatsky's cell-mates: Shubankov, Trubny, Gruzilov, Chernykh, Peisachenko, and seven others. Svetlov laughed – the names of the best plants in the Butyrka were well known to him.

He casually asked the woman working in the office: 'Who's the senior one of these?'

'Gruzilov,' she said, and even gave his nickname – the 'Teacher'.

But Svetlov himself knew Gruzilov – he had three escapes from prisons and camps, including this same Butyrka, and sentences from seven courts amounting to a total term of seventy-two years to his credit. But for successful co-operation with the militia Vitaly Gruzilov had been a free man for six years; he was registered in Moscow, had settled down with a home and family, and the cells of the Butyrka prison were just his place of work. Whenever he met Svetlov they liked to talk about old times – how Gruzilov once eluded capture by Svetlov by escaping down the Moskva River during the Moscow Regatta . . .

'Where is he now,' asked Svetlov. 'It's quite a while since I've seen him.'

'Having breakfast. In the Investigation Block, Office Six.'

'And where's Grandad? Snegiryov?'

'Briefing the wardens. Telling them not to take bribes. The prisoners they've rounded up this time are offering a hundred roubles for a packet of cigarettes! And do you remember Safonov, the warden? He got caught! He was passing messages. Apparently he'd got five thousand for taking one message . . .'

'Hm, yes! You're having fun here. Right, I shall go and have a chat with the Teacher, and talk about old times. Give me a shout when Snegiryov is free.'

The Teacher was sitting having breakfast in a separate room – Investigation Office Six. Brought here supposedly for interrogation, he had made himself comfortable at the investigator's desk, and was munching away with relish on an abundant breakfast that was clearly not prison fare: cabbage and red caviare pies, chicken cutlets, juicy fritters in sour cream.

And he was glancing with even more relish at the strongly-built figure of the pretty Cossack girl who had brought him this breakfast from the officers' kitchen, and who reminded him of Aksinya in *Quiet Flows the Don*.

'Ah, Colonel! Greetings, my dear friend!' he greeted Svetlov. 'Another bandit's bullet got you in the arm? You'll just about make it! Sit down and have some breakfast with a grass, while you're still alive! Don't be shy! Lyuska, quick march to the kitchen! Bring whatever's left! And don't forget the Narzan! I don't drink Essentuki, I have an acid stomach. How many times have I told you, you fucking idiot!'

Darting a glance at the colonel out of her green lynx-eyes, and impudently twitching her backside, Lyuska obediently vanished through the door.

'A prisoner, or from outside?' asked Svetlov, following her out with his eyes.

'A lovely girl, eh? One of the prisoners. They've put her on remand. For good work. She's got such good results, especially with her backside, that she'll be going home altogether in a month. Except now you'll never get her back to normal mating. Have a word with your friend Snegiryov, he'll fix you up with her, he's not such a mean sod.'

'All right. I've come to you on business,' said Svetlov, and asked point-blank: 'Have they cracked Buryatsky yet?'

The Teacher put his fork down, looked intently at Svetlov. and said cautiously: 'That little question is not in the book of rules, Chief . . .'

'Of course it's not,' replied Svetlov calmly. 'And assaulting and murdering a six-year-old boy – is that in the rule-book?'

The Teacher clenched his fist, brought it crashing down on the table, and shouted at the top of his voice: 'That's enough! Why the fuck do they try to pin someone else's crime on me? They've been trying to hang that one on me for seven years! But they haven't made it stick! They're not your sort. I'm going to write to the Minister, Nikolai Anisimovich!' White spots appeared on his red cheeks as he spoke, a true sign that the Teacher had taken fright. And he had reason to – eight years ago the residents of Komsomolsky Prospect were shocked by an incident involving a six-year-old boy called Kostya Zuyev, who had been found in a rubbish-bin behind a fish shop. The boy was dead, naked, and had been viciously sexually assaulted.

'Quiet,' Svetlov said to the Teacher. 'Why are you making all this song and dance? I'm not trying to pin anything on you. I was not concerned with the case at the time. But if you start shouting – I shall concern myself. There is no amnesty yet for the man who did that. The prescription's still in force.'

'I'm not afraid!' said the Teacher, calming down, and he angrily waved away a fly that was buzzing round his breakfast: 'The swine! They're breeding flies in the prison! Flies – in January! What do you want to know?'

'Well, something else,' said Svetlov. 'I need to know all the instructions Krasnov or Baklanov gave you for this Buryatsky.'

'Buryatsky!' said the Teacher contemptuously. 'And it's for such filth you're threatening me with that case, Marat Alekseyevich?'

'You're the one who blew your top. I asked you as man to man, and you start throwing the rule-book at me.'

'You're right, of course,' agreed Teacher reasonably. 'Well, the first instruction was to break this artist down, make him shit in his pants. Well, that's kid's stuff for us, as you know. We put on such a show for him yesterday as soon as he got here! Made out we were all murderers and queers. By night he was already crying on the investigator's shoulders and was ready for anything, but so long as they would transfer him to another cell. It's obvious – an artist, weak psyche, he cracked up. Then Chernykh started to milk him. He had different instructions: to take this artist and pretend to protect him from us, then squeeze him for every detail. Especially about his friendship with Tsvigun. And hiding-places – where Tsvigun might have certain tapes hidden away. Well, he's easy to squeeze. He stays awake all night, afraid we're going to give him a gang-bang. But he knows fuck all about the tapes, that's certain.'

'And is that all?'

'In our line – yes.'

'What do you mean – in your line?'

'Well, we did our job – he's not a man any more. We told him so many lies about camps and torture that he'd sign his own mother's death-warrant to get out of it, let alone take responsibility for a hit-job.'

'So they're trying to pin a killing on him?'

'I never said that! Colonel!' said the Teacher reproachfully. 'I'm no sucker. You came just to get that out of me. Grandad may be your friend, but he'll never tell you who they're trying to pin a killing on, especially one like that! So now you're in my debt.'

'But you haven't told me anything yet,' laughed Svetlov.

'That's good. I told you nothing, and you understood everything. If they're going to collect professors and Teachers from the whole Butyrka for the sake of two men . . .'

'Two?' said Svetlov in amazement.'Why two? One! Buryatsky. Who else is there?'

'His little friend is sitting in cell 503; he also knocked around with Tsvigun – Sandro Katauri. A different bunch is working on him, as insurance. If one lets them down, they've got the other in reserve. Like astronauts – they have doubles. Unless they're both going to appear together, I don't know, the authorities will decide that one . . .'

'And at Tsvigun's place there was a Sveta playing cards with them too, red-haired, about forty. Who was she?'

'Search me, I don't know. I'm not lying, cross my heart! I don't know. I didn't have any instruction to squeeze him on any Sveta. Maybe Chernykh did, but he won't tell, he deals directly with the authorities. Well, where's that tart Lyuska? My tea's cold.'

Svetlov got up – he had found everything that interested us. On the way back he once again caught the aroma of roast tabaka chicken, home-made

152

pies, and other delicacies in the parcel-reception-room and thought how, by the irony of fate, the greater part of these victuals would go, not to those for whom they had been brought, but to the crackers, grasses, and plants who were sharing their cells.

10.17 a.m.

Taras Karpovich Vendelovsky was a small, wizened old man of seventy-two who stubbornly refused to retire, and his office was a reflection of the man himself – piled high with old, yellowing folders, legal codes, directives, a coffee-machine, a teapot, doughnuts, felt boots with rubber galoshes standing in the corner, a bottle of yoghurt, processed cheeses, and some other packages between the windows, and an electric fire glowing orange at his feet, which Vendelovsky used to plug in illegally, behind the backs of our bursar and safety officer.

'Shamrayev – outside call!' came over the intercom. 'Igor Iosifovich, pick up the outside phone! You've a call from the Forensic Institute.'

I gasped inwardly – could it be Sorokin? Had he changed his mind?

I picked up the receiver and said cautiously: 'Hello?'

'Hi!' said the cheerful voice of Alla Sorokina. 'It's impossible to reach you in your office! Where have you been? Running after women, or something?'

I said nothing – her voice sounded oddly cheerful, just as though I had never quarrelled with Sorokin that morning.

'Listen, are you interested in the results of the biologists' tests on the bullet or aren't you? You were yelling at us that it was so urgent, and then you don't even ring!'

I caught my breath – of course! Sorokin himself refused to take the risk of ringing, but he told his wife about my request, and she . . . good girl!

'Of course I'm interested!' I said with a slight catch in my voice; I still didn't know the results of Svetlov's expedition to the Butyrka prison.

'Only remember: it's strictly secret!' Alla began acting it up, not for me, but for the third person who was listening in to our conversation. 'I'm not supposed to divulge the results of a test until the report's been signed.'

'OK, cut the cackle! Give us the goods!' I said, playing along with her.

'Anyway, I happened to see out of the corner of my eye that the blood-groups didn't coincide. The dead man was group II, and the bullet had traces of group I. That means he didn't die from that bullet! Can you imagine?'

'Got it,' I said. 'When will they have the report ready?'

'Well, you know how long things take over here. First it's written out by hand, then it's sent for typing, then everyone has to sign it. Don't expect it before lunch. That's why I'm ringing you.'

'Thanks! Kiss on both cheeks!'

'At least!' she laughed.

'Alla, remind Sorokin to send the ballistics men over to 16-A, Kachalov Street, I put in a request on Friday, together with inventories . . .'

'OK, I'll tell him. Cheers!'

I listened to the dialling tone and carefully replaced the receiver. Ha! Good old Alla! The most she risked if the KGB really were listening in was an official reprimand. And even then, for what? So, she confused the numbers I and II – that could happen to anyone. And she rang Shamrayev because he ordered her to – after all, he's working under special instructions from Brezhnev. He has a document to say that all organizations are obliged to help him . . . So, relax. What's the first thing to be done? Of course, pretend I'm really excited by this fact! And so . . .

I dialled Andropov's reception-room: 'Chairman's reception-room,' a dry male voice replied immediately.

'Good morning. This is the Public Prosecutor's Office. Special Investigator Shamrayev speaking. I need an urgent meeting with Comrade Andropov.'

'On what matter?'

'I am conducting the case on the death of Semyon Kuzmich, and I have something of extreme importance to communicate.'

'All right. When Yury Vladimirovich sets a time we'll get back to you.'

Oh, I didn't doubt it! If they need someone they find him. I dialled the Third Section of CID and heard Nina's voice: 'Hello, Third Section.'

'Take this telegram please,' I began, trying to alter my voice. 'For outstanding services Nina Makarycheva is awarded the Order of Hero of the Soviet Union.'

'Oh! It's you! And I actually began to take it down in the telegram-book. Now, thanks to you I've got to cross it out!'

'No need to cross it out. Take down: "To Captain Laskin, One: request you go to the Forensic Institute at eleven o'clock to expedite report on the blood-groups. Two: for outstanding services Nina Makarycheva . . ."'

'There you go again!' she said, annoyed. 'Shall we have lunch together?'

'I don't know. I'll ring you. Bye!' I put down the receiver and settled back comfortably in the armchair opposite Taras Karpovich Vendelovsky – now I could sit listening to his story about the fire in the Rossiya Hotel.

He launched himself eagerly into his account. 'That fire did not start by accident. Now that both Tsvigun and Paputin are gone I can tell you – it was not a fire, it was a war between them, between Tsvigun and Paputin. I don't know how and when Paputin received permission to create a new Internal Intelligence Section within the MVD. I only know the following facts: from the end of 1975 the entire tenth floor of the west wing of the Rossiya Hotel was taken over by the new Intelligence Section of the MVD. There they set up their own operations headquarters and installed the very newest listening and surveillance equipment – they brought it from Japan, America, and even got some in Israel. The rumour was that Suslov helped them with the equipment; I didn't check this rumour, but I saw the equipment with my own eyes, and even made use of it when I was conducting the affair of the Uzbek drug-traders: the lads from Intelligence helped track down the leader of the gang. Well, when I was sitting with them on the tenth floor I realized what they were up to – they were like a Gestapo within the MVD. They had set up a surveillance of all Party and State leaders, they had dossiers on everyone that was in any way close to the government. I even saw my own file, they showed it to me themselves since it had the letters "N.D." on it, i.e. "Not Dangerous". In other words, a second KGB! And where? In the Rossiya, which as you know has always been the KGB's turf, where one spy spies on another and threatens him with a third! The director of the hotel, Nikiforov, is an ex-general in the KGB, and they won't even hire a cleaner without KGB clearance. Naturally! The Rossiya is full of foreigners, you've got to keep an eye on them. But besides foreigners many of our people stay there too – leaders, artists, scientists from all the republics – and all sorts of operators, underground millionaires. In other words all the riff-raff that Cascade is mopping up right now. It's finally coming out that they were all under Tsvigun's protection, but at that time I had to dig it out for myself. Anyway, a couple of months after the fire I realized that the Rossiya was not only KGB turf, but also a hornets' nest of unofficial business. For instance, Rakhimov, a so-called "timber procurements official", arrives from Central Asia and immediately takes eight de-luxe rooms in the Rossiya. Every day he gives receptions in these rooms, or to put it simply – booze-ups. And these booze-ups were attended by just about the whole State Planning Commission, the Forestry Ministry, the Transport Ministry, and even Galina Leonidovna Brezhneva herself with her uncle Yakov Ilyich, Leonid Ilyich's brother. And after these "receptions" whole trainloads of scarce saw-timber roll out to Central Asia, where it goes on to the unofficial market at speculative prices, and all parties to the operation earn a million each. Or another example, about that black caviare which was going to the West illegally in cans labelled "Herring" or "Sprats". Where did that all begin? In the Rossiya – eight years ago our operators met up with their opposite numbers from the West right there and fixed up that whole underground operation. In other words, the Rossiya is not just for international film festivals, it was also the headquarters of the unofficial economy and the central point of contact between our underground businessmen and the western traders. The deals that were done there! In gold, furs, diamonds, icons, even imported contraceptive pills! Well, part of these operations the KGB exposes – if they don't receive their cut. But the rest – you can guess . . . And it's that very hornets' nest that Paputin wades into with his new Intelligence Section. So? Two forces, a clash.

'Well, in May '76 Paputin moves against a really big diamond speculator, the wife of Mzhavanadze, former First Secretary of the Georgian Central Committee. By this time Mzhavanadze had already been removed, and if Brezhnev hadn't interceded for him the Georgian security men would have just put him behind bars. And I should think so too! When Shevarnadze, the Chairman of the Georgian KGB, ordered a search of this Mzhavanadze's apartment in Tbilisi, he found gold ingots in the shape of pigs, cows and other animals weighing five or six kilos apiece! So First Secretary of the

155

Central Committee is a very profitable post, as you can see. I just mention that in passing. Even so, the main valuables escaped Shevarnadze – Mzhavanadze's wife managed to flee to Moscow with a suitcase of diamonds and moved in with none other than her friend Galina Brezhneva. And her husband, Vasily Mzhavanadze, lives at Brezhnev's brother Yakov's *dacha* outside Moscow. Now try to touch them! What does Shevarnadze do? Grabs their son in Tbilisi, holds him in prison as a hostage, and pins a case of illegal hunting in a State park on him. He also sends a brigade of Georgian detectives to Moscow to catch Mzhavanadze's wife red-handed in her contacts with diamond speculators. So these Georgians sit day after day in the Rossiya, in Intelligence Headquarters, watching this Mzhavanadze but unable to pick her up, because she never goes out without Galina; wherever she goes, it's always arm in arm with Galina. I remember them cursing about that, Georgians cursing in perfect Russian! But they did hook a few contacts, and as I recall, Intelligence helped them a lot, and they helped Intelligence. And I think it was all up for Mzhavanadze, they were just about to pick her up; and she would have brought with her whole mafias of course, right up to Tsvigun, Galya Brezhneva, and above, exactly like in Cascade right now. But the fire ruined everything. At dawn on 25 May a fire of incredible intensity broke out on the ninth floor of the hotel's west wing, right under-neath the tenth-floor rooms where Intelligence had its operational head-quarters. And it just so happened that at the time the fire-fighting system in the west wing was switched off for repairs, while all the fire-engines with ladders reaching above the seventh floor had been sent from the Moscow Fire Department depot to Serpukhov on summer exercises, an hour away from Moscow. How's that for coincidence? Well, while the firemen were unwinding their hoses and dragging them up through the Rossiya, which took forty minutes, three whole floors had been destroyed – the ninth, tenth, and eleventh. All the Intelligence Section's equipment had perished, includ-ing their card filing systems, surveillance equipment and also fourteen people from the Georgian Interior Ministry and Moscow Intelligence who were on duty that night. Apart from that, twenty-seven foreigners died in the fire, and seventy-one people received burns and injuries. There was a meeting of the Politburo in connection with the foreign deaths, the director of the hotel was immediately sacked, and the Prosecutor's Office was given the job of investigation, a job that Rudenko dumped on me. Well, it's all part of our job, as you know.

'I began digging around – why wasn't the fire-fighting system working? Sure enough, it was being repaired. Why were all the fire-engines with long ladders in Serpukhov? Sure enough, they were doing exercises. But you know I'm like a mole. In a couple of months I knew every floor lady in the Rossiya, not only by name, but when and from which guests they had taken bribes in exchange for letting them keep a girl in their room after eleven. Anyway, I finally found out that the day before the fire broke out some carpet-cleaners had been on the ninth floor of the west wing in the very

156

rooms where the fire had broken out. Well, they cleaned the carpets on the floor – that's quite normal. The hitch was that those particular cleaners – one described by the floor lady as a Georgian of about thirty, the other a Russian, but dark-haired – were not on the staff of the Rossiya Hotel. All right, I burrow further, like a mole. I question one floor lady after another. What were they carrying, I ask, how were they dressed? And then one of them recalls that on the Georgian's trolley, apart from a vacuum-cleaner and various brushes, there was a sort of large metal tin, like a small barrel, only with a handle. And when they were leaving, he was carrying this tin in his hand and swinging it around, and the buffet lady Dusya said to him: "Let me have that tin, dearie, I have a rubber plant at home that's suffocating in its pot." And he says to her: "No way, mum, that's government property, needed for the job," and then five minutes later he chucked it into the garbage himself. Well Dusya's no fool – she apparently went and got the tin and took it home with her. Only the rubber plant was still suffocating.

'Well, you can understand that in twenty minutes I was at that Dusya's place. And I carried off the tin, together with its rubber plant, straight to the Forensic Institute. And a few days later the chemists gave me their findings, that the tin had contained "Delayed Action Inflammable Liquid – DAIL-12". That is, the liquid ignites twelve hours after coming into contact with fabric, wood, or plastic. Fine, I began looking for who issues this liquid, and came to the Ministry of Defence's "PO Box 41" in Baku. And there in the sales department I found the following entry in the accounts book: "17 January, by personal order of Comrade Geidar Aliyev, fourteen litres of DAIL-12 issued." I ask: who was it delivered to? They don't remember exactly, they say: he looked like a Georgian. Well, I wasn't going to start questioning Geidar Aliyev – you understand, I'm not such an idiot that I would question the First Secretary of the Azerbaidzhan Central Committee, who moreover was until recently Chairman of the Azerbaidzhan KGB! He wouldn't have let me out of Baku alive! No, I quietly slipped home to Moscow and started looking for the Georgian and the dark-haired Russian, but . . . just then Roman Andreyevich Rudenko called me in and told me to hand all my investigative materials over to the KGB. Tsvigun had got Brezhnev to have him entrusted with finishing the investigation. Well, the late Rudenko and I quietly burned everything in the file that concerned the liquid DAIL-12 in his office. Otherwise I would have long since been "late" myself. Geidar Aliyev, in case you didn't know, was a close friend of Tsvigun, and it doesn't take long to guess who the liquid was issued to and why Operational Headquarters of MVD Intelligence went up in flames. Right after that fire Mzhavanadze's wife got a military aircraft from Ustinov and flew to Tbilisi accompanied by ten colonels of the General Staff. There they released her son and got back the gold cows and pigs that had been confiscated from her. And at that point the whole affair died down . . .'

10.55 a.m.

'Personal delivery for Shamrayev! Igor Iosifovich, go down for your mail!' Once again my name sounded over the intercom.

'You're really in demand today,' observed Vendelovsky. I left his office and went down to the Reception Centre. Rekunkov's assistant on duty handed me an envelope.

SECRET
URGENT

To: Com. I.I. Shamrayev, Special Investigator at the Public Prosecutor's Office of the USSR, by special messenger

In connection with the operation on 24/1/82 for the capture of the dangerous criminal A.I. Vorotnikov, alias 'Korchagin', of which you were in charge, I request you to oblige the members of your force, M. Svetlov, E. Arutyunov, and P. Kolganov to submit without delay to the Special Personnel Inspectorate of the MVD reports explaining the reasons for the use by them of firearms exceeding the limits of essential self-defence, which led to the death of the criminal.

P.M. Lubachov, Major-General of Militia,
Head of MVD Special Personnel Inspectorate

Moscow, 25 January 1982

I crumpled up the letter and was about to throw it into the waste-paper basket, but changed my mind, sat down at my typewriter, inserted a Prosecutor's Office blank into it, and typed out:

URGENT
SECRET

To: Com. P.M. Lubachov, Major-General of Militia
Head of MVD Special Personnel Inspectorate, by special messenger

Dear Pavel Mikhailovich,

During the operation for the arrest of A. Vorotnikov, alias 'Korchagin', the force under my command were obliged to use their weapons only because Colonel Oleinik, Deputy Head of MVD Intelligence, ineptly organized the ambush to catch the criminal.

I request that you set the investigation of the operation for mid- or late February.

Respectfully,
I. Shamrayev.

Moscow, 25 January 1982

'Quite right, too,' said Svetlov's voice above my head. 'I'll really rub their noses in it at the investigation!'

I raised my head. Svetlov, his hand in bandages, was standing behind me with his coat over his shoulders. Snowflakes melted on the epaulets.

158

'Well? What happened at the Butyrka?' I asked quietly.

But Svetlov had no time to answer: the assistant on duty handed me the telephone and said: 'For you again, Igor Iosifovich.'

'This is Captain Laskin,' came from the receiver. 'I'm ringing from the Forensic Institute. Unfortunately, Igor Iosifovich, it is not possible to get the report of the blood-group test now.'

'Why not?'

'Colonel Malenina of the Anti-Fraud Squad sealed the biology lab half an hour ago and is doing an inspection of all chemicals. So it's impossible to get a single scrap of paper.'

I laughed. 'Cinderella's Trap' had worked – now I knew the people who killed Tsvigun. I didn't suppose, or guess, or construct hypotheses; I knew: he had been killed by those who heard my telephone conversation with Alla Sorokina and decided the biological experts had gone off their heads. After all, murderers know their own blood-group well enough!

'Fine,' I told Laskin. 'Go back to CID,' and I turned to Svetlov: 'Marat, if you have photos of all the Georgians Tsvigun was friendly with, I'll tell you who set fire to the Rossiya Hotel in '76.'

'Unfortunately his very closest Georgian friends are vanishing one after the other,' he laughed. 'The Finance Minister of Georgia, Bagrat Ananiashvili, was jailed a week ago; the meat-king Nukzar Baratashvili I personally arrested in Sochi; the painter Sandro Katauri, with whom Tsvigun used to play cards, is already in the Butyrka too; and a certain Givi Mingadze has disappeared altogether from the memory of the MVD computer and the Records Office of the Central Address Bureau.'

'What?' I exclaimed in amazement.

'Just imagine,' he said. 'Yesterday, when I poked my nose in at the Computing Centre looking for data on this Mingadze, I was told that the computer had broken down, and today I nipped in there again on my way back from the Butyrka and saw that right after the name "Mingabov" the computer had "Mingadyan". And the same thing in the Central Address Bureau. And "Mingadze" seems to have gone down with the bath-water! I get the impression that someone's running along ahead of us pulling out Tsvigun's whole bunch under our very noses. The only one left is a certain "Sveta", but I'm afraid even to say her name aloud by now.'

11.25 a.m.

What do you think, where can you find a hard-currency prostitute at eleven in the morning in Moscow? And not just one, but thirty? I'll give you three guesses.

Driving along the snowy boulevard of Patriarch's Ponds, the driver of Svetlov's Volga turned into a small side street, and we found ourselves in front of a high stone wall with a sign on it: 'Clinic Number Seven for Skin Infections and Venereal Disease'. Next to the main gateway was a small gate, and Svetlov and I went into the courtyard. Here we caught the sound of

159

happy female squeals: several young girls in grey hospital gowns were having a snowball fight, and three others were laboriously building a huge snowman. Seeing us, they squealed even louder, someone shouted, 'Hey, girls, look who's come!' someone threw a snowball at us, and someone else greeted Svetlov: 'Hey, Marat Alekseyevich!' while the youngest, a kid of about fifteen, ran up and tugged him by the coat: 'Colonel, let's go behind the bushes! I'm clean already, or I fucking will be soon!'

'You will be but you're not yet,' Svetlov said to her.

We entered the clinic and the duty nurse issued us with white gowns which we had to put on over our suits, then she led us down corridors smelling of carbolic to the office of the head doctor, Lev Aronovich Goldberg, a fat, pot-bellied old man of about seventy with a pince-nez that was attached to the collar of his doctor's gown by a little gold chain. We explained to Goldberg why we had come, and he asked: 'And how did you find out that the batch you are looking for is being treated at this clinic?'

'From the card index of our Whores' Section at CID,' said Svetlov, and laid before him several cards that had been extracted that morning. 'Look, it says here: "1979, sent to VD Clinic Number Seven". And here – same thing, and here . . . Then these girls moved to the KGB, but they couldn't change their clinic: people don't like changing doctors, especially those who have cured them even once. And especially VD doctors!'

'It makes sense,' laughed Goldberg. 'I do indeed have a branch of your Whores' Section, as you like to call it. And that's not all – these girls bring their friends too, KGB girls who I am not obliged to treat at all. They have their own hospital at the KGB. But we treat them, what else can you do? Otherwise they carry gonorrhoea round Moscow for months. It's not too bad right now, in the winter, but in the summer it's an epidemic. Sometimes Arabs bring the virus, sometimes Cubans . . . Do you want to question them all together, or singly?'

Svetlov and I shared them out; Goldberg let us use his office and the house-surgeon's room, and following his instructions the duty nurse began bringing us the clinic's batch of whores. The very first patient gave me a shock. A tall, tough twenty-year-old walked into the house-surgeon's office, efficiently shed her hospital gown and panties and, naked as the day she was born, sat herself down in the gynaecological chair, throwing her long legs wide apart.

I looked her in the eye, dumbfounded, and she said: 'Well, what are you staring at my eyes for? I don't have gonorrhoea in the eyes. Have a look down there.'

Only then did I realize that I was wearing a white doctor's gown, so I took it off and said curtly: 'Get dressed. I am an investigator from the Prosecutor's Office, I need to ask you a few questions.'

Without even blushing she calmly got up from the chair, put on her panties and gown, and sat down at the desk opposite me. With her chin propped on her fist, she said innocently: 'Right. Go ahead, Comrade Investigator.'

I saw a sparkle of laughter in her eyes, and then heard a loud female guffaw outside the door.

Nevertheless, thirty minutes later, having questioned only half the batch, Svetlov and I already had data on four thin, red-haired, forty-year-old Svetas, who could have had their own Lada and who could have supplied Tsvigun with hard-currency girls: Svetlana Arkadyevna, manageress of the Budapest Hotel; Svetlana Antonovna, the madam of a secret brothel at 217, Peace Prospect, Apartment 67; Svetlana Nikolayevna, gynaecologist at the first-aid post in the Ukraina Hotel; and Svetlana Frantsevna, in charge of the women's cosmetics section of GUM. When the next patient, balancing the hospital slipper on the end of her toe, began recollecting another Svetlana, the driver of Svetlov's car walked into the house-surgeon's room, and said: 'Comrade Investigator, Investigator Baklanov is ringing you over the radio-telephone. He wants you to take the call.'

On the way to the car I looked into the head doctor's room and said to Svetlov: 'Have you heard? Baklanov's on the phone! It looks as if Buryatsky has already "confessed" to the murder of Tsvigun!'

'Or Sandro Katauri,' he said.

12.57 p.m.
DOCUMENT OF SPECIAL PARTY IMPORTANCE
TOP SECRET

Typed in 5 (five) copies
To: The Presidium of the Plenary Session, CPSU Central Committee,
Summary of the Results of Operation Cascade

During the course of 1981-2 on the instructions of Com. M.A. Suslov, Secretary of the CPSU Central Committee, the Intelligence Section and Anti-Fraud Squad of the MVD conducted the investigative Operation Cascade with the purpose of exposing corruption and the links between persons in authority and underground operators – representatives of the so-called 'unofficial' economy.

As a result of the operation it was established that: over the last ten years economic formations of the unofficial economy, the activities of which have involved thousands of people, have been functioning in various spheres of our industry, agriculture, services, and bodies responsible for culture, education, and sport.

The economic activity of these formations may be expressed in the following figures.

The total profits of underground economic and administrative mafias for 1981 alone amounted to 25 billion (25 thousand million) roubles. Moreover, bribes received by various persons in authority for co-operating with the illegal activities of these organizations amounted to 42 million roubles, from which the highest leaders of the Administration received cuts as follows:

S. Tsvigun, First Deputy Chairman of the KGB:	3,420,000 roubles
A. Shibayev, Chairman of the All-Union Central Soviet of Trades Unions:	1,760,000 roubles
A. Ishkov, Minister for Fisheries:	6,312,000 roubles
N. Mokhov, First Deputy Minister of Culture:	2,980,000 roubles

The remaining 28 million roubles were received by workers in the higher and medium echelons of party, government, and administrative organizations in the form of direct bribes, presentations, and valuable gifts.

A total of 1,507 leaders of the 'unofficial economy' have been arrested in Operation Cascade; they are all being held in investigative solitary confinement cells in Moscow and will appear before the courts in the near future.

In the course of the operation numerous links were discovered between operators of the 'unofficial economy' and members of the family of Comrade Leonid Ilyich Brezhnev, Secretary General of the CPSU Central Committee. According to the most conservative estimates, members of the Brezhnev family were given, in the form of direct bribes, gifts, and presentations of valuables, furs, antiquities, and museum exhibits, amounts as follows:

Galina Brezhneva-Churbanova:	to the value of 2.7 million roubles
Yury Leonidovich Brezhnev:	to the value of 3.2 million roubles
Yakov Ilyich Brezhnev:	to the value of 1.8 million roubles
Semyon Kuzmich Tsvigun:	to the value of 3.4 million roubles

In return for this the above-named persons afforded those involved in the underground unofficial economy protection in various ministries and authorities and helped them to obtain high positions and also to procure extraordinary deliveries from reserve supplies of raw materials, heavy equipment, and machinery in short supply.

217 leaders of the unofficial economy arrested in Operation Cascade testified that to achieve their criminal aims they entered into direct contact with Galina Leonidovna Brezhneva, Yury Leonidovich Brezhnev, and Yakov Ilyich Brezhnev, and a further 302 persons testified that they were acting through the mediation of Boris Buryatsky, Sandro Katauri, A. Kolevatov, and others.

The fact that all the closest relatives of Com. L.I. Brezhnev are giving assistance to criminal elements and thus contributing to the collapse of the planned Soviet economy, while some of them, notably Galina Brezhneva, are leading an openly immoral life – all this reflects unfavourably on the authority of Com. L.I. Brezhnev as Head of the Soviet State and on the prestige of the Communist Party and the Soviet Government.

Appendix: Materials on Operation Cascade – interrogation protocols, reports of confrontations, reports of candid confessions of 1,507 accused, and evidence of 3,788 witnesses in 32 volumes and 6,383 pages.

Signed
Leaders in command of Operation Cascade:

But there were no signatures at the foot of the document, and Baklanov, holding out his hand for the paper, said: 'There are no signatures yet, but there will be.'

He took the document from me, placed it carefully in a bulging leatherette folder, and put the folder away in his briefcase. Then, pouring us a glass of wine, he continued: 'Let's be blunt, it's a rare document. Even the members of the Politburo haven't read it yet. And you of course are wondering why I am showing it to you and why I have invited you to this restaurant at all. Right?'

Indeed, for Baklanov, who was such a skinflint that he rarely even paid for his own beer, it was very extravagant to seek me out through CID and then over the radio invite me to lunch at the best Caucasian restaurant in Moscow – the Aragvi. And here we were sitting in a private suite, and on the table was a bottle of twelve-year-old Armenian brandy, hot sulguni cheese, aromatic roast chicken in *satsivi* sauce, lobio beans, Caucasian green vegetables, fresh tomatoes (in January!), and fine Georgian wine. And in the main room, through the wall of our separate suite, a party of Caucasian traders that had not yet been picked up by Cascade were celebrating: 'To Suliko! Ha-ha-ha! Such a clever fellow! Made a hundred thousand in a week by bringing two hundred crates of flowers in through Vnukovo Airport!'

Baklanov put the bottle on the table and said: 'You don't believe I invited you here purely out of friendship. But I did! Bear in mind – we're playing for high stakes, very high! But in this sort of game pawns like you and me are the first to go.'

Through the wall another extravagant toast was drunk to Papa Suliko who had produced such an amazingly talented son . . .

Baklanov frowned: 'You see what's happening? The people are used to stealing. In one Georgian film this man says quite openly to his neighbour: "How do you survive? There's nothing to steal at your factory except compressed air!" And even if you jail three million of them it won't help, because the rot starts at the top. Now do you see which team you're playing for? Every two months Brezhnev puts out a rumour that he's at death's door, hardly breathing, and nobody touches him. They all wait . . . for years! Meanwhile this ruling family has created a vast unofficial industry in the country, something like a second New Economic Policy. Every crook is making a hundred thousand a week, and because of all this shit you and I have almost become enemies. But we need to unite, old man, unite and bring the country back to health. So that we have people in power with clean hands.'

'Hands or fists?' I asked.

Baklanov stopped dead, and the *shashlyk* he was holding in his hand froze in the air. 'What do you mean?' he asked.

'Kolya,' I said. 'If you're so clean, why are you afraid of me?'

'Where did you get that idea?'

'Quite simple. This is the second time you have tried to persuade me to get out of this case. On Saturday you put an obvious tail on me and you've been bugging my telephone. And now you even reached me by radio.'

He put the *shashlyk* on the plate, wiped his hands with his napkin, and spoke: 'All right. You honestly don't understand. So I'll tell you: you're not getting in our way at the moment, but you soon will be. Because you're like a tank – you push straight through obstacles, and the only thing that will stop you is a shell. A direct hit.'

We looked each other in the eye, and there was a long drawn-out pause.

'Kolya,' I said, 'about this direct hit – what's that meant to be? A warning?'

'You're mad! I meant it figuratively!' he exclaimed with exaggerated heat and immediately lowered his eyes, starting on his *shashlyk*. 'It's just that as a friend I'm asking you for the last time: this game is for high stakes, and if you have any cards we could make first-class partners. I'll slip you such an ace of spades that it'll take your breath away! And if you play that ace I guarantee everything will have changed in a week. Well, you won't make it to Public Prosecutor perhaps, because of your background, but you'll get Karakoz's job. And you're going on about "direct hits"! I suppose if a brick falls on your head tomorrow it'll be my fault?'

He went on to say some other things about our work together and got quite carried away, waving his *shashlyk* in the air as he painted bright prospects for the future, but I hardly heard him. I realized what he was offering me. If I said yes now and made a deal with him, they would hand me over Tsvigun's 'murderer', perhaps today – Boris Buryatsky, the lover of Brezhnev's daughter. And I, the 'unbiased' investigator appointed by Brezhnev, would secure a 'candid confession' from Buryatsky. And then at the Politburo meeting on 4 February, apart from the Cascade materials, they would also have a killing to hold against the Head of State's family. Nice? And if I said no – I could receive a direct hit on the head tomorrow from an 'accidental' brick. It was a game for high stakes in which Tsvigun had already been got rid of and Galina Brezhneva was being openly interrogated, so what could it cost them to finish me off if I really began to get in their way?

I rose. 'Thanks, Kolya. If you're warning me off your own bat, thanks, and if someone else authorized you do it, tell them I'll think about it. Most likely I'll say to hell with all of you – you, Tsvigun, and Brezhnev. And I'll start bringing flowers up from the Caucasus – there's more money in that.' And I pulled about fifty roubles out of my pocket and put it on the table, dismissing Baklanov's half-hearted attempt to protest: 'This is from the future flower-speculator to the future Public Prosecutor, settle up for lunch with it.'

He took the money, and I laughed to myself: when they came to power they would be taking bribes just like this one today, or even bigger . . .

2.50 p.m.

I walked out of the restaurant to Sovetskaya Square. Hungry pigeons, cooing loudly, walked about under the snow-covered statue of Prince Yury Dolgoruky, the founder of Moscow. An old woman, looking like a beggar herself, was throwing them handfuls of breadcrumbs, but a flock of sparrows flew down before the pigeons could get there and pecked the crumbs out of the deep, fresh snow.

I stood there, wondering where to go. To the right of the square was Pushkin Street and the Prosecutor's Office, but what was the point of my going there now?

I set off to the left towards Gorky Street, crunching the snow with my boots. Pedestrians were streaming along it, and I felt drawn towards ordinary people who didn't have all these Kremlin intrigues and passions. Of course, the simple realization that I had funked it soured my soul with a bitter after-taste. I had funked it precisely when it was clear that Tsvigun had not been killed accidentally, and when Baklanov himself had admitted that I was "about to get in their way", in other words, unlock the mystery of this crime. On the other hand, if I proved who killed Tsvigun and who was plotting against Brezhnev, the most I could expect would be promotion to Senior Investigator and a rise of sixty roubles a month. Was it worth risking my life for those sixty roubles? And anyway, why risk my life at all? Why risk losing this clean snow, the cooing pigeons, Gorky Street, and the smell of those oranges they were queueing for outside Yeliseyev's? What difference would it make to me whether Brezhnev survived or whether on 4 February he was charged with ruining the economy and condoning bribery and corruption. What the hell if the Red Square parades were taken, not by him, but by Suslov, Kirilenko, Gorbachov, Andropov, Grishin, or Romanov? Would they take away my son, my Ninas, the crunch of snow underfoot, the chilling glance of that passing blonde on Pushkin Square, and that crazy ice-cream seller in the white coat who stamped his felt boots and shouted in the midst of all this snow: 'I-i-ce-crea----m! The iciest ice-cream in the world!'

I crossed Pushkin Square and opened the door of the International Telegraph building. This tiny branch of the Central Telegraph appeared here five years ago, at the height of the Jewish emigration, in order to separate those ringing abroad from the rest of the public. Too many people were phoning abroad these days: to the USA, Austria, Italy, and Israel, and it was demoralizing the general public. Whereas in this small International Telegraph on Pushkin Square only present and future emigrés heard each other. I entered this cramped building with its five kiosks and immediately heard in one of them a loud female voice with an indestructible Jewish accent: 'Monya, I've got it! I've got permission! I'm coming out in ten days!

What? No, they don't give you a month to get ready any longer, forget it! Now they give you ten days, and then – scram! But I'm happy. I only waited sixteen months for permission, but the Gureviches have been waiting for two years already! But no more for now! I'll be with you in ten days!'

I had the impression the woman in the kiosk was crying with happiness, and I almost envied her.

From another kiosk I could hear a clear male voice dictating: 'Zaferman, Yevsei Ivanovich, send invitation to 6, Pirogov Street, Moscow; Kapustin, Oleg Yakovlevich, invitation to Shevchenko Embankment.'

I went up to the telegraphist's counter and suddenly thought: why not ask that nut to get me an invitation from Israel too? That would solve all my problems at once: they would chuck me out of the Prosecutor's Office, take away the Tsvigun case, and I really would be left selling flowers at the Collective Farm Market. But the telegraphist was already speaking sternly into the microphone that was attached to her earphones and sticking up in front of her lips: 'Citizen, your time is up! I am disconnecting you!'

A red beard was thrust out of the kiosk and a young man said: 'You have no right to do that, I still have four minutes! I paid!'

I picked up a telegraph form and, with my elbows on the counter, wrote:

TOP SECRET

To Herman Karakoz Head of Investigation Section Public Prosecutors Office of the USSR 15A Pushkin Street Moscow
AM FLYING SOUTH URGENTLY TO FINISH SCREWING GIRLS REQUEST YOU RELIEVE ME OF PRESENT POST AND IN GENERAL YOU CAN ALL GO AND TAKE A RUNNING JUMP
SHAMRAYEV

I wondered what other rude things I should add to the text, but decided that these three lines were certainly enough to get me sacked – I didn't even need an invitation from Israel. But the telegraphist, reading the text, flung the cable back at me nervously: 'I won't accept a telegram like that!'

'Why not?'

'It's hooliganism, not a telegram! One sends rude telegrams to the Prosecutor's Office, another dictates addresses to Israel! Hey, you, red-head, leave the kiosk.'

'I won't come out until you connect me!' came the reply. 'I still have four minutes!'

'And I shall call the militia! With no more Stalin breathing down your necks you've all got completely out of hand. And there's no one to lock you up. God, when will you all clear off to Israel?!' She looked at me and repeated: 'I told you, I'm not taking that telegram, get out of here!'

'You will take the telegram,' I said in quiet rage. I laid before her my red identity card from the Prosecutor's Office and my second mandate – the personal headed sheet from Brezhnev, saying that all bodies in the land had to carry out my demands since I was on a government assignment.

Seeing this document with Brezhnev's personal signature, the telegraphist went numb, quickly counted up the words, and choked out: 'An ordinary telegram, or urgent?'

'First connect that man, let him finish his four minutes,' I said.

She obediently rattled the receiver cradle, to get through to the Central Telegraph: 'Operator! Give me Israel again, please, Tel-Aviv . . .'

And I thought to myself, you can only survive in this country with such powerful mandates. But the question of my service to Soviet justice was already decided – I sent that telegram and went out into the street. The traffic was roaring, pedestrians were hurrying about, a militiaman on point duty was blowing his whistle. I had nowhere to hurry to. I set off slowly down the deserted Tverskoi Boulevard, along a narrow path trampled in the snow. On either side of me, along the snowy avenue, Party newspapers of all fifteen Soviet Socialist Republics were displayed on boards behind glass: *Pravda Ukrainy*, *Pravda Moldavii*, *Latviiskaya Pravda* and so on. The snow was sticking to the stands, but you could read the headlines. They were similar in all the papers: 'TRUE TO THE BEHESTS OF LENIN!' 'FOR COMMUNIST IDEALS!' or 'ONWARD TO COMMUNISM!' In a children's playground to one side some teenagers were flinging snowballs and obscenities at each other.

4.45 p.m.

I don't know how it happened, but about five o'clock I found myself on Kachalov Street. Evidently, just as the criminal is drawn to the scene of the crime, so my subconscious had brought me to the scene of an unfinished investigation. Early dusk had already blackened the Moscow sky, the lamps were lit in the streets, and round them in the black air hung crystals of falling snow. Loaded down with heavy shopping-bags, people walked cautiously along the slippery, snowy pavements and crowded at trolleybus stops. But on quiet Kachalov Street there weren't many people. The pavements had been sprinkled with sand, the windows of the tall 'government' houses blazed with bright yellow lights, and through the glass window of the bakery I saw a small queue of people buying bread, and in the back, in the cafeteria, the figures of the tireless Pshenichny, Marat Svetlov, Nina, Ozherelyev, and Laskin. They were standing round a plump nine-year-old girl in pig-tails and a squirrel coat. The girl sat at a table with her child's violin on her knee, munching away at a pastry and swinging her legs in the air while she related something to the members of my team. They didn't know that their leader, Shamrayev, had already surrendered and broken off his investigation. Now I had to muster the courage to tell them everything, in front of Nina.

I drew a deep breath and entered the bakery.

'Igor!' Nina immediately called excitedly. 'Here! Listen to this!' and she told the girl: 'Katya, this is our very top leader. Now, you repeat to him what you saw on the evening of the nineteenth here.'

'But I've finished my pastry,' said Katya, brushing the crumbs off her black violin case and beginning to get down.

'I'll buy you another one, Katyusha,' Svetlov told her. 'But you'll burst, that'll be your fifth already.'

'I'll take it home,' announced Katya.

'Only first repeat what you told us.'

'Phew!' Katya sighed deeply, as if she were talking to idiots. 'How many times do I have to repeat the same thing? Well, I saw two men dragging a third man out of that building over there, and he was limping on one foot and there was blood on his trousers. And that's all I saw.'

'And where did they drag him to?' asked Svetlov.

'But I've told you already: they put him in a car and drove away.'

'And what sort of car was it, a Volga?'

'You promised me a pastry,' replied Katya.

Svetlov laughed and went to the saleswoman to get the pastry, while Pshenichny, his blue eyes shining, triumphantly handed me 'Report of the Interrogation of Witness Yekaterina Uzhovich, minor, nine years'. And he had reason to be triumphant – three days of round-the-clock questioning of the residents of these houses had certainly produced results. Nine-year-old Katya Uzhovich testified as follows:

'. . . On Tuesday, 19 January, at approximately five o'clock in the evening I was on my way from music school to buy my French pastry at the bakery, when I saw, outside 16-A, two men of medium height, without coats, wearing jackets, leading a third man out of the building, also without a coat, in a jacket, and tall. This man was limping on his left foot, and there was blood on his trousers. I stopped and looked at them, because this man was making funny faces from the pain. He wasn't very old, about thirty. But I don't remember what the other men were like, because I was only looking at this man who was bleeding. They put him in a car, a black Volga, and drove off, and I went into the bakery . . .'

'That's not all, Igor Iosifovich,' Pshenichny smiled softly, and handed me another sheet of paper.

TELEGRAM

RE YOUR ENQUIRY ABOUT THE CAR ACCIDENT 16 JULY 1978 IN THE
REGION OF KACHALOV STREET MOSCOW INVOLVING VOLGA
REGISTRATION GRU 56-12 I HAVE TO REPORT THAT SAID VOLGA
BELONGED TO GIVI REVAZOVICH MINGADZE LIVING AT 7 PIROSMANI
STREET TIFLIS AND WAS CONFISCATED BY SENTENCE OF MOSCOW
MUNICIPAL COURT DATED 20 JULY 1978 TOGETHER WITH OTHER
PERSONAL POSSESSIONS OF MINGADZE IN CONNECTION WITH HIS
CONVICTION FOR FOREIGN CURRENCY OPERATIONS UNDER ARTICLE 88
OF THE CRIMINAL CODE OF THE RSFSR
D I ABASHIDZE GENERAL OF MILITIA
HEAD OF DIRECTORATE STATE CAR INSPECTORATE
GEORGIAN SSR

Tiflis 25 January 1982

'How do you like that?' said Svetlov, coming back with the pastry. 'He's inside under Article 88, but he doesn't figure either at the Address Bureau or in the MVD Records! What are they doing to us? Do they think we're idiots? Sorry, little girl, here's your pastry. One thing I don't understand – if he's been inside for three years already, why are they hiding him from us?'

Captain Laskin came up to me from the other side and placed in my hand the report of the test on the blood-traces on bullet number two:

Data from the microscopic examination of the surface of bullet No. 2 indicate that on the surface of the said bullet there are micro-particles of human blood belonging to group II (β-2).

Examination of the blood sample taken during the post-mortem of the victim Cit. Tsvigun, submitted by the Laboratory of the Bureau of Forensic Medicine, indicates that the victim's blood group was also II (β-2)

A. Sorokin, Director of Laboratory

E. Abdikrina, Senior Analyst, Candidate of Biological Sciences

And while I was running my eye down these lines, Major Ozherelyev added: 'Of the five Svetlanas you and Colonel Svetlov found this morning, only one has a blue Lada. That is the gynaecologist at the first-aid post in the Ukraina Hotel. But we didn't find her at work, and she hadn't arrived home yet. Yet the Lada is standing outside the house under the snow, so this Sveta's not going anywhere, Captain Arutyunov is waiting for her.'

I looked silently at Svetlov, Pshenichny, Ozherelyev, Nina, Laskin. They were all in a state of elation, with lively faces and sparkling eyes. And why not! It was clear even to Nina that on all fronts of the investigation we were coming out into the final straight.

'Let the little girl go,' I told them.

'Why?' asked Svetlov, surprised. 'We're just going to take her along to Gusev in the technical department, to do an identikit. I've already rung him; he's expecting us.'

'Marat, no discussions,' I said, and repeated to Pshenichny: 'Valentin, let the girl go. Katya, Uncle Laskin is taking you home now, and you just forget all about what you told them here, all right?'

Katya shrugged her shoulders and left with Laskin, holding her violin in one hand and the bag with the pastry in the other.

The team gathered round me with anxious faces. 'What happened?'

'Well, lads,' I uttered with some difficulty. 'We're no longer investigating this case.'

'Wh-a-a-t?' exclaimed Nina.

'What did Baklanov say to you?' asked Svetlov.

'That is already immaterial,' I said. 'The main thing is that the team is disbanded and we are no longer working on the case.'

'But why not?' said Nina, jumping up to me.

169

'Perhaps you've taken a bribe from Baklanov?' laughed Svetlov.

'I have . . .' I said.

'How much?' asked Svetlov.

'Life,' I said, looking him in the eye. 'Mine and yours.'

'Interesting . . .' said Svetlov, raising his injured hand slightly. 'Yesterday you were risking my life and Kolganov's, and Laskin's, and Arutyunov's. And today . . .'

'Well yesterday was enough,' I replied. 'An hour ago I sent a telegram to Karakoz resigning from the Prosecutor's Office. So excuse me – I'm no longer an investigator.'

They all gazed at me for about fifteen seconds – Svetlov, Pshenichny, Ozherelyev, Nina. Then Nina turned, took her handbag from the table, and without a word walked out of the bakery. The glass door slammed behind her.

Svetlov and Ozherelyev began to follow her towards the door.

Valya Pshenichny silently gathered up his piles of papers from the table, put them away in his worn leather briefcase, got up, and left the bakery, slightly dragging one foot.

I got out a cigarette and struck a match, but immediately heard the coarse voice of the saleswoman shouting: 'Hey you! No smoking here!'

'Oh yes, sorry . . .' I said, realizing that everyone would be shouting at me now; saleswomen, tram conductors, militiamen, cashiers, and even yardmen. I sighed and got into the queue for bread – it was time to get used to the stern business of living, since special supplies from the buffet of the Prosecutor's Office were a thing of the past.

As I approached the door with a white baton and two buns, I saw a long black limousine – a government Chaika – slowly come to a halt outside the bakery.

The head of Brezhnev's personal guard, Major-General Ivan Vasilyevich Zharov, got out and came hurriedly towards me. 'At last!' he said. 'I've been looking for you for a whole hour! Suslov died at five past four.'

'Forgive me,' I said, and pulled out of the inside pocket of my jacket the almost unused bundle of money and the mandate signed by Brezhnev, and handed both of them to him. 'I have resigned from the Prosecutor's Office.'

'I know that! We've already read your telegram!' he said dismissively. 'Leonid Ilyich is expecting you at six this evening.'

5.00 p.m.

In the car Zharov opened the drinks cabinet and poured us both a full glass of brandy. 'Well, thank goodness I found you!' he said with relief. 'Otherwise we would have had to drag you up from the south. I'll be honest: I gave the order through military channels, and the commandants of all the southern airports are waiting for you.'

'But what's happened?'

'I'll show you in a second . . .' Zharov downed his glass in one, took snuff from the back of his hand, and, reaching into his tunic pocket, drew out some sheets of paper folded in four. 'As soon as Suslov died I straight away organized a search of his office and apartment. Look what I found!' and he switched on the light in the back of the car as it bowled along the Tverskoi Boulevard towards the city centre.

On large ruled sheets, in the handwriting of an obviously old and highly-strung person, was scrawled the following:

POINTS FOR 4 FEBRUARY

1. Report: 'Evils of L.I. Brezhnev's cult of the leader'
   a. Defeats in foreign policy:
      - failure of peaceful occupation of Afghanistan in 1978, feet-dragging in active Sovietization of Afghanistan today;
      - delayed reaction to outbreak of anti-Soviet trade-union movement in Poland, prolonged liberalism towards Solidarity leaders;
      - indecisiveness over expanding Soviet spheres of influence in Middle East, leading to weakening of our bargaining positions for an outlet to the Persian Gulf and loss of control over Arab oil.
   b. In internal policy:
      - liberalism (afraid of the West) over anti-Soviet dissident movement. Solzhenitsyn. Sakharov;
      - permitting Jewish, Armenian, and German emigrations, which has led to re-emergence in Union Republics of nationalistic aspirations directed towards secession from USSR;
      - collapse of planned economy and emergence of 'unofficial' economy (figures and materials from Cascade);
      - members of Brezhnev's family involved in bribery and corruption (Cascade materials);
      - result of above points – weakening of ideological education of workers, destruction of Soviet people's faith in Communist ideals, critical attitude of people to existing authority.
2. Decisions of Politburo meeting:
   a. suggest L. Brezhnev retire. In case of agreement by him, not publish report 'Evils of the cult of the leader', see B. off with honour, awards, etc. In case of refusal, remove from Politburo, publish report 'Evils of the cult of the leader' to May Central Committee plenary meetings;
   b. form 'New Course Government' to ensure following measures as soon as possible.
      In foreign policy:
      - immediate total Sovietization of Afghanistan;
      - final destruction of Solidarity forces in Poland;
      - take decisive advantage of West's inability to oppose active moves by Soviet Union, as indicated by events in Afghanistan and Poland. Therefore, maximum military support for pro-

171

Communist popular movements in Middle East countries, including direct military intervention to secure control within next one to two years of Persian Gulf and Arab oil;
- extend military and other support for Communist and anti-Imperialist forces in countries of Latin America and Africa;
- take advantage of growing rift between NATO countries, widen it, and bring about isolation of USA in Capitalist world.

Successful realization of these points within a concrete timespan (1–2 years) will be final stage in preparation for Sovietization of Europe, Middle East, and American continent.

In internal policy:
- harsh eradication of dissident movements, religious and spiritual sects, cessation of all forms of emigration;
- census of population capable of working and mandatory attachment of workers to enterprises, collective and Soviet farms. This will guarantee sharp improvement of economy and permit supply of food products through network of industrial distributors exclusively to working population;
- eradication of all forms of 'unofficial' economy and other manifestations of anti-Soviet and Capitalist aspirations. For this purpose conduct series of exemplary trials with public execution of capital punishment;
- in connection with new foreign- and internal-policy tasks, increase numerical strength of Soviet Army by increasing compulsory service period from 2 to 5 years in land forces and from 3 to 7 years in Navy.

3. Form 'New Course Government' with following composition:
1st Secretary General of CPSU Central Committee: ....
2nd Secretary General of CPSU Central Committee: M. Suslov
Politburo:

The final ruled page of notes had been torn off at this point – right at the word 'Politburo'. Handing the paper back to Zharov, I thought: yes, the only thing missing from the list of charges against Brezhnev to complete the witches' brew was the killing of his daughter's lover. The rest of the text would do admirably for any anti-Brezhnev speech, even if the first initiator and author of this document, Suslov, had surrendered his evil Party soul to God an hour ago.

'Where did you find this?' I asked Zharov.

'Right in his desk, in the office. That bastard Suslov! He tore off the most important part! Otherwise we would know who else was in the plot, who discussed these fucking "points" with him!'

I laughed: 'Ivan Vasilyevich, it wasn't Suslov who tore it off. It was whoever slipped those papers into his drawer . . .'

'What are you talking about, that's Suslov's writing!' he objected.

172

'I'm not disputing that. It may well have been Suslov who wrote that, more than likely in fact. But the fact that these papers were lying openly in his desk drawer indicates, as I see it, that they were placed there specially. In other words, whoever needed them has a copy, several copies, and he can make use of Suslov's ideas for his coup. And for Brezhnev – it's a hint, not to dig his heels in, but to go quietly into retirement.'

Zharov blinked. With all his batman's diligence, it seemed he was as slow-witted as a batman, despite his general's insignia.

'Then who put it there?' he asked.

I sighed.

The government Chaika was rolling up to Red Square.

5.37 p.m.

TELEGRAM

To O G Abolnik Duty Colonel of Militia Moscow

AT 1737 HOURS AT MAYAKOVSKAYA METRO STATION TWO WOMEN FELL OR WERE THROWN FROM THE PLATFORM UNDER THE WHEELS OF A TRAIN STOP HAVE HALTED TRAIN MOVEMENT STOP SEND INVESTIGATION TEAM URGENTLY

F Abramov 2nd Lieutenant of Militia

Duty Officer at Mayakovskaya Metro Station

5.38 p.m.

Passing under the Spassky Tower, we came out into the inner territory of the Kremlin. Immediately I realized why Brezhnev's messenger had hesitated two days ago when Nina and Anton had asked him to give them a ride round the Kremlin in the government limousine: the entire inner territory of the Kremlin was filled with troops – tanks, armoured cars, groups of soldiers smoking in silence beneath the luxuriant Kremlin firs, and then more tanks, armoured cars, and soldiers. Just over there, beyond the Kremlin's embattled wall, was the usual solemnity of Red Square, the well-dressed foreigners converging on the Mausoleum to stare at the ceremonial of the changing of the guard and the remains of the great Lenin, the windows of GUM decorated with garlands, and the feeling of total stability conveyed by the brickwork of the Kremlin wall. But immediately behind the Spassky Tower – snow creased by tank-tracks, the uneasy glow of soldiers' cigarettes; and above all – total silence, no laughter, no voices, just the crunch of snow beneath soldiers' boots.

But there was a bustle of life in the corridors of the Central Committee, with the hurried footsteps of employees and the crackle of typewriters and telexes behind closed doors. Even though I was with the very head of Brezhnev's personal guard, there was a three-fold document check on every floor, a body-search, 'hand your coat in at the cloakroom', another search, until finally we were on the fourth floor, in the reception-room of the Secretary General of the CPSU Central Committee. Once again it was surprisingly quiet here, the sound of footsteps absorbed by grey carpeting.

'This way, please,' Zharov said to me, opening yet another door, but instead of an office we found ourselves in a small, comfortable hall with a moulded ceiling and windows overlooking the Kremlin and Red Square. In the middle of the room, at a green conference table covered with old newspaper files, cups of coffee, and bottles of Narzan, sat Yevgeny Ivanovich Chazov, my old friend, and Brezhnev's favourite journalist, Vadim Belkin, together with three other middle-aged men I didn't know. Belkin was tapping something out on his typewriter, Chazov was writing something by hand, but they all rose when we appeared.

Belkin came over to me: 'Igor Iosifovich. Hello! Let me introduce . . . These are Leonid Ilyich's advisers, Pavel Romanovich Sintsov, Suren Alekseyevich Pchemyan, Eduard Yefimovich Zolotov. And Chazov you know . . .'

The advisers shook my hand, they were all about the same age, about forty, wearing good suits and fashionable ties. Sintsov was thickset and looked like a film actor, Pchemyan was tall and dark-haired, with an intelligent Armenian face, Zolotov was a plump, freckled man with fair hair.

'Please sit down,' Sintsov said to me. 'Tea? Coffee? Are you hungry?'

'No, thank you,' I sat down in a chair and looked out of the window at the clock on Spassky Tower. There were still twenty minutes to wait until six o'clock.

'Then excuse us,' Sintsov said to me. 'We will just finish the paragraph and then we'll talk.' And he turned to Belkin. 'So. Where were we?'

Belkin sat down at his typewriter and read out what he had typed: ' "On 25 January 1982 the death occurred, in the eightieth year of his life, of Mikhail Andreyevich Suslov, Member of the Politburo, Secretary of the CPSU Central Committee, Deputy of the Supreme Soviet of the USSR, twice Hero of Socialist Labour. A man of great heart, crystal purity of morals, extreme humility, he won the deep respect of both Party and people." Any good?'

'Very talented!' laughed Pchemyan, and picked up an old newspaper with an obituary of Kirov: 'Now you could take some from here: "In every post which the Communist Party and the people entrusted to him he showed himself to be an outstanding organizer, an inflexible fighter for the great cause of Lenin and for the successful building of Communism . . ." '

With an ironical smile Belkin punched this out on his typewriter like a machine-gun, then asked: 'Could we add that he firmly and uncompromisingly defended the purity of Party ranks?'

'Go ahead,' agreed Pchemyan.

'Perhaps leave out the "purity of Party ranks"?' asked Sintsov. 'Otherwise it sounds like a reference to the Party purges of '37 and '46, when that paranoid destroyed thousands of the best Communists.'

'Write: "firmly defended the purity of Marxism–Leninism",' said Zolotov. 'It's more or less the same, but without the direct reference.'

174

'You see that, Igor Iosifovich?' Belkin complained cunningly. 'No freedom of creativity, even in obituaries!'

5.42 p.m.

TELEGRAM REPORT

To: Com V I Abyzov Duty Controller Metropolitan Underground
Railway Moscow
TWO FEMALE PASSENGERS HAVE FALLEN UNDER A TRAIN AT
MAYAKOVSKAYA METRO STATION STOP OWING TO ARRIVAL OF
AMBULANCE AND MILITIA PLUS FAINTING OF TRAIN DRIVER
ALEKSANDRA AVDEYENKO TRAIN IS UNABLE TO LEAVE STATION STOP I
REQUEST YOU CLOSE TRAIN MOVEMENT THROUGH MAYAKOVSKAYA
METRO STATION STOP ACCESS TO MAYAKOVSKAYA STATION HAS BEEN
CLOSED BY MILITIA
M AVERBAKH STATIONMASTER
MAYAKOVSKAYA METRO STATION

5.43 p.m.
Belkin, Pchemyan, and Zolotov continued to put together an official obituary for Suslov from old obituaries on Kirov, Ordzhonikidze, Zhdanov, and other Party leaders. Chazov was writing a 'Medical Report on the illness and cause of death of M.A. Suslov'.

Sintsov detached himself from the others and came over to me. 'Igor Iosifovich, It seems to us you are having difficulties at work. Are you?'

'I don't quite understand,' I said. 'Zharov told me I had been invited here by Leonid Ilyich.'

'He will be having a chat with you, but a little later . . .'

'I think you started the wrong way round,' Pchemyan said to him. 'Igor Iosifovich doesn't yet know who you are and who he is dealing with in general. I'm sure he's thinking it's simply a question of whether Brezhnev should remain in power or not. Right?'

'Not exactly,' I said. 'I've already seen Suslov's points.'

'Ah, then it's easier. Now you realize that it's not so much a struggle for the throne as a struggle for whether your son will be fighting somewhere in Saudi Arabia, or whether he will be going to study at an institute. Whether total serfdom, public executions, and other charms of the Middle Ages will be introduced, or whether we walk the tightrope of a more or less human life . . .'

I laughed to myself, and Belkin simply took the words out of my mouth that I was afraid to utter. He darted a glance at Pchemyan and asked scornfully: 'And do you consider we have a human life here? No meat, bread-lines, theft at every step.'

'I said "more or less human",' Pchemyan replied. 'At the moment we face a dilemma: whether we take care of our own back garden, sow wheat and breed cattle, or conquer other people's cattle and back gardens. Moreover,

175

the whole machinery of power is geared to the second course: in order to send troops to Afghanistan, Colombia or Saudi Arabia there is no need to change a single regional committee secretary or even call a meeting of the Supreme Soviet. And it would cost nothing to introduce serfdom – no revolts, no demonstrations. And if a few Lithuanians go on strike, there are Kirghiz troops stationed on their territory, and Lithuanian troops in Kirghizia – Stalin was a genius to think that system up. War for the world victory of Communism will justify the rationing system, serfdom, the death-penalty for dissidents, anything you want. And the main thing is that it will strengthen the Party's control, that is, all the Party officials will keep their seats and will receive officer's ranks as well. That's why it was so easy for Suslov to plot Kremlin coups or insist on the invasion of Afghanistan: the generals want to fight so as to become marshals, and the Party lieutenants want to control the army generals . . .'

'Suren, repeat that. I want to write it down for posterity,' said Belkin ironically, and his hands hovered histrionically over the typewriter.

'Wait,' said Pchemyan, waving him away. 'The man's really got to under-stand who he's dealing with. Otherwise he will argue to himself: why the hell should I save Brezhnev if he started up the "unofficial" economy and his whole family is taking millions in bribes? Right?' he asked me.

I laughed. To be honest, I had heard frank conversations at the most varied levels, but in the Kremlin?! In the room adjoining Brezhnev's office! I noticed Chazov smiling to himself – now I realized whom he had in mind when he told me that Brezhnev was not just Brezhnev, but that there was a whole army of invisible men standing behind him . . .

5.48 p.m.
EXTRACT FROM THE TESTIMONY OF CITIZEN YU. S. AVETIKOV,
WITNESS TO THE MURDER ON MAYAKOVSKAYA METRO STATION.

The time was rush-hour, there were crowds of people on the platform, and these two women were standing next to me, on my right. One was quite young, a blonde, the other a red-head of about forty. The train had just appeared from the tunnel when I heard the older one say to the young one: 'They all went to Mikhail Andreyevich's *dacha* for the New Year, and Semyon made these recordings there secretly. Take them and give them to your Igor.' And she gives her a bag. And suddenly a peasant type standing behind them grabs this bag from them and shoves them both in front of the train. It all happened in a moment! There was a scream, screeching of train-brakes, everyone rushed to hold on to these women – they thought they must have fallen or jumped. And I wanted to grab the man, but two women pushed me aside and shouted: 'Ambulance! Suicide!' And the man darted into the crowd with the bag, and then these two women disappeared too . . . I don't remember what the man looked like, but he was about thirty, had a grey rabbit-fur cap on, grey eyes, a round face.

5.49 p.m.

'All right,' Pchemyan poured himself a glass of Narzan. 'A word about the "unofficial" economy. What is it? A chance phenomenon? A cancer on the body of Socialism? Or the consequence of the fact that the collective farms have not justified themselves and our planned light industry is totally useless. Here we are, six men, and not one of us is wearing a Soviet suit or a Soviet shirt! So? Does that make us ponces? No, it's just that our stuff is impossible to wear – every new shirt-style has to be passed at ten different levels, which takes five years. And it's the same with everything. But the Party bureaucracy does not permit U-turns like abolishing the collective farms or introducing a fresh New Economic Policy – they're afraid to lose their seats at the controls. And so the "unofficial" economy appears, to compensate for the shortcomings of the official one: it meets seventeen per cent of the population's needs in food and industry today. Besides, they've learned to make jeans in Odessa no worse than the American ones! And things turned out all right – Soviet rule hasn't collapsed just because young people are wearing jeans and dancing in discos. But they were afraid it would collapse, they fought against it, and in my day people who wore jeans were taken along to the militia! It's the same with the "unofficial" economy. If we remain in power we shall have to take the final step – legalize a certain amount of private enterprise . . .'

'Phew!' whistled Belkin. 'The Kremlin dreamer! That will never happen, so stop trying to blow the man's mind!'

'Why not?' said Sintsov. 'With State control over the banks and heavy industry, no Soviet government would collapse from that. On the contrary – it would get stronger. And bribery would be sharply reduced.'

'There have always been bribes in Russia and there always will be!' said Belkin.

'Well, all right, all right!' answered Pchemyan. 'What business is that of the State? Let's say the Head of State or some minister receives a hundred million in bribes. Or I do. Where does that money go? Nowhere. It stays in the country. Your friend Svetlov arrested a dozen managers in Sochi. But what were they doing? They had set up unofficial enterprises in their district, and incidentally, they paid their workers handsomely, 500 roubles a month, and they kept all their profits in a so-called "unofficial" account at the bank. But it's a State bank! In other words, all those profits went into circulation within the State! So they kept some for binges and to buy gold for their wives. But even that gold stayed inside the country. You could go and search them any time and pick it up . . . Well then, Igor Iosifovich? Have I persuaded you to save the whole Brezhnev shower, or not?' he asked me point-blank, and I realized what all the long speech was for: they were trying to recruit me. And I had to admit they were not doing a bad job.

But I laughed, nodded at the window where the tanks and soldiers were standing inside the Kremlin, and said: 'In my opinion, you don't need saving. You're already well protected.'

177

'That's just Zharov doing his nut,' said Pchemyan dismissively. 'Zharov, Ustinov, and to some extent Leonid Ilyich. They're afraid Andropov will move a KGB division into the Kremlin. Don't worry about them, they're just nervous old men! Andropov's not such a fool, he knows now is not the time for violent coups. How would he rule the country afterwards? They've had a military coup in Poland, and now one here? No, foreign Communist Parties would immediately break away and he would become the most unpopular Secretary General ever. Like Jaruzelski. No, the battle for power will be a silent one, at the Politburo meeting on 4 February. They'll either shove Brezhnev off into retirement or they won't. If they do, by using Cascade and other charges, then that's it. The "New Course Government" will come in legally, and so will the serf regime and other delights. Not immediately, not all in a day, but . . . But if we have proof that they murdered Tsvigun, none of them will open their mouths. They'll just blame it all on Suslov and wait quietly for another six months or a year.'

'And then?' I asked.

'But we just need that year, two at the most,' said Svintsov suddenly. 'During that time we'll try to legalize private enterprise and introduce a new NEP. It's hard, almost impossible, given the present Party machinery, but . . . we'll give it a whirl! Of course we're only advisers, and on each question we give Leonid Ilyich two or three alternative solutions and he chooses one. But think for yourself: whose solutions are they? His or ours?' He gave a cunning smile and asked: 'Well, are you joining the team? Make up your mind, because it's nearly six. Time to go in to Leonid Ilyich.'

5.58 p.m.

FROM THE REPORT OF G. V. AVILOV, CAPTAIN OF MILITIA

HEAD OF THE INVESTIGATION TEAM, CONTROL ROOM, MOSCOW CID

Apart from the witness Yu. Avetikov, none of the passengers detailed at Mayakovskaya Station saw the criminal who pushed the two women in front of the train and stole the handbag of the older one. No documents were discovered in the handbag of the second victim, therefore it has not been possible to identify the victims. Their bodies were taken by ambulance to the mortuary of Medical Institute Number One at 17.43 hours.

At 17.56 hours a telephone communicaton was received from the reception at the mortuary of Medical Institute Number One, to say that the pathologist on duty, A.A. Bogoyavlensky, recognized one of the victims as the girl who visited the Dissecting-Room of Medical Institute Number One on 23 January in the company of Special Investigator I.I. Shamrayev of the USSR Public Prosecutor's Office.

The telephone rang, Zolotov picked up the receiver, and said: 'Igor Iosifovich, for you. From CID.'

Without answering Sintsov's question in the end, I took the receiver.

178

'Igor Iosifovich, this is Colonel Glazunov. I am on duty for Moscow today. When you are free, please go along to the Dissecting-Room of Medical Institute Number One to identify a body.'

'What body?'

'I'm afraid it's the girl who has been with you for the last few days. Svetlov has already gone.'

I stood, stunned, the receiver in my hand. Outside the window the Kremlin chimes were beginning on the Spassky Tower – the hands of the clock had reached six. The relief guard of honour marched towards the Mausoleum, stamping each step on the snowy cobbles of Red Square. The first strike of six fell at their feet like a drop of resonant metal.

'Igor Iosifovich,' said Svintsov. 'It's time for us to go to Comrade Brezhnev.'

I replaced the receiver and said, moving towards the exit: 'Tell him I shall do everything in my power. Even more.'

7.00 p.m.

What two hours ago had been young Nina – that little miracle of life who used to cast impish, devoted looks at me with her little blue eyes, or fling her hair over her shoulders in a gesture of independence, and blow the fringe off her forehead, the girl who lovingly massaged my tired shoulders in the bathroom, pushed aside the crowd of young people outside the Blizzard, sunbathed on the Black Sea beach, and somersaulted on the trampoline beneath the vault of the Vologda Circus – what remained of all this after a cruel encounter with the wheels of an underground train now lay before me, covered with a sheet on a table of the Dissecting-Room at Medical Institute Number One.

Next to me stood Svetlov, Pshenichny, Ozherelyev, Laskin, Arutyunov and Kolganov. At the next dissecting-table Bogoyavlensky and Gradus were working on the disfigured corpse of Svetlana Nikolayevna Agapova – redhaired, thin, just a short while ago Tsvigun's beautiful forty-year-old woman, doctor at the Ukraina Hotel. Gradus and 'Sandy' Bogoyavlensky worked miracles, but, despite a thick mask of make-up, powder and rouge, the faces of Nina and Svetlana had been disfigured by the catastrophe.

I looked at them. I forced myself to look at those two mangled corpses.

They lay side by side – my little Nina and Tsvigun's woman.

And by some link beyond the grave I now felt a kinship with Tsvigun.

The registrar of the Autopsy-Room came up and said to Svetlov and me: 'We need her address in Vologda, in order to inform her parents.'

Svetlov shook his head: 'Wait. Give us a couple of days. When the one who killed her is lying here . . .'

He didn't finish, and I turned and went out to the duty office. There I took the telephone and dialled my ex-wife's number. She had left me nine years ago and, after living it up for about six months, married a Major Sokolov in the medical service.

Now I could hear his voice down the telephone: 'Major Sokolov speaking.'

'This is Shamrayev,' I said. 'I have a favour to ask of you, Colonel. Take Anton to school tomorrow morning.'

'Hm . . .' he said. 'He's no longer a child, you know . . .'

'Please, it's important. Take him to school in the morning, and in the afternoon I'll meet him and bring him home. It's important.'

Svetlov came over to me, took the receiver, and hung it up. 'Don't lower yourself,' he said. 'We'll solve this problem another way.'

8.00 p.m.

That evening Svetlov visited three ex-convicts – murderers – and three current bosses of the petty black-market riff-raff in Sokolniki, and on Trubnaya Square and Begovaya Street, in the area of the Hippodrome.

9.00 p.m.

The official militia Volga brought Nikolai Afanasyevich Baklanov to the entrance of 78, Vernadsky Prospect. Baklanov stepped wearily out of the car and, with a heavy briefcase in his hand, went in through the door and up to the seventh floor to his apartment, number 43. He unlocked the door, entered the apartment, and stopped in surprise in the hallway: through the closed sitting-room door he could hear the happy, excited voice of his four-year-old son Vaska, the laughter of his wife Natalya, and a male voice that he didn't recognize. His son was pretending to be shooting, and shouting: 'Da-da-da-da-da!' the man's voice was making train-noises: 'Sh-sh-sh! Oo-oo-oo!' and Natalya was laughing and shouting: 'Oh, I'm wounded! I'm wounded!' They never heard him come into the apartment.

Baklanov was fifty-three, his wife Natasha thirty-four, and, as always in late marriages, especially when there is such an age-difference, Baklanov was jealous, worshipped his son, and tried to do all the housework if he could. On hearing the happy laughter of his wife and the voice of a strange man, Baklanov frowned, went straight through into the kitchen, and began unpacking his briefcase which contained products acquired at the top-grade buffet of the MVD – Bulgarian tomatoes and apples, canned fish, and a Dutch chicken wrapped in shiny cellophane, as well as a carton of Camels, his favourite American cigarettes. He put the food in the refrigerator and the cigarettes on the top shelf of the kitchen cupboard, where he also put several official folders marked 'Secret'. Only then, observing with surprise that there was not a single chair in the kitchen, did he light a cigarette and, finally, go through to the sitting-room. There he was doubly surprised: all the furniture in the sitting-room had been moved around, all the chairs were standing in a row down the middle of the room like a train, and Vaska was sitting on the last 'coach', facing backwards, shooting at the 'pursuers' with his toy automatic. The driver of the train was Marat Svetlov, puffing and hooting like an engine.

180

Seeing his father, Vaska joyfully aimed his automatic at him and shouted: 'Bang, bang, bang, bang!'

About ten minutes later, when Natalya had taken the struggling Vaska off to bed, Svetlov and Baklanov stood smoking by the open window, talking quietly.

'You understand, Nikolai,' Svetlov was saying calmly, 'I have been in the militia for seventeen years. In that time I have personally caught five hundred and three criminals. Eighty-four of them were murderers. Some of them have already done their time and are free again. Why do you think they haven't liquidated me? After all, sixteen criminals have perished from my bullet, and they have friends, gangs, the thieves' code of revenge . . .'

He looked Baklanov in the eye, but he shrugged his shoulders, not knowing what Svetlov was driving at.

'I'll tell you. It's because the whole professional world of crime knows that my killer will survive me by exactly twenty-four hours. Or less. Why? Because I've got several old cases in my "hush-up" file. A backlog of cases that are considered to be unsolved. The criminals have gone straight long ago, they're working, they have little Vaskas like yours, and they don't want to end up behind bars again. But these are ex-"fathers", and in the world of crime their word is law. And they know quite well that if a brick falls on me or my friends, their old cases will be on the Prosecutor's desk tomorrow. And every one of them will get the maximum sentence – the prescription period on them has not yet elapsed. Now do you understand what I'm driving at?'

'But that's crime committed in office,' said Baklanov. 'You are concealing criminals from the law . . .'

'Nikolai, who are you to talk about crimes committed in office?' laughed Svetlov, moving his injured hand: 'I redeem these crimes committed in office with my own blood. Besides, they've already done their time for other cases and now they're working honestly. Why lock them up again? Anyway, here's what I want to tell you: today I extended this contract. If anything happens to me, Shamrayev, Pshenichny, or anybody else in our team, it makes no odds who throws the brick at our heads. You, Krasnov, and Malenina will survive us by just twenty-four hours, no more.' And Svetlov turned round towards the bedroom, from where the voices of Baklanov's wife and son could be heard. 'And you have a nice kid, a happy little boy . . .'

Outside the window, above the Vernadsky Prospect metro station, glowed a large red neon 'M' – just like at the Mayakovskaya metro station. Thick snow was falling.

Part 6

The Bridegroom from the Camps

Tuesday 26 January, 9.00 a.m.

URGENT

TOP SECRET

The Minister of Internal Affairs of the USSR General N.A. Shcholokov
To: the Chief Public Prosecutor of the USSR,
Comrade A.M. Rekunkov, by special messenger

Dear Aleksandr Mikhailovich,

In the course of Operation Cascade which we are conducting, on Sunday 24 January, one Boris Buryatsky was arrested while attempting to extort diamonds from the well-known circus artiste and Bolshoi Theatre soloist Bugrimova. Over the last six years Buryatsky has been one of the middlemen operating between the leaders of the underground economic mafia and former First Deputy Chairman of the KGB, General Tsvigun. It has been established, and his own evidence confirms the fact, that in the period 1976–82 the leaders of our underground economy handed to Tsvigun via Buryatsky valuables to the tune of about four million roubles. With his criminal activities now revealed, Buryatsky testified that on 19 January of this year a quarrel took place between himself and General Tsvigun in the house at 16-A, Kachalov Street, apartment 9. Not realizing that mass arrests of the leaders of underground enterprises were being carried out without Tsvigun's knowledge by the Intelligence Section and the Anti-Fraud Squad of the MVD, Buryatsky accused Tsvigun of organizing these arrests and threatened that the leaders of the economic mafia would never forgive either Tsvigun or Buryatsky for them. In the course of the ensuing quarrel, Tsvigun drew his gun and shot at Buryatsky, probably in an attempt to scare the latter – the bullet flew out of the window without hitting Buryatsky. Buryatsky testifies that in order to defend himself he was forced into a wrestling-match with Tsvigun, and during their struggle Tsvigun accidentally shot himself in the head. Buryatsky maintains that the fatal shot was fired by Tsvigun at a moment when Buryatsky was twisting his arms behind his back in order to wrest the gun from him. Following this, fearing that any inquiry would reveal

185

his role as middleman between Tsvigun and the underground economy, Buryatsky set things up to make it look like suicide: he seated Tsvigun at his table in the drawing-room in the attitude of one who might have committed suicide, and forged a suicide note. Then, since nobody, including Tsvigun's bodyguard, had heard the sound of the shots because of the music and noise at a wedding-party in the neighbouring apartment, Buryatsky left Tsvigun's apartment unobserved, taking with him the blood-stained rug from the entrance where the killing had taken place. Buryatsky then went with this rug to the eleventh floor of the same house, to the apartment of his friend the actress Snezhko, who at that time (and up to the present) has been away filming on location. Buryatsky testifies that he remained in this apartment until 11.30 p.m., and that that same night he threw the incriminating rug through a hole in the ice on the Moskva River near the Karamyshevskaya Embankment . . .

Reading this document under the gaze of Karakoz and Rekunkov, I could not restrain a sarcastic smile at this point – it looked as if I was now the equal of Baklanov in my experience as an investigator. He and I had both invented legends that were amazingly similar. Even the robbing of Bugrimova now looked simply like 'extortion' . . .

'Why do you smile?' asked Karakoz in surprise, then looked over towards the Chief Public Prosecutor who was sitting sullen and motionless, like a grey tree-branch arched across the writing-desk of his office.

Without taking my eyes off the letter, I felt in the pocket of my jacket, took out my notepad, opened it at the last page and handed it to Karakoz.

'What is it?' he asked.

'Read it,' I said with a laugh. 'I have legible writing.'

Sometimes in a spare moment I draft plans of action on this pad, and on the previous evening already I had written the following: 'In the course of the next day or so, Buryatsky or Sandro Katauri admit to the killing of Tsvigun. Their version tells of a quarrel with Tsvigun; Tsvigun fires the first shot – at the window; the second, fired by accident, causes his death. Then it is rigged to look like suicide; the rug is taken to Snezhko's. Next door there is a wedding-party, noise, champagne bottles popping, so nobody paid attention to the shots fired in Tsvigun's apartment. At night the rug is burned somewhere out of town, or else thrown into the river. Our best action is not to let ourselves become involved by searching for alibis for Buryatsky and Katauri, but to continue searching for the real murderers.'

Karakoz read this note and silently laid it on the table in front of Rekunkov. Meanwhile I carried on reading Shcholokov's letter. What I read filled me with admiration. No, I thought, I still have a long way to go to match these boys from the Intelligence Section and Kolya Baklanov!

However, the version of Tsvigun's accidental killing recounted by Buryatsky raises certain doubts. The fact is that in the course of secret surveillance of Buryatsky carried out during December and January as part of Operation Cascade, his numerous contacts came to light with foreign correspondents, members of the American, West German and Italian Embassies, and also with foreign tourists. Thus, during the month of January alone it was noted that Buryatsky had meetings with the American television correspondent John Canter in the foreign-currency bar of the National Hotel, with Italian diplomat Uno Scaltini in the country restaurant Arkhangelskoye and with a group of West German tourists in the buffet of the Bolshoi Theatre. In his testimony Buryatsky justified these meetings by reference to his life as an artist, and his ambition to go for voice-training and experience at La Scala, Milan. However, according to Section Eight of the KGB, John Canter works for the CIA; Uno Scaltini is married to the daughter of an American Admiral, Ted Cole; and among the group of German tourists who met Buryatsky in the Bolshoi Theatre were two agents of West German Intelligence. Thus a genuine fear arises that Boris Buryatsky is an agent in the pay of one of the western Intelligence services who are immensely interested in his close association with the daughter of Comrade Brezhnev, his friendship with Tsvigun and other leaders of the Soviet State. The fear arises that the true reason for the killing of Tsvigun was the fact that he began to suspect Buryatsky of having contacts with western Intelligence. This version is also supported by the fact that on the very next day after Buryatsky's arrest, rumours began circulating among foreign correspondents in Moscow about the suicide of General Tsvigun, about his contacts with arrested leaders of the 'underground' economy, the close relationship between the arrested man Buryatsky and the daughter of Comrade Brezhnev, Galina Leonidovna, and about the latter's being summoned for questioning at the USSR Prosecutor's Office. It is not excluded that these rumours are being spread in order to conceal Buryatsky's connections with one of the western Intelligence agencies.

Since uncovering the activities of foreign Intelligence agencies lies outside the competence of both the MVD and your own Office, I consider it necessary to hand the materials of the preliminary investigation of Buryatsky's case not to Special Investigator Comrade I. Shamrayev who is conducting the inquiry into General Tsvigun's death, but to the KGB. I consider that the materials of the preliminary investigation into the Tsvigun case which are held by Investigator Shamrayev should also be handed over without delay to the KGB, in order to carry out as quickly as possible Comrade Brezhnev's instruction that the true causes of General Tsvigun's death be brought to light.

Yours respectfully,
N. Shcholokov
Minister of Internal Affairs

Moscow, 26 January 1982

Hmm, yes, I thought, they have really fooled that poor man Buryatsky. They've persuaded him to admit only to having had a fight with Tsvigun, but then they have drawn the foreign Intelligence agencies into the whole business. And so the trap had closed on Buryatsky: the KGB would even get him to confess to the fact that he was an agent of international Zionism – they were quite capable of that . . .

'What do these notes of yours add up to?' Rekunkov nodded towards my notepad when I finally laid Shcholokov's letter on his desk.

I said nothing. But I evidently looked sufficiently eloquently at the four telephones standing on his desk, for he too slowly turned to look at them, sighed, then bent down underneath the desk, and pulled all four telephone leads out of the socket and laid them down next to the actual handsets. The Prosecutor's Office was now cut off even from the direct line to the Kremlin.

'You can say everything openly,' he said. 'Yesterday evening we were summoned by Comrade Brezhnev and instructed to give you our full co-operation. So that everything in my power – the whole Prosecutor's Office – is at your service. In addition he asked me to convey to you his condolences on the death of your girlfriend . . .'

'He said that you must find the murderer, and that the murderer will get capital punishment, whoever he is . . .' interjected Karakoz.

I laughed to myself – when I found the murderer, I would do without any court sentences. 'The murderer was only carrying out someone else's wishes,' I said. 'The situation is as follows: I shall not hand over to them any of the materials of my inquiry. Yesterday I might have done so. But today, after the murder of Nina, I shall not hand anything over, even if Brezhnev himself instructs me to . . . and that, really, is all.'

'At twelve o'clock we have been invited to go and see Andropov about this case,' said Karakoz. 'Shcholokov, Krasnov, Kurbanov and goodness knows who else are going to be there. But if this Buryatsky really was connected with foreign Intelligence agencies, then they are entitled to demand that we surrender the materials of our inquiry. What do you say to that?'

I nodded towards my notepad. 'As you can see, I knew the day before yesterday that they would try and make out Buryatsky was the killer. I also put down my conclusions there: not to get involved, and not to waste time on refuting their claims.'

'Very well,' said Rekunkov. 'What can we give you in the way of concrete assistance?'

'First of all,' I said, 'I need Vendelovsky as a member of my team. Secondly: when you go to see Andropov, try to draw out the discussion for as long as possible.'

'Aren't you going to go too?' asked Karakoz, surprised.

At the same time
Nine-year-old Katya Uzhovich who was so fond of French pastries, sat on a

soft seat in the half-darkened film-theatre of the CID technical department at 38 Petrovka Street. Next to her sat her mother, fully aware of how important a person her daughter had become. But nobody here paid any attention to the mother. Everyone – Pshenichny, the senior scientific consultant in the technical department, Captain Nora Agisheva, and Captain Laskin – looked only at Katya, following every movement of her face.

Across the screen in front of Katya flashed a series of human lips of every imaginable shape – full, then thin, then broad, then narrow. Operating remote control levers, Nora Agisheva was able to send these lips floating like magic across the screen and match them up to the nose that Katya, our only nine-year-old witness, had already identified.

'Now then, try and remember, Katya. Did the man who limped have lips like this?' asked Agisheva. 'Or like this? . . . Or were they like this?'

'No,' said Katya firmly. 'That man was definitely biting his lips when I saw him . . .'

'Biting his lip?' Nora asked animatedly. 'Did you see his teeth? What were his teeth like? Were they large ones?'

'He had one metal tooth,' said Katya. 'That's right!' she exclaimed gaily, evidently trying to turn the whole of this laborious and concentrated task into some sort of game. 'Come on, let's have a look at what sort of teeth you have. Where are your teeth?'

In the viewing-room next door another technical adviser, Lieutenant Agranovich, was at work with a witness of the murder at Mayakovskaya metro station, Yury Averikov. And on the screen could already be seen the identikit reconstruction of the murderer with his round face and light-coloured eyebrows.

Meanwhile
Natasha Baklanova was taking her son Vasya to the kindergarten. She held his hand, but the little lad tried to break free in order to slide down the slippery, polished ice-slide that the youths had made. A long queue of snow-covered figures were standing outside the Leipzig store which had still not yet opened. People came here early in the morning from all over Moscow in the hope of buying imported women's and children's underwear, cosmetics, haberdashery and toys. Natasha went to the end of the queue with her son and discovered that today they would be 'offering' women's boots. She took her place in the line. A bewhiskered old man in a leather coat damped the tip of his indelible pencil and wrote on her palm 'her' number – 427

'But we call the numbers out each half-hour!' he warned her.

'I'll be back in time,' said Natasha, 'I'm just taking him to kindergarten, I'll be back in a jiffy . . .' And off she went with Vasya.

Moving along in the same direction on the opposite side of Vernadsky Prospect was a car carrying one of the 'bossmen', whom Svetlov had visited the previous day.

189

Meanwhile, the former king of the Rostov housebreakers, Volodya Azarin, alias 'Gold Fang', who was now an agent in the pay of Moscow CID, was at work in house number 78. With the fine touch of a jeweller he had forced the door of the Baklanovs' apartment with his jemmy, and was starting on an illegal search of the premises.

'After the murder of Nina there are no holds barred,' Svetlov had said the previous night. 'We've got to find out what he carries round in his briefcase, what he keeps in his desk at home, and if necessary I'll force the safe in his room right here in the Prosecutor's Office!'

Meanwhile

In the office records of the Moscow Circus Training School, Marat Svetlov sought out the personal file on Tamara Bakshi, who had graduated there in the art of bareback riding. This was the same Tamara who had been introduced to him five days previously by my little Nina, and with whom he had spent the night at my place from the Friday to the Saturday. Yesterday at 7.45 a.m. Nina had been rung supposedly on behalf of Tamara by Svetlana Agapova, Tsvigun's red-head friend. And it was on her behalf that she had fixed up that fatal meeting with Nina. Or maybe it had been Tamara herself who rang? Svetlov telephoned the Moscow Address Bureau and promptly obtained her details: Tamara Viktorovna Bakshi, born 1962, unmarried, official address: 6, Gagarin Street, Apartment 3, Moscow.

Meanwhile

FROM THE REPORT OF CAPTAIN E.A. ARUTYUNOV TO COMRADE
I. SHAMRAYEV, INVESTIGATION TEAM DIRECTOR

In the course of an inspection of the dwelling of citizeness Svetlana Nikolayevna Agapova who was killed at Mayakovskaya metro station, I was able to establish the following: Agapova, born 1921, was a gynae-cologist working at the medical centre in the Hotel Ukraina. She was single and lived alone in a three-room apartment at 62, Chistye Prudy, Apartment 17. Her quarters were expensively furnished, with several original pictures apparently given to Agapova by various well-known artists, as confirmed by the various signed dedications on them. The artists included Ilya Glazunov, Rasim Hassan-Zade, Yakov Maisky-Katsnelson and others. Among the pictures were also works by Sandro Katauri. In the dressing-table and cupboards a large quantity of valuables was discovered, and some unique items of jewellery, which have been handed by me to the Diamond Board to have their value estimated.

Also discovered were: 6 (six) men's suits size 56, two dozen men's shirts and two military uniforms of the same size (one dress uniform and one everyday) together with the insignia of an army general, a medal 'Merit-orious Chekist of the USSR' and twelve decorations. These uniforms, the men's clothing, and also a man's silver shaving-set engraved 'to dear Semyon on his birthday from Svetlana', a second toothbrush in the bathroom, and pictures in photograph albums leave no doubt that:

1. The above-mentioned male articles belonged to General Tsvigun;

2. Agapova's apartment was also a temporary or permanent residence used by General Tsvigun.

One notable feature is the fact that although the apartment of Agapova was full of valuables, fur coats made of mink, fox, and silver fox, and imported stereophonic tape-recording equipment, there was a total absence in the apartment of any recording-cassettes and tapes, and also of any notepads, notebooks or any other form of handwritten material. It may therefore be assumed that the above-mentioned items were removed or seized *before* I made my own inspection, and possibly by the same people who stole citizeness Agapova's handbag at Mayakovskaya metro station, which according to a witness of the killing, Yu. Avetikov, contained tape-cassettes with recordings made secretly at the *dacha* of Mikhail Andreyevich Suslov.

Meanwhile

Vera Petrovna Tsvigun came out of Kievskaya metro station, went up the escalator to Kievskaya Square and joined the queue waiting for the 119 bus. Five yards away was one of Moscow's fixed-route minibus taxi-stands, but Vera Tsvigun preferred to stand in twenty degrees of frost and wait for the bus. There she stood, an erect, stern and elderly lady in her worn astrakhan coat, and the frosty snow-laden wind made the arid features of her face and thin, pursed lips seem even sharper. Finally the bus arrived and the noisy crowd crammed into it. In the course of the journey people had loud discussions about the recent unprecedented snowfall and Israel's annexation of the Golan Heights. One passenger read aloud from his newspaper: 'Over the last five days more than thirty million cubic metres of snow have fallen on Moscow. The depth of snow covering the streets is thirty-six centimetres, while in some places snowdrifts three metres deep have formed.'

Five stops later the bus struggled up the steep snow-covered brow of Vorobyovy Gory, which in clear weather commanded the finest view over the whole of Moscow. It went past the USSR Ministry of Foreign Affairs Guest House and halted on the opposite side of the street, at the entrance to the Mosfilm cinema studios.

All the passengers got off the bus, and Vera Tsvigun went with them. But unlike these regular employees of Mosfilm, she had no staff-member's pass; so she could not go straight into the studios and had to join the 'crowd scene' queue. Here, by the staff-entrance, a bright and vociferous female assistant was registering extras for the crowd scenes in the film version of *Ten Days that Shook the World*. She unceremoniously reviewed the group of pensioners in the frost. They came here every morning in the hope of earning a modest three roubles per session to add to their pensions.

The woman assistant harangued them: 'I need soliders for Admiral Kolchak! I need White guards officers! Russian aristocrats! And what do

191

you lot look like? Like a queue waiting to collect your social security! The same old faces day after day!'

Then she spotted two or three new faces in the crowd and pointed a finger at them: 'You, you and you! Come this way! Here are your passes! Go to Bondarchuk in studio number six – *Ten Days that Shook the World.*'

And so Vera Tsvigun, official wife of the former Central Committee member and First Deputy Chairman of the KGB, joined the forces of Admiral Kolchak and found her way into the Mosfilm studios. But she didn't go to studio number six. Instead she made her way to the main administrative block and went up to the third floor, to the reception-room of the director of Mosfilm, Nikolai Trofimovich Sizov. However, Sizov never came to work as early as this, so his secretary told her. The director would be there by ten o'clock, but would not be able to see her – at ten he had a production-conference on the new film of *Lenin in Paris.*

Vera Tsvigun left the reception-room and waited by the lift. A porter passed by her, heading for the director's private viewing-room. He was wheeling a trolley piled high with metal cases holding the rushes of *Lenin in Paris*, the latest film spectacular. Then a thin, tousle-headed assistant ran into the projection-room shouting 'Have they brought the sound?' and the directors of the studios and those producing the film began assembling in the viewing-room: the seventy-five-year-old producer Sergei Yutkevich, creator of *Lenin in Poland* and *Lenin in Zurich*; with him was another elderly man, the short, rotund scriptwriter with intelligent eyes, Yevgeny Gabrilovich; and after him came Naum Ardashnikov, a young cameraman who moved with a jauntily bouncing gait.

At ten o'clock precisely a black Volga rolled up to the main administrative entrance, and the former chairman of the Moscow City Council, former general and head of the Moscow militia, and now director of Mosfilm and member of the Soviet Writers' Union, Nikolai Sizov, got out and came up to the third floor in the lift.

As he emerged, Vera Tsvigun blocked his passage: 'Hello, Nikolai . . .'

Sizov was a fat, morose man, who never looked at the faces of subordinates. He made to walk past, but Vera Tsvigun grabbed him by the sleeve: 'Wait! You recognize me, don't you?'

'Ah!' Sizov was forced to stop. 'Yes, I do recognize you. I'm sorry though, I have a meeting at ten to discuss *Lenin in Paris.*'

'Never you mind. Lenin will wait,' Vera Tsvigun said drily. 'What about it? Aren't you going to make the film of Semyon's book? I rang the producer and he said the film had been stopped.'

'Well, it's been put on one side for a time.'

'Put to one side?' Vera Tsvigun gave a wry laugh. 'Oh, you . . . young Nikolai! Once upon a time we took a lousy little collective farmer called Sizov and we really made him into somebody! And what do you go and do?'

'Sorry, I have to go,' Sizov said abruptly and made as if to walk on.

But then Vera Petrovna suddenly broke into a whimper. Completely losing her Cheka agent's self-control, she became a pathetic little old lady. 'Kolya! I ask you – please don't cancel his film! It's surely no trouble to you? And it'll be such a splendid picture! All about the Cheka and the days of our youth! I beg of you! The story was printed in the literary magazine *Znamya*, and there was a good review in *Literaturnaya Gazeta*. Kolya, please!'

'It doesn't depend on me at all. I've had my instructions. I'm sorry. I'm in a hurry!' Sizov said irritably, and he wrenched the sleeve of his suit out of her hand and stalked off into his director's private viewing-room. The lights immediately went down, and from the projection-room the start of the soundtrack could be heard – the strains of 'The Internationale'.

Vera Tsvigun wiped away the tears with the sleeve of her astrakhan coat and sadly plodded down the corridor leading to the production area. She gave the impression of having been here on more than one occasion and found her way easily through the maze of corridors from one building to another. Major Ozherelyev, dressed in civilian clothes, was following her. The previous night we had decided to keep a secret watch on all the people connected with Tsvigun whom the MVD Intelligence Section had not yet arrested, or who could not be arrested by them. But there were hardly any such people apart from Vera Tsvigun and Brezhnev's daughter Galya.

In the studio production area Vera Tsvigun moved confidently down the corridor past the doors with their various signs: *Ten Days that Shook the World, Rebirth, The Lieutenants, The Mistakes of Youth, Communists Are We, Love at First Sight*, and so on. Behind these doors telephones were ringing; there was the sound of shouting, laughter and discussion; in through the doors went a constant procession of actors, assistants, make-up girls, heroes of the revolution, German and Soviet generals, American spies, and a variegated assortment of cinematic beauties of all ages. Vera Tsvigun even came across two Karl Marxes together, both of them desperately pursuing a comely young assistant and heading for *Communists Are We*.

And only in one room with a sign on the door reading *The Invisible War* was there a dull and funereal silence. The doors of this room were wide open. A cleaning-woman was sweeping out into the corridor a pile of papers with the letter-head *The Invisible War*, together with photographs of actors and actresses, pencil notes of frame-sequences, and various other litter. Inside the studio a workman in dirty overalls was busy up a step-ladder tearing down scenery sketches for the film that had now been cancelled and colourful posters advertising the other films based on Tsvigun's earlier work; *Front without Flank*, and *The War behind the Front*. The faces of two of the country's most popular actors, Vyacheslav Tikhonov and Natasha Sukhova, looked down from these posters at Vera Tsvigun. Sukhova, with her young, round face and dressed in Cheka uniform distantly resembled Vera herself.

10.00 a.m.
In the printing department of Moscow CID foreign-produced photographic

duplicators were stamping out the identikit portraits put together from descriptions by Katya Uzhovich, Yury Avetikov and Aleksandra Avdeyenko. According to Katya, on the evening of 19 January, a tall blond man of about thirty-five with light eyebrows, closely set eyes and a metal tooth in his right upper jaw, had come out of 16-A Kachalov Street. Armed with this portrait and description sixteen staff-members of the Third Section of Moscow CID headed by Valentin Pshenichny set out to visit all the hospitals and mortuaries in the city.

At the same time
At the main office of the Soviet State Automobile Inspectorate on Moscow's Peace Prospect, seventy-year-old Senior Special Investigator Taras Karpovich Vendelovsky extracted from the card-filing system a copy of the licence issued in October 1975 to citizen Givi Rivazovich Mingadze, together with a list of fines imposed on him from 1973 to 1978 for various traffic offences. His driving licence also carried a photograph of Mingadze, who was a native of Tiflis, born there in 1945. Vendelovsky put the documentation on Mingadze in his briefcase and slipped into the card-file a note on official headed paper of the USSR Prosecutor's Office confirming removal of the documents by official decree.

Meanwhile
The former king of the Rostov housebreakers, Volodya Azarkin alias 'Gold Fang' carefully closed the door of the Baklanovs' apartment behind him, went down to the entrance and out on to blizzard-blown Vernadsky Prospect. There he sat with 'Bossman' in the waiting car and said with a sigh: 'There's nothing – no papers, no tapes.'

'Did you go over the lot?' asked Bossman, who after a career in crime now worked as a car assembly technician at the Likhachov Motor Works.

'Do me a favour!'

'That means we've got to get his briefcase,' said Bossman, and he got out of the car and went to a telephone booth. He dialled: 'Ignat?' he said. 'It's empty. Where are the sneakers?'

'In Kolpachny Lane, by the Visa and Registry Office.'

Among the million telephone conversations going on in Moscow, this short exchange probably excited nobody's attention. None the less, Bossman had got the message that the 'sneakers' – a second group of Moscow criminals drafted in by Svetlov – were now following Nikolai Baklanov and were at the present moment in Kolpachny Lane.

At the same time
A crowd of relatives and friends of those leaders of the 'underground economy' arrested in Operation Cascade were for the second day running besieging the four small windows of the parcel-reception-room at the Butyrka prison. In the queue Captain Kolganov spotted Brezhnev's

daughter Galya. She looked suddenly tired and aged. Her heavily powdered face was tear-stained, her eyes had a faraway look, and she was holding a parcel containing food.

Not far away from her the man on duty, an elderly sergeant-major figure, was making a strident announcement: 'Only parcels from direct relatives! I warn you now: we take no parcels from friends and acquaintances! We don't feed prisoners on caviare either, not bloody likely! They're already constipated from all the parcels they've had so far!'

With a sigh, some of the visitors left the queue. Several others surrounded the man on duty, trying to persuade him they had only brought medicines.

But the sergeant-major was immovable: 'We've got our own doctor here! He'll prescribe whatever they need!'

But Galina Brezhneva did not leave the queue and seemed not to have heard the announcement. When there were only two people left between her and the window, Captain Kolganov pushed his way through to her side and said in a low voice: 'Give me your parcel. I'll hand it in for you. They'll not take it from you anyway.'

'And will they from you?' she asked.

'Let's try,' he smiled. Then he bent down to the low window and said to the girl in charge: 'Zoya, this is for Boris Buryatsky, cell 317.'

The girl glanced up in surprise and recognized Kolganov: 'Petya! And what relation are you to this Buryatsky?'

'Step-brother!' said Kolganov, looking her straight in the eye.

'How d'you mean, step-brother?' she said, failing to grasp.

'Just what I said – same father, different mothers. Here's the parcel.'

The receptionist hesitated then took the parcel. She opened up the various packets and began cutting open the sausage from Finland and the Bulgarian tomatoes.

'What are you cutting the tomatoes for? How can I smuggle anything in a tomato?'

'You'd be surprised!' said the girl. 'Some of them have had spirits and liquor injected into them! They've got it to a fine art.'

Kolganov left the Butyrka together with Galina Brezhneva and walked with her out onto Lesnaya Street.

Kolganov pointed to a waiting militia car and said: 'A certain gentleman would like to have a talk with you. Get in and let's go.'

Meanwhile

At 6 Gagarin Street, far away on the working-class outskirts of Moscow, nobody answered the repeated rings at the door of apartment 3, where Tamara Bakshi had her home. Suspecting that perhaps the corpse of Tamara might even be lying behind the door, Svetlov called out her neighbours and ordered his driver, a sergeant in the militia, to break down the door. But there was no body in the apartment, and all three rooms looked deserted and neglected – there was dust on the furniture, the flowers on the window-sill had withered, the freezer was switched off and from its open door came the stench of rotten cabbage.

'Well, she's 'ardly ever 'ere,' the old woman from next door told Svetlov. "Er father works somewhere on the frontier, 'e's a colonel, an' 'er mother's wi' 'im. An' tha' young tart comes 'ome once a month per'aps.'

'And where does she work?'

The old woman laughed: 'Where does an 'ore work? Wherever she lies down, that's where!'

11.00 a.m.

The trolleybus brought Vera Tsvigun to Pushkin Square. She got out and walked along the snow-covered pavement of Gorky Street, taking little mincing steps for fear of slipping. She went down past the display windows of the confectionery containing glowing plaster models of cakes; and in the windows of the Ocean fish shop streams of water played over a huge plaster model of a sevruga sturgeon. But there were no real cakes, and there was certainly no sturgeon. The shops stocked only biscuits and tinned fish, so there were no queues. Nevertheless, worried looking housewives with purses and string shopping-bags trotted on their usual fixed route from shop to shop. They had keen and roving eyes, and well-trained ears. The slightest indication from the behaviour of deliverymen or saleswomen was sufficient for them to work out that something had been delivered, some sort of fresh fish would be on the counter, or that sausages and chicken would be on offer at Yeliseyevs'. Gorky Street was a display sign for the whole of Moscow. It was supplied far better than any of the suburbs, and with the experience of a daily hunt for food here one could occasionally 'net' even such things as mandarins.

But Vera Tsvigun was uninterested even in the suspicious activity round the Crystal shop. She dismissed the temptation to be one of the first in the queue for a new consignment of Bohemian cut-glass. Extricating herself from the gathering crowd, she turned the corner and walked away down Gnezdikovsky Lane. Here, two hundred yards away from the bustle of Gorky Street, stood a quiet three-storey house behind a wrought-iron railing, the State Committee for the Cinema, which had under its control all twenty-three film studios in the country.

Vera Tsvigun went in at the main entrance and immediately bumped into the tall one-armed janitor.

Drily though politely he asked: 'Who do you want to see?'

'The Minister, I want to fix a time to come and see him.'

'There's the phone.' The janitor nodded towards an internal phone attached to the wall.

Vera Tsvigun lifted the receiver and told the switchboard: 'Yarmash's reception-room . . . Is that the reception-room? I'd like to see Comrade Yarmash . . . My name? Tsvigun – Vera Petrovna . . . Yes, the wife . . . What about? It's a personal matter.'

196

There was a short pause, and the Minister's secretary asked her to hold the line.

Then she heard: 'Comrade Yarmash is away at the moment. He'll be back in a week's time.'

'Very well,' said Vera Tsvigun, 'put me down to see him in a week.'

'Well, unfortunately, he'll be here only one day and then he's leaving again for Bulgaria, to attend a festival.'

'I see,' said Vera Tsvigun and hung up the receiver.

At the same time

At the Moscow CID on Petrovka, there was the clump of officers' boots and the jangle of telephones. In the corridors could be heard the sound of effing and blinding as various thieves, hooligans and prostitutes picked up during the night were escorted from the cells and taken for interrogation.

Somebody's trained tracker-dog barked on the staircase. And on the second floor, in Svetlov's office, I interrogated Galina Brezhneva, the Premier's daughter. Actually it would be difficult to describe it as an interrogation, since Galya for most of the time just wept and implored me to 'Save him! Save him!'

'Galya, who is Givi Mingadze?'

She turned to face the window and said shortly: 'I don't know.'

'That's not true. It's because of this man Givi that your friend Buryatsky tried to rob Irina Bugrimova and landed up in prison.'

'He didn't rob her. He came to collect his diamonds.'

'Which you gave to her in order that she could "get Givi out with the help of her fancy-man". These were your own words to Buryatsky on Saturday morning, and the MVD Intelligence Section were listening in. And so they knew in advance that Buryatsky would be calling on Bugrimova, and they set a trap for him there.'

'Really? I thought that Irina herself had called the militia, in order not to have to surrender the diamonds.'

'Galya, let's go back to the beginning again. Who is this Givi? And how could a circus artiste like Irina Bugrimova help him?'

'Givi is a former friend of Buryatsky's and of Uncle Semyon – Tsvigun. Three years ago he was imprisoned for some currency dealings. Boris Buryatsky was left to keep his diamonds, and he asked me to hand them over to Bugrimova, in order that she could get Givi out of gaol. That would be no trouble to her to do – the head of all the camps and prisons in the country is in love with her. What's the name of the organization?'

'It's called the Main Directorate of Corrective Labour Institutions,' I said. 'But wouldn't it have been easier to ask your uncle? One word from Tsvigun, and Givi would have been free. And anyway I can't understand how they could have put him in prison in the first place if he was a friend of Tsvigun's?'

'They'd quarrelled, and my uncle didn't want to hear the name mentioned even.'

197

'What did they quarrel over?'

'I don't know!' she shouted, almost as if something had snapped. 'Stop tormenting me! I shan't tell you anything anyway! I don't know anything!'

'You know all right, Galya. Only Baklanov put the wind up you so much yesterday that you're afraid to talk. But just bear in mind that they are carrying out this Operation Cascade, and now they are going to blow up this business of your Boris simply in order to topple your father. I have to know what it was Baklanov talked to you about yesterday.'

She gave no answer. She turned away to the window again. Outside Svetlov's office it was still snowing, shrouding the already snow-covered Petrovka and the Hermitage pleasure-gardens opposite in soft white flakes.

'So you are prepared to betray your own father . . . for what?' I asked.

'They are going to remove Papa anyway!' She turned round suddenly. 'Today, tomorrow, in two months' time! But they promised me that they would soon release Boris.'

'Who are they?'

She looked down and said: 'I can't say.'

'Galya, they are going to deceive you,' I said. 'Baklanov, Krasnov and Shcholokov are pulling the wool over your eyes. They are already trying to pin some dealings with foreign Intelligence agents on Boris.'

She was silent. Well, I thought, if she is so in love after all with this Buryatsky, they might have persuaded her to say nothing; they might have promised her that however disastrous the Buryatsky affair may be for her father, the better it will be for her: after Brezhnev's resignation, Churbanov will immediately divorce her, Buryatsky will be set free, and she can live happily ever after with the man she loves. And anyway, it is time that Papa Brezhnev retired, so it's not really a question of betraying him. On the contrary, Brezhnev needs medical treatment and a rest.

But if that is the case, then it is useless talking to her now – the love of a fifty-year-old woman is even more blind than that of a seventeen-year-old.

I then asked, less as a matter of form, than out of pure curiosity: 'Galya, just tell me if you can: your father is the Head of State. Your husband is the Deputy Minister of Internal Affairs. And you yourself are a senior employee of the Institute of American Studies and draw a salary of three hundred roubles a month. That means that in addition to your salary you have everything served on a plate – you live in government apartments and *dachas*, and you use government cars and boats. Why on top of that did you have to start speculating, taking bribes, diamonds, gold?'

She looked me straight in the eye, got up and said contemptuously: 'Listen to me! How is it you pretend that you're so honourable? Wouldn't you take it if it was on offer? I'm just an ordinary woman – I like men. I like enjoying life. And I like diamonds. I'm not pretending to be pure as the driven snow! Rada Khrushcheva made out that she was straight, and look where it got her! Now she just lives on what she earns and stands in the queue to buy butter in the morning! I don't give a damn for my father. He's had his fling.

But you save Boris for me and I'll shower you with gold!'

And for the second time in the last couple of days I thought why shouldn't I just tell them all to get stuffed – Brezhnev and the whole of his 'holy family'? If Nina had not got killed yesterday . . .

Staring fixedly at this fifty-year-old fool, I said, 'And what about Baklanov? Did you offer *him* a bribe?'

Meanwhile

At the personnel department of the Bolshoi Theatre investigator Vendelovsky was given a whole wad of photographs of Boris Buryatsky – full-length, in profile, and facing. Certainly Eleonora Savitskaya who tipped off the burglars, had been right: Buryatsky was an imposing figure. It was immediately evident from the photos that he was a man of proud and theatrical bearing; the hands and face looked well groomed. He had large, dark and slightly protruding eyes, long black hair, and an imposing chin over the lace-frilled shirt. Looking at these photos, any prison-warder would have confirmed the immediate diagnosis of Teacher Gruzilov, who was one of the best men at 'cracking' supposed fellow-prisoners in the whole of the Butyrka. His verdict was: 'Artist type, feeble personality, will fold inside a day.'

From the Bolshoi, Vendelovsky went to the Union of Soviet Artists to pick up a photograph of another of Tsvigun's friends now under arrest – the Georgian painter Sandro Katauri.

Meanwhile

Svetlov arrived at the Moscow CID in a towering rage. 'Where's Shamrayev?' he asked Captain Laskin down in the duty office.

'Sitting in your office. He's interrogating Galina Brezhneva.'

Svetlov laid a wad of photographs in front of Laskin, which he had taken from the family photo-album in Tamara Bakshi's apartment.

'Look up under "Whores" in your photographic files, please, and see if you can't find this little slut,' he ordered Laskin. 'If she's not there, go to the Hotel Ukraina and show the photos to the manager. And have a snoop around the other sleazy spots – we've got to get this hooker in by tonight!'

Laskin went out, and Svetlov, left in the duty office of his own Third Section, immediately lifted the outside phone receiver, glanced in the directory and dialled the number of Dr Goldberg, chief consultant at VD Clinic Number Seven.

'Lev Aronovich? Hello, this is Svetlov from Moscow CID. How do you do? Just one question. How many days after contact does one begin to show symptoms of gonorrhoea or syphilis? Internal pains? No, no pains at all yet. Colour of the urine? Goodness knows!'

When he had heard all Goldberg had to say, Svetlov replaced the receiver, took a tumbler from the table and went off to the toilet.

Meanwhile

Nikolai Baklanov came out of the Visa and Registry Office and went to his official Volga which had meanwhile acquired a powdering of snow. His driver, Sergeant Andreyev, had grown drowsy with the heating, and had dozed off at the steering-wheel; and the car meanwhile was listing over on the flat tyre of its offside rear wheel. Baklanov woke the driver and silently pointed to the flat.

'Ugh, shit and sand!' The driver suddenly came alive. 'Where the hell did that nail come from? It won't take a minute, though, sir. I'll put the spare on.'

He rushed to the boot and pushed the key into the lock. But the key refused to turn and the boot would not open. 'Damn it!' the driver swore and beat the lock with his fist. Water must have got in and frozen, damn it!'

Andreyev then tried a few other tricks of the Moscow chauffeurs' trade. He struck a match and heated the key, then pushed it into the lock again, but it was of no avail. Nor did hot oil from the engine dripped into the keyhole help.

Baklanov stood on the pavement, still holding his indispensable black leather briefcase, and looked drearily at the driver's feverish attempts to free the jammed lock. He was hungry and it was almost midday. But at that moment, a smart little bright green Zhiguli that was passing down Kolpachny Lane pulled up next to him. A well-dressed man in a deerskin hat got out and came towards Baklanov, obviously delighted to see him.

'Nikolai, old son! Long time no see! Don't you recognize me? I bet you won't in a thousand years! But I recognized you straight away! Well, can you guess my name? Try! Ha! No, you'll not get it! I'm Mikhail Belyakov!'

Neither the name nor the jolly man's face meant anything to Baklanov. But these sort of meetings happen to an investigator at least once a month – people you have dealt with recognize you on the street, in restaurants, at the cinema. And depending on the length of sentence they received, they either spit after you, or rush up with arms outspread. This looked like one of the second type.

'Goodness me, surely you remember? The Rostov Wine Trust business in '69? There were a hundred and forty of us brought up then. But you didn't send me down for actual fraud, but just for mismanagement, and I only got three years. But that was the end. I'm now an honest man, I've been to the institute and now I'm working for Moscow Clothing Traders. Anyway, to celebrate our meeting, I'd like to invite you to any restaurant you name, it's all on me!'

Baklanov did remember that in 1969 he had been in charge of the Rostov Wine Trust case, but now he had no recollection at all of who he'd sent down for what.

'I'm sorry, but I can't come to a restaurant with you. I'm busy,' said Baklanov.

'Oh, come on! We're all busy! But life goes on! It slips away all the time, damn it!' Belyakov insisted. 'Well, at least let's go and have a beer! I'll really be hurt if you say no! You've actually been like a father to me – you've taught me a lesson that'll last a lifetime. There's a beer bar quite close, on the Taganka, I'm on my way there now. I'd love to have a beer.'

Baklanov saw the pleading look in his eyes, then saw that his driver was still cursing and struggling unsuccessfully with the lock of the car's boot.

He turned again to his tempter and asked: 'Have they got stocks of beer in at the moment?'

'For me?' Belyakov exclaimed. 'There's always some there for me! Come on! Let's go! Get in! Afterwards I can drop you off wherever you like.'

And seven minutes later Baklanov and Belyakov were already sitting in the noisy, crowded beer bar not far from the well-known Theatre on the Taganka. The moist air laden with beer fumes, the cramped space round the tables, the dim light of the lamps wreathed in cigarette-smoke, the people queueing for draught, and that special sense of cameradcrie among beer-drinkers always had a relaxing effect on Baklanov.

Belyakov's keen eye took the scene in at once and he spotted a free space at one of the tables. He told Baklanov: 'Nikolai Afanasycvich, you keep the places, and I'll be there in one second. I can get us a beer without having to queue.' And he lunged forward to the bar: 'Now then, lads, I was standing here just now, it's my turn!' And he shouted to the barmaid, 'Olya! I had six beers on order!'

Baklanov wiped clean the corner of the table he had just managed to claim for them. He placed his black leather briefcase between his legs, and Belyakov was already coming back, beaming and carrying six tankards of foaming beer – three in each hand.

Baklanov was tired, and those first few gulps of cool beer were so very gratifying – he never noticed Gold Fang, the one-time Rostov housebreaker standing behind him, neatly exchanging the briefcase at his feet for an identical one made of the same black leather.

And next to Baklanov the exuberant Belyakov kept up an unbroken stream of chatter: 'So when I came out of the jug, I told myself: there's an end of it! Go and get yourself an education, I thought.'

Meanwhile, in the toilets, Gold Fang and Bossman bolted the cubicle behind them, took all the papers out of Baklanov's briefcase and without pausing to study them, photographed each one.

12.00 noon
The large free-standing clock in its antique mahogany cabinet tunefully chimed midday. The light oak door of Andropov's office opened and the figure of his assistant appeared, a dignified, rosy-cheeked major who announced in subdued tones: 'If you'd like to come in, gentlemen, Comrade Andropov is ready to see you.'

The men sitting in the ante-room rose to their feet and made their way towards the door, carefully observing the unwritten protocol: first the guests – Rekunkov, Chief Public Prosecutor, and with him Shcholokov, Minister of Internal Affairs. Then came the head of MVD Intelligence, General Krasnov, and with him the head of the Investigatory Section of the Prosecutor's Office, Herman Karakoz. And bringing up the rear were the hosts, Andropov's Deputies, Tsynyov, Pirozhkov, and Matrosov, and the head of the KGB Investigation Directorate Boris Kurbanov.

At the far end of the room a solidly-built, elderly man with a round face, thin grey hair and horn-rimmed spectacles on his full broad nose, looked at the guests attentively and rose from his desk to greet them – Yury Vladimirovich Andropov, Chairman of the KGB, the USSR Committee for State Security. He shook hands with the visitors and broadly gestured towards the conference table that stood some distance away from his writing-desk.

From the windows of this office there was a splendid view of Moscow and the Kremlin, almost like a picture. Down below on the square the stone statue of Feliks Dzerzhinsky in his long greatcoat stood with its back to Andropov's windows and also gazed out towards the city centre and the Kremlin. Inside the office a portrait of that same Dzerzhinsky together with pictures of Lenin, Brezhnev and Suslov (the latter with a decorous black ribbon over one corner) hung on the walls. Beneath the portraits, on broad bookshelves, stood the *Large Soviet Encyclopaedia*, the complete collected works of Lenin, the works of Brezhnev, Dzerzhinsky, and a large number of books in English including John Barron's *The KGB*, Robert Conquest's *The Great Terror*, and *Gorky Park* by Martin Cruz Smith. On a separate newspaper table were the latest editions of the *New York Times, Washington Post* and *The Times* – all of them clear signs of Andropov's command of English.

The guests stepped across the Persian carpet that covered the whole office floor, and took their places at the conference table. Andropov, ever the polite host, was last to take his seat. and he sat not at the head of the table, but next to the Chief Prosecutor and the Minister of Internal Affairs, in order not to flaunt his commanding position. His assistant handed him a red leather folio stamped 'Secret'.

Before opening it, however, Andropov said: 'Actually, the business on which I've invited you over here is familiar to you already. I have to say that this January has turned out to be a critical, testing time for us. Quite apart from all sorts of complications in Poland and Afghanistan, we have had two losses within a single week – Semyon Kuzmich Tsvigun and Mikhail Andreyevich Suslov. Some western correspondents have even been trying to link the two events, and in this way they've provided material for their own papers and radio-stations to make certain insinuations. I begin by mentioning this because any unhealthy sensation attaching to the names of the leaders of our State is a reflection on the prestige of the Party and the country. And in the light of this, it is extremely important that we unite our efforts in investigating the circumstances of General Tsvigun's death. From

202

the very outset I must say that his suicide has struck me as strange. And now after Comrade Shcholokov's report about the admissions of this Buryatsky . . .'

The portraits of Lenin, Brezhnev and Suslov stared fixedly through the window at the stone figure of Dzerzhinsky. And Dzerzhinsky in turn gazed down Marx Prospect towards the centre of Moscow with a look of stone, and a blizzard-laden wind swept the snow from the deep hem of his greatcoat . . .

Meanwhile

In the broad ground-floor windows of the *Izvestiya* editorial office, large and garish photographic displays were given over entirely to 'A New and Shameful Act of Aggression by Israel – Annexation of the Golan Heights'. Vera Tsvigun paused a moment by them then went into a telephone booth and dialled a number she had known by heart for the last seventeen years.

At the other end of the line, in Leonid Brezhnev's home on Kutuzovsky Prospect, there was an immediate but guarded reply: 'Hello.'

'Viktoriya Petrovna please.'

'Who is calling?' the male voice asked.

'Her sister.'

'Viktoriya Petrovna is not in Moscow at the moment '

'Where is she?'

'I can't tell you.'

'But perhaps she is out at the *dacha*? This is the third time I have rung.'

'I know. And I am telling you for the third time, Vera Petrovna, that she is definitely not in Moscow. She is . . . in the south.'

Vera Tsvigun slowly replaced the receiver and stood in the cold phone booth – one of the glass panes was shattered and an icy wind blew through the gap. She had already given up hope that *The Invisible War*, the film devoted to the days of her own youth, would ever be made. But the most hurtful thing was that her own sister Vika didn't wish to see her. Oh well, Vera Tsvigun decided, so much the worse for her, and for Brezhnev. And with this thought in mind, she took from the pocket of her old astrakhan the slim envelope without stamps which she had found this morning in her postbox. Unhurriedly she tore the envelope into tiny shreds. Then she left the telephone booth, and with the usual tidiness of older generation Muscovites she threw the shreds of paper into a litter-bin. Then, without looking back, she set off for the Rossiya cinema to see *Pirates of the Twentieth Century*.

Meanwhile

REPORT

To Comrade I.I. Shamrayev, i/c Investigation Team

Today, 26 January 1982, I carried out the task assigned me and showed to the staff and employees of Hotel Rossiya 26 mounts with photographs of 10 men of Georgian nationality aged between 30 and 45, and of 16 men with brown hair of Russian and Jewish nationality. Among the photographs shown to the staff were pictures of Givi Mingadze, Boris Buryatsky and Sandro Kataur. Elizaveta Konyayeva on floor duty on the ninth floor, buffet waitress Kseniya Masevich and cleaning-woman Darya Shirokova unmistakably recognized Givi Mingadze and Boris Buryatsky as the 'carpet cleaners' who had cleaned the carpets on the ninth floor of the hotel on the eve of the fire of 26 May 1976.

T. Vendelovsky
Senior Special Investigator in the USSR Chief Prosecutor's Office, Juridical Consultant

'We'll use this report to put the squeeze on Vera Tsvigun,' I told Svetlov. 'The old crone must surely know that the fire in the Rossiya Hotel was her husband's work, and I would very much like to have that jacket of his which split down the back. So get in touch with Ozherelyev and tell him to invite her along for a talk.'

At that moment though, Svetlov was forestalled by a ring of the telephone. He listened as someone made a report, and frowned. 'They've gone and lost Vera Tsvigun somewhere in the Rossiya cinema, the idiots!' he said. 'But they *have* found some letter which she threw away on her way there. They'll bring it round right away.'

12.32 p.m.
EXTRACT FROM MAJOR OZHERELYEV'S REPORT

At 12.17 hours, as she left the telephone booth, Tsvigun dropped into a rubbish-bin small fragments of some paper and then went to the ticket window of the Rossiya cinema. Junior Lieutenant P.O. Sinitsyna, dressed as a housewife, who was shadowing Tsvigun, was forced to remain behind by the rubbish-bin in order to gather up the fragments of paper that had been scattered by the wind. Meanwhile, Tsvigun had bought a ticket and entered the crowded cinema where she was lost among other members of the audience. I am taking every step to relocate Tsvigun. All entrances and exits to the cinema have been sealed off. If you so instruct, the show can be halted and all members of the audience will be let out through just one exit.

I enclose the fragments of paper and am sending them by special messenger. Awaiting instructions,

Yours,
Major V. Ozherelyev

There were twenty-seven pieces of paper. Working together in the office, Svetlov and I set to to stick them together on a clean sheet of paper. It was a tedious and complex piece of work. Svetlov was fidgety and obviously found such 'balderdash' a considerable trial. Then the telephone sounded again.

After listening to another report, Svetlov announced: 'I'm off to see my tame crooks. They've returned Baklanov's briefcase, and now I've got to have the film developed. You can finish sticking this yourself!'

'Wait,' I said. 'There seems to be something interesting here.'

And sure enough the text of the letter torn up by Vera Tsvigun provided us with a new conundrum. The single sheet of paper carried the following text, written in a rounded feminine hand:

Dear Vera Petrovna,

I hope that you remember me still. I am Anya Finshtein, and I worked on the film version of your husband's script *Front without Flank*, and my father was one of the sound technicians for the film. But I am sure that you recall my fiancé Givi Mingadze. On 18 July 1978, on the very eve of our marriage, your husband arrested him and put him in prison, and we were obliged to emigrate at short notice from the USSR.

For more than three years I never knew how father managed to obtain an exit visa for Israel inside a single day, and why we left the Soviet Union in such haste. A month ago my father died and before the end he told me everything. Of course, I could immediately have informed Israeli Intelligence, the CIA, or western correspondents of the whereabouts in Moscow of twenty-four spools of recording-tape which my father did not manage to destroy in the rush to leave. And you will understand that they could find a way of getting these tapes out of the Soviet Union. But I did not do this, and instead wrote your husband a letter directly addressed to the KGB. I believed that even if the censors opened this letter, they would still hand it to Tsvigun, since they are under his authority. In this letter I suggested to your husband an exchange: he would release Givi Mingadze back to me, and I would let him know the whereabouts of these tapes. Of course, knowing your husband and realizing what the KGB was, I did not give my home address but only a box number in a post office where I have a friend in charge. On 12 January, a reply came to this address – a postcard which said: 'Anya, we must discuss the exchange:– At 2.00 p.m., 14 January, the Pinaty cafe at the corner of Disenhoff and Fischman in Tel-Aviv.' But the same day, my friend noticed some unfamiliar men and women who took turns to hang about the post office near the wall where the boxes were. They kept watch there on the 12th, 13th and 14th, and of course I did not keep that rendezvous. Apart from that, your husband never called me 'Anya'. On the 15th and 16th there were telegrams in my box with urgent requests to get in touch, and on the 17th I discovered some suspicious-looking women hanging about my home. (You may know that in Israel we have a large population of Arabs some of whom have brought wives back from Russia, and these two women were like weavers from Voronezh dressed up in Arab clothing.) That same day I left Israel.

It was in Europe already that I heard of your husband's death.

I do not know who sent those people – whether it was Tsvigun or someone else. But if they were interested in making an honest exchange, they would not have started trailing me, would they? And your husband would have addressed me in the way he did when he called in at our production department.

I have fled to escape these KGB agents. Your husband is no longer living, but I am still anxious to get Givi out of prison and out of the USSR. I am therefore making one final attempt via yourself.

Please tell your brother-in-law, Leonid Brezhnev, that if Givi does not rejoin me within a week, I shall reveal the address where the tapes are hidden to western correspondents and Intelligence agencies.

And they will begin broadcasting these recordings on 'Voice of America' and will publish them in the western press. And the whole world will hear how Brezhnev, his son, daughter, brother and other friends Ustinov and Tsvigun talk in their family circle about the Soviet regime, the members of your Politburo, the internal and foreign policies of the Soviet government, the military plans of the General Staff, and the so-called international Communist movement.

The telephone number through which you can contact me in western Europe is a West German number: 0611-33-18-19. But please bear in mind that this is only an answering service for leaving messages.

You will receive this letter on the 26th, and I shall wait precisely one week for Givi to be released. If I do not get back my fiancé, I go to the American pressmen on 6 February.

Anya Finshtein

23 January, 1982

P.S. Have no fear, this letter will not be delivered to you by the CIA. I have found someone who leaves today on a tourist trip to the USSR.

'Ha!' said Svetlov. 'The naive fool! I'll get the lists of tourists sent who arrived in Moscow in the last two days, and I'll find this character.'

'Wait,' I said. 'Do you understand what this letter's about?'

'What is there to understand?! Her father somehow managed to record Brezhnev's conversations at home, and then for some reason fled from the Soviet Union, but didn't take the tapes with him and didn't have time to destroy them. And now she's going to try and blackmail us with these tapes in order that we hand over to her the criminal who set fire to the Rossiya Hotel! To hell with her! Tsvigun didn't hand him over to her, and we . . . Wait!' He suddenly screwed up his eyes and began to read the letter through again. 'But, you know, maybe her first letter didn't actually get through to Tsvigun . . . and then . . . and then these would be those very tapes which Krasnov, Baklanov and Malenina are searching for.'

I lifted the receiver of the telephone, searched quickly in the directory, and dialled the number of Meshcheryakov, Director of the Head Post Office in Moscow: 'Viktor Borisovich? Sorry to trouble you. This is Shamrayev speaking from the USSR Prosecutor's Office. On Saturday I sent off to you an order concerning the interception of all postal and telegraph communications addressed to Tsvigun.'

'I know, I know,' his deep voice responded. 'I am just sending a reply. You see, actually, all the mail for Comrade Tsvigun since 19 January has been picked up by the Investigation Directorate of the KGB.'

'And prior to the nineteenth?'

'Prior to the nineteenth all mail was delivered to him, personally.'

'All?'

'Why, of course! Certainly!'

'Thank you.' I replaced the receiver and turned to Svetlov. 'Come on, we're going to see the postal censors at Komsomolskaya Square.'

'But my crooks are waiting for me!' he said. 'And apart from that, what is Ozherelyev to do with Tsvigun's wife? He is waiting for instructions. I'll be going right past him.'

'First of all we'll go to the censors,' I said. 'And in the meantime she can watch her film. In any case we've no time to be bothered with her just at the moment. Let Ozherelyev leave her be for the time being.' I folded Anya Finshtein's letter and slipped it in my pocket. 'Off we go!'

Svetlov looked at me and sighed: 'As if we didn't have enough on our plates! Not content with looking for two murderers, we're after these tapes! Why the hell have you involved yourself in this business now?'

'We are not going looking for these tapes,' I answered. In response to the surprised look he gave me, I went on: 'If these are the same tapes that Krasnov, Baklanov and Malenina are looking for, we're not going to bother racing against them. We'll simply hand this girl her Georgian and have done with it. If he's still alive, that is.'

Captain Laskin came into the office and reported: 'Comrade Svetlov, we've identified this Tamara Bakshi in the Hotel National. She's there every evening in the foreign-currency bar. We'll pick her up there this evening.'

'Oh, no you don't!' exclaimed Svetlov. 'I shall do the picking up! In person.'

1.00 p.m.

The meeting in Andropov's office continued. Here, in this spacious room sat the men who in effect wielded the highest authority in the land – to control, supervise and punish. And they were aware of this. And for that reason their speech was unhurried, no one strained his voice, and there was no altercation. All of them were perfectly polite and considerate to one another.

General Kurbanov, head of the KGB's Investigation Directorate, was speaking: 'I have to confess that when I inspected the scene of events on the nineteenth of January, I personally made a few slips. I failed to notice both the signs of a struggle and of a second bullet on the window-frame. And since I didn't suspect that this might be murder, I didn't send Semyon Kuzmich's suicide note for examination. As I now gather, Investigator Shamrayev has done all these things. And if it were not for these suspicious contacts of Boris Buryatsky with foreign agents, I would have been the first to tell Comrade Krasnov to hand him over to the Prosecutor's Office and let them sort it out. But if this Buryatsky has been recruited as a foreign agent, everything becomes more complicated. There's not only the prospect of uncovering the hostile activites of foreign Intelligence services, but also the more interesting one of 'turning round' these agents that Buryatsky had contacts with, and we could then run a counter-intrigue against western Intelligence. But that is entirely in the hands of our Section Eight. Of course,' he said smiling, 'the Prosecutor's Office or the MVD might get the impression that they actually did all the basic work, and that we were just skimming the cream . . .'

Everyone laughed, and Krasnov went on: 'But we personally are quite prepared to forego the rewards for the sake of the cause.'

Everyone present now looked at Chief Public Prosecutor Rekunkov and the head of his Investigation Section, Herman Karakoz. Rekunkov took from Shcholokov who was sitting next to him a red cloth binder marked 'Top Secret' and headed 'Case of B. Buryatsky'.

Leafing through it, he cleared his throat gently and said: 'Hmm! To be quite honest, I would have liked to shed this matter from the very outset. Get it off our backs, so to speak.'

Again there were smiles all round. Krasnov had even leaned back in his chair with relief.

But Rekunkov went on: 'I see, however, that in his inquiry, my investigator Shamrayev has made a number of blunders. For instance, there are no reports of any interrogation of Tsvigun's bodyguard, or of his chauffeur.'

'They are both on vacation, somewhere in the south,' said Pirozhkov, becoming slightly uneasy.

'That doesn't matter, they can always be sent for,' Andropov observed.

'Indeed,' said Rekunkov. 'They must be summoned and questioned. How was it that they never heard any shots? There were after all two shots fired, if this Buryatsky is to be believed. And in addition to that, the inquiry should carry out an experiment and take Buryatsky to the safe apartment, and let him demonstrate to us minute by minute exactly what happened. And we should place another man down below where the bodyguard was sitting, and he can listen to ascertain whether shots are audible from there or not.'

'We can do all that as well,' said Kurbanov. 'But if it's for us, he'll show us not just minute by minute, but second by second.'

There were some more smiles, but the Chief Prosecutor went on in the same tone, drawing out the words slightly: 'I understand . . . But you must also understand me: it would have been for me to go and tell Leonid Brezhnev that I was abandoning the affair. But in order to do that, I have to have some fairly weighty arguments' – and he looked Shcholokov in the eye – 'so put into the file the reports from interrogating the bodyguard and the chauffeur of Tsvigun, and the results of this experiment with Buryatsky in the apartment and that will do it. I'll go out and see Brezhnev, and report that the murderer has been found, and that we are handing him over to the KGB.'

'But that could take a devil of a long time yet,' said Kurbanov.

'And why all the hurry?' Rekunkov asked him. 'I hope Buryatsky isn't going to escape and run away?'

Meanwhile

On Komsomolskaya Square, to the left of the Leningradsky Station, in the courtyard of the old brick building of the Customs freight section, there stands a grey concrete block with many storeys and narrow windows: the USSR Ministry of Communication Postal Inspection Department. But although the employees of this Department actually receive their pay from the Ministry of Communications, it is no secret to those who know about their work, that this Department is subject not to the Ministry, but to the KGB.

Once upon a time, before the Khrushchev détente and the large-scale Jewish emigration, the flow of letters from abroad was fairly small. People still feared to correspond even with close relatives living in the West, and at that time the Inspection Department made do with a fairly small staff and occupied only half of one storey in the main Customs building. But over the last ten to fifteen years the Soviet Union has been inundated by an avalanche of letters from America, Canada, Israel and western Europe. The staff of the Department did not expand to keep step with the increase, and even in the new hastily built wing things were frightfully cramped, with up to six postal censors sharing the same office. Now seventeen million emigrants from Russia lived abroad, and even if only half of them wrote only one letter per year back to the Russia that they loved, nearly eight million letters would come teeming into the Department. Each letter had to be opened without leaving tell-tale evidence, read, assessed and a decision taken whether to deliver it or not to the addressee – and in all cases a copy had to be made and sent to a special department of the KGB where this material was sorted and filed in the dossiers of its intended recipients, and it would lie in the files for days, months and years, until the moment came when all this had to be converted from archive material into evidence for a prosecution.

Svetlov and I showed the military-style guards our credentials and went up to the second floor, heading down a long corridor to the office of the Department head, Sukhorukov. To left and right were doors marked 'English Sector', 'Japanese Sector', 'German Sector', 'Jewish', and so on. No telephones rang behind these doors, and according to the rules there should have been an atmosphere of quiet labour. In fact, though, through almost every door one could hear merry voices – the staff in the various sectors were either exchanging the latest local gossip, or else reading out to one another anything specially amusing in the letters they had to process. Just as we went by, a young female Customs lieutenant dashed from the American Sector to the German, holding a letter. She was helpless with laughter, and from beyond the door we heard her voice: 'Listen to this girls! From America. "Last night I dreamed of a Moscow meat-pie . . .".'

When I opened the door marked 'R.V. Sukhorukov, Director, Postal Inspection Department', I had a surprise. The familiar figure of Roman Sukhorukov, former fighter-pilot, war invalid and Hero of the Soviet Union, was not to be seen. Into his small and modest office were crammed four tables piled high with letters, and at one of these tables sat his deputy, Inna Borisovna Figotina. She was a small, dried-up woman of about sixty, and wore the uniform of a major in the Customs and Excise Service.

'Hello,' I said. 'Where is Sukhorukov?'

'Hello, Igor. Roman Viktorovich is no longer working here.'

'How is that? I saw him here just before New Year.'

'That was *before* the New Year,' she said sadly. 'Now we have another boss – Ksana Aksenchuk. If it's her you want to see, she's chosen a different office for herself, a bit bigger than this, room 302. But she's hardly likely to be in.'

I sat down at Figotina's table and said: 'Inna Borisovna, actually I don't *have* to see her. I am dealing with the case of Tsvigun's death, and I need to take a look at the register books for last December and this January.'

'What is it you're looking for?'

'All the post addressed to Tsvigun – when it came, from whom, and who it was passed on to.'

Figotina looked straight at me, then over towards Svetlov.

I suddenly realized, and introduced him: 'Oh, this is Marat Alekseyevich Svetlov, my close friend and head of the Third Section of Moscow CID. We are both dealing with the Tsvigun case, on Brezhnev's instructions.'

She looked at both of us again, paused to think, and then said: 'Then please shut the door firmly.'

Svetlov obeyed and she then asked: 'What is it in Tsvigun's mail that you're interested in?'

'A letter from some Anya Finshtein in Israel. It must have come in either immediately before, or immediately after the New Year.'

Figotina silently felt in the desk, took out some 'Belomor' cigarettes, lit up, wreathed herself in a cloud of smoke, screwed up her eyes, and then finally asked: 'Igor, how did you find out about that letter?'

'Well . . .' I answered evasively, 'we simply found out.'

'Oh,' she said, 'so God's in His heaven after all! That is a surprise!'

I smiled: 'Actually, though,' I said, 'we have come not from God, but from Brezhnev. And therefore a few details about this letter might not come amiss.'

'Very well,' she said. 'I would never have come to seek you out, but since you're here . . . you won't find anything about this letter in the register books. But there *was* such a letter. In general we long ago stopped ascribing any importance to threatening letters from abroad addressed to Brezhnev, Andropov or to Zotov, head of the Visa and Registry Office. There are whole bundles of such letters every day, mainly from Jews. They threaten to kill whoever it is unless their brothers, husbands and relatives are let out. Even children write in saying: "Brezhnev, if you don't let my Daddy go, I'll put an evil spell on you." And nonsense of that sort. But the letter from that Finshtein woman was something special. It came immediately after the New Year, on January the first or second. It was a sort of *cri de coeur*, and we all read it here and passed it round. She wrote asking Tsvigun to release her fiancé from prison, some Georgian, and in exchange offered some tape-recordings of Brezhnev's conversations at home. Well, of course, we all had a laugh at this – what would these crazy, love-sick Jewesses get up to next? And Sukhorukov was going to send the letter on as usual to Tsvigun's private office. Then suddenly the letter disappeared. Search as we might, we couldn't find it. Well, you know Sukhorukov – the old man got nervous, he started shouting and held an inquiry into who was the last person to have the letter in his hands. And he discovered it was Ksana Aksenchuk, a junior censor in the Arab Sector, and niece of Pirozhkov the Deputy Chairman of the KGB. But she would have none of it. She maintained she'd never seen the letter. So the matter was forgotten. But on the nineteenth Tsvigun died, and the same day Sukhorukov received an instruction to redirect all mail addressed to Tsvigun immediately to the KGB Investigation Department without opening any of it. Then there came rumours that Tsvigun had not just died but had done himself in after a conversation with Suslov. And then, three days ago, on Friday, Sukhorukov was told that he was being pensioned off, and in his place as Head of Department they appointed – can you imagine? – Ksana Aksenchuk! I hope you get the message? So she's our new boss, and Sukhorukov has had a heart-attack and is in the Botkin Hospital.

1.45 p.m.
The lights went up in the auditorium of the Rossiya cinema. The film *Pirates of the Twentieth Century* had ended. The audience – mainly youths between twelve and fourteen – rushed to leave. But of the dozen broad exits, only three were opened, and then only one of each set of double doors. Members of the audience could thus only get out one by one, so that Major Ozherelyev could find Vera Tsvigun again. But he underestimated what twelve hundred youths who have just seen *Pirates of the Twentieth Century* are capable of. A fearful whistling and stamping started up inside, and youths began beating on the doors with their fists and feet. Then, emulating the pirates' recent rampage across the screen, they set out to 'storm' the doors.

The management's appeals to the young people over the public-address system to calm down had no effect. The locked oakwood doors started bending as the crowd pressed against them, and the desperate shouts of half-crushed youngsters could be heard from the midst of the press. Another few seconds, and it seemed as if the crowd would come bursting out of the exits, trampling children underfoot and sweeping aside the feeble cordons of militia.

But Ozherelyev saved the situation. He tore into the projection-room and shouted: 'Start the film! Restart the fucking film!'

The frightened technician immediately switched on the projector again, and once again the pirates rolled across the screen. And that same instant, the young people rushed back to their places with the same impetus with which they had stormed the exits, and there were jubilant shouts and ecstatic whistles. A chance to see the *Pirates of the Twentieth Century* a second time – for free!

'But at this rate they'll never come out!' said Junior Lieutenant Polina Sinitsyna to Ozherelyev.

'Very well, let them stay there,' he answered. 'But the old woman will come out. Why should she want to watch this twaddle a second time?'

He was right. When the auditorium had quietened, Vera Tsvigun made her way to the exit. But this time she was the only person to leave the cinema, and the faces of the agents in disguise hanging about near the exit put her on her guard. Whatever else, Vera Tsvigun was a former Cheka worker and the wife of the First Deputy Chairman of the KGB, and at such close range she detected something unmistakably familiar in these characters – something that smacked of the KGB. And she also realized for whose benefit the cinema doors had to be turned into a control-point just now. Her heart froze, and expecting that any second she would be arrested, she stepped slowly through the doors and out on to the street.

But no one did arrest her. No one seized her arms or gagged and hurled her into a waiting car. Strained, walking erect, and with the pounding of her elderly heart echoing through her chest, she moved away from the cinema and set off down Strastnoi Boulevard.

Her suspicion was confirmed. As she walked along in a semi-daze, from the corner of her eye she noticed on the far side of the Boulevard an ordinary Moskvich which followed her progress, neither hurrying nor falling behind. Her heart sank somewhere below the cold pit of her stomach. In those moments Vera Tsvigun felt the presentiment of arrest and the ordinary Soviet man's sense of desperate helplessness before the all-powerful KGB, which for so many years had given delight and satisfaction to her husband. Vera Petrovna had no doubt that it was the KGB who were following her – they had evidently already arrested the man who that morning had put the cursed letter from Anya Finshtein in her postbox. And now they were going to seize her too, and they would grill and grill and grill her about those cursed tapes.

'But why? Why don't they pick me up here right now?' the thought beat through her grey head. She did not know that the man in the Moskvich was Major Ozherelyev, not of the KGB, but of the Moscow CID. Nor could she know that at that moment he was vainly trying to establish radio contact with his chief, Marat Svetlov, and with Investigator Shamrayev in order to find out whether or not to pick her up.

212

Meanwhile
Svetlov and I developed and printed the films taken by Bossman and Gold
Fang not in the professional laboratory of the CID, nor in the Forensic
Institute, nor even in the Institute of Criminology. We did it at the home of
our exuberant Belyakov, in a tiny cell which his elder son Alyosha maintained as an amateur photographer's darkroom. And on the still wet
printing-paper we could already read some extremely intriguing documents.

First of all there was a document certifying confiscation of valuables from
the home of General Zotov, Chief of the Visa and Registry Office. These
included one item of material evidence – a platinum tiara with the following
words engraved on the rear: 'From Givi to my dear Anya'.

Secondly there was a report on the interrogation of General Zotov. Its
seven pages established that Baklanov had revealed Zotov as guilty of taking
bribes. On 18 July 1978, Zotov had in a single day rushed through the issue
of exit visas to Israel for Arkady Borisovich (or Borukhovich) Finshtein, his
wife Raisa Markovna, and his daughter Anna Arkadyevna (or Anya). In
return for this service he had received the above-mentioned tiara, three gold
bracelets encrusted with diamonds, and eight men's and women's gold rings
set with precious stones.

The third item was a series of photographs of Anya Finshtein, her mother
and father, extracted from the Finshtein family's Emigration Application
No. 56197, also several photographs of Anya Finshtein obtained by
Baklanov in the course of questioning and interrogating all members of the
filming team that had shot *Front without Flank*, starting with producer Igor
Gostev and finishing with film star Nikolai Tikhonov.

The fourth item consisted of the reports on interrogations of former
neighbours and colleagues of Anya Finshtein and her father Arkady. From
these reports one could tell that Baklanov had attempted without success to
establish with these people's help: A) where Finshtein might have hidden a
box containing tapes; and B) the present address of the Finshteins in Israel.
In one thing, however, Baklanov had been successful: Arkady Finshtein's
colleagues in the film studios had confirmed that he was a remarkable radio
engineer and inventor, and for his future son-in-law he had in 1978 made a
unique miniature tape-recorder with a supersensitive microphone; he had
also regularly boosted his earnings from Mosfilm by repairing his friends'
and acquaintances' foreign-made stereo equipment; and he had also fitted
private cars with stereo and radio.

But the fifth and most intriguing item was Baklanov's letter, and the short
notes he had made in it revealed the methods used by KGB agents to trace
Anya Finshtein in Israel.

Baklanov had argued as follows: Anya Finshtein can be found through the
Israel telephone directory (difficulty – namesakes, since Finshtein is a
common name; also possibility of name changed); via Soviet film people
emigrated to Israel; collect list from Boris Maryamov at Union of Cinema-
tographers; in view of father's recent death, inquire with administration of

213

Tel-Aviv cemeteries, who may have noted addresses of relatives; also she is bound to visit the grave; Finshtein had driving licence. Hence may have had car in Israel. Bribe one of staff at vehicle licensing office.

'Hmm, yes!' said Svetlov, looking at the photographs of Anya Finshtein. 'This little beauty has got herself into a fine scrape! If they see fit, they'll bring her back from beyond the grave even! If they've not already done so.'

The strikingly beautiful, pure face of a twenty-year-old girl gazed at us from the photographs. Her large dark eyes were set in a fine and slightly elongated face, and the lips were slightly parted. Her face was framed by a luxuriant growth of fair hair which came down to her shoulders.

'But it looks as though they haven't yet done so,' I said, pondering an idea I had had on my mind for more than an hour. 'At any rate, it's clear that these tapes actually exist, and that Baklanov, Krasnov and the KGB have done everything conceivable to find them. So we're left with one possibility.'

I went out of the tiny darkroom into the main room, lifted the receiver of the phone and dialled the number of Suren Pchemyan at the CPSU Central Committee.

'Suren Alekseyevich? This is Shamrayev calling. I need to see Leonid Brezhnev urgently.'

'How urgently?' asked Pchemyan.

'Extremely.'

'Good. Come to the Spassky Gates at half-past five this evening. You'll be met.'

'Can't we make it earlier than that?'

'Unfortunately not. At the moment Gromyko is holding discussions with Haig in Geneva, and he keeps conferring constantly with Comrade Brezhnev over the phone. And in addition, in Warsaw General Jaruzelski is speaking before the Sejm again, and the situation there is very tense. So there's no chance of anything before half-past five.'

'OK, I'll be there.'

I glanced at my watch. It was ten minutes to two, and at two o'clock my son would be coming out of school.

I told Svetlov: 'I have to rush over to Presnya to meet my son. Can you drop me off there?'

'One moment,' he said, and he grabbed an empty glass flask from Alyosha Belyakov's darkroom and went out to the toilet looking worried.

'How is it you keep going to the lav every ten minutes?' I asked in surprise as he went out.

'Goldberg said that with gonorrhoea flakes of tissue appear in the urine. But so far there's no sign of any,' he answered.

1.58 p.m.
When they had seen off the guests and their subordinates, Yury Andropov and Nikolai Shcholokov remained behind on their own. Andropov removed

214

his spectacles. He seemed tired as he rubbed the bridge of his nose and his brow.

'Strange how that man Rekunkov bristles,' said Shcholokov.

'He seems to be playing for time. But it's a disgrace that your section of the Moscow CID is working against us.'

'Nothing to worry about,' said Shcholokov and shook his head dismissively. 'And you can *see* what they're up to. They've knocked together a few identikit pictures and gone rushing round the hospitals. They won't find a thing. It's a wild goose chase, so why not just let them keep running. What's more alarming is that the bloody Jewess has got lost in Israel.'

It sounded like an answering thrust – a hint that for over a week Andropov's 'residents' in Israel had been unable to find a simple émigré girl.

But Andropov answered calmly: 'She's not in Israel any more, she's in western Europe. My people have found out at Port Ben Gurion that on the seventeenth she flew to Rome on an Alitalia flight, and she had a ticket just as far as Rome. That's all in our favour: it's far easier to smuggle her back to the Soviet Union from there, than it is from Israel.'

He glanced at his watch, and turning in his leather armchair, he opened up the oak doors of a bookcase. Behind them on the shelf stood the latest Grundig radio-receiver. The set was already adjusted to the right wavelength, and at the touch of a bright metal key, the call-sign of Radio Liberty in Munich issued from the speaker, overlaid by the heavy, monotonous howl of the Soviet jamming stations. And through the howling a baritone speaking voice could be heard. 'This is Radio Liberty. This is Radio Liberty. We are now broadcasting on the 16, 31, 41 and 49 metre bands. This is Oleckso Boyarko and Mila Kareva, and here is the latest news. In Moscow . . .'

At this point the speaker's voice was drowned out completely by the jamming. But Andropov dialled an internal extension number on the intercom and quietly gave the instruction: 'Kachalov, stop the jamming.'

And in the same instant, the howling of the jammers disappeared, and Andropov's office was filled by the pure, strong and well-modulated voice of the newsreader from that most hostile of all radio stations: 'The Soviet press agency TASS has announced the death yesterday at the age of seventy-nine of the Kremlin's chief ideologist, CPSU Central Committee Secretary Mikhail Suslov. Western Sovietologists note that this is the second death in the Kremlin in the last few days. On 19 January, Leonid Brezhnev's brother-in-law, First Deputy Chairman of the KGB, General Semyon Tsvigun also died. Foreign correspondents in Moscow connect the death of Tsvigun with the mass arrests of leaders of the Soviet Union's "underground" economy which have been taking place in the country recently. It is reported that a close friend of Galina, daughter of Brezhnev, one Boris Buryatsky, alias "The Gypsy", has been arrested, Galina Brezhneva herself is undergoing interrogation, and Brezhnev's son Yury, who is First Deputy Minister of Foreign Trade, has not appeared in his office for several days. It is supposed that they were closely connected with the activities of the underground

215

economic mafia, and that KGB General Tsvigun was the initiator of the revelations, which have angered both Mikhail Suslov and Leonid Brezhnev. In Moscow rumours are circulating that after a sharp conversation on this subject with Mikhail Suslov, Tsvigun committed suicide, and this allegedly explains why neither Brezhnev nor Suslov signed the obituary of Tsvigun, who was a member of the CPSU Central Committee and a close relative of Brezhnev. Moreover, the body of Tsvigun, second-in-command of the KGB and member of the government, has not been buried at the official government cemetery. It is now announced that the chief ideological watchdog of the Kremlin, Mikhail Suslov, has not survived by long the man who dared to reveal the corruption on the highest level among the Soviet leadership.'

'Warsaw . . .' a female voice took over from the first newsreader.

'Kachalov, you can carry on jamming. That's one thing. The second is: they will probably be saying the same thing today on the BBC and 'Voice of America'. These reports should not be jammed.'

And he leaned back in his armchair and looked at Shcholokov with a glimmer of pride. Meanwhile the air was filled again with the renewed noise of jamming, through which the hostile radio station attempted to inform Russian listeners of another wave of arrests in Poland.

'Nicely managed . . .' said Shcholokov with a hint of envy.

'That's only the beginning,' said Andropov. 'We'll be throwing them another interesting titbit. Especially about Galya and this "Gypsy". They like that sort of thing. And with that sort of dressing her father won't look his best either, will he?'

'Hmm, yes . . .' pondered Shcholokov. 'You don't have an Armenian mother for nothing! To twist even the mouldy Tsvigun story round for one's own benefit and make the western press praise a general of the KGB for revealing corruption in the Soviet government – only an Armenian, or perhaps a Jewish mind is capable of that sort of thing! We simple Russians have a long way to go!'

The secretary's voice quietly announced: 'Lunch is served, Yury Vladimirovich.'

'Let's go through and eat.' Andropov rose and led his guest through to the back of his office suite where there was both a dining-room and retiring-rooms.

From the windows of the dining-room there was a view of the Kremlin and of crowded Dzerzhinsky Square. The dining-table was covered with a white linen cloth and was set for two. In an elegant soup-tureen of Bohemian porcelain hot *borshch* steamed, another porcelain dish contained vegetables, and on several other plates, dishes and pots lay hors d'oeuvres and black caviare. And in the centre of the table stood bottles of cold vodka, Johnny Walker, Soviet Narzan mineral-water and American soda-water. The snow-white linen napkins were enclosed in silver rings and lay next to the silver cutlery.

Andropov went up to the table and poured some Johnny Walker into a

216

crystal glass – just a little in the bottom. Since the doctors had diagnosed diabetes in him, he could no longer drink as he had in his youth, but his long-standing love of Johnny Walker was stronger than any medical prescriptions.

With glass in hand he moved away to the window and said to his guest: 'Make yourself at home.'

Shcholokov poured himself some vodka from the carafe, placed a pickled gherkin on his plate, and a spoon of black caviare on his bread – a first snack to accompany the first glass of vodka. He knew that Andropov would wait by the window while he drank and ate what he, Andropov, had been forbidden by his doctors. His diabetic condition, Shcholokov thought, made Andropov resemble Suslov even in outward appearance – from a one-time puff-cheeked Party prodigy Andropov had turned into a stern ascetic with almost hollow cheeks.

But Shcholokov said aloud: 'All the same I think that after the death of Suslov it would be better for us to retreat.'

'But what is there actually for us to retreat *from*?' Andropov laughed. 'You and I never made any advance! We are innocent in the eyes of Brezhnev and the Party. You started Operation Cascade on Suslov's instructions. He gave the orders – you carried them out. And the fact that this operation ended in the death of Tsvigun is not your fault – Suslov simply purged the Party of a bribe-taker. And anyway, when power is handed over, a lot of things will have to be cleaned up. Over the last eighteen years the Party apparatus has really turned into a caste of bribe-takers. For them the rule of Brezhnev has been a golden age. Whatever people may say about Stalin, under him Party jobs were never put up for sale. But today in Azerbaidzhan the post of Secretary of a Party District Committee can be bought for 120,000 roubles. We shall put an end to this as soon as we get there.' He nodded through the window towards the Kremlin. 'Not straight away, of course, but . . . first of all it will be necessary to let the people have just a little rest, put provisions in the shops – even from military stores if necessary – and offer a few minor economic reforms. And it's urgent that we modernize our ground-to-air missiles. I gather that a story is going round the country that after the Israeli air force knocked out several Soviet-built rocket installations, the Syrians sent Brezhnev a telegram: 'CEASE DELIVERIES OF "GROUND-TO-AIR" ROCKETS. PLEASE SEND ROCKETS "GROUND TO AIRCRAFT!"' ' . . . But I merely mention that in passing . . . However, the main thing is that the people should realize that at last an honest government has come to power, which will put an end to thieving and bribery in the Party apparatus. And here we shall be greatly helped by western radio stations. They are in fact already helping. We provide them with their information, and each day we throw them some spicy morsel. And these western radio stations are believed by the people here much more than our own radio . . .'

He fell silent. Outside the window, through the white rippling snowfall the

Kremlin stood before him – not at all far away, no more than three blocks, only a few steps. And looking at the Kremlin with his grey-blue eyes, Andropov took a tiny sip of Johnny Walker.

Meanwhile

The school bell could be heard even from the street, and a minute later a noisy band of youths poured out of the five-storey building like a barbarian horde. They whooped, shouted, leap-frogged, hurled snowballs at one another, pushed the girls over into the snow, and knocked one another's fur helmets off. And through this roaring, laughing and whooping crowd came a group of four boys, stooping and shielding their faces from the hail of snowballs. Meanwhile the fourteen-year-olds pelted them with weighty lumps of snow and ice and clouted them across the back and shoulders with their briefcases, and one youth took a run and hurled one of them into a snowdrift. Among the attackers I saw my own son Anton. 'Beat the Yids! Give them a thrashing!' he yelled, and tripped one of them so that he tumbled on to his face in the snow while the others around him laughed.

I rushed forward and grabbed my son forcefully by the scruff of the neck: 'What do you think you're doing?'

'And what have they gone and seized the Golan Heights for, the bastards?' he said, and tore himself free of my grip.

'And who are "they"?' I asked.

'Who else d'you think? The Yids!'

I looked at my son, dumbfounded. And maybe for the first time I saw standing before me an almost grown-up lad, too old to give a box on the ears to, or administer a belting. He looked up at me, sullen and morose, and the gang of schoolboys raced on past us to the schoolyard exit, shoving the Jewish boys and yelling: 'Clear off to Israel! Get out!'

'Wait,' I said to my son. 'And what are you? You're part-Jewish yourself!'

'I'm not a Jew!' he shouted in my face, and his voice was full of anger and bitterness, and he looked around to see whether anyone could overhear our conversation.

'Just stand here and calm down,' I said, trying to get a grip on myself as well. 'Your grandma, my mother, was a Jewess. That means I am half-Jewish, and you – well, you are a quarter-Jewish. And apart from that . . .'

'I am not a Jew, and you are not a Jew!' he interrupted. 'Your wife was Russian and all your mistresses are Russian! You sleep with Russians, you live in Russia, and you think and speak in Russian. Tell me one Jewish word that you know! Or perhaps you sit up at night studying Hebrew?'

'Well, in theory I wouldn't mind knowing Hebrew . . .'

'Well, I don't want to know it!' he interrupted again. 'I don't want to know either the Jewish language, or my Jewish grandmother! I am Russian! My mother was a Russian! And I want to be Russian!'

'Go ahead, nobody is stopping you. You can consider yourself Russian and you can love Russia. I love Russia as well. But why do you have to be an anti-Semite? That's not at all a Russian characteristic. I have Russian friends all over the place, and none of them beat me for being half-Jewish.'

'They *will* beat you,' he said. 'You'll see! What have you come for anyway? To introduce me to the next of your Ninas? Or to circumcise me?'

I looked him in the eye and said nothing. His eyes blazed with frustrated puerile frenzy.

'Very well,' I said, bending down and picking up a stone caked about with snow, and holding it out to Anton. 'Take this and throw it at me. I'm a Yid after all. Come on! Throw it! Call me a filthy Jew. What are you waiting for?'

He turned and walked away. I remained standing, still holding the stone in my outstretched hand, and watched him go. My son – my *son*! – walked away from me, the Moscow snow crunching under his feet as he went.

'Anton!' I shouted.

He did not turn round, but only quickened his step.

It became clear to me that the Suslovs, Andropovs, Shcholokovs, Maleninas and Krasnovs had not only killed Nina, they had also taken my son away from me. And while they had been smashing his soul, I had been serving them, and still continued to serve . . .

I hurled the stone hard into a snowdrift, and my first thought was to try and blow my mind with a tumbler-full of vodka.

Outside the school gates on the street, Svetlov's car was waiting.

When I went back to the car, Marat said: 'You're looking awful. What's happened?'

'To a pub!' I said. 'Take me to any pub in the area!'

Meanwhile

EXTRACT FROM A REPORT BY V. PSHENICHNY TO
I. SHAMRAYEV, INVESTIGATION TEAM LEADER

Nurse Dina Temnogrudova of District Clinic No. 49 told me upon questioning that shortly after 5.00 p.m. on 19 January of this year, at the surgery at Arbatskaya metro station, where she also helps out, a militia colonel appeared, escorting a young man with a gun-shot wound right through the right thigh. The man had lost a lot of blood. Dr Levin carried out initial treatment, and Temnogrudova applied a temporary bandage, after which the patient, still accompanied by the militia colonel, departed, allegedly heading for the Sklifasovsky First Aid Institute where Dr Levin had referred them.

In the series of photos shown to her, Temnogrudova identified the injured man with the identikit portrait assembled from the description by junior witness Ekaterina (Katya) Uzhovich . . .

2.17 p.m.

Seeing that nobody tried to seize or arrest her, Vera Tsvigun was slightly reassured. The memory of her own youthful Cheka experience returned, and without altering her step or showing in any way that she realized that she was being tailed, she began considering. There could be no question of running or hiding from the KGB agents. Even if she gave her pursuers the slip just now – a fairly easy matter (she had been taught that years ago by Berzin himself, the teacher of Colonel Abel and Richard Sorge) – the KGB would then cover all the airports and stations, and she would never make it to a train or aircraft . . .

Vera Tsvigun struggled to think of a loophole in the system which she and her husband had given their whole lives to constructing. And she came to the bitter conclusion that over the decades the system had been perfected and polished to the point where it had no more gaps. There was only one thing to do – turn round and go to meet them. Let them take her and arrest her – if only this depressing uncertainty would end.

At that moment she thought of the Prosecutor's Office. The investigator who recently came to see her was from there. What was his name? Damn! She had forgotten the name of that man who had come on Brezhnev's instructions to inquire into the death of her husband. And in fact she had practically had to throw him out of her house. But the Public Prosecutor's Office was somewhere here nearby, on Pushkin Street. Only she must not show her agitation or change her pace. Don't hurry, don't run, don't look back – that was what Berzin had taught her. Keep calm. Until they seize you and put in handcuffs, you are still master of the situation . . .

She turned right and there were now only two blocks to go to reach the Public Prosecutor's Office. But those two blocks with the same Moskvich still in stealthy pursuit seemed to take her ten years to walk.

At twenty-eight minutes past two, though, as Vera Tsvigun passed by 15-A Pushkin Street, she suddenly made a sideways dash to the tall brown wooden doors of the Prosecutor's Office, seized the bronze handle, pushed against the door, and literally fell inside and said to the guard on duty: 'I am the wife of Tsvigun. I need to find the investigator who . . .'

Meanwhile
The investigator whom Vera Tsvigun was looking for – to wit, myself – was sitting with Marat Svetlov in the fusty, half-empty Arrow Cafe. Of course, we could have gone to the fashionable Arbat, or the élite private restaurants at the House of Journalists or House of Writers, but I had no desire at present to see the well-fed and fragrant physiognomies of the men who educate the Soviet public. The unpretentious Arrow Cafe suited me perfectly, with its dirty tablecloths and slovenly impudent waitresses, its warm Streletskaya vodka, and its single meat dish – a rump steak tough enough to sole one's shoe. We were already on our second glass of Streletskaya, but I was still in a fever and had not yet cooled off from the encounter with Anton.

Nevertheless the vodka seemed gradually to take effect, and I drunkenly leaned across the table to Svetlov: 'Listen. Are you put out by the fact that I'm Jewish?'

'What are you going on about? Calm down, have a bite to eat.'

220

But I turned to the half-empty dining-room and asked loudly: 'And who here is put off by the fact that I'm a Jew?'

'Quiet!' Svetlov implored me, but the manager was already hurrying across to our table. His face was round-cheeked, and speckled with blackheads, his lips were full, his little eyes were the colour of pale lead, and he wore a resolute expression as he crossed the room. But when he saw the colonel's epaulets on Svetlov's uniform, he became confused, and when he got to our table he merely asked: 'What's all the noise about, Comrades?'

Svetlov took from a pocket his red CID identity card, showed it to the manager and said simply and quietly: 'Push off.'

'I understand,' the manager made a grovelling reverence. 'And may I possibly bring you some refreshments, Comrade Colonel?'

'Do.'

The manager disappeared, and a moment later emerged bearing a tray of salmon, pork, gherkin salad and a steaming plateful of Siberian meat dumplings, none of which figured on the official menu.

'There we are, Comrades,' he cooed, placing all this on our table. 'What a splendid evening it is! The Central Sports Club side have beaten Dynamo 3–2. So relax and enjoy it, Comrades. May I perhaps bring you some *shashlyk*? They've just brought in some fresh meat a moment ago.'

'What is your name?' Svetlov asked him.

'N-n-neznachny, C-comrade Colonel.' For some reason the fleshy-cheeked manager began to stutter as he answered.

'Christian name and patronymic?'

'F-f-Frol Isayich . . .'

'A Jew?' Svetlov asked.

'E-e-eh . . .' something seemed to stick in the throat of the frightened manager. 'Yes, a Jew, but er . . . I am a Party member, Comrade Colonel!'

'Well, how is it? Do you find that being a Jew interferes with life?'

'Not in any way whatsoever, Comrade Colonel! Why! I even have a Russian wife, and she treats me wonderfully! I am not at all hampered, I am totally unaware of my nationality . . .' The lackey hunch of his spine had straightened out, he puffed out his chest and his pancake face with piggy eyes even assumed an expression of outrage, as if to say: 'How could Soviet life fail to please Neznachny, Soviet citizen, Jewish national, and member of the Communist Party of the Soviet Union?' Indignation caused even the blackheads on his face to pale.

'There, you see,' Svetlov turned to me. 'Nobody here minds at all that you're a Jew.' Then to the manager: 'OK, go and fix the *shashlyk* for us.'

'Right away.' And Neznachny disappeared into the kitchen, shoulders back and chest puffed out.

'What a bloody country!' I said, looking after him.

'Why?' asked Svetlov in amazement. 'It's a splendid country! Where else would they serve you like that at the mere sight of your red identity card?'

'Marat,' I said, pouring out the vodka into our cut-glass tumblers, 'I

221

couldn't care a damn at the moment whether the Jews like it in this country, or not. Or who is in power here – Brezhnev, Chernenko or Andropov. Nothing will change here anyway. But one thing I have to do – and that is settle accounts with them for taking Nina and Anton away from me. Will you help me? You realize of course that it was not the man who pushed her off the platform that killed her, but those who sent him to push her.'

'We shall certainly settle accounts with them for Nina,' he said. 'I made that vow yesterday at the mortuary.'

3.40 p.m.

EXTRACT FROM THE REPORT BY VALENTIN PSHENICHNY

Dr Sergei Levin of the medical surgery at metro station Arbatskaya identified the identikit picture shown to him as the man who, on 19 January of this year shortly after 5 p.m. required first aid for a gunshot-wound through the right thigh. Levin also supplied details of the militia colonel who accompanied the patient and described him as tall with brown hair, about fifty years of age, stooping hazel eyes, hooked nose. According to Dr Levin, the above-mentioned colonel forbade him to enter the patient in his register book, failed to show his militia identification papers, and was scornful of Dr Levin's offer to write a note referring him to the Sklifasovsky Institute. A check of the register books and thorough questioning of all the medical staff of the Sklifasovsky First Aid Institute established that neither on the 19th, nor 20th or 21st January was a single man treated by them for a bullet-wound in the region of the right thigh.

Despite the fact that all trace of the injured criminal has at present been lost, I have come to the following conclusion: since the medical surgery at Arbatskaya metro station is situated close to Kachalov Street where the killing of General Tsvigun occurred at 16-A, and since the injured man had, in Dr Levin's words, lost a lot of blood, the malefactors must have been forced along the way to apply for emergency treatment at some other hospital which we have not yet managed to locate.

The team of Moscow CID investigators under my command is continuing the search for the criminal in the hospitals of Moscow and the surrounding area.

Dr Sergei Levin and nurse Dina Temnogrudova have been taken to the Moscow CID's technical department in order to establish an identikit portrait of the militia colonel who was escorting the injured man.

3.45 p.m.

I was given emergency treatment at sobering station number nine in the Krasnopresnensky District of Moscow for food and alcohol poisoning. That blasted rump steak which had been like an old shoe, combined with impure vodka and salmon of doubtful freshness had caught up with me. The hazards of daily life could cause hiccups even in the work routine of Brezhnev's personal investigator – as the proverb has it, ''Tis but one step from greatness to absurdity!' But Svetlov was quite untouched! He had no signs of poisoning.

And not content with that, while they used the stomach-pump on me and I kept rushing between my bunk and the toilet, he proceeded to stand there and make fun of me.

'You see, you've got a Jewish stomach,' he said. 'It won't take our Russian food!'

Shortly after 4 p.m.
In the film-theatre of the CID technical department, Dr Sergei Levin and Nurse Dina Temnogrudova were busy putting together on the screen an identikit portrait of the militia colonel who accompanied the injured man on the evening of 19 January.

In the semi-darkness Valentin Pshenichny had dozed off in his seat. I think it was the first rest he had had since our investigation began. Svetlov and I stood by the door and looked at the face taking shape on the screen, with its dark hair, hooked nose, fine nostrils, low brow and sharp transverse crease on the prominent chin.

'Oleinik,' Svetlov whispered in my ear. 'Colonel Oleinik, one and the same.'

I nodded to him and went up to Pshenichny's seat. I did not feel like waking him, but I had to. I touched him on the shoulder, and he immediately twitched, and shot me a glance with his blue eyes that were now sunken with tiredness.

I sat down next to him, and said quietly so that only he should hear: 'Valya, when the portrait's ready, don't show it to anyone and don't have copies made. Hand it to me and then you go home and sleep.'

'But I haven't found the criminal yet . . .'

'You have found him now. Only we can't touch him for the time being. Finish off here, hand me the identikit picture and go and sleep. That's an order. I need a man who's fresh and well-rested.'

He nodded, and Svetlov and I left the viewing-room. We went off down the empty corridor of the technical department which at the same time was set up as the Moscow CID's criminological museum. Here in the glass cases and cupboards stood the most varied exhibits and trophies from the CID's struggle against crime. As Marat and I headed for the other wing of the building which housed the Third Section, we passed by an exhibition of guns of various calibre, Finnish daggers, knuckle-dusters, defused mines, home-made guns, jemmies, traps, strangling-cord, aerosol cans with the poisonous liquid now removed, dynamite charges without detonators and detonators without dynamite.

'Take your pick,' laughed Svetlov, pointing to the exhibits. 'I've got masses more stuff like that in my own private store of material evidence.'

'Yes, I'll choose,' I said, 'when the time comes.'

223

Then, turning a corner in the corridor and going through a series of doors and passages, we emerged into another world and found ourselves among the usual everyday CID atmosphere of heavy oaths, telephone calls, clumping boots and a thick fug of tobacco.

In the duty-room leading to Svetlov's office we also found a strange scene: almost half the operational staff of Third Section – about twenty officers – were huddled round a table with a large Spidola radio-set from which issued a clear voice, uninterrupted by jamming: 'And that KGB General Tsvigun was the initiator of the revelations, which have angered both Mikhail Suslov and Leonid Brezhnev. In Moscow rumours are circulating that after a sharp conversation on this subject with Mikhail Suslov, Tsvigun committed . . .'

4.25 p.m.

Hardly had Vera Tsvigun convinced herself that she was not threatened by interrogation and grilling from the KGB, and that all her fears had been in vain, when she adopted a quite different frame of mind. Amid the routine din of the CID corridors, the heavy steps of prisoner-escorts, lusty male swearing, officers' uniforms, telephone calls, shouts and tobacco-smoke, she came alive, straightened her back, and even seemed to get younger, as though she had returned to the fighting days of her youth in the Cheka.

And she followed me into Svetlov's office with an easy, free gait, sat down in front of the desk, lit a cigarette, and said: 'I can give you some valuable information. Extremely valuable. Not just about the murder of Tsvigun, but even more vital. So vital, that perhaps Brezhnev might even survive in power after all. But – on one condition: only if Mosfilm resumes the shooting of *The Invisible War* based on Tsvigun's story 'We Shall Return', and, of course, if there's a guarantee that the film will be released and shown publicly.' And with these words she produced from her handbag a copy of the journal *Znamya*, No. 5, for 1981, where the story first appeared. 'I repeat, in exchange for this I have some very valuable information.'

I looked at her straight and said: 'If you mean the letter from Anya Finshtein, then you've already provided us with this information.'

'How do you mean?' she started in surprise.

I drew from my pocket an envelope containing the carefully folded sheet on which the shreds of Anya Finshtein's letter had been mounted, and I showed it to her: 'Vera Petrovna, in another place not far from here – we won't be too precise – they would try and pin on you a charge of illegal dealing with foreigners. And the fact that you're Brezhnev's relative would not help you. But I don't intend to do that. Nor do I even intend to try and extract from you how your husband used to address Anya Finshtein – "Anyuta", "Anna", or some nickname. It would be intriguing but it's not essential – I can find that out from the film producer or cameraman – or I simply needn't bother. All that interests me – and even that merely from the psychological angle – is the figure of her fiancé Givi Mingadze. Of course, he'll soon be telling me about himself in person, but some preliminary information would not come amiss.'

She sat silent, evidently crushed.

'Well?' I asked. 'Shall we have some tea perhaps? Would you like something to eat?'

'Yes, I would . . .' she said quietly, and with despair in her voice: 'What about the film?'

I shrugged. 'I'm not the Minister of Culture,' I said and glanced outside the room and asked the sergeant on duty: 'Sergeant, bring us two buttered rolls from the canteen and two glasses of strong tea. Here's the money.'

'What has the Minister of Culture to do with it?' asked Vera Tsvigun in a temper. 'It's not he who decides, it's decided in the Central Committee. And what difference does it make to them – a film based on Tsvigun's story or another writer's? But for me the whole of my life is now in these films! If they agree to do this film, I'll do anything for you you care to name, my word of honour! And Brezhnev can carry on ruling, damn him! Of course, I could have taken this letter to Andropov and come to some agreement with him, but I'm convinced that all this Cascade business and the death of Tsvigun are his doing. And I couldn't go and see a murderer!'

'All I can promise you,' I said, 'is that I will talk about this with the Central Committee this evening. But without an ultimatum from you.'

A knock at the door was followed by the entry of the duty sergeant, carrying a plate of rolls and butter and two glasses of tea on a tray. I felt a stab of heartache – the last person to bring in tea on this tray had been Nina . . .

Sipping her tea, Tsvigun's widow told me her tale.

'Givi Mingadze . . . In 1975 Galina Brezhneva brought two characters to see us. They were down-and-out and half-broke – Boris Buryatsky and this Givi Mingadze. Where she picked them up, I don't know. Probably in some restaurant where Buryatsky used to sing gypsy songs. Both these characters were about thirty, and Galya at the time was forty-five, but she was head over heels in love with this gypsy singer! And Givi . . . Well, I must say that he was an extremely witty and easy-going young man. A loafer without any special occupation, but he was a splendid card-player, and Semyon my husband was an inveterate preference-player, as you know. To put it briefly, this Givi became Semyon's regular preference partner, and they played mainly at the house of Yasha Brezhnev, Leonid's brother. Yasha, or Yakov, had once been an engineer specializing in metallurgy, but now he had retired and settled down to write his memoirs and play cards. Both of them are fond of writing their reminiscences – both Leonid and Yakov. But in Leonid's case the journalists ghost-write for him – whereas Yakov wrote his own stuff – but that's not the point. This Givi got so friendly with Yakov, he became simply one of the family. And he set up a business based on this friendship: he took bribes from all sorts of crooks and with Yakov's assistance set them up in important positions. It cost Yakov Brezhnev nothing to lift the receiver and ring up some minister and say: "This is Yakov Brezhnev speaking.

Listen, I have here an excellent man, very intelligent, a friend of our family, and I believe you have a post going free as director of a brewery in Leningrad . . ." And that did it. A phone call like that was sufficient. Who could refuse the brother of the Secretary General of the Central Committee? But Semyon my husband knew nothing about this. It went on behind his back, and . . . well, they simply enjoyed a game of cards together in the evenings and that was all. Galya fixed her "Gypsy" up at the Bolshoi Theatre, and this Givi supposedly was helping Yakov Brezhnev to write his memoirs. Then once he saw on our bookshelves Semyon's book *Front without Flank*. Semyon wrote it back in the fifties, when he and I went on holiday to Valdai. That is, well, really, he and I wrote it together – it was about our years at the front. We altered one or two things, finished it off and thought up a joint pseudonym for ourselves, so that there would be no gossip about a KGB leader using his authority to get his memoirs printed. Briefly, Givi took this book to read, and three days later brought to us some friend of his, a producer at Mosfilm called Igor Gostev. And this man began telling us what a splendid film one could make based on this book, about the work of the Cheka. And that's how they shot this film. There were all sorts of complications of course. For instance, the actor Vyacheslav Tikhonov – you know him, he played Prince Bolkonsky in *War and Peace* – he refused to take the main role. And the main part in it is that of a Cheka agent, the commander of a SMERSH unit – that was really Semyon himself, of course. Well, Gostev went to Tsvigun and told him what had happened: Tikhonov refused to play the main part, and did not even turn up for rehearsal. Semyon was not a proud man. He rang up this actor, invited him along to the KGB and explained that they placed great hopes in him – it was necessary to build up a positive image of the Soviet Cheka agent. Well, as you can well understand, it was hard to refuse Semyon Kuzmich! And especially when Tikhonov was immediately allocated a splendid apartment . . . To cut a long story short, they gathered the best actors together, and I also got completely involved in the work. First we made *Front without Flank*, then a sequel called *The War behind the Front*, and then we began a third – *The Invisible War*. And this work completely engrossed me and reconciled me with the fact that . . . well, that the husband and wife relationship between Semyon and myself had completely fallen apart. He did not want an official divorce, but simply lived with this . . . what's her name? . . . well, anyway, he had some woman and I knew about it. But they don't like it in the Politburo when members of the government get divorced and marry younger women. You know how it is. Well, briefly, he kept two homes – he and I stayed on purely comradely terms, and where he was the rest of the time – that didn't concern me. We didn't use to talk about it at all. I got keen on the cinema and – incidentally, Semyon and I never got a kopeck for those films – we gave the entire fees to a fund to help the children of Vietnam, so that they wouldn't say in the Central Committee that we were making a fat living out of the cinema. And incidentally, when we were shooting the second film in early

1978, it was on the sets that Givi Mingadze got to know our cutting technician, Anya Finshtein. She was a very beautiful girl – a Jewess with enormous eyes, hair down to her shoulders, a real Princess Esther! – That was what Tsvigun called her incidentally. Well . . . this Givi turned out to be a good-for-nothing. He played us a dirty trick as thanks for all the good we had done him, especially Yakov. He hid a tape-recorder in Yakov Brezhnev's apartment, and for two months this tape-recorder recorded all the conversations there. And Brezhnev himself used to go there, and Ustinov, and Galina and Yury Brezhnev. Well, my husband uncovered this, of course. He took all the tapes off him and handed them to Brezhnev. And we took pity on Givi himself – Boris Buryatsky went down on bended knee to Tsvigun to spare his friend, and we did. Instead of executing him for creating a political diversion, we sent him down for ten years on a currency speculation charge. But now it turns out that not all the tapes were taken off him, and some of the originals were in the hands of Anya Finshtein's father . . . But Semyon did not receive any letter from her. That's for certain. He would have told me . . .'

'That letter was intercepted by the postal censors and delivered to Pirozhkov at the KGB,' I told her.

'So you see! So those were the tapes they were searching for at my place. But the tapes we had were handed to Brezhnev long ago. Because of them he has kept his brother for three years under house arrest at his *dacha*. But they went looking for them at our house, the idiots!'

I laughed: 'Vera Petrovna, you have told me only part of the truth. If you and your husband were on comradely terms, then you must definitely have known that in 1967 on your husband's instructions Givi Mingadze and Boris Buryatsky burned down the entire headquarters of the MVD Intelligence Section in the Rossiya Hotel. Apart from that you must know how the coincidence came about that on 17 July 1978, Givi Mingadze was arrested, and the very same day Fyodor Kulakov died of a heart-attack, and a day later Suslov was admitted to hospital. Was it on their orders that Givi Mingadze recorded the Brezhnevs' family conversations?'

'I know nothing about that,' said Vera Tsvigun drily.

Meanwhile
In the office next door Marat Svetlov was giving Captain Arutyunov a telling-off: 'You idiot! A splendid idea like that, and you blurt it out in front of everyone! You realize that they have got all of us under the microscope! They are following our every step and reporting if not to Krasnov, then to Shcholokov! We have to outplay them – outplay them in their presence! And you! It's a dead simple matter to hide this injured man in a prison hospital, in a place where no investigator, not even I, can get in without a pass! But you, you stupid bastard! You Armenian peabrain!'

Svetlov's eyes blazed with passion. 'Right now! I personally entrust you with this – but not a living soul must know, not even Pshenichny! Tomorrow morning first thing you take the City Health Authorities – three doctors – by the short and curlies, and you quietly explain to them their task, which is to arrange a sanitary inspection in every single prison hospital. They can check for plague, cholera, lice, dysentery or gonorrhoea – that doesn't concern me. They can think something up for themselves. The important thing is that they should go round all the hospital wards in prison medical wings and examine all the patients. And if this injured man doesn't turn up among *them*, he might be in one of the Moscow Region prisons, so you check there too. But don't you dare show your face at even one of the prisons, so as not to frighten the geese, do you understand? And Pshenichny and all his team can go round the public hospitals, and Vendelovsky can do the military hospitals. As a cover, to distract attention . . .'

Svetlov glanced at his wristwatch and without any break in the flow of his speech said: 'Here, you don't know what time the hard-currency whores gather in the Hotel National do you?'

5.40 p.m.

'Perhaps you'd like a brandy to give you courage?' suggested Chazov just outside Brezhnev's study.

I made a wry face. After the incident in the Arrow cafe, the very thought of alcohol made my stomach heave. 'No. But I wouldn't mind a glass of mineral-water,' I replied.

'There's some of that in Brezhnev's study,' he said. 'Let's go in.'

General Zharov frisked me once again, saying: 'Don't take offence. It's the rules. You don't search one, you don't search another – and then, before you know where you are . . . That's that,' he continued. 'Please go in.' And he opened the door for me.

The warm, spacious room was bathed in a reddish half-light. Outside the windows, about fifty yards away, you could see the red star shining on the Spassky Tower, and it was the light from this that dimly illuminated the study, along with a desk lamp of the same colour. In this one bright pool of light sat Konstantin Chernenko, a round-faced, grey-haired individual with moist lips and skin which looked pinkish in the light. He was writing something, rapidly and silently. Leonid Brezhnev sat sleeping, wrapped in a checked blanket, his fleshy features relaxed in sleep. A decrepit old man, he was breathing with his mouth open and his chin protruding slightly over the edge of the woollen plaid. A ginger kitten was asleep on his lap, holding his small puffy hand between its paws.

Chazov walked silently over the thick piled carpet, nodding to Chernenko at the desk as he did so. Then he went right up to where Brezhnev was sitting and stood over him for a moment, listening to his breathing. Then he moved a chair from the wall and placed it a couple of yards away from the Secretary General, motioning me to sit in it. I did so. With the same silent authority, Chazov opened a cupboard in the wall, which turned out to be a refrigerator. He removed a bottle of mineral-water from it, and poured me some in a tall

228

wine glass. The sound of the mineral-water effervescing awoke Brezhnev.

'What is it?' he said, twitching those bushy black eyebrows of his which have become known all over the world. Then he looked at me with curiosity and began to suck his lips sleepily. 'Who are you?' he asked.

'It's the investigator, Igor Shamrayev,' said Chazov.

'Hello,' I mumbled, not knowing what to say. My voice sounded unnecessarily loud in this quiet room. The frightened kitten wanted to jump off Brezhnev's lap, but he held on to it.

Then he said very slowly: 'It depends . . . on you . . . now . . . whether . . . I shall stay well . . . or . . . take to my . . . bed . . .'

His lower jaw moved with obvious effort, as if something were preventing it meeting the upper part, and this was why he had such difficulty pronouncing words. The consonants almost disappeared. But his eyes were penetrating and held me fast in their gaze. 'Well, what happend to Tsvigun? . . . Was he murdered?'

'Comrade Brezhnev,' I replied, 'I must speak to you alone.'

From the depths of the room Chernenko looked at me in astonishment.

'Don't worry,' said Brezhnev. 'I can trust everybody here.'

'I can wait outside,' said Chazov.

'Comrade Brezhnev,' I continued, 'there are certain facts I have to report, which are for your ears only. There mustn't be witnesses. It is my duty as an investigator to say this. I'm sorry, Comrade Chernenko,' I said, turning towards him.

'Well, all right, if it's your duty . . .' said Brezhnev, motioning Chazov and Chernenko to go. 'And does the cat have to go too?' he asked mockingly.

I finished the glass of mineral-water, as Chazov and Chernenko were leaving.

'Well,' said Brezhnev, without moving in his chair. 'Have you found out . . . who . . . murdered him?'

'Yes.'

'And . . . And . . . Andropov?' he continued, his lower jaw obviously having great difficulty with this combination of consonants.

'I can only deal in facts, Comrade Brezhnev,' I said, opening the file I had brought with me and showing him the identikit picture. 'This is a likeness of the wounded man. This is the individual whom Tsvigun shot, when trying to defend himself. And this one,' I said, showing him another picture, 'is a likeness of Colonel Oleinik, who accompanied the wounded man to hospital.'

When he saw this actual evidence, Brezhnev's reaction wasn't at all what you would have expected from a decrepit semi-invalid. He sat forward energetically in his chair and asked, without any pronunciation difficulty at all: 'And who put them up to it?'

'I don't know the identity of the wounded man yet, but the second picture is of Colonel Oleinik of the MVD's Intelligence Section.'

'Has he been arrested yet?' he asked in a flash. Even the 'r' was clipped and clear.

'Not yet, Comrade Brezhnev. It's too early.'

'What do you mean . . . "too early"? I gave you until February the third.'

'Comrade Brezhnev, it's not so much a question of who did the actual killing, as of *why* he was killed . . .'

'No!' he shouted harshly. 'It's the question equally of *who* actually did it *and* whose orders they were following. Shcholokov's? Suslov's? Andropov's? Grishin's? Kirilenko's? Whose? Good for you Leonid Ilyich! It wasn't for nothing that you feigned illness this month! Let's have the whole MVD Intelligence Section arrested! We'll soon discover whose orders they were carrying out!'

He started moving energetically in the rocking-chair, and I was amazed at the sudden transformation. Just a moment ago I'd been talking to a decaying old man with sunken features, somebody half in his grave who could scarcely move his jaw, yet now . . .

'What are you looking so surprised about?' he asked with a laugh. 'It's an old trick of Begin's. Whenever there's a vote of no-confidence in the Israeli Knesset, he has a heart-attack. Chazov had the brilliant idea of using the same tactic here. Whenever Suslov, Kulakov or some other bastard is making a play for my position, I pretend I'm dying. Then they decide to wait for it to happen. After all, what's the point in removing me by force, if I'm likely to go to my grave any day? Meanwhile, we alter the balance of power, and before you know where you are . . . As soon as I was told that Tsvigun had shot himself, I realized right away that they were done for! Now I've got them where I want them – in my fist.'

As he said this, he gripped the kitten so hard by the scruff of its neck, that it started to hiss and claw at the air with its paws.

But Brezhnev only looked at it and laughed.

'So your claws have been cut, eh? You can't scratch? That's just what we'll do to that crew. They've come unstuck with this suicide of theirs. And I certainly fooled them. I pretended to believe their version of events, and I even insulted the memory of the deceased by staying away from the funeral. On the other hand, this made your task a lot easier, didn't it Shamrayev? Otherwise, they would have made a much better job of destroying all the evidence . . . Carry on, Shamrayev! I need to know everything by February the third, and I need documentary proof. You can go.'

'Excuse me, Comrade Brezhnev,' I replied. 'I need to ask you a few questions.'

He looked at me in astonishment. 'What, you want to cross-examine me?'

I said nothing in reply.

He sat back in his rocking-chair. His heavy features drooped again and his lips parted a little.

'All right, carry on, if you must . . .' he said with an obvious effort.

All the same, I put my questions. 'At the end of 1978 Tsvigun gave you tapes of conversations recorded by one Givi Mingadze at your brother Yakov's apartment. Do you have the tapes?'

He didn't say a word. The reddish light from the star on top of the Spassky Tower was shining on us both, and I couldn't work out whether it was this light or a rush of blood to the face that made him turn red. His breathing got even louder and more stertorous.

Then he threw the cat off his knees, closed his eyes and said: 'All right . . . What else . . . do you want to know?'

'Perhaps I should summon Chazov?'

'No,' he replied, shaking his head. 'Carry on . . .'

I had it on the tip of my tongue to ask him how these tapes were connected with death of Kulakov, but I took pity on the old man.

Instead, I said: 'About a month ago a letter addressed to Tsvigun arrived from Israel, sent by the fiancée of this Mingadze. In it she told him that copies of these tapes were hidden somewhere in Moscow, or perhaps it was the originals, I don't know. She asked Tsvigun to release her boyfriend to the West, and in exchange she promised to give him the address of the place where the tapes were hidden. But the letter didn't reach Tsvigun. Instead, it ended up in Pirozhkov's hands. Now the KGB is on the lookout for Mingadze's fiancée in Israel, while the MVD Intelligence Section is searching for the tapes here. I think that Suslov may have asked Tsvigun for these tapes during their last conversation together.'

'And have you . . . found these tapes?' asked Brezhnev, without opening his eyes.

'No. I only found out about their existence a few hours ago.'

He opened his eyes and said very quickly and harshly: 'They must be found. Above all, they mustn't fall into Andropov's hands . . .'

'Comrade Brezhnev, the whole of MVD Intelligence has been searching for them for three weeks. I'm not competing with them and can't undertake to find them.'

'But these tapes *must* be found,' he said, lurching forward in his rocking-chair with the full force of his body. 'Do you understand me? They must be found *at any price*.'

General Zharov put his head round the door with a worried look on his face, but Brezhnev waved him away with his hand, as if to say: 'Shut the door!'

'Comrade Brezhnev, there is only one way of finding these tapes before the KGB or MVD get their hands on them. And that is quite simply to hand Mingadze over to his girlfriend.'

Brezhnev looked at me without blinking. 'Look,' he said at last in a hoarse whisper. 'Pour me out a glass of Borzhomi water.'

I got up and opened the refrigerator in the wall. This was surrounded by book-cases containing all Brezhnev's works in the language of each Soviet republic: *Dire Straits*, *The Rebirth*, *At the Sound of the Factory Whistle*, *Speeches of L.I. Brezhnev* – they were all there. I poured the old man his

231

mineral-water. He took a few swigs and then handed the glass back to me. In the reddish gloom of the study the kitten was playing about at the foot of a chair, attempting to scratch one of the legs with its claws. But its paws slipped over the wood without doing any harm.

Brezhnev turned away from the kitten and began to look at me again. 'Hand him over to her?' he asked. 'Isn't there any other way?'

'Not that won't involve the KGB and Intelligence finding out what's going on,' I replied. 'As it is, you can't exclude the possibility that they'll find this Anya Finshtein at any moment . . .'

'I understand. But if *they* can't find this Finshtein woman, then how will you?'

I told him briefly about Anya's second letter and also expounded my own plan. 'I must meet this Anya as quickly as possible in West Berlin, and in exchange for information about the whereabouts of the tape, Mingadze will be released to her from East Berlin.'

'And what if she deceives you and gives you the wrong address?'

'When she tells me the address, I shall ring through to my assistants in Moscow straight away. As soon as they find the tapes and call me back, Mingadze can cross the Berlin Wall to the West. Only this must all be done as quickly as possible, before the KGB have a chance to find Finshtein.'

Brezhnev leant back in his chair and began to rock slowly backwards and forwards, as he thought over my plan. Then he asked: 'Do you think . . . she'll . . . believe you? . . . And what if we . . . take the tapes and don't . . . release Mingadze? . . .'

'But I will be her hostage, Comrade Brezhnev.'

He stared at me hard for a moment. Then he said: 'Are you married?'

'Divorced.'

'Are your parents alive?'

'Not any longer, Comrade Brezhnev.'

'So, you're divorced . . . Your parents are dead . . . Your girlfriend has been killed . . . What guarantee . . . do we have . . . that . . . you won't defect to the West?'

'I've got a son here, Comrade Brezhnev.'

This was the turning-point in our conversation, the moment which decided everything that was to happen subsequently.

'A son? . . . Hm, yes . . . Children are a hold on people . . . though not on everybody . . . it's true . . .'

He carried on rocking in his chair and stared out of the window. The hands of the clock on top of the Spassky Tower were approaching 6.00 p.m. He noticed this, nimbly threw off his blanket, and stood up with scarcely any effort. I didn't even have to support him by the arm. He was wearing an open-necked woollen shirt over his light, worsted trousers. On his feet he had thick woollen socks. With short, light steps, he went over to the writing-desk, where Chernenko had been sitting a few minutes earlier. He opened one of the drawers and got out a small, colourful box, obviously

232

imported from abroad. Inside it were a number of tiny white ear-plugs, so soft that they could have been made of cotton wool. Then I watched with amazement as he stuffed two of these objects into his ears. At that very moment the bells of the Spassky Tower began to strike. Brezhnev stood by his desk, in the pinkish light of his reading-lamp, and pushed the plugs further into his ears. But each stroke of the bells made his face contort with pain. After the sixth stroke he removed the stoppers from his ears and emitted a sigh of obvious relief.

'What a bastard Lenin was!' he said. 'Inventing these chimes to sound right above my head! They split my head open every hour! . . . All right, so you'll be her hostage, and your son will be ours . . . That's OK. Now which prison is her boyfriend in?'

'I can't find out. It's being concealed from me. But if you sign a decree from the Supreme Soviet declaring him pardoned, I'll find Mingadze, don't you worry. All I'll have to do will be apply a little pressure on Bogatyryov, the head of the Main Directorate of Corrective Labour Institutions.'

He sat down at the desk and began to ponder, without saying a word.

Then he said: 'And are you sure that there is no other way to do it?'

'Quite sure,' I said, with as much firmness as I could muster.

'And are you certain that they'll surrender this Mingadze to you alive, and that you won't get killed yourself?'

'They won't do anything like that for the moment,' I replied. 'Neither the KGB, nor MVD Intelligence will try to stop me. They'll want to trump me in the final stages, when we're about to get the tapes. But I've already made preparations for that . . .'

'Well, I'll out-trump them myself, when it comes to it. Tell me, have you heard any recent anecdotes about me?'

'About *you*?' I said, doing my best to feign amazement.

'That's enough, stop playing the fool with me. I know very well there are thousands of stories about me going around. Particularly that I'm an old duffer, who doesn't have any inkling of what's going on any more . . . For instance, have you heard this one? Brezhnev comes to work and the secretary says to him: "Leonid Ilyich, one of your shoes is brown and the other is red." "Well, yes . . ." answers Brezhnev, "But I've got another pair just like it at home." Do you get it? Brezhnev is now so old, that he can't think straight, he's turned simple in the head. But that is splendid! It means that in the eyes of the people he is guilty of nothing – not responsible for the food shortages, or for the business in Afghanistan, or in Poland. Like to hear another story? At a meeting of the Central Committee Brezhnev says: "Comrades . . . we would like . . . to reward Comrade Chernenko with the Order of Lenin and the Order of First Chevalier of the Soviet Union . . . You ask us why? . . . Because when we were burying Comrade Suslov and the music started up . . . Comrade Chernenko was the first to get up and invite a lady to dance . . .".'

I burst out laughing, but he looked at me with satisfaction and said: 'Do you like it? . . . I thought of it today. Only don't tell it to anyone before Suslov's funeral, OK? But overall, I can tell you that I am very much afraid for the country when I die, if Andropov seizes power – oh!' He sighed heavily. 'He worked for twelve years with Suslov, in complete harmony. Together they worked out all our international policies. Suslov ran the international Communist movement and through it brought over here all sorts of young Communists from the Arab countries and Latin America; and once they were here, Andropov made terrorists of them. Now we shall have to throw him a bone, give him Suslov's post. While I am in power – that's all right. But if I die tomorrow, what will happen to the Party? And to the country? . . .' He was obviously tired. He pressed the button on his desk, and at the same instant Zharov opened the door.

'Send Ustinov and Belkin to me urgently,' said Brezhnev wearily. 'And that . . . what's his name? . . . the boss of camps and prisons? . . .'

'General Bogatyryov,' I prompted him.

'Yes, him . . .'

'But why do we need Belkin?' I asked.

'He has a journalist's passport with entry visas for every country in Europe,' Brezhnev explained. 'He can fly out today to Paris or London and ring this Jewess from there. She can't be rung from Moscow – the KGB will listen in. Who else do you need?'

'Marat Svetlov,' I said, and I thought: this old man of the Kremlin is certainly not at all as simple as he seems, even to his advisers.

6.45 p.m.

In a corridor on the second floor of the Hotel National, Marat Svetlov had a worried expression as he spun KGB Major Shakhovsky the following yarn: 'I need your help urgently, Major! You scratch my back, I'll scratch yours, as they say. You won't be the loser by it.'

'Well, what's the problem?' asked Major Shakhovsky, the section leader in charge of 'servicing' foreign tourists with prostitutes. The Hotel National was his headquarters.

'This morning a gold icon-case and four sixteenth-century icons disappeared from the Voznesensky Monastery. According to my information, the thieves intend to smuggle them abroad through foreigners, using the resources of this beauty here.' And Svetlov showed the major a photograph of Tamara Bakhshi. 'Is she one of yours?'

The major looked at the photograph and uttered three syllables: 'I'll kill her.'

'That's precisely what you mustn't do,' said Svetlov. 'Just hand her over to me. I want to have a few words with her. And if you ever want anything, the CID is at your service, it goes without saying.'

'Let's go,' said the major and led Svetlov to the end of the corridor. As they were walking along, he said: 'I don't think she's here at present. She's busy with some Swede.'

234

At the end of the corridor, sitting on a small sofa in front of the entrance to room 321, reading a copy of *Vechernyaya Moskva*, was a well-built young man dressed in a grey suit. He looked inquiringly, first at the major, then at Svetlov.

Then Shakhovsky said: 'Carry on reading, it's all right. He's one of ours.'

He then opened the door of 321 and let Svetlov go on ahead.

They found themselves in a spacious and luxurious, three-bedroomed suite. The décor was quite out of keeping with a hotel. There were consoles for operating remote-controlled television cameras and television monitors of all shapes and sizes flickering overhead. Next to these were a number of large, built-in recording-machines and other devices for covert surveillance. The consoles were manned by KGB operatives, dressed in civilian clothes, but the whole atmosphere was informal. Two KGB employees were sitting on a sofa, playing draughts and drinking tea, while another, sitting next to them, was reading a recent issue of *Playboy*. Only a few of the room's occupants were actually 'working'. The television screens in front of them covered nearly every part of the Hotel National that could be of interest to them – the main entrance with foreign tourists going in and out all the time and a constant flow of Intourist cars; the foyer with its souvenir kiosks, the hotel administrator's desks, the corridors, the restaurant and the hard-currency bar.

The bar had soft lighting to give it an intimate atmosphere and jazz was being played in the background. There were several groups of foreigners sitting at the tables with Russian girls. You could hear the music from the bar in Shakhovsky's 'apartment', too, but it didn't interfere with those who were monitoring the screens, as they had headphones on.

When they saw Shakhovsky come in, one of them turned to him and said: 'That Brazilian isn't interested in Lyusya either, the bastard! That's the third woman I've set up for him, and still we get nowhere. If you ask me, he's a poof!'

'Well, ring up headquarters and get them to send some queers along,' said Shakhovsky.

Then he went up to one of the other consoles, manned by a fat, bearded man with tousled curly black hair. In spite of the headphones he was wearing, he looked as if he was working with only half an ear, because he wasn't looking at the screens at all. Instead he was leafing through an English book with one hand, and writing something down on a big piece of paper with the other. Underneath you could see that he was making a carbon copy of it, too.

'Kozyol, are you writing rubbish while you're on duty again?' Shakhovsky asked spitefully. 'Switch on the camera in the Swede's room, the one that Tamara's working on. Perhaps they're there already?'

'No, they pushed off this afternoon. She was taking him round the museums. But they've got a table reserved in the bar for seven o'clock this evening,' replied the bearded man, without looking up from his book.

'We'll have to wait,' Shakhovsky said to Svetlov. 'Take a seat. Make yourself at home.' Then he turned to the bearded man again. 'What are you reading?'

'A fucking good book. It's a new American detective novel about life in the USSR,' he replied, carrying on writing as he did so. He was scribbling so fast that his hand was actually quivering with the effort. 'I'm an ordinary fellow, as you know, but I can tell you without any embarrassment that I stayed up all night reading it, till eight in the morning. I couldn't tear myself away from it. Every page simply breathes authenticity.'

'So what are you doing? Have you decided to copy it out by hand?' Shakhovsky asked sarcastically.

'No, I'm writing a review of it. For the Novosti Press Agency, *Novy Afrikanets*, *Moskovsky Komsomolets* and the English language section of All-Union Radio. Somebody's got to expose the book for stirring up hatred of our country. It's just a question of taking a few phrases out of context and slating the book for being full of sex.'

'But Vova, what the fuck do you need so much money for?' asked a tiny, Korean-looking man at the other end of the room. 'You're getting paid by the newspapers, radio, the KGB, and I dare say you're even translating for films.'

'Well, what do we get paid for working in the KGB? Fuck all!' said the bearded man, doing up one of the buttons of his shirt, forced open by the enormous pot belly protruding over his belt. Suddenly he became all attention and pressed the headphones closer to his ears, saying to the major: 'The girls have started, Chief. Do you want to listen in?'

Moving a handle on the console, he trained the invisible camera on a table in the hard-currency bar, at which a couple of foreigners were sitting with two Russian girls, a blonde and a brunette.

'Switch on the sound,' said Shakhovsky.

'But what about . . .?' said the other, nodding in the direction of Svetlov.

'That's all right, he's one of us,' said Shakhovsky. 'Switch it up.'

The bearded man turned up the volume control, and immediately the sound of four voices came over the loudspeaker.

'His mother was a settled gypsy, but his father was Russian,' said the big-breasted, dyed blonde, as she sipped her cocktail from a tall wine glass.

'How do you mean "settled"?' asked the young foreigner. 'What does that mean?' He was tall with aristocratic features, and was writing something in a notebook.

'Well, how shall I put it?' said the blonde. 'You know, gypsies are usually nomadic, they wander around from place to place. His mother had stopped doing this and now stayed in one spot. She *settled down*, you see. Anyway, that doesn't matter. What's important is that before he got to know Galya, nobody knew him at all. He simply sang gypsy songs in some restaurant or other. But Galya got him fixed up at the Bolshoi Theatre. And how!'

'Wait a minute,' said the foreigner again, interrupting the blonde girl.

236

'How do you mean: "got him fixed up"?'

'Got him a job there by string-pulling,' replied the other girl impatiently, trying to fish a tiny sliver of cherry out of her empty cocktail glass. 'Anyway, I've heard that this Galya has got up to such tricks, that if the KGB was allowed to get it all out of her, well . . .'

'What tricks?' asked the other young foreigner, puffing at his cigar. He wasn't noting anything down, but there was a portable tape-recorder lying in front of him, next to his drink.

'Comrade Major, the Japanese have arrived,' said another operator, the one who resembled a Korean. One of his screens showed four Japanese men about to sit at an empty table, each of them holding a document case.

'What are they talking about?' asked Shakhovsky, immediately walking over to this other console.

'They're not talking about anything. Completely silent.'

'Bastards!' said Shakhovsky in disappointment. 'They drag these document cases about with them all over the place, and don't put them down for a moment. Fucking physicists!'

Then he turned towards the men on the sofa playing chess. 'Come on, you two. Stop swinging the lead! The foreigners have arrived.'

There, on the screen showing the entrance to the hard-currency bar, were several groups of foreign tourists, mostly strapping Americans and Canadians, with a few solid Germans and aesthetic-looking Frenchmen thrown in. They were all wearing expensive fur hats and smart suits. Some of them were accompanied by girls who were obviously Russian.

'Look,' said Shakhovsky to Svetlov, and pointed to the television screen. 'God knows what food they're brought up on, these foreigners! You can tell they're not Soviet straight away. Ah! Here comes the one you're looking for.'

Holding the hand of an enormous Swede, a shapely, dark-haired girl was approaching the entrance to the bar, her hips swinging slightly as she walked. It was Tamara Bakhshi, the girl that Svetlov had slept with that Friday night at my apartment. Svetlov got quickly to his feet and started to head for the door, but Shakhovsky stopped him. 'Stop! Don't be a fool! How can you go in there dressed in military uniform? Are you crazy, or what? Go into that room over there, it's full of spare clothes. They're all from abroad, by the way. Go and choose a suit and tie for yourself. Do you know how to knot one?'

A few minutes later, Svetlov was downstairs, dressed now in civvies and a tie. The dimly-lit bar was full of noise and people. A small jazz quartet was performing on a stage and a few couples danced in front. Svetlov looked up at the ceiling trying to figure out the position of the concealed television cameras, but he couldn't find any. The ceiling was concealed in darkness. He drank a glass of vodka at the bar and then, as if by chance, caught sight of Tamara, sitting at a table with her forty-five-year-old, pock-marked Swedish companion.

237

Putting on a polite expression, Svetlov went up to their table and said to the Swede: 'Excuse me, but may I ask your lady to dance?'

The Swede looked at him uncomprehendingly. Tamara turned pale, as Svetlov softly said to her: 'Tell him that I'm an old friend of yours, and that you're happy to have a dance with me.'

In broken English Tamara did as she was told.

'Oh, sure, sure!' said the Swede. 'OK.'

Svetlov took Tamara over to where the band was playing, so as to get as far away as possible from the microphones concealed beneath every table. The music drowned out people's voices, so Svetlov held Tamara close to him with his one good hand and said into her ear: 'OK sister, first question: have you got the clap?'

Tamara gave an indignant start, but Svetlov had a firm hold on her.

'And no lying!' he said, smiling all the time. 'I'll send you to the clinic for a check-up tomorrow, whatever you say. So, have you got it?'

'No, word of honour . . .' she said, almost on the point of crying.

'No tears, that's all I need! How do you know you haven't got it? When did you last have a medical examination?'

'Last week. In any case, I always take an antibiotic before doing it . . .'

'Where do you have medical checks, and where do you get the antibiotics from?'

'I've got my own doctor.'

'Who? Svetlana Agapova, eh?'

Tamara said nothing in reply.

'Second question,' said Svetlov. 'Who put you up to sleeping with me that night?'

'Nobody! Word of honour! Nina gave me a ring. You were with her at the time. You had called by, and she rang me while you were there . . .'

'How did she get through to you? You're never at home.'

Around them there were foreigners madly dancing with Russian girls or their own wives, talking all the while, or laughing and drinking cocktails and pure Russian vodka. Meanwhile, Svetlov was smiling absent-mindedly at those around him, while he held Tamara's waist in a vice-like grip.

'She happened to catch me while I was at Irina's. You must remember,' begged Tamara, 'it wasn't me she was ringing, but Irina, a friend of ours.'

It was quite true. Svetlov remembered that evening, when he had dropped in at my place with a bottle of brandy and some of the fried chicken that had been left over from the flight from Adler. Nina had been ringing round her old friends from the circus school and had dragged Tamara away from some party to meet Svetlov. It looked to Marat as if she wasn't lying and didn't even know that Nina and her doctor, Svetlana Agapova, had been killed.

'Question three,' said Svetlov. 'Did Agapova ever introduce you to Tsvigun? Be honest now.'

'Yes . . .' said Tamara in a scarcely audible voice.

'In that same apartment at 16-A, Kachalov Street?'

'Yes, but it happened a long time ago, six months at least. Word of honour! And I only went there twice . . .'

'And did you sleep with Tsvigun?'

Tamara said nothing. Svetlov was furious at the thought that he had probably 'shared' this girl with Tsvigun. He squeezed her so tightly round the waist that she had to gasp for breath.

'I'm asking whether you *slept* with Tsvigun?'

'No. Let go of me, Marat. It hurts. What have I done wrong?'

'Who did Agapova take you along there for?'

'There was a whole group of people there, Marat. I don't quite know how to say this but . . . Well, you know, there are some men who can't have it off alone with a woman. They only get their pleasure if somebody else is present . . . And Tsvigun was one of those . . .'

'I see. When did you last see Agapova?'

'On Saturday. But what's that got to do with it? I only told her that I'd been to Tsvigun's flat with you.'

'And did you give her Shamrayev's telephone number?'

'Yes, but so what?'

'And why did you phone Nina yesterday morning?'

'Me?' said Tamara with surprise. 'But I didn't, I swear to you!'

'All right. But can you get away from this Swede right now?'

'No. He's leaving tomorrow. After that I'll have three days off. Shall I give you a ring?' she added coquettishly.

'Yes. But before you do, go along to Clinic Number Seven to see Dr Goldberg. He'll give you an examination. Tell him that I've sent you.'

'Why? Svetlana Agapova will give me a check-up.'

'She won't any more,' said Svetlov, directing her towards the table where the impatient Swede was already sitting, gloomily drinking his third vodka. Svetlov smiled at him, and for some reason said in French: '*Merci.*' Then he sat Tamara down at the table next to the Swede and added in Russian, for her benefit: 'And after you've seen Goldberg, go home and clean up your apartment. Give the flowers some water.'

After leaving the bar, Svetlov took the lift to the second floor, and went along to room 321 to change back into his military uniform.

'Well, what happened?' asked Shakhovsky. 'Will you take her in?'

'No, not this time,' replied Svetlov, as he got changed. 'I don't want to interfere with your work. Besides, she's clean – in the sense that she's got nothing to do with icons. We must have made a mistake. All the same, I'm in your debt, and if I can ever do anything for you, don't hesitate to ask.'

'Thanks,' said Shakhovsky.

Outside, Svetlov's police Volga was still parked to one side of the brightly-lit hotel entrance. Its radio-telephone was buzzing. Before answering, Svetlov started up the engine and began to warm the inside of the car. It was freezing inside as well as out. Shivering from the cold, Svetlov lifted the receiver off its hook and said rather rudely: 'What do you want?'

'Colonel Svetlov,' replied duty officer Kremnyov. 'You're summoned urgently to the Kremlin. Drive up to the Spassky Gates.'

After 7.00 p.m.

Paris Soviet Embassy

Embassy Secretary Comrade A P Gonchar

ON COMRADE BREZHNEVS PERSONAL INSTRUCTIONS KOMSOMOLSKAYA PRAVDA JOURNALIST VADIM BELKIN WILL BE LEAVING MOSCOW TODAY AT 20 10 HOURS ON AEROFLOT FLIGHT NO 81 STOP HIS TASK WILL BE TO PROVIDE PRESS REPORTS ON THE POSITIVE REACTION OF THE FRENCH PEOPLE TO THE SIGNING OF THE CONTRACT OF THE CENTURY IE THE CONSTRUCTION OF THE TYUMEN-PARIS GAS PIPELINE STOP MEET HIM AT ORLY AIRPORT AND RESERVE A HOTEL ROOM FOR HIM

Director of L. I. Brezhnev's Private Office

M.V. Doroshin

Dispatched from the Kremlin 26 January at 19.22 hours.

Received in Paris by Embassy Duty Officer Comrade M.E. Speranskaya.

EXTRACT FROM THE VERBATIM REPORT OF THE CROSS-EXAMINATION OF LIEUTENANT-GENERAL I.D. BOGATYRYOV, HEAD OF THE MAIN DIRECTORATE OF CORRECTIVE LABOUR INSTITUTIONS, MVD, USSR

Questions put by Investigator Shamrayev

QUESTION: You are suspected of concealing information concerning the whereabouts the convicted prisoner Givi Rivazovich Mingadze, and also of removing this information from Central Files and the MVD Computer Department. What do you have to say about the disappearance of this information?

ANSWER: I personally took no part either in concealing the information or in removing it from Central Files. Around the beginning of January the MVD Intelligence Section sent me a request for information about this Mingadze, and I informed them that he was at the strict regime camp in Tyumen. I subsequently received information from the camp commandant that Senior Investigator Comrade Baklanov had arrived at the camp from the USSR Public Prosecutor's Office. At the request of the Investigator, the prisoner was then transferred to the Balashikhinsky strict regime camp near Moscow. But information about his change of whereabouts could have been delayed at head office and not yet have reached the computer.

INTERVENTION: FROM GENERAL ZHAROV, HEAD OF THE KREMLIN GUARD, PRESENT AT THE CROSS-EXAMINATION: Stop this . . . (expletive). Could have been delayed?! Who ordered you to do it? Tell us, or else . . . (expletive).

ANSWER: I was simply making a conjecture, Comrade General. Information about the transfer of prisoners is sent via the Directorate's Registration Office to MVD Central Files. Perhaps one of the employees there may have . . .

QUESTION: Is the prisoner to be found at the Balashikhinsky strict regime colony at the present moment? This camp comes under the control of the KGB Dzerzhinsky Division, does it not?

ANSWER: No, the prisoner is not detained there now. Three days ago, on Saturday, I received a telegram from camp commandant Skvorchuk informing me that, in the interests of the prisoner's security and on the personal instructions of General Krasnov, head of MVD Intelligence, Mingadze had been transferred to extra strict regime camp No. 274 at Ferganu in the Kirghizian SSR. As you know, there are uranium mines there. However, I do not think that in three days he will have reached that destination. Convicts are transferred by train, in special coaches . . . I doubt whether in three days he has got further than the Urals . . .

EXTRACT FROM THE REGISTER OF DOCUMENTS ISSUED BY
L.I. BREZHNEV'S PRIVATE OFFICE
TELEGRAM-DIRECTIVE

To the Head of the Railway Police Directorate Lieutenant-General V U Solomin

ON THE PERSONAL INSTRUCTIONS OF COMRADE BREZHNEV YOU ARE TO IMMEDIATELY HALT ALL TRAINS CONTAINING CARRIAGES FOR THE TRANSFER OF PRISONERS AND TO DISCOVER THE WHEREABOUTS OF PRISONER GIVI RIVAZOVICH MINGADZE BORN 1945 CONVICTED UNDER ARTICLE 88 OF THE RSFSR CRIMINAL CODE STOP YOU ARE TO KEEP ME PERSONALLY INFORMED EVERY 20 MINUTES OF THE RESULTS OF YOUR INVESTIGATION

Director of L. I. Brezhnev's Private Office M. V. Doroshin.
Dispatched from the Kremlin 26 January 1982 at 19.47 hours, received by Railway Police Directorate duty officer Colonel I.P. Maslennikov.

By eight o'clock in the evening Vadim Belkin had received my instructions and was already leaving Sheremetyevo Airport for France. Meanwhile I was sitting in the Kremlin cafeteria with Svetlov and Zolotov, devouring soup and croutons and mugging up some German phrases.

'*Guten Tag* – Good day. *Guten Abend* – Good evening. *Guten Morgen* – Good morning. *Wieviel kostet das* – How much does it cost?'

'*Wo kann man telefonieren* – Where can I phone?' prompted Zolotov.

General Bogatyryov, who had now recovered from his cross-examination, was drinking brandy with Svetlov. Wiping his brow, he said to the latter: 'I haven't got a thing to do with this business, I swear!'

'But what about Irina Bugrimova?' Svetlov asked slyly.

'Well, I have a comradely relationship with her . . .'

241

'All right, Comrade General, who are you trying to kid? Comradely relations with a circus artiste?'

'Well, she is a lion-tamer! I'm afraid to get near her!'

The telephone rang. One of the waitresses lifted the receiver, listened to what was being said and passed it over to me.

'It's for you, Comrade Shamrayev.'

I took the receiver and listened.

'This is Doroshin. A telegram has arrived from the head of the Sverdlovsk railway police. Train No. 32 containing coach No. 94621 for the transportation of prisoners has arrived at Sverdlovsk station No. 22 with Mingadze on board. The city is closed for defence reasons and is garrisoned entirely by KGB troops. Please call on Comrade Brezhnev.'

EXTRACT FROM THE REGISTER OF DOCUMENTS ISSUED BY
L. I. BREZHNEV'S PRIVATE OFFICE
TELEGRAM-DIRECTIVE

To Stationmaster Sverdlovsk – 22 Major D U Sytin

Copy to Military Commandant Sverdlovsk – 22 Lieutenant-Colonel D M Radovsky

ON COMRADE BREZHNEVS PERSONAL INSTRUCTIONS YOU ARE TO IMMEDIATELY UNCOUPLE PRISON COACH NO 94621 AND ITS OCCUPANTS FROM TRAIN NO 32 STOP THEN SURROUND THE COACH WITH ALL THE SOLDIERS AND RAILWAY POLICE AT YOUR DISPOSAL STOP ALLOW NO UNAUTHORIZED PERSONNEL TO APPROACH THE COACH UNTIL THE ARRIVAL OF THE COMMANDER OF SVERDLOVSK MILITARY DISTRICT LIEUTENANT GENERAL B B MAKHOV STOP INFORM US IMMEDIATELY WHEN THESE INSTRUCTIONS HAVE BEEN CARRIED OUT

Director of L. I. Brezhnev's Private Office M. V. Doroshin.
Dispatched from the Kremlin by railway-telephone 26 January at 20.39 hours.

TELEGRAM – DIRECTIVE

To Commander of Sverdlovsk Military District Lieutenant-General B B Makhov

I ORDER YOU PERSONALLY TO TAKE A PLATOON OF SOLDIERS IMMEDIATELY TO RAILWAY STATION SVERDLOVSK – 22 AND TO RELEASE FROM CUSTODY CITIZEN G R MINGADZE STOP HE IS TO BE FOUND IN COACH NO 94621 WHICH IS SURROUNDED BY RAILWAY POLICE AND SOLDIERS FROM THE UNIT ATTACHED TO THE STATION STOP IN THE EVENT OF ANY RESISTANCE FROM THE PRISON ESCORT THIS RESISTANCE IS TO BE CRUSHED AND THE ESCORT ARRESTED STOP THE ABOVE-MENTIONED MINGADZE IS THEN TO BE TRANSFERRED BY MILITARY PLANE TO MOSCOW ARRIVING AT ZHUKOVSKY MILITARY AIRPORT STOP TIME AVAILABLE FOR THE RELEASE OF CITIZEN MINGADZE 1 HOUR STOP

242

TIME AVAILABLE FOR TRANSPORTING CITIZEN MINGADZE TO
ZHUKOVSKY AIRPORT – 3 HOURS STOP
CITIZEN MINGADZE IS THEN TO BE PLACED IN THE PERSONAL CHARGE OF
SPECIAL INVESTIGATOR TO THE USSR PUBLIC PROSECUTOR'S OFFICE
COMRADE I I SHAMRAYEV
Chairman of the USSR Defence Council Marshal Brezhnev
Moscow Kremlin, 26 January 1982, 21.00 hours

DIRECTIVE
To Head of the Moscow Passport Office, Comrade I. A. Medvedkin.
Draw up passports within the next two hours for the following: Citizen
Shamrayev, Igor Iosifovich, born 1935, Special Investigator at the USSR
Public Prosecutor's Office.
Citizen Mingadze, Givi Rivazovich, born 1945, of no fixed occupation.
Deliver the passports today to Comrade L. I. Brezhnev's Private Office in
the Kremlin.
Director of L. I. Brezhnev's Private office M. V. Doroshin.
Dispatched from the Kremlin by special messenger 26 January 1982 at
21.00 hours.
Delivered to Comrade Medvedkin at his apartment 21.17 hours.

Evening
Bogatyryov, Zharov and I were asleep in armchairs in the reception-room
outside Brezhnev's study. Leonid Ilyich himself, as well as Zolotov, Chazov
and the rest of his entourage, had left for home long before. The machinery
which they had set in motion to avoid the KGB was now working perfectly
well without them. But we remained here along with the Central Committee
duty officer, and only the hourly-ringing of the Kremlin bells made us twitch
in our sleep. I'm sure it's true that these chimes can eventually drive you
mad. Only their creator in his Mausoleum on Red Square could possibly
sleep soundly. Every hour, too, the military guard of honour at the Mausoleum was changed as the bells chimed. The clear-cut sound of their
goose-stepping rang out loudly in the frosty silence of the night. We could
hear it echo through an open window in the reception-room. At 9.35 p.m.
we heard via military telegraph that the Commander of Sverdlovsk Military
District, Lieutenant-General Makhov, had released Mingadze from custody
and had met with no resistance from the escort. At 10.40 p.m. Makhov
informed us that a military plane flown by fighter-pilot and Hero of the
Soviet Union, Colonel Pchelyakov, had left Sverdlovsk military aerodrome
with Givi Mingadze and eight sub-machine-gunners on board, and was now
heading for the airport at Zhukovsky. At 10.50 p.m. the terrified head of the
Moscow Passport Office, Medvedkin, drove personally to the Spassky
Tower with two red-coloured passports, one for myself and one for

Mingadze. In his briefcase he had several other spares as well as the official seal, just in case they should be needed.

Everything was going smoothly and without a hitch, just as you would expect once the Kremlin intervenes.

Not a word from the KGB.

I knew, however, that this silence did not mean they had given in.

At 6.00 a.m. Vadim Belkin phoned the editorial office of *Komsomolskaya Pravda* from Paris. He dictated his first report to the duty typist, which consisted almost entirely of extracts culled from the latest French newspapers: 'BASED ON THE PRINCIPLES OF RECIPROCITY. The French press continues to give extensive coverage to the Soviet gas pipeline agreement signed recently in Paris. It has made both economic and political headlines. The Paris newspapers note both the magnitude of the agreement, which they are calling the "contract of the century", and its long-term nature. In a television interview the French Economic and Finance Minister remarked that the signing of this agreement embodied the principle of reciprocity and foresaw in his turn the "entry of western industry into eastern markets"' – and so on: 120 lines in all, signed 'Your Paris Correspondent, Vadim Belkin', telephone 331-37-34-05.

The typist made two copies of the report and gave one of them to Marat Svetlov, who had spent the night in the typist's office for that very purpose.

At 6.20 a.m. when the snow-filled Moscow streets were empty apart from a few shadowy figures hurrying to work, Svetlov himself was driving rapidly down Gorky Street towards Red Square and the Kremlin.

By 6.40 a.m. we had already deciphered Belkin's relatively transparent message. Thus interpreted, Belkin was telling us that, on arriving in Paris, he had phoned the number given by Anya (0611-34-18-19) and had dictated the phone number of his own hotel room. Anya Finshtein had then dialled through to him. Two pre-arranged phrases in the report informed us that she was willing to meet me in West Berlin after 1.00 p.m. on that very day, 27 January.

I sensed that the game which I had begun to play with Nina's murderers was reaching its climax. It only remained to make a few final moves. They would prove fateful either for me, or for them.

At Zhukovsky Airport, guarded by a squad of sub-machine-gunners and the airport military commander, an uncomprehending Givi Mingadze had already been waiting three hours for me to arrive.

But only after I had received the signal from Belkin in Paris did it make sense to rush to Zhukovsky and thence by military aircraft to East Berlin.

I dialled Kolya Baklanov's home number. He obviously wasn't asleep, as he lifted the receiver right away, and his voice sounded quite alert. 'Hello . . .'

'This is Shamrayev,' I said. 'Kolya, I can't get to sleep. I keep on remembering that conversation we had on Saturday morning at the Prosecutor's Office. Listen, why don't you take your wife and child away on holiday today, to a rest-home or somewhere. You must be exhausted, too. How about it?'

He said nothing. Nor did I. I had told him everything I could, even more than I should.

'Well,' he replied at last. 'Anything else?'

'That's all I've got to say, old lad. You've got a fine boy. It would do him good to go walking with his dad in the fresh country air.'

'Fuck off!' he said and calmly replaced the receiver.

TELEGRAM

To Commander Aviation Division No 69 Major-General USSR Armed Forces G S Yanshin

Zhukovsky

Urgent Secret By Military Telegraph

IN CONNECTION WITH THE IMMEDIATE DEPARTURE OF A GROUP OF GOVERNMENT OFFICIALS FOR EAST BERLIN WHERE THEY WILL BE MET BY REPRESENTATIVES OF THE SOVIET ARMED FORCES YOU ARE TO PLACE A MILITARY TRANSPORT PLANE AND AN EXPERIENCED AIR-CREW AT THEIR DISPOSAL STOP THEY WILL BE ARRIVING AT ZHUKOVSKY MILITARY AIRPORT FORTHWITH ACCOMPANIED BY COMMANDER OF THE KREMLIN GUARD MAJOR GENERAL ZHAROV

Duty Officer CPSU Central Committee B. T. Artseyulov

Moscow Kremlin 27 January 1982

Dispatched by Special Military Telegraph at 6.45 hours

Received by Duty officer Aviation Division No. 69

Colonel USSR Armed Forces Sh. Zh. Otambekov.

'Let's go!' said General Zharov. 'It'll take us half an hour to get to Zhukovsky even in a Chaika.'

'And can I go home now?' asked Lieutenant-General Bogatyryov.

'You stay put until you receive instructions from Colonel Svetlov!' said Zharov. 'When he needs you, he'll come to pick you up. And don't go with anybody else. I've already issued instructions to the guard. Understood?'

'Yes, sir!' replied Bogatyryov in some trepidation.

Marat Svetlov had three operations to perform in Moscow, and one of them could only be carried out in the personal presence of Bogatyryov.

I went to the duty officer's desk and picked up his copy of the telephone directory for Greater Moscow. 'I'll let you have it back, all right?' I said to him.

'That's OK. There's no need,' he replied.

Svetlov, Zharov and I went downstairs and climbed into the Chaika which was waiting for us. It was still dark outside and it was snowing as hard as ever. The red star on the Spassky Tower looked down at us uneasily.

As I shook Svetlov's right hand, his face contorted with pain. 'Go easy! It still hurts . . . Off you go to Berlin then. I'll be waiting for your call, and don't get into a panic. Everything will be all right here, you can be certain of that. I'll arrange to fire a salute in memory of Nina.'

From the window of our limousine I could see him heading for his Volga, which was parked by the Spassky Tower check-point.

'Don't get your own fingers burnt, Marat,' I thought.

Part 7

Checkpoint Charlie

Wednesday 27 January, after 9.00 a.m.
Low cloud concealed the whole of snow-covered Russia, and the same was true of Byelorussia and Poland. There were only two passengers being carried in the military transport plane, Givi Mingadze and myself. Givi was thirty-seven years old and of average height. His head was completely shaven. Constant transfers from prison to prison had given him a thin and wasted look. His chin and cheeks were covered in stubble. He was wearing a quilted camp jacket, padded trousers and heavily patched canvas prison boots. In fact, the first impression was that of an escaped convict, only belied by his dark luminous Georgian eyes, and his slender hands which were covered in scratches and nervously clutched the quilted grey cap on his lap . . .

GIVI MINGADZE'S STORY

When people say that all Georgians are racketeers, it isn't true. I know that nowadays the Moscow markets are full of Georgians selling flowers and mandarin oranges from Sukhumi. But what was it like before? The Georgian, the real Georgian, was a warrior, a horseman with a dagger, a man who would help the poor and pay court to a pretty woman. He was a *man*, you understand. For thousands of years we lived in the mountains, and our rulers were knights and poets. And now they've made profiteers of us. Of me, too, I admit, though I must add that I resisted it for a long time – until I was thirty in fact. I used to live the life of a poverty-stricken student. I graduated from music college, played the clarinet and wanted to conduct a variety orchestra – or become a film actor. I don't know. I was pretty thoughtless when I was young, but I wasn't involved in any underhand deals. What does a Georgian need, after all? A little money, a bit of success, and a lot of friends. And I had all this, especially friends. I wasn't officially registered in Moscow so I used to move around a lot, from one friend's flat to another. But in 1975, my friend Boris Buryatsky had an affair with Galya Brezhneva and used to take me along to the flat of her uncle, General Tsvigun. What did I have in common with Buryatsky? Well, we were basically two good-for-nothing idlers, you see, as free as birds! He used to sing gypsy songs in restaurants, and I used to play first the clarinet, then the drums. And where did the two of us end up? At Tsvigun's place, with Galya Brezhneva. At first we just used to play preference together, but then Tsvigun started to give me little commissions. Phone up this person, collect ten thousand roubles from that one, twenty thousand from another. And so it went on. Six months later I had my own car, a Volga. Do you know what a young Georgian is in Moscow, if he's got his own Volga? He's a king! Especially if he's got influential backing, like one of the KGB bosses. I just couldn't stay home. The whole of Georgia would be calling me on the phone. It wouldn't stop ringing from morning till night. Yes, it was a fine life. I can't say anything against it. I could drive my Volga anywhere, even over public gardens. And a very great deal of Georgian money passed through my hands into Tsvigun's. I wasn't without funds myself. I was pretty rich.

Then in 1976 Tsvigun made use of my services in a way that I'll never forget! I'll never forgive him either, or his wife! To cut a long story short, you said that I set fire to the Rossiya Hotel. OK, listen to me. It's true, we'd already been involved in some underhand dealings at the Rossiya. Then MVD Intelligence set up its headquarters on the tenth floor of the hotel and started to spy on us. They almost caught Mzhavanadze's wife and nabbed a lot of others besides. They had quite a bit on me, of course – photographs, cine-films and tapes of my conversations and dealings with Georgian fruit-racketeers, and so on.

Anyway, one fine evening Tsvigun and his wife said to me: 'Givi, something terrible has happened. MVD Intelligence is on to you, and through you they'll get to us. Don't forget that if they arrest you, we won't be able to do anything about it. Brezhnev will help us out, but we won't be able to rescue you, because somebody has to get locked up in order to divert attention from the others. So you'll be the lynch-pin in the affair. You'll have to take responsibility for everything. There is another way out, however. A secret factory in Baku has developed a chemical reagent which can destroy tapes and optical instruments at ten yards' distance. If you place some of this chemical on the floor below the Intelligence Section, all their machines will go wrong after a few hours, their tapes will turn black and even the glass on the windows will shatter. If you manage to do this, you'll destroy all the information they've got on anybody.'

And, fool that I was, I believed them. How we laughed when we thought of their windows smashing and all their secret dossiers going to hell. The rest you know. I flew to Baku, collected the chemical, and then Boris and I dressed up as workmen, whose job it was to clean the floors. They wouldn't let us in to the Intelligence Section itself, of course, but we were able to gain access to the ninth floor. We spread the liquid over all the carpets in the rooms immediately below the MVD. The next morning

I heard that there had been a fire at the hotel and that dozens of people had died. Boris and I had a fit. And there was Tsvigun telling us that it had all happened by accident. Some drunken foreigner was supposed to have dropped a lighted cigar on the carpet in one of the rooms, and the chemical had caught fire.

Well, however it happened, I had committed a crime and Tsvigun had me just where he wanted me. What does a real Georgian do in a case like this? Commit suicide? Turn to drink? No! He takes revenge! And I decided to have my revenge on all of them – Tsvigun, his wife and their whole family. I'd seen the kind of life they lived. Tsvigun's wife might have been wearing the the same coat for ten years, but you just examine the frame of her bed. It's old and made of iron, but the legs are hollow and full of diamonds and gold. Some of it was left over from the war, when she and Tsvigun worked together in SMERSH. She was the one who wrote Tsvigun's books about the heroic deeds of Cheka agents, and I was the one who arranged for films to be made of all this rubbish. I brought a producer from Mosfilm along to see them. She and Tsvigun were already millionaires at the end of the war, of course. Their job was to check all the luggage which our soldiers brought back from Germany with them in 1945. You know yourself all the gold and jewellery that found its way into Russia at that time. Well, Vera Tsvigun used to take all the best things for herself not watches and clothing, but precious stones and diamonds.

However, getting back to the point again, I had decided to get my revenge. I was playing cards with Brezhnev's brother and handing over the money he'd 'earned' for fixing people up with various jobs, when I thought of the form my vengeance could take. What a fool I was! You should just hear what the Brezhnevs would say at home about the Soviet system, the Soviet people and that whole Communist Party of theirs! This was at the time when Kulakov was going up in the world, pretending to make an honest man of himself, like Suslov. But I didn't believe any of them. All I dreamed about was toppling both Tsvigun and Brezhnev. I told Kulakov that I would let him have tapes of the conversations they had at home. Kulakov was no fool, he grasped the possibilities right away. Once when he was drunk he painted me a picture of what a marvellous ruler he would be, if he got Brezhnev out of the way and came to power himself . . . Anyway, I rushed along to Mosfilm to see Anya's old man. He was a sound technician, a radio engineer, and what I needed was a tape-recorder which would switch itself on automatically at the sound of voices, and then switch itself off when people stopped talking. I didn't tell him that I intended to place the recorder at Yakov Brezhnev's flat, of course. Instead, I spun him some yarn and brought him a couple of dozen of the best foreign tape-recorders and a hundred or so microphones. He made me the tiniest machine with an especially sensitive microphone. But it had one drawback. The microphone picked up the slightest noise, even the sound of traffic in the street. So deciphering what was actually said was very difficult. When I'd recorded a hundred or so cassettes and couldn't make any sense of what was on them, I went back to see Anya's father. He started transferring the sound from one tape to another in an attempt to improve the quality. But when he heard the voice of Brezhnev he nearly had a fit. I swore to him that nobody would ever find out, not a single soul, including Anya. If only he could really improve the quality, I'd let him have everything I had, jewels, diamonds, gold, the whole shebang.

On 17 July he gave me ten cassettes with really good sound reproduction, which I took with me straight away to the Sandunovsky Baths. I'd arranged to meet Kulakov there. He was a strong, sturdy fellow who worshipped real Russian baths. As strong as an ox, he could outsit anybody in the sweating-room. Of course, whenever he visited the Sandunovsky Baths, the management knew in advance, and they closed them to the public. I was allowed in, naturally! There he was, sitting in the sweating-room and waiting for me. He didn't know, of course, that the KGB were watching him. When I handed over the tapes we were caught. They threw some liquid in his face, and he fell down on to the bench, unconscious. I was tied up and taken to Tsvigun for interrogation. I told him everything, except for the part Anya's father had played in the affair. I kept my promise there. Otherwise he and Anya would have been done away with, that goes without saying. I invented a story about having bought the tape-recorder from a foreigner, which wasn't so far from the truth, since the whole machine was made up of parts from abroad . . . Two days later the papers announced that Kulakov had suddenly died as the result of a heart-attack.

Meanwhile, I was already en route for the camps. Tsvigun himself had drawn up the sentence, which was passed by the Moscow court. It was a miracle that I wasn't shot. Boris Buryatsky managed to get off . . . Three weeks ago Investigator Baklanov arrived at the camp to interrogate me about the tapes and Anya. Then he had me flown to the Balashikhinsky prison near Moscow, where I was cross-examined by some generals and colonels. But what could I tell them? I didn't have the slightest idea where old Finshtein might have hidden those tapes . . .

At 10.23 a.m. we landed in the West at a military aerodrome on the edge of East Berlin. In the capital itself it was only three degrees centigrade.

At the steps to the plane we were met by a smiling red-cheeked colonel, a big fellow aged about fifty, with a strong Vyatka accent. 'Colonel Boris Trutkov – at your service,' he said. 'It's my job to look after you. What's it like in Moscow? As cold as charity?'

'Let me introduce you,' I said. 'This is Comrade Givi Mingadze. He'll need to change into a decent suit.'

'We'll find one for him, don't worry! And we'll give him a good bath, too. We've got excellent saunas here with real birch switches and everything else.

I never thought that birch trees grew in Germany – but there you are. There are as many here as in Vyatka.'

There was indeed a birch forest surrounding the aerodrome. Elsewhere in the forest was a military camp complete with brick-built barracks two storeys high, just as there had been at Zhukovsky, which we had left two and a half hours earlier. The garrulous Colonel sat us in his green army Volga and took us to have breakfast in the officers' mess.

'First you've got to have something to eat. Feeding is a man's first duty. The girls have cooked pancakes for us this morning, just like Shrove Tuesday. You'll be licking your fingers, they're so good.'

He carried on talking like this without stopping, engulfing us in his Vyatka accent, and yet not once during our whole conversation did he look me straight in the eye.

At the same time in Moscow

EXTRACT FROM THE REPORT GIVEN BY CAPTAIN E. ARUTYUNOV
TO HEAD OF CID THIRD SECTION, COLONEL M. SVETLOV

On your instructions, a group of doctors from the Moscow Public Health Inspection Centre, acting under your guidance, today, 27 January 1982, conducted an examination of the medical facilities in the Butyrka prison, the Krasnaya Presnya prison and the special isolation prison 'Sailors' Rest' Those who took part were Senior Doctors Aida Rozova and Aleksei Speshnyov, Dr Gennady Sholokhov and Laboratory Assistant Konstantin Tyrtov. As a result of this inspection and the examination of prisoners held in these medical wards, Dr Rozova was able to identify a prisoner with a bullet-wound in his thigh, who resembles the identikit picture of the criminal described by the witness Katya Uzhovich. This prisoner is to be found at the special isolation prison 'Sailors' Rest'.

Following my instructions, Dr Rozova showed no interest in the patient, but continued her rapid inspection of the medical facilities at the prison and the seven prisoners receiving treatment there. She concluded this examination at 10.11 a.m., whereupon she returned to the Moscow Public Health Inspection Centre by ambulance and informed me that the prisoner, whom she had identified, was in a serious medical condition, with gangrene developing rapidly in the right leg.

'The bastards!' said Svetlov, when he had read this report. 'They abandon their own man in a prison hospital, like a dog, and are even afraid to call ordinary doctors to help him!'

'But how are we going to get him out of there?' asked Arutyunov. 'The prison guard won't let us have him.'

'Oh yes they will,' said Svetlov. 'That's why Bogatyryov is sitting in the Kremlin under arrest! Let's go!'

Forty minutes later Lieutenant-General Bogatyryov, accompanied, or rather, escorted by the head of the Kremlin guard, General Zharov, was being taken to Sokolniki on the outskirts of Moscow, to Special Isolation Prison Number One, which is situated on a street bearing the poetic name of 'Sailors' Rest'. General Bogatyryov was the only person in the USSR for whom the gates of any prison immediately open, with the governor standing smartly to attention outside. Without so much as a single word to this particular prison governor, Bogatyryov and Zharov gloomily walked across the snow-covered courtyard to the dilapidated single-storey building, which formed the prison's medical wing. Zharov's Kremlin Chaika swung in noise-lessly beind them. The warders rushed to remove the inquisitive prisoners from the barred windows.

A few minutes later Generals Bogatyryov and Zharov were carrying the wounded man outside, supporting him in their own arms. He was unconscious.

Siren sounding, the Chaika screeched out of the prison courtyard and hurtled towards Moscow. Destination – the Kremlin Hospital's surgery wing on Granovsky Street. This was the first occasion when the Kremlin doctors had had to deal with a patient transferred directly from a prison bed to a surgical one. The duty surgeon ordered his assistants to prepare the patient for a leg amputation, and then informed Svetlov that there was no chance of cross-examining the patient for an hour or an hour and a half. Swearing loudly, Svetlov left the surgeon's room and said to General Zharov: 'It would be as well to place someone on guard here, Comrade General. He's as much a Sidorov from Sakhalin as I am.'

'I'll have one posted. We'll have to get Krasnov and Oleinik now.'

'No,' was Svetlov's reply. 'Not yet. It's too early.' He looked at his watch. It was ten to twelve. Less than forty-two hours had elapsed since the murder of Nina Makarycheva. And it wasn't long now to the moment of reckoning, to the 'salute' which Svetlov and I had talked about early that morning beneath the Kremlin wall.

Leaving Captain Arutyunov at the hospital, Svetlov returned to CID headquarters to await the telephone call from West Berlin.

East Berlin, 12.50 p.m.
Colonel Trutkov's army Volga drove out of the fortress containing the Soviet Embassy, sped down Unter den Linden and turned into Friedrich-strasse. I was already fed up with the talkative colonel's over-meticulous solicitude. You might have thought that he had been born and brought up in this city, which was astonishingly like Stalingrad, or Kuibyshev, or some such town, not so much in the detail of its architecture, as in the general impression which the buildings made. They were built of the same heavy grey stone. Shop windows contained the same photo-montages from provincial newspapers and the same pictures of outstanding representatives of local Socialist labour. You might have been looking at material published in the Krasnodar or Voronezh *Pravda*. On the streets people wore the same anxious, unsociable expressions. Practically every junction was dominated

by an identical police observation tower made of concrete and glass, just like in the Soviet Union. Who copied whom, I don't know.

Colonel Trutkov distracted me from these thoughts. Ever since we had driven into Berlin two hours before, to get our West German visas and register at the Soviet Embassy, he had been spewing forth the names of streets, squares and places of historical interest. He pointed out the Brandenburg Gates here, the Humboldt University there, the Comic Opera, the Leipzigerstrasse, the ruins of some department store, the remains of the Jewish synagogue, and so on. And there, in front of the State Opera, was an 'Eternal Flame', with soldiers goose-stepping to change the guard, just like in the Aleksandriisky Garden near the Kremlin or outside Lenin's Mausoleum in Red Square. Then we drove through streets lined with Prussian buildings and empty apart from a few clapped-out old cars. We might have been in Voronezh or some place like that.

I kept on thinking that, although we had flown over Poland, I hadn't actually travelled west at all. I felt as if I were somewhere south-east of Moscow, in the German region of the Volga, say, where some red-cheeked official from the local regional committee, dressed in colonel's epaulets, was obsequiously showing his domain to a visitor from the Moscow Public Prosecutor's Office. Even the avenue of lime trees on Friedrichstrasse looked somehow Russian. I was half-Russian after all, I thought. That was why these lime trees looked so familiar. God knows what trees grow in my other genetic homeland! Cactuses, avocadoes? I had never seen them and didn't think I could regard them as being even partly my own . . .

'People say that there used to be some marvellous hotels along here before the war,' Trutkov chattered on. 'I've seen photographs of them, and it's quite true. They were really luxurious. The restaurants were fantastic! Still, never mind, Comrade Shamrayev. When you return from West Berlin we'll wash away your memories at the Ratskeller. That's on the Alexanderplatz, and it's the best restaurant in Berlin. Even West Germans reserve tables there.'

It was extraordinary how he managed to address himself to me all the time, completely ignoring the presence of Givi Mingadze. It was as if Mingadze were some inanimate object attached to me, like a second brief-case, something it would be necessary to exchange in half an hour or so, over there, beyond the red and white painted wooden barriers, which now came into view as we drove down Friedrichstrasse on to the Potsdamerplatz. When we had been choosing a civilian suit for Givi earlier that morning, at the Soviet garrison shop, Trutkov had said: 'What size is it you need, Comrade Shamrayev? What colour shall we choose?' Somebody about to depart for the West was obviously not a real person in his eyes.

At one o'clock we crossed the Potsdamerplatz and arrived at Checkpoint Charlie. A high concrete wall stood before us. So this was the famous Berlin Wall! All along it were watchtowers equipped with searchlights. A series of small, square-shaped huts with a narrow passage between them lay between

255

us and the check-point itself. Again there were the red and white painted barriers, and vehicle-traps as well. Practically every couple of yards you met East German border guards and duty officers dressed in grey military uniforms. For the first time I thought of Anya Finshtein, whom I would soon be meeting in the strange and unfamiliar world that lay beyond the Wall. For the first time I thought of her as a living, flesh and blood human being. Her love for this Georgian, the love of a simple Russian-Israeli girl, sought for three weeks by the KGB network in Israel and Europe, had not only shaken the whole Soviet State machine, from the KGB, MVD and CPSU Central Committee down to military headquarters in Adler, Sverdlovsk and Berlin. It was also about to break through this enormous concrete wall, patrolled by guards armed to the teeth. How that State machine had grated and ground, unwilling to yield to Anya Finshtein. The blood of Tsvigun and his mistress, Suslov's heart-attack, the deaths of Vorotnikov and my Nina, these were the price which had to be paid for the State's struggle to maintain its face. And there were more deaths to be exacted yet. In a world without Nina Makarycheva, forty-four hours since they had given her that simple push in the back, her murderers were probably sitting at their desks or being driven about in their cars, dreaming, as the clock struck one, about the ministerial posts that would be theirs under the 'New Course Government'.

Holding our red Soviet passports in his hand, Colonel Trutkov confidently led us past the East German officers and soldiers towards the door of a metal hut where several foreign tourists were queuing for their passports. There was a smell of disinfectant and tobacco here, and the floors were covered with cigarette-ends. The Colonel left us and disappeared into the room occupied by the Chief Customs officer. I looked at Givi. His cheekbones stood out sharply against his pallid, almost grey complexion. His fingers appeared white, as he clutched the canvas mitten, which he had somehow hung on to, after we had replaced his prison clothes with a raincoat and suit bought at the garrison shop. I was becoming nervous myself.

Next to us some foreign tourists asked a question of an idle duty officer: '*Ich warte bereits vierzig Minuten. Wo sind meine Dokumente?*'

'*Noch nicht fertig*,' came the reply.

'Listen.' I said to Givi. 'While we're waiting, write a message for Anya.'

I opened my briefcase. It contained nothing apart from the Moscow telephone directory, a Russian-German phrase-book, a map of West Berlin and a heap of typewritten sheets – the notes I had taken on the Tsvigun affair.

I started to search amongst them for a clean sheet of paper, but Givi said: 'Don't bother. If you've got a felt-tip pen . . .'

I gave him one, and he flattened out the canvas mitten in his hand. He wrote three words on it: 'I'm here. Givi.'

I put the mitten into the pocket of my shabby, fleece-lined coat and just had time to exchange glances with Givi before Colonel Trutkov came along, with a single passport in his hand. It was mine.

'Everything is in order,' he said to me. 'I shan't be accompanying you any further. The customs-hall is over there, as well as the exit to the West. But they won't be checking you. I've already given the order. Let's go over everything once more. I've told you how to use a German telephone. You can change money for West German marks over there. Don't forget to ask for as much small change as possible. You'll need it for the phone. You've got a phrase-book. You'll be checked by the Americans as you arrive, but that's nothing to worry about. A formal examination of your papers, that's all, and your papers are all in order. You've already written down my telephone number. I think that's about all. Oh yes, once you're on the other side, you can take a taxi or a twenty-nine bus to the Kurfürstendamm, that's the main street in West Berlin. It's full of expensive-looking shops, but don't forget that they're swarming with pickpockets – mainly Russian emigrés from Odessa. A friend of mine had his back pocket cut away with a razor-blade, wallet and all. He didn't hear or feel a thing. I don't know whether they chose one of their own countrymen on purpose, or whether . . .'

I thought that he was never going to shut up and let me go. I couldn't stand it any longer, so I interrupted him fairly rudely: 'OK, that's enough. I'm off.'

'I'm sorry, but what about me?' said Mingadze. Following Colonel Trutkov's example, he, too, would only address himself to me. I looked at Trutkov in an attempt to force him finally to face the anxious Givi and explain the order in which things would come.

But Trutkov avoided doing so yet again and said to me: 'He will stay here. When I receive the signal from Moscow, I shall ring through and he'll be given his passport. After that – good riddance!'

With these words, the Colonel offered me his hand and, I think for the first time in our short acquaintance, looked me in the eye. 'Well, good luck!' he said.

In spite of his genial and, indeed, almost paternal smile, Colonel Boris Ignatyevich Trutkov – head of Intelligence Directorate First Special Section attached to the Soviet Forces General Staff in East Germany – had perfectly cold, light grey-blue eyes. I have seen eyes like that only a few times in my life, always in the north, staring out of the faces of the bastards who run the extra strict regime camps there.

A minute later I was walking across the narrow wooden floor of Checkpoint Charlie. I showed the last East German border guard my passport. He then pressed a button to open the metal gate of the security complex. Beyond these gates lay the strange world, which we Russians refer to simply as 'the West'.

Paris, at the same time
In room 202 at one of the best hotels in Paris, the telephone rang for the first time that day. Vadim Belkin had spent all day sitting in the room waiting for that phone call. After the frosts of Moscow it seemed amazingly warm outside – ten degrees centigrade! Waiting for him out there were beautiful

257

Parisian women, cafes and boulevards, the fragrance of spring and the flowers being briskly sold by two young Arabs, who were actually rushing up to the windows of cars as they stopped at the junction. But Belkin was glued to the phone, and could only peer out at Paris through his window, staring at the pâtisserie opposite his hotel, or lie on his bed reading the fifth issue of the journal *Znamya* for 1981, which had published General Tsvigun's story 'We Shall Return'. Sintsov had asked Belkin to read it through so that a decision could be made about the possible filming of it. The book described the heroic exploits of KBG Major Mlynsky, the commander of the Special Regiment which smashed the advance of German troops on Moscow, led by General von Horn.

Belkin started to read as follows: 'Kempe, we must immediately recover the lost ground at whatever cost. It's not just me giving the order, it is the Führer himself. We must strain every nerve. The moment of decision is approaching.'

Belkin threw the journal on to the floor in contempt. Reading this bombastic nonsense in Paris was simply too much! Why, it probably hadn't even been written by Tsvigun, but by some hired hack, who wrote it with as much distaste as Belkin himself had felt over the last few months while he'd been composing Brezhnev's mawkish and trite biography. For all the cynical, consumer attitude which he had brought to bear on the task ('the worse, the better' had been his watchword), he had noticed several times that it was becoming more difficult for him to write the simple, human Russian words, which, as little as two years ago, had done so much to distinguish his own reporting from the grey, journalistic clichés of others. Only two or three years ago Belkin had been one of the most remarkable journalists in the country. He flew all over the place, wherever the action was; fires in the *taiga*, drug-addicts in the Caucasus, frontier guards on the Chinese border, fishermen and reindeer-breeders in Yakutia, oilmen in Tyumen, you name it. His reports and articles were remarkable for their simple, precise and colourful Russian, their energetic style and unusual subject-matter. This was what made him Brezhnev's favourite journalist at the time, and Brezhnev took him from the editorial offices of *Komsomolskaya Pravda* and put him in a special literary team set up to write his own memoirs. But since Belkin had started writing the 'Life of Brezhnev the Blessed', he had got more and more used to filling his pages with phrases like 'implementing decisions', 'mobilizing reserves' and 'straining every nerve'. Finding the same expressions in Tsvigun's piece published in *Znamya*, Belkin flung it to one side. It was too much like a mirror in which he saw the reflection of his own face, stuffed with Kremlin special rations.

The telephone saved him from more fruitless self-contempt. He grabbed the receiver.

'It's me,' said a female voice.

'Anya?'

'Yes.'

'Where are you ringing from?'

'It doesn't matter.'

'I mean, are you already in Berlin?'

'That doesn't matter,' she repeated suspiciously. 'But is your friend in Berlin yet?'

'He ought to be! In fact he ought to be in West Berlin by now. I'm expecting him to phone any minute.'

'All right, I'll ring you back in ten minutes.'

'Hang on! What am I supposed to tell him, when he does ring?'

'Describe his appearance to me.'

'His appearance?' repeated Belkin slowly. Simple human words were what he needed now, just the ones he had handled till two years ago. 'What does he look like? Well . . . Nothing very special . . . You know, about middle height, aged forty-five, brown hair . . .' He couldn't think of anything else.

'Is he wearing a fleece-lined jacket?' she asked.

'Yes, he does have one of those. And he was wearing it yesterday, you're quite right. How did you know?'

'What colour is it?'

'Er . . . dark brown, knee-length . . . And he's got a briefcase the same.'

'A knee-length briefcase you mean?' the voice exclaimed with a laugh.

Belkin began to sweat. Here was a simple emigrée, catching him out on language.

'No, of course not!' he said. 'I mean that his briefcase was the same *colour* as his coat, dark brown . . .'

'I see. Thanks.' Then he heard the dialling tone.

'Hello, hello!' he shouted into the receiver, before slamming it down in anger. Then all at once he took several swigs of Armenian 'Ararat' brandy straight from the bottle. He wiped his lips with the back of his hand and said aloud to himself: 'You bloody idiot!'

At the same time in Moscow

EXTRACT FROM THE REPORT OF CAPTAIN E. ARUTYUNOV

TO HEAD OF CID THIRD SECTION, COLONEL M. SVETLOV

When he had recovered consciousness after the operation, the prisoner suspected of taking part in the murder of General Tsvigun gave evidence that he was not 'Sidorov', but Pyotr Stepanovich Khutorskoi, born 1947 at Podlipki, Moscow Region, and that he was a Captain in the MVD and a permanent employee of MVD Intelligence.

Since the duty surgeon would only allow me five minutes in which to cross-examine Captain Khutorskoi, I was unable to elicit more than the following information during preliminary questioning:

On 19 January 1982, Captain P. Khutorskoy took part in an illegal search of Comrade S.K. Tsvigun's safe apartment. In charge of the search was Major-General A. Krasnov, Head of MVD Intelligence, assisted by his deputy, Colonel B. Oleinik and Intelligence agent, Captain I.M. Zaporozhko. At the same time, similar searches were being carried out by other MVD Intelligence operatives at Tsvigun's *dachas* near Moscow and Yalta, his office, and also at the flats of his wife and his mistress, S.N. Agapova. The purpose of these searches was the confiscation of tapes containing conversations which took place between the Secretary-General of the CPSU, Comrade Brezhnev, and others; also the removal of material connected with the secret surveillance which Tsvigun had been conducting, of Comrade Suslov and other members of the Politburo. According to Khutorskoi's testimony, Tsvigun arrived at 16-A, Kachalov Street at the beginning of the search, when it had been assumed that he would be delayed at Comrade Suslov's office for at least two or three hours. Having entered the apartment and discovered the search going on, General Tsvigun stood in the entrance hall and managed to fire two shots, one of which wounded Khutorskoi in the thigh. As a result of this, Khutorskoi was not able to see who actually fired the shot which killed Tsvigun. After that, the corpse was carried into the living-room and a hurried attempt made to stage a suicide. Colonel Oleinik and Major-General Krasnov then went down to the main entrance hall and disarmed Tsvigun's personal bodyguard, Major Gavrilenko and his chauffeur, Captain Borovsky. The suicide note ostensibly written by General Tsvigun, and the reports of Major Gavrilenko and Captain Borovsky, are therefore spurious. Since Khutorskoi was losing blood, Colonel Oleinik and Captain Zaporozhko carried him out of the building, and Colonel Oleinik drove him first to the first-aid post at the Arbatskaya metro station, to have his leg bandaged, and then to the hospital wing of the Lubyanka prison. There, under the guise of medical aid, he was given a general anaesthetic. When he recovered consciousness forty or fifty minutes later, he found himself alone in a room in the medical wing of Special Isolation Prison Number One ('Sailors' Rest').

When Khutorskoi was presented with a copy of the Identikit picture provided by witness Yu. Avetikov, purporting to resemble the person suspected of murdering N. Makarycheva and S. Agapova, he immediately identified the person as MVD Intelligence operator, Captain I. Zaporozkho.

Note 1. I have to report that Captain Khutorskoi is seriously ill and that he expresses himself for the most part in obscene language (especially when referring to General Krasnov and Colonel Oleinik, who were responsible for transferring him to 'Sailors' Rest'). For these reasons it was impossible to carry out a more detailed cross-examination.

Note 2. According to the doctors, Khutorskoi has the same blood-group as General Tsvigun (blood-group II). I assume that deliberate use was made of this coincidence when the suicide was staged.

West Berlin, 1.15 p.m.

I have often heard it said that Soviet people are stunned and astounded by their first encounter with the West. A friend of mine once told me that, after she had returned to Moscow from visiting London and Paris as a tourist, she could not leave her flat for a whole week . . . I am neither a snob, nor a Party propagandist, but I have to say that I was not in the least bit shattered by West Berlin. On the contrary, from the moment I walked past Checkpoint Charlie, past the blocks of houses patrolled by American soldiers, and reached Kochstrasse, where there were no longer any soldiers at all, and West Berlin proper begins – from that very moment, I could not help feeling that I had arrived in a perfectly natural, normal, human world. And this was not because the shining shop windows were filled with an abundance of meat, smoked sausage, fish, salad, vegetables and fruit, the like of which has not been seen in Moscow for decades. Nor was it because there were bright advertisements everywhere, and thousands of gleaming Mercedes, Volkswagens, Peugeots and Toyotas going along the streets. It was simply because there, at the metro station, was an unbelievably beautiful flower stall filled with masses of brightly-coloured flowers. There were carnations, asters, roses, tulips. It was a veritable paradise of flowers, a celebration of spring – and in January at that! I couldn't understand where all the nervous tension of the last few days had disappeared – the strain of pitting my wits against the KGB, the MVD, Rekunkov, Zharov, Bogatyryov and Brezhnev himself. And all this for the paltry pleasure of revenge, revenge which had already been planned by Svetlov and myself down to the last moment. Dozens of people in Moscow, Belkin in Paris, Trutkov in East Berlin, Givi Mingadze at Checkpoint Charlie and Anya Finshtein, somewhere here in the western sector – all of them were awaiting my phone call, ready to act, take off in cars, send coded telegrams via special military telegraph, or whatever. Even that Kremlin schemer, Leonid Ilyich Brezhnev, was waiting for the results of my mission. And yet here was I, standing about in front of this beautiful flower kiosk and wondering whether Comrade God had sent me into the world to do anything other than live amidst the resplendence of these brightly-coloured flowers. Then I thought of something else. I had a rendezvous with somebody. Yes, indeed. I was about to meet a woman whose love had been strong enough to break through two walls – those of the Kremlin and Berlin! I was not the one she loved. Nobody had ever loved me as passionately as that, nor, I dare say, would anybody ever do so. With Nina there had been a hint that such love and devotion might eventually come my way, but . . . Wasn't this why I had to avenge her death? Let Anya have this lover of hers, this good-for-nothing former speculator and henchman of Semyon Tsvigun, what difference did it make? And I stepped towards the kiosk, prodded one of the gorgeous bouquets of red tulips and said, using one of the phrases I had learnt the day before: '*Frau, wieviel kostet das?*'

She said something in reply, but to tell the truth, I couldn't work out what it was equivalent to in Russian money, so I simply handed over the small bundle of German marks which I had just received at Checkpoint Charlie, in exchange for those roubles of Brezhnev's. While she was extracting three of the notes and wrapping up the bouquet in pale blue paper with an embossed design, I couldn't help laughing to myself. There was I, buying flowers for Israeli citizen Anya Finshtein, using money provided by Leonid Brezhnev. He was giving her this bouquet, too, as it were. Not a bad touch for anybody writing a heart-rending novel. I took the flowers, heard her say, '*Danke schön*' (it wasn't often that I heard anybody say 'thank you') and asked: '*Wo kann man telefonieren*?'

The flower-seller pointed towards the nearest phone booth. Holding the bouquet and my briefcase in one hand, I went up to the telephone and started to slip the unusually light-feeling German coins into the box.

'If you're phoning Paris, you might as well spare yourself the expense,' said a woman standing behind me. She spoke perfect Russian. There before me was a blonde, sun-tanned girl, dressed in a dark cherry-coloured suede coat. She had magnificent hair and big dark eyes. It was Anya Finshtein. She looked just as she did in the photographs, which had been removed from Baklanov's briefcase by the happy-go-lucky Belyakov, the former king of the Rostov housebreaking fraternity, known as Gold Fang, and the Boss-man, and now a technician at a Moscow car factory. I looked at her dumbly, not understanding how it was that this meeting was actually taking place.

'You've got a terribly stupid expression on your face,' she said with a laugh, and I could see that there was something different about her eyes. The photographs had shown her with big, beautiful, dark, Jewish eyes, whereas the eyes I could see now seemed to flash with the light of bright, sun-drenched sands and the warm sea.

'It was all very simple,' she continued. 'I saw you come out of Checkpoint Charlie and rang your friend in Paris. Incidentally, I needn't have rung. It's not difficult to pick out Russians in the West. It's true that your friend is waiting for me to phone him to arrange some cafe or other for us to meet in, but . . . If you'd been sent to kidnap me and torture me into revealing the whereabouts of the tapes, then I don't think you would have bought those flowers, eh? Let's introduce ourselves. I'm Anya Finshtein.'

She held out her slender, bronzed hand.

'Shamrayev, Igor Shamrayev,' I replied and clumsily offered her the bouquet of flowers, nearly dropping my briefcase as I did so.

'What, you bought these for me?' she said in amazement. 'In that case I can dismiss my escort.' With these words she turned towards a diminutive old Volkswagen, which was parked nearby. There were two young men and a woman sitting in it. She waved to them and said something in a guttural language, which was completely incomprehensible to me. They said a few words in reply, which she translated for me.

'They don't want to drive off, just in case. But they won't interfere with us, don't worry. They're friends of mine from Israel. Let's go to a cafe . . . And thank you for the flowers. They're tulips of ours, imported from Israel. We export flowers to every country in Europe . . .'

She said 'we' with a special pride.

'Wait, Anya,' I said. 'We'll go to a cafe, but I must ring Moscow first . . .'

'But I'll only give you the address of the tapes in exchange for Givi,' she replied sharply.

'I know. We'll talk about that a bit later. Take this for now.' And I produced Givi's canvas mitten from my pocket and offered it to her.

'What's this?' she asked with a frown.

'Read it.'

She read the three words which Givi had written on it fifteen minutes before. She said nothing, and there were no tears. She simply grasped the mitten in her hand and stared at me.

I turned back towards the telephone and dialled the code for Moscow, 7095. Then I added Svetlov's number. He replied straight away, as if he'd been holding on to the receiver. 'Hello.'

'It's me.'

'Well, what's happening?' he asked quickly. His voice was so clear that he might have been in the next building, instead of half-way across Europe.

'Everything's OK. She's standing next to me. Make a note of the address: page 227, eight lines from the top. In the left-hand corner of the garage loft there is a big iron case of the kind used by film people for storing old reels of film.' I was speaking very calmly and audibly, so that those who were listening in to our conversation in Moscow would be in no doubt as to what we were talking about.

'OK, I'm on my way. Salutations!' said Svetlov in a broken voice.

I replaced the receiver very slowly. Some small change came tumbling out at the bottom. I paid no attention to it. Svetlov was about to make the last move in Moscow, but the slightest hitch could still ruin the military 'salute' which he had planned.

'I don't understand,' said Anya. 'What was the address you dictated to them? I haven't told you anything yet.'

'Let's ring my friend in Paris now,' I said, 'to stop him getting worried. Then we can go to a cafe and you can tell me everything.'

Moscow, at the same time

Marat Svetlov's police Volga was travelling fast down the priority lane of Peace Prospect towards the Yaroslavl Highway. Across Kolkhoz Square and past the Riga Station, he squeezed as much out of his souped-up engine as he could. The windscreen wipers kept sweeping off the falling snow. At the lights on Krestovsky Bridge there was a traffic-jam. The red light refused to change to green, and the traffic-controller had disappeared somewhere. Cars were hooting impatiently, but Svetlov was quite content to sit it out. In his wing mirror, a few cars back, he could see the two Volgas which had started out of a side street off the Petrovka, as soon as he had driven away from the CID office. They kept well behind him, however, and so as not to

263

give themselves away, they avoided the priority lane, driving along in the stream of traffic. This was why the traffic-controller had been ordered to slow Svetlov down. As soon as the two unmarked, grey Volgas had caught up, the traffic-controller appeared in his booth, and the lights turned green. Svetlov laughed. The fish had obviously swallowed the bait. The only thing now was to keep up the pressure and not make them suspicious. Wincing somewhat with the pain from his right hand, Svetlov went into first, second and then third gear and accelerated off down the priority lane, laughing again as he did so. At the Exhibition of Economic Achievements, next to the French-built Cosmos Hotel, it was the same story. There was another traffic-jam and the cars were hooting furiously, especially the taxis, which were always in a hurry. But until the two grey Volgas had once again settled on Svetlov's trail, the traffic-lights stayed at red. In any case, he mustn't get too far ahead of them now, as it was essential that they see him turning off down Rostokinsky Passage, towards the area the Finshteins had lived in before they emigrated to Israel. He made a quick turn and glanced in the rear mirror to check that the grey Volgas were still following him. Then he drove past the apartment block where the Finshteins had lived, towards a row of private and co-operatively-owned garages, spread out like little boxes along the frozen River Yauza. The Finshteins had never had their own car, but the father had often done work on the side, installing radios in other people's cars. So it all appeared completely logical and simple, and the two Volgas carried on following Svetlov without hesitation. Before they entered the garage area, they stopped, so as to stay hidden, while Svetlov drove right into the garages over the icy ruts made by other cars. There was nobody else around. It was daytime, after all, and people were at work. Every garage was padlocked. Svetlov pulled up to Number 117, a plush-looking garage, made of stone with a loft added on and a dovecote on the roof. It was padlocked, like all the rest. Svetlov shot through the lock four times, and the pigeons flew up in alarm, with a great flapping of wings. He opened the garage door and in the half-light climbed up a ladder to the loft. There in the corner, covered by some old rags, was a large, cylindrical metal box covered in ancient rust. I had put it there myself yesterday. This was our secret. Svetlov looked out through the tiny, snow-covered window. Two grey Volgas were heading slowly and almost noiselessly down the snowy tracks to garage Number 117. He laughed, picked up the heavy iron reel-case and slowly descended the ladder with it. When he came out of the garage, he saw two revolvers trained on him. There stood Krasnov, Oleinik, Zaporozhko and Kolya Baklanov.

'Quietly does it, Colonel,' said Major-General Krasnov. 'You've got two alternatives. Either you give us the tapes, and in a week you'll be receiving your general's epaulets, or – a bullet in the head. The choice is yours.'

Svetlov looked at them all intently. The pigeons had quietened down and were gradually returning to the dovecote. He looked at Kolya Baklanov's eyes. They were as pitiless as the bright, pale eyes of young Captain

Zaporozkho. Svetlov offered the reel-case to the latter. He took it and, surrounded by the others, carried it to one of the cars. Svetlov looked at the pigeons, picked up a lump of snow and hurled it at the dovecote with all his strength. Krasnov and Baklanov looked round in bewilderment, as the pigeons flew up once more into the lowering, snow-laden Moscow sky. Somewhere in the distance you could hear the rumble of an electric train. Almost running, Svetlov rushed towards his car, whose engine he had left ticking over. Before he had even had time to sit down properly at the steering-wheel, Marat went into first gear. In his rear mirror he could see that the four of them had placed the reel-case on the bonnet of their Volga and were trying to open the frozen lid. He managed to switch into second gear and press his foot down hard on the accelerator. A second later Captain Zaporozhko managed to wrest off the lid, and there was the most deafening explosion. The four figures dressed in police uniform were hurled into the air along with the grey case. The salute in memory of poor Nina had been fired.

West Berlin, at the same time
'My father took half of Givi's diamonds straight to Zotov's room at the Visa Office, and we got all our exit papers the same day. The rest of the diamonds he left with Buryatsky so that he could somehow get him out of gaol. We left the country with nothing apart from the clothes we were wearing. We didn't even take suitcases, as we were afraid that there would be some fuss at the customs.' Thus Anya Finshtein ended her story.

We were sitting together in a comfortable little cafe, which was almost empty at that time of day. On the table in front of us were some coffee cups and two glasses of a liqueur, while next to them, in a pretty vase, were the Israeli tulips which I had presented to Anya. They had been placed in water by the thoughtful waitress, which was also a sign of the new, more human environment in which I found myself.

'Anya,' I said, 'there is only one way for you to get Givi back. And that is to tell me the address where the tapes are to be found. I'll then ring General Staff in East Berlin. They will immediately telephone the coded text to my assistant in Moscow. If the tapes really are there, then your Givi will be allowed to pass through Checkpoint Charlie to the West.'

'But what if they don't let him through? What if they get the tapes and refuse to send him over?'

'Then I'll be in your hands. I'll be a hostage, and you and your friends can do what you like with me.'

She thought for a moment and said: 'It looks as if there isn't any other alternative. OK, write down the address. The tapes are in the basement of the film archive at Mosfilm. Stack 693, case Number 8209. On the case it says: "Soundtrack of the film *Tchaikovsky*", only there isn't any *Tchaikovsky* in it, of course. it's Brezhnev.'

I opened my briefcase and took out my Moscow telephone directory. On

265

page 306 there was a long column of telephone numbers, all of them relating to the Mosfilm studios. At the very end of the column, on line thirty-eight, it said: 'Film archive' along with the relevant phone number. But I didn't need the latter. I wrote the page and line number in my notebook, went up to a telephone, and dialled the number given to me by Colonel Trutkov a few hours earlier.

His loud, Vyatka accent immediately assaulted my ears. 'Well, how's it going? How do you find Western Europe? Are they all stuffing themselves, the bastards?'

'Write this down,' I said coldly. 'Page 306, line thirty-eight. Have you got it? And also write the following: stack 693, case 8209.'

'Listen, Shamrayev,' he replied. 'Can't you send this bloody Yid packing, and come back yourself? There's no point in letting her have the Georgian, now is there?'

'I can't do that,' I replied. 'There are eight of them, and they're holding me at gunpoint.'

He said nothing. It looked as if he was weighing up what they'd have to lose if Anya's friends really did bump me off.

'Bear in mind, Colonel,' I said, 'that if Givi doesn't come across there will only be one way for me to save my own skin, and that will be to tell western journalists everything I know. Neither Brezhnev nor Ustinov will forgive you for that.'

'OK,' he replied hoarsely. 'We'll have to let her have her Georgian then. To hell with him! I'll get the message coded and sent to Moscow. Let me have the number you're phoning from.'

I looked at the number on the dial in front of me and dictated it to him.

'All right,' he said. 'Wait for me to phone.'

Moscow, one minute later
Next to Arbatskaya Square, in the massive stone building of the Soviet Army General Staff, the Codes and Ciphers Department dealt with the message from Berlin and passed it on to Valentin Pshenichny, who had been sitting in the entrance hall. He opened his Moscow telephone directory, looked up page 306 and walked out of the building. Zharov's Chaika was waiting for him at the stone steps. The general himself was asleep on the back seat. Pshenichny opened the door and woke him up. Eight minutes later the government Chaika was entering the gates of the Mosfilm studios. The frightened head of security at Mosfilm showed them where the archive was – right at the far end of the courtyard, beyond the film lots. At that very moment the famous producer, Sergei Bondarchuk, Lenin Prizewinner and Candidate Member of the CPSU Central Committee, was actually shooting a crowd scene for his latest spectacular, *Ten Days that Shook the World*. Bondarchuk was hovering over the scene, seated in the cab of a crane, alongside its driver. The Kremlin Chaika tore into the frame as it was being shot, and headed straight for the tiny mock-up of an armoured car con-

taining the actor Kayurov. He was made up as Lenin and was attempting to imitate one of the latter's demagogic performances, speech impediment and all. Lenin's famous peaked cap was clutched in his hand as he gesticulated at the crowd.

'Stop!' cried Bondarchuk through his megaphone. 'Where did the car come from?! Get rid of it!'

'Go to hell,' growled Major Zharov from the Chaika. 'Drive on, drive on!' he ordered the chauffeur.

Interrupting the fiery words of the great leader of world revolution, the Kremlin Chaika crossed the square and drove up to the long, grey, two-storey building, which housed the film archive. There, in the enormous rooms with their own moist microclimate, amongst the thousands of cases containing film and sound tapes, Pshenichny and Zharov found stack 693 and in it a large reel-case of standard design, 8209, with the words 'Soundtrack to *Tchaikovsky*' written on the label. The case contained reels of brown magnetic tapes.

'Do you want to listen to the music of *Tchaikovsky*?' the head of the film archive, Matvei Aronovich Katz, asked in some surprise.

'Yes, please,' came the reply.

So Comrade Katz took the tapes out of the case and placed the first one on to the heavy recording-machine. He pressed the 'play' button. Instead of the music of Tchaikovsky, the loudspeakers echoed to the muffled sound of Brezhnev's laboured voice.

'Turn it off,' ordered Zharov. 'I'm taking these tapes with me.'

'Wait a moment,' said the astonished Katz. 'This case is supposed to contain recordings of Tchaikovsky's music . . .'

West Berlin, 3.00 p.m.

Anya Finshtein and I were waiting opposite Checkpoint Charlie. Between us and the iron gates of the Berlin Wall there was nothing apart from some American officers, the white line indicating the neutral strip and the avenue of birch trees which stretches along the western side of the wall. Anya looked tensely towards the firmly shut iron gates. The Volkswagen with her friends was parked behind us.

At last, the iron gates opened and Givi Mingadze walked cautiously and tensely through.

'Givi!' Anya cried.

He turned his head sharply in our direction, and the setting sun hit his eyes. An American officer went up to him, held out his hand to examine the passport, looked at it for one moment and returned it immediately, saying to Givi, as he had to me a few hours earlier: 'Welcome to the West.'

I looked at them running towards each other, Anya and Givi. She dropped the scarlet tulips from Israel, and they fell on to the roadway, in the white neutral zone. I laughed and remembered the words of a popular song: 'And in the neutral zone flowers of unusual beauty . . .' And that was where they were standing, hugging each other. Then they both came up to me, and Anya said:

'Thank you. We're flying to Israel tonight. Perhaps you'd like to come with us? How about it? Make up your mind. It's warm there. The tulips are already in flower.'

In her eyes I could see again reflections of the hot sand, the sweltering sun and the warm, southern sea.

I shook my head. 'I'm sorry, but I'm afraid I can't go with you. My son is over there,' I said, nodding towards the Berlin Wall.

EPILOGUE

By special military telegraph
To the Chairman of the USSR Defence Council Marshal Leonid Ilyich Brezhnev
To the USSR Ministry of Defence Marshal Dmitry Fyodorovich Ustinov
REPORT CONCERNING PRIORITY MISSION No. OS371 OF 27 JANUARY 1982
On your orders, at 15.19 hours today, 27 January 1982, Special Investigator of the USSR Public Prosecutor's Office, Senior Juridical Counsellor, Igor Iosifovich Shamrayev, sent to Berlin on your instructions, died in a car accident on the Friedrichstrasse near Checkpoint Charlie.

Investigation of the accident is in the hands of the Main Police Directorate, GDR Ministry of Internal Affairs.
Head of First Special Section, Intelligence Directorate,
Attached to Soviet Forces General Staff in East Germany
Colonel B. Trutkov

East Berlin, 27 January 1982

By special messenger
To the Head of First Special Directorate Ministry of Internal Affairs GDR Colonel Heinrich Schorr
Having examined the evidence in your report concerning the accident to USSR citizen I.I. Shamrayev, knocked down by an un-numbered car of a type used by the army, I suggest that you take action to halt the enquiry into this road accident on the grounds that the exercise is pointless. I also request that all documents relating to the preliminary investigation carried out by the police should be sent to me personally as quickly as possible.
Head of First Special Section, Intelligence Directorate,
Attached to Soviet Forces General Staff in East Germany
Colonel B. Trutkov

East Berlin 28 January 1982

On 29 January with great sorrow, the Soviet people accompanied Mikhail Andreyevich Suslov on his last journey. M. Suslov was a prominent member of the Communist Party, the Soviet government and the international Communist movement. Workers of Moscow and the surrounding region, representatives of the Soviet republics and other Party, governmental and social organizations filed past his coffin in a silent, unending stream. The funeral ceremony on Red Square was opened by the Secretary General of the CPSU Central Committee, Chairman of the Presidium of the Supreme Soviet, Comrade L.I. Brezhnev. In his funeral oration to Mikhail Suslov he said the following:

'The life of Comrade Suslov was filled with great deeds. It is painful and distressing to say farewell to such a person. We valued and loved this charming man who, while being extremely modest, was always exacting, both towards himself and towards others. Adhering to firm principles in everything, he was a loyal and trustworthy comrade. As we now say farewell to him we would want to add the following words: "Sleep soundly, dear friend! Your life has been great and glorious. You accomplished a great deal for your party and people, and they will revere your memory."'

SUICIDE OF BORIS THE GYPSY
EXTRACT FROM THE NEWSPAPER NOVOYE RUSSKOYE SLOVO, NEW YORK, 10 APRIL 1982

Moscow, 9 April. Foreign correspondents in Moscow have discovered that a friend of Galina Brezhneva, Brezhnev's daughter, the thirty-five-year-old Bolshoi Theatre singer Boris Buryats[ky], known as 'the Gypsy', committed suicide at the Lubyanka prison, soon after his arrest at the end of January . . .

EXTRACT FROM A LETTER WRITTEN BY V. ILYICHOV, HEAD OF THE PRESS SECTION OF THE CPSU CENTRAL COMMITTEE TO L. KORNESHOV, CHIEF EDITOR OF KOMSOMOLSKAYA PRAVDA

According to information supplied by the Soviet Embassy in Paris, today, 31 January 1982, your special correspondent, Vadim Belkin, has requested political asylum from the French government. When he met representatives of our Embassy, Belkin informed them that he was taking this action after careful consideration, as a sign of protest against the lack of artistic freedom in the USSR and because of his desire to become an honest writer. His action must be condemned at a general meeting of the party and Komsomol at your editorial office. I suggest also that you should increase the level of ideological awareness amongst employees of the newspaper.

EXTRACT FROM DIRECTIVE OF THE MINISTER FOR INTERNAL AFFAIRS,
N. SHCHOLOKOV, TO THE HEAD OF THE MAIN DIRECTORATE OF
CORRECTIVE LABOUR INSTITUTIONS, GENERAL I. BOGATYRYOV

Former Police Colonel, M. Svetlov, charged with murdering employees of the MVD Intelligence Section A. Krasnov, B. Oleinik, and I. Zaporozhko, and also Investigator N. Baklanov, sentenced to detention in a strict regime camp for a period of fifteen years, and former Investigator of the Public Prosecutor's Office, V. Pshenichny, charged with violations of administrative duty during his work as investigator and sentenced to detention in a general regime camp for a period of ten years – should be transferred to extra strict regime camp Number 274 at Ferganu, in the Kirghizian SSR, and be made to perform hard labour. Both are to be deprived of the right of correspondence.

EXTRACT FROM A SPEECH MADE BY YURY ANDROPOV AT A CEREMONIAL
MEETING HELD AT THE KREMLIN PALACE OF CONGRESSES IN HONOUR OF
THE 112th ANNIVERSARY OF V.I. LENIN'S BIRTHDAY
(PRAVDA, 23 APRIL 1982)

Comrades! It is not easy to tread paths which nobody has yet taken. There is much which it is impossible to calculate or predict in advance. In order to move forward with greater confidence, the Party teaches us to combine boldness with flexibility.'

EXTRACT FROM AN APPLICATION BY ANTON IGOREVICH SHAMRAYEV,
AGED FOURTEEN, TO ENTER THE ALL-UNION LENINIST KOMSOMOL

I ask to be accepted into the ranks of the All-Union Leninist Komsomol as a loyal servant of the Communist Party of the Soviet Union. I solemnly swear to uphold the regulations and programme of the Komsomol, to follow the precepts of the great Lenin in everything, to observe the moral code of a builder of Communism, to live like Lenin, to learn, labour, struggle and conquer under the leadership of the Communist Party of the Soviet Union. I promise religiously to observe the Komsomol's watchword: 'If the Party says "we must", the Komsomol replies "we will".'
Anton Shamrayev
Moscow, 28 May 1982

AFTERWORD

On publishing this book about the Soviet Investigator Igor Shamrayev, based on the notes written by Shamrayev himself, which he gave to Miss Anya Finshtein in West Berlin on 27 January 1982, I must make a few confessions to the reader.

I knew Shamrayev well. It is true that he came to my aid at a difficult moment. But he did so, not for my sake, but for the advantages he would gain from successfully fulfilling a mission, entrusted to him by the Central Committee: promotion, a new flat, increased salary, and so on.

None the less, I felt that I had a definite moral duty to undertake the immense labour of transforming his artistically feeble jottings into some semblance of a literary work. I do not think that I have always succeeded in this task, and not just because my own literary abilities are modest, but because, in my estimation at least, the real-life prototype of the book, that is to say Igor Shamrayev himself, did not square with the image of the noble, talented, brave and honest Soviet investigator which Shamrayev attempts to portray in his writings.

In actual fact Igor Shamrayev was an uninspiring example of the typical Soviet lawyer, the immutable product of his twenty years' work in the legal organs of the country. He was a self-assured, fat-cheeked member of the Communist Party, who was always willing to make use of the talents of his friends and colleagues – Svetlov, Pshenichny, Sorokin and others. It is precisely people like Shamrayev who thrive in Soviet life, not as a result of their own talent and professional know-how, but because of their good knowledge of the Soviet State machine and their ability to use this knowledge to their own advantage. Thus it was that Shamrayev, while he was investigating the death of Tsvigun, did not himself make a single discovery genuinely interesting from the point of view of a specialist in crime-detection. Nor was he capable of doing so. I remember one occasion when Shamrayev and I were having a pint of beer at the House of Journalists in Moscow. I asked him to invent an original plot for a detective story, or to remember one from his own experience. 'There's no such thing as originality when you're investigating a crime,' he said, with all the aplomb of one who might have invented Soviet crime-detection. 'Everything an investigator does is written in the Criminal Code.' Those words epitomize Shamrayev. As a person he was insignificant, being nothing but a petty bribe-taker, one who had no scruples about accepting small change, even from Brezhnev. Although he was a lackey at work and in his domestic life, he was somebody who tried to compensate for his sense of professional inferiority by writing such paeans to himself as are offered to the reader in this book.

Vadim Belkin,
New York, September 1982

GLOSSARY

'Beacon' (Russian *Mayak*), a well-known radio programme for young people.

Cheka, the name of the Secret Police founded by Feliks Dzerzhinsky in the early stages of the Soviet regime 1918–22. The name is formed from the first two initial Russian letters of the Extraordinary Commission for the Struggle against Counter-Revolution and Sabotage. The terms Cheka and Chekist are still occasionally used to refer to Soviet security organs and their agents.

Chistye Prudy, literally 'Clear Pools'.

CPSU, initials of the Communist Party of the Soviet Union.

GUM, Russian acronym for State Universal Store, the best-known of the Moscow stores, situated opposite the Kremlin in Red Square.

KGB, Russian initials of the Committee for State Security, the main Secret Police organ in the USSR. Its chairman bears full ministerial status. The KGB's main functions are control and surveillance of the Soviet people, intelligence and counter-intelligence. Its officers hold military-style rank.

Korchagin (Pavel Korchagin), boy-hero of a well-known Stalinist work of literature, notorious for setting his absolute faith in the Soviet Communist Party before any family and personal loyalties.

Komsomol, Communist Youth League. Membership – open from the age of fourteen – is widespread, but often merely nominal and evidently half-hearted. Usually only the ideologically committed or career-minded go on to become CPSU members at the age of twenty-eight.

Komsomolskaya Pravda, one of the best-known national newspapers published by Komsomol.

Lemon man (Russian *limonshchik*), rude term for Georgians, analogous with 'kraut' or 'frog'. Based on the trade pursued by many of them in bringing fresh fruit to Moscow and the north. Here specifically denotes a fruit millionaire.

Lubyanka, the KGB headquarters, situated on Moscow's Dzerzhinsky Square.

Militia, the name of the main police force in the USSR.

MOS, letters on a number-plate distinguishing government cars from the Moscow City Council Garage from all others.

Moskovsky Komsomolets (The Moscow Komsomol Member), local Moscow periodical published by Komsomol.

MVD, initials of the Soviet Ministry of Internal Affairs, equivalent body to the British Home Office and responsible for internal order in the country. Staff usually have quasi-military rank.

New Economic Policy (NEP), period in the 1920s when some free enterprise was encouraged in order to revitalize the economy after the disasters of war, revolution and civil war.

Novy Afrikanets (The New African), Soviet periodical.

Politburo, the political Bureau of the CPSU Central Committee, and the main ruling Party organ consisting of approximately a dozen members. It is responsible for running the Party between the plenary sessions of the full Central Committee.

Satsivi, Georgian culinary delicacy consisting of chicken in cream and nut-meg sauce.

Shashlyk, popular dish of Caucasian origin made of mutton roasted on a spit.

Slavyansky Bazar, well-known Moscow restaurant.

SMERSH, Russian acronym for the organization *Smert Spionam* (Death to Spies) set up by Stalin in 1941, when the USSR entered World War II. Its function was counter-espionage, terror and the capture of refugees from the Soviet regime.

Sobering stations, widespread in Soviet cities to deal with drunks. Treatment of offenders may involve locking up for the night, shaving of the head and the imposition of fines.

Vorobyovy Gory, Sparrow Hills.

Znamya (The Banner), one of the leading Soviet literary journals.